W9-ATP-642

Fifty Years of Russian Prose

Volume 1

Boris Pasternak

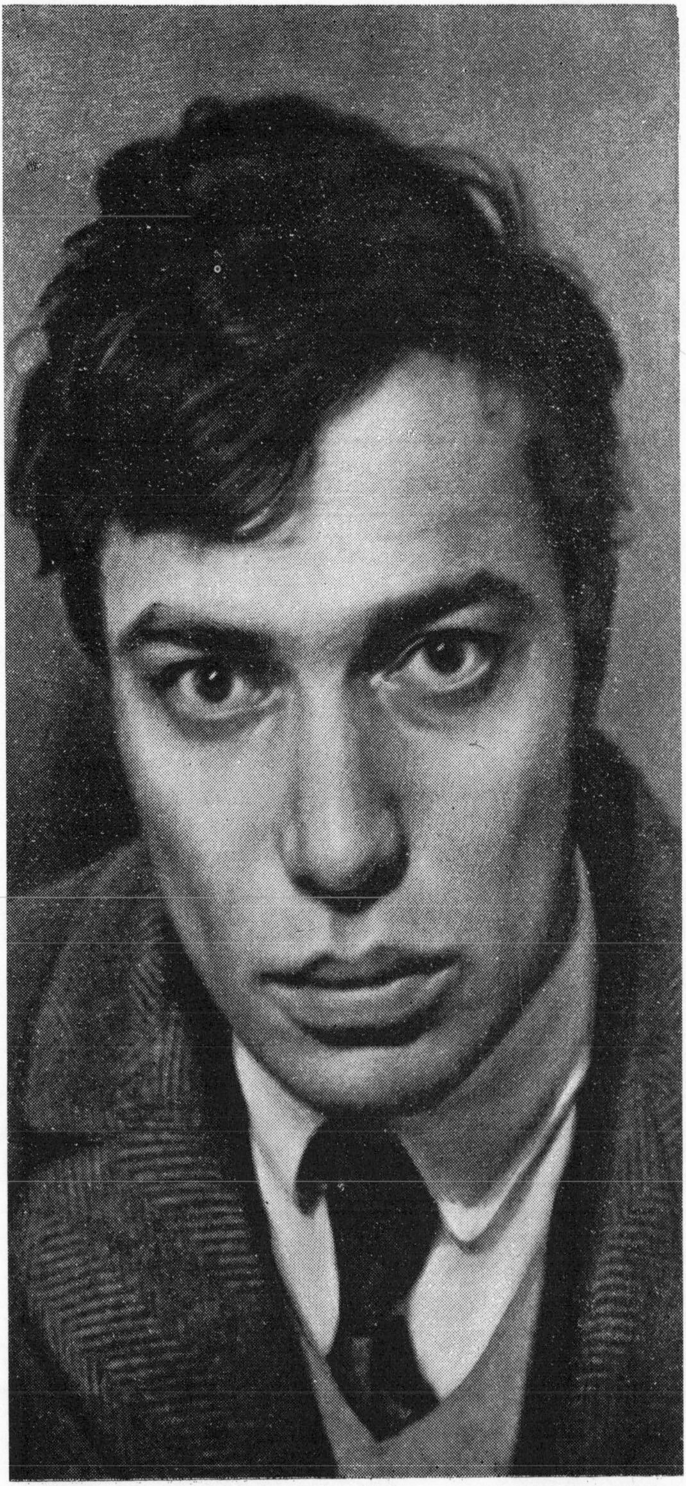

Fifty Years of Russian Prose:

From Pasternak to Solzhenitsyn

Edited by
Krystyna Pomorska

Volume 1

The MIT Press
Cambridge,
Massachusetts,
and London,
England

Set in Lumitype Optima
Printed by The Apine Press Inc.
Bound in the United States of America by The Colonial Press Inc.

Second printing, first MIT Press paperback edition, October 1973

"Il Tratto di Apelle," reprinted by permission of Ernest Benn Ltd., London; "Aerial Tracks," reprinted by permission of Anchor Books, Doubleday and Company, New York; "The Cave," reprinted by permission of Ginn and Company, Boston; "Second Lieutenant Likewise," reprinted by permission of Peter Owen, Ltd., London.

ISBN 0-262-16037-4 (hardcover)
ISBN 0-262-66019-9 (paperback)
Library of Congress catalog card number: 70-122263

Contents

Introduction

This anthology does not pretend to offer what might be called a "faithful picture" of Russian prose after the 1917 Revolution. It would hardly be possible to present such a picture without giving the reader a heavy academic volume of selections with commentaries, a literary panorama, with many pieces as bad as they were "representative."

Instead, the present volume shows the output of writers belonging to different schools, different groups, and professing different creeds. All, however, beginning with Pasternak—once associated with Mayakovsky and the Futurists—as well as the proletarian writer Platonov, Vsevolod Ivanov (a member of the Serapion Brotherhood), or such independent writers as Tsvetaeva and Grin—all are united by one particular aspect: they create their own vision by experimenting with verbal material, freeing themselves from outdated conventions, sometimes called "realistic."

The abundance of literary phenomena after 1917, the outburst and rapid growth of innovations and experiments, is equaled only by the diversity and unevenness of their value. Yet it is definitely a period that Maurice Bowra has felicitously termed "the period of the great experiment." This spirit of experimentation and innovation was certainly stimulated by the social and political changes of the times. One must not forget, however, that the era of literary revolution in Russia began well before October 1917.

By the late twenties two powerful trends had left their impact on Russian literature: Symbolism, which may be said to date from the 1890s, and Futurism, the first manifestations of which were shocking the public and shaping opinions around 1912.

In spite of the many differences between the two schools (the Futurists emerged as the main adversaries of their Symbolist predecessors), they both re-established the idea of pure literary values—whether those of Symbolist aestheticism or those of strict Futurist craftmanship. Together they brought about the true revival of the cult of verbal art and of the poetic word in itself. Characteristically enough, the Russian Symbolists and Futurists were first and foremost poets. Symbolist prose, such as that of Sologub and especially Bely, was but a byproduct of the poetry. This fact becomes even more significant if we recall that before Symbolism the literary horizon in Russia was dominated for half a century by realistically oriented prose and by a criticism heavily charged with ideological and didactic issues.

Since the turn of the century the outstanding figures in Russian literature have been poets. The names of Balmont, Bryusov, Blok, Khlebnikov, Mayakovsky, and Pasternak, to mention only a few, are known to the world as symbols of the new poetry.

Until the famous First Congress of Soviet Writers in 1934, when the doctrine of Socialist Realism was introduced, Russian prose developed under the influence of experimental poetry as well as of similar phenomena in cinema, theater, and painting.

It is fitting that two stories from Pasternak's early prose should open this selection. Very few English-speaking persons know that before he wrote *Doctor Zhivago* Pasternak had been greatly occupied since his earliest years with a kind of prose reflecting the ideas and the style of his poetry. Metonymical relations are predominant in both genres in Pasternak's writings. "Il Tratto di Apelle," his earliest attempt in prose, already displays this quality to a considerable extent. Various phenomena, related by simple contiguity and commonly considered thus unrelated, start acting *for* each other and *in place of* each other. People of Pisa "burned the fragrant Tuscan night" – instead of just living in a brightly lit night. "The leaning tower of Pisa had pushed its way through a chain of medieval fortifications" – a part of a cityscape is given the power to act for the whole.

In a later tale, "The Childhood of Luvers" (1918),* marginalia changed places with those aspects commonly considered central. Zhenya, the little heroine of this charming story, lets pass unheeded what the adults consider the main theme of conversation, but she watches and listens with eagerness for what the others disdain as "unnecessary details," mere trifles. She also does not look on facts as having causal relationships, an association accepted by adults as obvious common sense. This point of view is supported by the very structure of the story, which develops in parallel fragments rather than in causally connected elements that are the usual components of plot.

In "Aerial Tracks," a story written six years later, Pasternak presents the same problems and emphasizes the same conceptions, only under another guise. The plot suggests that coincidence rules people's lives – coincidence, another form of the contiguity, opposed to the cause-and-effect beliefs people hold with fervor despite the facts. It is coincidence that brings the former lovers together at the precise moment in which the little son of Lolya and her present husband is lost. The desperate mother tries to intensify her companion's effort to find the baby by telling him that the lost child is his son. This startling news, however, produces a result opposite to what was intended: the man loses all zeal in looking for the child. What might have been a mysterious event and a disinterested deed becomes a boring cliché when the man is exhorted to "do it *because* he is yours."

*This tale, frequently published in other collections, was not included in our anthology.

The repetition of a similar pattern "fifteen years later"—this time with more serious implications leading to a tragic dénouement—confirms Pasternak's belief in the coincidental and contiguous structure of the universe. Once more we are faced with a free pattern of contiguity whose elements freely shift in time and space and are tossed "like sand in an hourglass." The events in our lives are comparable with the pure forms in the universe, and he sees them as hazy configurations without names, which at times bend "from past to future, and from future to past." Their position may be changed not only in time but also in space: "They were resting . . . the distances between them, compared with the daytime distances, widened." ("Aerial Tracks").

The principle of the free relations among phenomena explains the ruling power of coincidence. The novel *Doctor Zhivago* is constructed on this principle. This is precisely what connects Pasternak with the experimental art of his time. The idea of contiguity as the basis of metonymic structure was introduced by the Cubists in painting, and was applied by the Futurists to poetry. Braque is declared to have said, "I do not believe in things. I believe only in the mutual relations between things." This is one way of defining the metonymic principle, by virtue of which either entities are presented as parts instead of wholes (synecdoche) or else they arbitrarily change their spatial relations. In Futurist poetry the "parts of words" often stand for the words themselves. The imagery and organization of Mayakovsky's and Khlebnikov's poems embody the same principle. The only distinction is that the Futurists treated metonymy on a purely aesthetic level, whereas Pasternak elevates it to a philosophic postulate of the pattern of the universe.

Zamyatin's famous story "The Cave" (1920) presents a theme different from Pasternak's. Zamyatin's is the theme of people on the periphery of life. Ever since the author of *We* published his first collection of stories, entitled *Things Provincial* (1913), this theme was always his main interest. In recent history it took on factual reality, when people were reduced to a cave existence during the civil warfare of the twenties with its freezing cold and starvation. The plot of "The Cave" rests on two dramatic episodes: the theft of firewood and the suicide of the heroine. It unfolds in a remarkable manner. Two sets of imagery are invoked: a cave and a siege. The siege is expressed as the constant battle against cold and starvation. In its course man is steadily pushed back as he gives up one room after another so as to preserve the minimum warmth for existence. The metaphor of the cave is reflected in a series of images—

"the iron god," or "the animal hides," within which man huddles, or the final image, that of a mammoth.

Another remarkable feature of Zamyatin's technique is his elliptical style. Neither the characters nor the events are represented explicitly. For example, the theft is not referred to directly but is intimated in the following: "And he—one log, then—the other. . . ." Similarly, we learn of Masha's suicide indirectly, so that only the pathetic pill bottle signifies the means of death. The characters themselves are described by an emblematic indication: Martin Martinych has a "clay face," Masha's is "like paper," and Obertyshev's is "all teeth."

Various critics have noted that Zamyatin employs a cinematic technique in this story. Again it is notable that this technique is based on the metonymic principle. In a sense it is dictated by the natural facilities of the cinema. On the one hand, the speed and mobility of the camera and the limits of the frame on the other compel a creator to display only a part of the whole, thus producing a special artistic effect.

The early twenties were a time of magnificent development of films as an art form, and of Soviet films in particular. Eisenstein produced his *Potemkin,* Dovzhenko and Dziga Vertov enchanted the audiences of Moscow, Petrograd, and Western Europe with their fantastic visions. Zamyatin, with his tendency toward implicitness of style, certainly owes a great deal to the cinematic vanguard.

Boris Pilnyak occupies a special position in Soviet literature. Once he was acclaimed as the leading writer of his time, the founder of modern Soviet prose. The setting of his stories, like Zamyatin's, is provincial Russia with all its idiosyncrasies and backwardness. His first collection, *Things Long Forgotten* (1915–1919), appeared before the Revolution, but it was his novel *The Naked Year* that made his reputation (1922). Pilnyak's interpretation of the Revolution, however, was thought to be too far removed from the official line. Like some other writers of his time, such as Esenin, Klyuev, or Klychkov (whom Trotsky called "the peasant singers"), Pilnyak saw it as a primal movement in which the peasants played the chief role. He compared the period with the time of Peter the Great, a time of mutinies, a time influenced by religious sectarianism. This point of view was reinforced by Pilnyak's negative appraisal of modern civilization with its rapid technological development, and he predicted man's defeat by the machine. In his novel *Machines and Wolves* (1924), the machine ravages a man. Shortly thereafter Pilnyak's position was defined as "neo-Slavophilism," and he himself was attacked for proclaiming the defeat of civilization.

"The Death of the Army Commander"—or, to cite its poetic

subtitle, "A Tale of the Unextinguished Moon" — has a special place among Pilnyak's writings. Instead of the usual provincial scene, he chooses the very center, the Moscow Kremlin, and official personages are his actors. As the story too closely resembled actual events,* it was confiscated immediately after its appearance (1926) in the journal *Novy Mir*. Even though Lunacharsky, then the Commissar of Education, was its editor, the issue was destroyed, and the editorial board published a special note of self-criticism for having committed "an obvious and flagrant error."

Whatever the actual story is behind this brilliant piece, its salient feature is its depiction of the destiny of the Party member, the devoted Communist, and consequently a tragic figure during the period of "personality worship." In the war years his fate is subject to the imminence of death "for the sake of the Revolution." Yet even as a civilian he is compelled to bend to the inexorable "will of the Revolution." He learns that orders have already been issued with regard to his "security," his health, his life, and his death. He reads in the newspapers of his own destiny, already ordained, before any notification is sent him.

Pilnyak's narrative technique makes use of montage. As in his larger work, *Ivan Moskva* (1927), he employs newspaper headlines, slogans, or excerpts from army reports as stylistic contrast to the intimate dialogue and the scenes from the lives of two officials, Commander Gavrilov and his friend Popov. Such a contrast reinforces the reader's ever increasing horror at the regimented existence to which Gavrilov must submit, cut off from the stream of life, still free, that surrounds him.

The same device of contrast is seen in the style of the dialogue between Gavrilov and "a straight-backed man" (who obviously has Stalin's characteristics). While the latter's speech bears the stamp of newspaper headlines, Gavrilov speaks a language of freedom, as friend to friend.

It is worth noting that another device making "the straight-backed man" faceless and terrifying is the lack of a proper name for him. In Russian tradition, the tsar's name was a taboo, a notion arising from the belief in his divine origin. Up to the time of Alexander I the tsar was identified with God Himself. It is for this very reason that in Pushkin's famous poem "The Bronze Horseman," Peter the Great is never mentioned by name. The artistic effect is intentionally mystical. In modern times Pilnyak uses the same device to even greater effect.

*It was believed to have been based on the death of General Frunze.

Although the two stories represent quite different artistic values, "The Death of the Army Commander" and "Chocolate" (1922) by the proletarian writer Tarasov-Rodyonov are comparable. There is a sociological basis for such juxtaposition. Both stories present an analysis of the totalitarian ideology that penetrates an individual's deepest thoughts and takes possession of him. Another theme recurrent in twentieth-century literature is also present here: a party member—an ardent Communist, a soldier, "an iron man"—is shown in his intimate relations with his family and his friends. An inevitable conflict develops between his *privata privatissima* (to which he has no political right) and his duty to the organization. Zudin's case is even more interesting and significant. He is proved guilty of a crime against the Party, even though this crime is quite fictitious, and he agrees to sacrifice his life in order to serve as an example of crime and punishment, because the moment calls for it. The ensuing psychological complex—that of the revolutionary who agrees to repent of, and die for, his uncommitted yet conceivable faults—was later to be called "the Rubashov complex," after the character in Arthur Koestler's famous novel *Darkness at Noon*. Koestler wrote his brilliant and highly intellectualized story after the Moscow show trials of the "Trotskyite opposition" of the 1930s. Tarasov-Rodyonov, for all his literary shortcomings, had prefigured the Rubashov complex as early as 1922. It is mainly for this reason that the story "Chocolate" is included here.

Isaac Babel, a Jew from Odessa, represents an outstanding phenomenon not only in Russian but also in world literature. His *Red Cavalry* (1926), translated into most European languages immediately after its publication, raised a great controversy in his native land. On the one hand, Babel was praised for the rich romantic qualities of his prose and his characters, and on the other, he was attacked for proclaiming "banditism." A startling reaction came from Marshal Budyonny himself, the commander of the very cavalry unit Babel was describing and one in which he had served. In an open letter with the scornful heading "Babizm Babelya,"* Budyonny accused the writer of having slandered "the heroic Red Cavalry."

The reason for such violent attacks and sharp differences of opinion lies in the exceptional quality of Babel's prose. Romantically heroic, it is at the same time authentic and naturalistic. It displays both literary convention and striking

*An untranslatable pun, based on the word *baba*, a colloquial and derogatory term for "woman."

novelty, thus creating an ambiguity beyond the understanding of Babel's contemporaries—and often it is beyond that of his readers of today. The short, highly concentrated novella, usually built on a single event, strikes a balance between contrasting extremes. Cruelty goes side by side with human goodness and fidelity, just as the naturalistic, "forbidden" detail goes side by side with a lyrical landscape.

All these qualities may be observed in one of the most representative stories from *Red Cavalry*, "The Widow." As often happens in Babel's prose, the reader's attention is entirely focused on a detail that is placed in the foreground, whereas the background (the battlefield) remains in shadow. But the details themselves offer such a rich range of impressions that a concrete description of the battle, usual in a war story, becomes superfluous. Moreover, the event is presented without any psychological approach, almost purely "behavioristically," that is, without the author's omniscience.

As Babel himself testified, Chekhov and Maupassant, both masters of the short story, were his teachers. Yet another kind of affinity appears between Babel and Chekhov in their world outlook. In the latter's case, the trivialities and the incongruity of life are elevated to the tragic. Babel, on the other hand, shows tragedy and cruelty as inherent in everyday happenings.

"The Story of My Dovecote" comes from another cycle, *Tales* (1925). Its autobiographical character and introspective approach make it strikingly different from *Red Cavalry*. Yet many of the features of the latter book may also be detected in this extraordinary piece. A little boy's initiation into life is accompanied by the savage ruthlessness he experiences from some, whereas others, like the boy himself, show tenderness and high moral dignity.

"The Child" (1922) by Vsevolod Ivanov has certain parallels with some of Babel's writings. Here also the cruelty of man is presented with impartiality, like something as genuine as nature itself. The great difference between the two stories, however, lies in the fact that Babel's soldiers are strongly conditioned in their decisions, whereas Afanasy Petrovich and his comrades make theirs with much more freedom of will. They choose to kill one child in order to save another, and this choice is determined by the fact that one is "merely" Khirghiz, whereas the other, little Vaska, is "a Russian man." Vaska is also especially protected by Afanasy, who for some reason feels a particular love for him and decides to save him at any cost. This is precisely what makes the story strange and "exotic." Man appears in it as a "wild and joyless beast," like Mongolia itself. He is as whimsical and unpredictable as is nature in Asia, which Ivanov knew so well and describes so powerfully. The critical point, however, is that here man happens to be a Red Partisan, a revolutionary, who acts with pure and instinctive spontaneity. He is presented as a basically biological being, motivated subconsciously. This makes the Revolution itself "strange," and indeed it was Ivanov's intention to show it as such. A strong tinge of exoticism—for which he was severely criticized—colors all his early stories.

Ivanov was a member of the literary group "without vote or statute" that called itself the Serapion Brotherhood (founded in 1921) and promulgated the complete freedom of the artist to create his own reality according to his own vision. The Brotherhood chose Zamyatin as its patron and literary master, and not by chance: he was certainly an artist who remained faithful to his own vision and to his own inner discipline. Such a position could not go unchallenged, and the Serapions were soon attacked by certain other groups (for example, the "On Guard"), which eventually entered into the Russian Association of Proletarian Writers (RAPP), an all-powerful organization until its official abolition in 1932. Ivanov suffered one of the sharpest possible attacks for his "biologism" and for a more common crime, "the distortion of reality."

The years following the First Congress of Soviet Writers in 1934 were years of increasing indoctrination, when all talents were supposed to be leveled and all literary groups dissolved. The years of the great experiment were over. There were very few who withstood the powerful anti-intellectual oppression. One of these was Konstantin Paustovsky. Having rejected the fashionable "timely" themes and having retained his own vision, Paustovsky continued writing about man and his nature, about the strange and whimsical destinies of people, regardless of their class affiliation, their involvements, or occupations. This persistence gained him the label of "cosmopolitan," which, needless to say, was a dangerous category at a time of "personality worship."

"Rain at Dawn" (1945) presents Paustovsky's characteristic style and motifs. Every man is given a role that does not satisfy him—he longs for some other, one that belongs to a different man. What is apparently accidental or coincidental, momentary and elusive, is often what one most desires, something remembered vividly, even for one's whole life. Such is the sense of the parable about Kuzmin, Bashilov, and Olga Andreevna.

Both the philosophy and the structure of the story clearly echo Chekhov. The sad, subdued tone, the setting—a remote provincial town, the old-fashioned and slightly mysterious "house with the mezzanine," its emphatically symbolic accessories, an open volume of Blok's poetry, wild flowers on the piano, and most dramatic of all, the boat siren that mercilessly puts an end to the bitter-sweet meeting—these features are very close to Chekhov's lyrical prose. Paustovsky's choice of such a tradition is meaningful. In those years Chekhov was not a desirable example to follow. He was too ambiguous, too "pessimistic," and not heroic enough. He created ideological and didactic difficulties for the interpreters of literature. The fact that Paustovsky followed this aspect of the Russian classical inheritance signifies his creative independence.

The last story in the present volume comes from the pen of a writer of the new generation. Victor Nekrasov was entirely formed by the new era. Having fought with the corps of engineers during World War II, he had actually had the experiences of the soldier he describes. His first war story, *In the Trenches of Stalingrad* (a novel of 1946), is a narrative of day-to-day fighting, much in the manner of the literature of the war years. *Senka* (a story from a collection of 1950) differs markedly from most of the battle literature written before and during the last war. Its main theme—what is heroism and what is cowardice and treason?—is treated with a psychological insight and an analytical manner that are close to Tolstoy's. What might have been classified as plain treason by some didactic representatives of Socialist Realism is shown in Nekrasov's story as the natural reflex of a frightened boy. His later self-reproach is born of the feeling that he has been unfaithful to his brothers-in-arms, has displayed a lack of solidarity with the community, but not that he has committed a crime against the "Socialist Motherland." Senka's heroic deed, performed at the end of the story, is in part owing to his skill in throwing grenades.

This tale marks the beginning of the pacifist and "antiheroic" literature later continued by writers like Okudzhava, and also by such remarkable Soviet films as *The Ballad of a Soldier*.

Three writers included in this anthology are strikingly different from the others, both in style and content. Alexander Grin invents foreign lands and characters with foreign names. His prose in the Russian original sounds as if it had been translated. Yury Tynyanov's story is based on purely philological invention. His protagonist is created out of a mistake in spelling. And his subtlety in employing historical parallels sets his work apart from the transparent analogies of his contemporaries.

About the third writer, Marina Tsvetaeva, one might ask, why should she be included among the prose writers? The primary reason was given at the beginning of this Introduction: both the poetry and the prose of poets cast light on the general literary development of the times. We have chosen from Tsvetaeva's relatively abundant prose production her essay "On Gratitude." It is a rare and almost completely unknown text, first published in the émigré journal of Brussels, *Blagonamerenny* (No. 1, 1926).

The fragment "My Pushkin" is characteristic of Tsvetaeva's special attachment to Russia's greatest poet. A whole volume of essays by her on Pushkin appeared recently in the Soviet Union. Her interpretation of Tatyana's rebuff to Onegin throws new light on this most enigmatic figure from Pushkin's masterpiece. It also casts light on Tsvetaeva herself, whose prose is autobiographical through and through. Her understanding of literature and literary personages reflects her own being and is a psychological elucidation of herself.

Krystyna Pomorska
Ossabaw Island, Georgia
January 1971

Fifty Years of Russian Prose

Volume 1

Acknowledgment

I extend my sincere thanks to Mrs. Elsie Bowen for her editorial help in preparing this volume.
Krystyna Pomorska

Il Tratto di Apelle

Boris Pasternak

They say that when the Greek artist Apelles discovered that his rival Zeuxis was not at home, he drew a line on the wall, so that Zeuxis would be able to guess who it was who had come in his absence. Zeuxis did not remain long in debt to his fellow-artist. He chose a time when Apelles was known to be away from home and left his mark, which became the proverbial sign of art.

1

On one of the September evenings when the sloping tower of Pisa led a whole army of oblique colors and sidelong shadows against Pisa, when all Tuscany, irritated by the night wind, smelled like a frayed laurel held between the fingers, on one of these evenings, I even remember the date—23rd August—on this evening Emilio Relinquimini, not finding Heine in the hotel, demanded paper and light from the obsequiously fawning lackey. And when the lackey reappeared, bringing beside the objects he had been asked for an inkbottle and a penholder, a seal and a stick of wax, Relinquimini dismissed him with a gesture of the utmost fastidiousness. Taking the pin from his tie, he placed it over the candle and waited until it was white hot, pricked himself in the finger and, taking one of the innkeeper's cards from a pile of similar cards, he bent it round the end of his bleeding finger. Then he handed it nonchalantly to the lackey with the words, "You are to give Herr Heine this visiting card. Tomorrow I shall visit him at the same hour."

The leaning tower of Pisa had pushed its way through a chain of medieval fortifications. The number of people who could see it from the bridge was increasing every minute. The red glow of the sky, like a pursuivant, crawled along the square. The streets were blocked with tiptilted shadows, some of which were still fighting in the narrow alleyways. The tower of Pisa continued its march, mowing everything down, until at last one insane, gigantic shadow covered the sun. The day broke into pieces. And meanwhile the lackey, briefly and confusedly informing Heine of his recent visit, succeeded several minutes before the final setting of the sun in presenting the impatient guest with a card bearing a coagulating yellow stain.

"What an original!" But Heine immediately guessed the name of the visitor, who was the author of the famous poem "*Il sangue*." The accident by which Relinquimini arrived in Pisa from Ferrara on exactly the same day that Heine arrived from Westphalia—obeying the even more capricious whimsy of a poet on his holidays—this fortune did not seem strange to him. He remembered the anonymous person from whom he had received several days before a negligently written, defiant letter. The claims of the unknown passed the frontiers of the permissible. Speaking vaguely about the blood call of poetry, the unknown demanded of Heine . . . his Apelles-like *pièce d'identité*. "Love [wrote the unknown] this cloud stained with the blood which often overlays our cloudless blood . . . you must speak of it in such a way that it will be as laconic as the signature of Apelles. Remember only that you belong to the aristocracy of spirit and of blood (these things cannot be separated). This is the only thing about which Zeuxis is curious.

"*P.S.* I have profited by your stay in Pisa, of which I was so opportunely informed by my publisher Conti, to put an end once and for all to my tortures of conscience. Within three days I shall come to you and look at the signature of Apelles."

The servant who appeared at the summons of Heine was given the following communication:

"I am taking the ten o'clock train for Ferrara. Tomorrow evening, the bearer of the card, who is already known to you, will ask to see me. You will personally hand him this parcel. Please let me have the bill and call the *facchino*."

The ghostly weight of the parcel, which was apparently empty, was nevertheless due to a thin sheaf of papers, obviously selected from some manuscripts. And this sheaf of papers comprised only a part of a phrase, without beginning or end: "But Rondolfina and Enrico have discarded their old names and changed them into names hitherto unprecedented: he cried wildly, 'Rondolfina,' she replied 'Enrico . . .'"

2

On the paving stones, on the asphalt marketplaces, on the balconies of Pisa and the embankments of the Arno, the inhabitants burned the fragrant Tuscan night. Out of the burning darkness of the night, the scent lay heavily on the suffocating passageways, and under the dust-laden plane trees; and its burning, glittering splendor was crowned with scattered sheaves of light from the stars and clusters of thorny mist. These flashes of light overflowed in the bowl of Italian patience: from the heat of their fervor they uttered curses, as though they were prayers, and wiped the humid sweat from their brows before they had even glanced at Cassiopeia. Handkerchiefs gleamed in the dark like shaken thermometers. The readings of these cambric thermometers spread perniciously along the streets: they diffused oppressive heat, like snatched-up rumors, like panic fear. And just as the stagnating town disintegrated unconditionally, the streets, the houses, the courtyards, so in the same way the night air was compounded of separate and motionless collisions, ejaculations, bloody quarrels and encounters, whispers of laughter and dropping voices. Those echoes existed in dustladen and frequent *interweavings:* they stood out in rows, which grew out of the pavement like the trees in the street, suffocating and colorless in the light of the gasflares. Fantastically and powerfully, the night of Pisa traced a limit to human endurance. Beyond these frontiers chaos began. Such a chaos reigned over the railway station. Here handkerchiefs and curses disappeared from the scene.

People to whom a moment before a simple and natural movement would have seemed a torture, here, clinging to their bags and parcels, bellowed at the ticket office and like madmen stormed the charred carriages, made siege on the footboards and, covered with soot so that they looked like chimney sweeps, hurled themselves into compartments partitioned by burning brown veneer which appeared to be warped by the heat, by the violent language and the incessant jolting of the passengers. The carriages were burning, the sleepers were burning, the naphtha tanks and the locomotives in the siding were burning, even the signals were burning, while the engines from far and near uttered their lamentations through the steam. Hobbling with flashlights, like a buzzing insect, the heavy breath of the open furnace fell asleep on the engine driver's cheeks and the leather jacket of the fireman: the engine driver and the fireman were both burning. The clock dial was burning, the iron crossbars of the speedometer and the minute hands were burning; the watchmen were burning. All this was beyond the range of human endurance. All this could be endured.

A seat by the window. A moment later—an entirely deserted platform formed of massive stone, massive rumbling sounds and massive exhortation from the guard: *Pronti!*—and the guard runs alongside in pursuit of his own exhortations. The columns of the station slip smoothly away. Lights scurry along, intermingling like knitting needles. Gleams of light from the reflectors catch the carriage windows, caught up by the draught, proceed through, beyond and across the opposite windows, lie along the line trailing, slide on the rails, rise and disappear behind the cartsheds. Dwarf streets, misshapen and hybrid corners—the jaws of the viaduct swallow them with a hollow roar. The blustering of approaching gardens close to the blind. The restful space of the curling carpet of vines. Fields.

Heine travels in a happy-go-lucky fashion. He has nothing to think about, he attempts to doze, he closes his eyes.

"Something will certainly come of it. There is no sense in making guesses about the future, no sense and no possibility of a solution. The future is always a delightful mystery."

The wild oranges probably in flower. Scented gardens overflowing. From where the breeze temporarily sleeps on the close-clinging eyelids of the passenger.

This is playing for safety. Something will certainly come of it. It can't be without reason—Heine yawned—that in all the amorous poems of Relinquimini, there is the unchangeable annotation: Ferrara.

Rocks, precipices, his neighbors crestfallen in sleep, the stench of the carriage, the tongues of gaslight. The gaslight licks the rustling noises and shadows from the ceiling, it licks itself and is out of breath when rocks and precipices are followed by a tunnel: the rumbling mountain creeps down along the roof of the carriage, spreads smoke from the engine, drives it through the windows, clings between racks and pegs. Tunnels and valleys. A road with a single cart track wails monotonously above the small mountain river which breaks against the rock; it rushes down from some improbable heights, fast invisible in the darkness. And here the waterfalls smoke and churn, and all night their strident rumbling encircles the train.

"The signature of Apelles . . . Rondolfina . . . Probably I shall not succeed in a single day. And I have no more time. I must hide without leaving a trace . . . Tomorrow. . . . And how he will run to the station when the lackey informs him of my journey!"

Ferrara! The blue-black steely dawn. The sweet-smelling mist saturated with coolness. O, how sonorous is a Latin morning!

3

"Impossible, the issue of *Voce* is already in page proof."

"Yes, but I refuse to surrender my discovery to anyone or for any money; meanwhile I can't stay in Ferrara for more than a day."

"You say his notebook was in the carriage under the seat?"

"Certainly, the notebook of Emilio Relinquimini, a notebook possessing a large number of manuscript pages and an immense quantity of unpublished poetry, rough copies, fragments, aphorisms. The entries were made throughout the year, mostly in Ferrara, as far as can be judged from the dates written underneath."

"Where is it? Have you got it?"

"No, I left my things at the station, but the book was in the traveling bag."

"A thousand pities! We might have been able to send the book to the house. The publishers know Relinquimini's address in Ferrara, but he has already been away for a month."

"What, Relinquimini is not in Ferrara?"

"That's the trouble. I really can't understand how you can hope to succeed by publishing an advertisement on this discovery of yours."

"Just this—with the help of your newspaper it may be possible to arrange a trustworthy liaison between myself and the owner of the book, and Relinquimini may at any moment profit by the courteous services of *Voce* in the affair."

"Then there is nothing to be done with you. Please sit down and have the kindness to make a declaration."

"I'm so sorry to worry you, but the telephone—will you allow me?"

"Do anything you like."

"Hotel Torquato Tasso? Could you let me know whether you have any rooms free? What floor? Good, reserve number eight for me."

"*Ritrovamento*. The manuscript of a book by Emilio Relinquimini, recently prepared for publication, has been found. The person occupying room number eight in the Hotel Tasso will be expecting the owner of the manuscript or his representatives, while staying in the room throughout the day until eleven o'clock at night. Commencing with the following day the publishers of *Voce*, in common with the directors of the hotel, will periodically and in good time be informed by the above-mentioned person of each change of his address."

Heine was tired by the journey and slept a dead and leaden sleep. The venetian blinds of his room, warm with the breath of morning, were like copper membranes of a mouth-organ burning. A net of light from the small window fell on the floor, taking the shape of a raveled straw mat. The straw closes its ranks, crowds together, squeezes together. On the street—faint conversations. Someone loses the train of his thoughts, someone else gathers them together again. The straw is already compressed into a single mass and already the straw mat has become a pool of sunlight spilled on the floor. An hour passes. On the street men are talking nonsense, they nod their heads; on the streets voices are being lulled to sleep. Heine sleeps. The sunlight pool is let loose: it seems that the inlaid floor is impregnated with it. Once more it is a thinning straw mat of singed and crumpled straw. Heine sleeps. Conversations in the street. Hours pass. They grow lazy, together with the black patches on the straw mat. Conversations in the street. The straw mat fades, is covered with dust, grows dull. Already it is an old string mat inextricably entangled. Already it is impossible to distinguish the threads and the stitches from the knots. Conversations in the street. Heine sleeps.

In another moment Heine will wake up. In another moment

Heine will slip out of bed, remember my words. Let him but see the last chapter of his dream to the end. . . .

Desiccated by the heat, the wheel suddenly cracks as far as the nave. The spokes protrude like a cluster of split pegs, the barrow falls to one side with a thump and a crash, bales of newspapers fall out—a crowd, sunshades, shop windows, awnings—they take the newspaper boy away on a handcart and the chemist's shop is nearby.

Look! What did I say! Heine leaps up. "Just a moment!" Someone is knocking at the door furiously and impatiently. Heine, half awake, his hair tousled, still in his cups, reaches for his dressing-gown. "Excuse me a moment!" With an almost metallic rattling his right leg falls heavily on the floor. "I'm coming at once!" Heine walks to the door.

"Who is there?"

The voice of the lackey.

"Yes, yes. I have the manuscript. Give the signora my apologies. Is she in the drawing room?"

The voice of the lackey.

"Ask the signora to wait ten minutes. In ten minutes I shall be entirely at her disposal. Do you hear?"

The voice of the lackey.

"Wait a moment."

The voice of the lackey.

"And don't forget to tell mademoiselle that the signor expresses his sincere regret that he is unable to join her this very minute, that he feels deeply sorry, but he will try. . . . Do you hear?"

The voice of the lackey.

". . . but in ten minutes he will try to make complete amends for his inexcusable inadvertence . . . and say it very politely, lackey, because I am not from Ferrara."

The voice of the lackey.

"Very good, very good. Lackey, is the lady in the drawing room?"

"Yes, signor."

"Is she alone?"

"Alone, signor, if it pleases you. On the left, signor. On the left."

"Good morning, what can I do for the signora?"

"*Pardon*. Are you from room number eight?"

"Yes, that is my room."

"I have come for Relinquimini's notebook."

"Allow me to present myself—Heinrich Heine."

"Excuse me, are you related to the . . . ?"

"Not in the least. An accidental coincidence. Even an embarrassing one. I too have the pleasure. . . ."

"You write poetry?"

"I have never written anything else."

"I know German well and spend all my leisure reading poetry, but. . . ."

"Do you know *The Poems Which Were Unpublished during the Poet's Lifetime*?"

"Of course. Now I realize who you are."

"Forgive me, but I have an ardent desire to know your name."

"Camilla Ardenze."

"Extraordinarily pleased. Now, signora Ardenze, did you happen to see my advertisement in the *Voce*?"

"Of course. All about the notebook which has been found. Where is it? Give it to me."

"Signora! Signora Camilla, you—perhaps with all your heart—celebrated by the incomparable Relinquimini. . . ."

"Don't! We are not on the stage."

"You are mistaken, signora. We spend our whole lives on the stage and it is only with the greatest difficulty that some of us assume the naturalness which is bequeathed to us, like the character of an actor, on the day of our births."

"Signora Camilla, you love your native town, you love Ferrara, but (I must tell you this) it is the first town I have ever come across which definitely repels me—you are beautiful, Signora Camilla—and my heart shudders at the thought that you and this detestable town are both conspiring against me."

"I fail to understand you."

"Don't interrupt me, signora—this town, I was saying, which lulled me to sleep like the poisoner who lulls to sleep his boon companion when the hour of his fate draws near, doing it in order to awaken a spark of disdain with regard to his fate in the eyes of the unhappy man who has just entered the tavern, and fate betrays the man who has been lulled. Milady, the poisoner turns to the woman who enters—look at the lie-a-bed: it is your beloved; he beguiled the hours of waiting with stories about you; they were like spurs when they pierced my imagination. Did you not gallop here on its back? Why did you whip it so unmercifully with your gossamer whip? It is lathered in sweat—it is in heat!

"O these stories! But allow yourself to glance at him. Milady, he is pulled by his own stories about you—you see, the separation has the effect of a lullaby on your beloved. However, we can awaken him. It is not necessary, the poisoner answers for the fate of the man who was poisoned. Needless to alarm him. He sleeps so sweetly and perhaps he even sees me in his dreams. Far better to arrange that I should be provided with a glass of punch. It is cold in the street. I am numb. Please rub my hands."

"You are very strange to me, Herr Heine. But continue, please, for your exalted speech entertains me."

"Excuse me if I have forgotten Relinquimini's notebook. I shall go up to my room. . . ."

"Don't trouble, I won't forget about it. Continue, please. What an amusing man. Continue. 'Please rub my hands,' said fate. Isn't that what she was saying?"

"Yes, signora, and many thanks for listening so attentively."

"Well?"

"Well then, this town has treated me exactly as the poisoner treated his boon companion—and you, beautiful Camilla, are on the side of the town. The town overheard my thoughts of crumbling dawns, as old as robber castles and as solitary, and it lulled me to sleep because it wanted to take advantage of them stealthily, and it allowed me to speak to my heart's content about gardens, borne on immense sails from the red evening air into the night, and it hoisted the sails and left me lying in the port tavern, and I am sure you will refuse to allow it to awaken me, if the crafty rogue should propose such a thing."

"Listen, my dear. Where am I in all this story? I do hope the lackey definitely woke you."

"Ah, so you think the night comes, there may be a storm, one must hurry, the time is up, don't wake him."

"O signor Heine, what illusions you have! I say yes, yes, Ferrara, ruffle his hair if he is still asleep; I have no time, rouse him roughly; assemble all your crowds; rumble in all the city squares; rumble until he is awake, there is so little time."

"Ah, but the notebook. . . ."

"We'll talk about that afterward."

"O my dear signora, Ferrara has been cheated in its calculations, Ferrara has been duped, the poisoner runs away, I am awakened, I am awake—I am on my knees before you, my love."

Camilla leaped.

"Enough! Enough! All this becomes you—even these commonplaces—yes, precisely these commonplaces! But it can't go on! You are acting like a wandering buffoon! We are almost strangers to each other. Only half an hour ago—it would be funny even to argue about this—and still—and here am I arguing with you. I have never felt more stupid in my life. This whole scene is like a Japanese flower which blossoms instantly in the water. No more and no less! But they are paper flowers! Such cheap flowers!"

"I am still listening to you, signora."

"Signor, I might have listened to you all the more willingly. You are very clever and, it appears, sarcastic. And yet you have no contempt for commonplaces! It is strange but not at all contradictory. Your theatrical pathos!"

"I beg you, signora. Pathos in Greek means passion, but in Italian it is only an empty kiss. And kisses are compulsory——"

"Again! Spare your pains! Intolerable! You are hiding something from me—explain yourself. And listen, please don't be angry with me, my dear signor Heine. For all that—you do not blame me for my familiarity? You are such an unusual child. No, that is not the right word—you are a poet. Why didn't I think of the word at once? But to discover it, it was indeed sufficient to look at you. An idler chosen by God and spoilt by fate."

"Evviva!" Heine leaped on to the windowsill and leaned out with his whole body.

"Careful, signor Heine!" Camilla cried." Careful, you are frightening me!"

"Don't trouble yourself, my dear signora!"

"Hey! *Furfante!* Catch it!" Lyres flew over the square. "Only stay a moment! You will receive ten times as many if only you rob a dozen gardens in Ferrara. A *soldo* for each hole in your trousers! Quickly! Don't breathe on the flowers when you are carrying them. The countess has a mimosa-like sensitiveness. Hurry, you old fool!"

"Did you hear it, enchantress? That ragamuffin will return in the costume of Cupid. But let us speak seriously. What perspicacity! With a single line—the line of Apelles—I have to express all my being, all that is essential to my existence!"

"I don't understand you. Or is this one more piece of play-acting? What is it you really want?"

"Yes, one more piece of playacting. But why am I not allowed to stay for a while under the rays of a perfect illumination? Am I at fault because the most dangerous place in life—bridges and crossroads—are illuminated more strongly than any others? How crude is the light! All the rest is submerged in darkness.

"Imagine a stage with a man illuminated by perturbed flares, as though he were on exhibition—a man enclosed within balustrades, the panorama of the town, precipices and the signal lights on the quays.

"Signora, you would not have listened to one half of what I have to say if we had not encountered one another in such a dangerous place. I am obliged to imagine that it is dangerous although I have myself no knowledge of its danger: it is necessary to imagine it, because whole seas of flame were exhausted by people in imagining it, and it is not my fault if we are illuminated so clumsily and crudely."

"Good. Have you finished? All that is true. But it is all unheard-of nonsense! I want to confide in you. It is not just my fancy. It is almost a necessity for me. You are not lying. Your eyes don't lie. Yes, what is it I wanted to say? I have forgotten. Wait a moment. Listen, my dear, only an hour ago . . . "

"Wait, these are only words. Hours exist, but eternities exist too. Quite a large number of them, and not one has a beginning. At the first opportunity they break away. And this now is a good opportunity. And then away with words! Do you know, signora, when and by whom they are cast down? Away with words! Such revolutions are known to you, signora? Signora, all my fibers rise within me and I must yield to them as one yields to the crowd. And one more thing. Do you remember what you called me just now?"

"Yes. I am quite prepared to repeat it."

"Quite unnecessary. And you know how to look freshly. And already you are in possession of the line, the unique one, like life itself. Don't lose it, don't throw it away on me, repel it only as much as it will allow you to. And then trace the line farther.

"What did you get, signora? What is the result? Are you in profile? Or half-face? Or in some other way?"

"I understand." Camilla stretched out her hands toward Heine. "And yet—no, I am no longer a young girl. One must have control over oneself. Such magnetism."

"Signora!" Heine exclaimed theatrically at the feet of Camilla. "Signora!" he exclaimed in a piercing voice, while he hid his face in his hands. "Have you already drawn the line?"

"How terrible!" He sighed in a whisper, tearing his hands away from his face which had suddenly grown pale . . . looking into the eyes of the completely disconcerted signora Ardenze, noticing to his unspeakable surprise that. . . .

4

. . . that she was really beautiful, that she was beautiful to the extent of being unrecognizable, that the pulse of his own heart throbs like the sea under the stern of a boat, surges, rises, pours close to the approaching knees, rolls over her in lazy layers of waves, sways her silk dress, stretches the smooth contours of her shoulders, lifts her chin and—miracle!—gently raises it a little higher and higher—the signora is now up to her neck in his heart, a wave more—and she will choke and be drowned. Heine seized the drowning woman—a kiss—

a kiss which bore them out of the whirlpool, but he groaned under the pressure of their breaking hearts, twitched and tore himself upward, forward, devil knows in what direction: and she offered no resistance at all. On the contrary if you want it, her body sings, attracted by the kiss, straddled by the kiss, her outstretched body sings; if you want it, I will be a boat for such kisses, only carry me, carry me. . . . The words burst apart with a hoarse sound from Camilla's breast. "A knocking at the door!" "A knock at the door!" and she tears herself away from his embrace.

Then:

"A thousand devils! Who is it?"

"The signor has locked the drawing room, God knows why. It is not the custom here."

"Silence! I shall do as I please."

"You must be ill, sir."

There followed swearing in Italian, sensual, fanatical swearing, like prayers. Heine unlocked the door. The lackey in the corridor had already come to an end of his swearing, and a short distance behind him there was a little ragamuffin whose head was blossoming out into a small forest of liana, oleander flowers, orange blossoms, lilies. . . . "This good-for-nothing . . . roses, magnolia, carnations."

"This good-for-nothing asked to be allowed to enter the room which has windows overlooking the square, and the only room of the kind is the drawing room."

"Yes, yes, the drawing room," the boy snarled.

"Naturally, the drawing room——" Heine agreed. "I myself told him. . . ."

"Because," the lackey continued impatiently, "there could be no question of letting him into the office, the bathroom, or still less the reading room. However, owing to the obvious indecency of his costume . . . "

"Ah, yes," Heine exclaimed, as though he had only just at that moment waked up. "Rondolfina, look at his trousers! Who sewed those breeches of yours out of fish nets, a transparent conglomeration . . . ?"

"Signor, the thorns of the prickly hedges in Ferrara are sharpened every year by special gardeners."

"Ha! ha! ha!"

". . . In view of the obvious indecency of his costume," the lackey continued impatiently, laying special emphasis on this last expression because he saw the signora approaching: on her eyes there wrestled the shadow of a sudden perplexity with gleams of a wholly unquenchable mirth. "On account of the indecency of his costume, we suggested to the boy, transferring to our person the demand made by the signor, that he should wait for the answer in the street. But this little swindler. . . ."

"Yes, yes, he is right," Heine said, bringing the orator to a full stop. "I ordered him to appear personally before the signora."

"This swindler," the angry Calabrian was babbling, "even began to threaten us."

"Precisely how?" Heine asked. "Isn't this terribly characteristic, signora?"

"The little brat referred to you. Signor, he threatened us, he said that the signor merchant would make use of other *albergi* in the course of his travels through Ferrara if, in defiance of his wishes, he wasn't allowed to see the signor."

"Ha! ha! ha! What an amusing person. Don't you agree, Signora? You will carry this tropical plantation, wait a moment!" Heine, turning round, waited for Camilla's orders. "To room number eight," Heine continued without receiving any reply from her.

"In your room, for the moment," Camilla repeated, blushing.

"All right, signor. But what about the boy. . . . "

"As for you, you monkey, what do you think your trousers are worth?"

"Giulio is covered with stripes, Giulio grows blue with cold, Giulio hasn't any other clothes, Giulio has neither father nor mother. . . ." the ten-year-old ragamuffin whimpered tearfully and sweatily.

"Answer, how much?"

"A hundred *soldi*, signor," the boy exclaimed diffidently and dreamily as though hallucinated.

"Ha! ha! ha!" they all laughed. Heine laughed, Camilla laughed, even the lackey burst out laughing, the lackey particularly when Heine, bringing out his pocketbook, produced a ten-lire note and without ceasing to laugh offered it to the little ragamuffin.

As quick as lightning the boy's outstretched hand dived at the outstretched pocketbook.

"Stop!" Heine shouted. "This is, it seems, your first appearance in the field of commerce. In good time. . . . Listen, *cameriere*, your laughter at such a time is positively indecent. It stings the young merchant to the quick and don't you think, my dear fellow, it would be better if, in your future negotiations in Ferrara, you never showed yourself again within the inhospitable walls of the 'Torquato'?"

"Oh, no, signor, on the contrary. How many days is the signor still staying in Ferrara?"

"In two hours I shall have left."

"Signor Enrico."

"Yes, signora."

"Come out in the street. It is so much better to leave the stupid drawing room."

"Good. *Cameriere*, these flowers—to number eight. Wait a moment, this rose must still blossom; for this evening the gardens of Ferrara will ensure that you have it, signora."

"*Merci*, Enrico. . . . This black carnation is really devoid of all reticence; the gardens of Ferrara, signor, entrust you with the care of this licentious flower."

"Your hand, signora. . . . *Cameriere*, take it to number eight. And bring my hat. You'll find it in the room."

The lackey went out.

"You are not doing this, Enrico. . . ."

"Camilla, I don't understand."

"You will stay. Oh, don't answer me—you will stay at least for another day in Ferrara. . . . Enrico, Enrico, you have sullied your brow with pollen, let me wipe it away."

"Signora Camilla, there is a fluffy caterpillar on your shoes, may I dispose of it? I shall send a telegram to my home in Frankfurt—and those petals on your dress, signora—I shall send telegrams every day until you refuse to let me do it any more."

"Enrico, I can't see any engagement ring on your finger. Have you ever worn one?"

"A long while ago I noticed one on yours. My hat—and thank you!"

5

The perfumed evening filled all the corners of Ferrara and trickled over the labyrinths of her streets like a drop of sea-water, pouring into the ears and filling the skull with deafness.

The coffeehouse was a hubbub of noise. Only a single fragile side street led to the coffeehouse. The town, deafened and stunned, encircled it on all sides, holding its breath because the evening drove into one of the little side streets and precisely into this one where there was the coffeehouse at the corner.

Camilla was deep in thought. She was waiting for Heine, who had gone into the post office next door to the coffeehouse.

Why in the world didn't he want to write the telegram in the coffeehouse and send it over by messenger? Is it possible that he is not satisfied with an ordinary formal telegram? Was there a strong and really emotional liaison? But, on the other hand, he would have entirely forgotten about the telegram if she had not reminded him. And who was Rondolfina? She would have to ask about her. But could she? Obviously, these were intimate things. Heavens, I am like a little girl. I can, I must. Today I have obtained the right to know everything. They spoiled you, my dear—those artists. But this one. . . . And Relinquimini . . . ? What a remote person! In spring? Oh, no, earlier—perhaps on New Year's Eve? No, he was never really close to me. . . . And now. . . .

"What are you talking about, Camilla?"

"Why are you so melancholy, Enrico? Don't grieve. I shall let you free. You can write the telegrams by dictating them to the lackey. Send a telegram like that home, it will only be three hours late, there is a train which leaves Ferrara for Venice at night, and Milan too, and the delay won't be more than. . . ."

"What are you talking about, Camilla?"

"Why are you so melancholy, Enrico? Tell me something about Rondolfina."

Heine trembled and sprang from his chair.

"Who told you? He was here? He was here in my absence? Where is he, where is he, Camilla?"

"You turned pale, Enrico. Whom are you talking about? I asked you about a woman. Isn't that so? Or perhaps I didn't pronounce it correctly. Perhaps it is Rondolfino. It all depends on the vowel. Sit down. People are looking at us."

"Who told you about her? Did he tell you anything? But how did it come here? We are only here by accident—I mean, no one knows we are here."

"Enrico, there was no one, and nothing happened while you were in the telegraph office, I give you my word. But it is becoming curiouser and curiouser every minute. Are there two of them?"

"It's a miracle—incomprehensible to the reason . . . I'm losing my mind. Who told you this name, Camilla? Where did you find it?"

"This night, in my dreams. It's such a common name. And you still haven't told me who Rondolfina is. Miracles do still happen—but let us leave them alone. Who is she, Enrico?"

"O, Camilla, Rondolfina is you!"

"What an incorrigible actor you are! No, no! Let me go! Don't touch me!"

Both jumped up. Camilla's was a single movement, an irrevocably impetuous maneuver. Only the little table separated them. Camilla clutched the back of a chair, something rose between her and her decision; something stirred within her, and like a merry-go-round, in a circular wave, it drew the coffeepot upward, sideways. . . . She was lost. . . . Tear it away, tear her necklace. . . .

In the same loathsome merry-go-round, the chain of faces broke away, moved away, floated in the air . . . imperials . . . monocles . . . lorgnettes . . . ; then in large and ever-increasing quantities, the conversations at all the tables stumbled against their unhappy table: she still saw it, still leaned against it, it might pass . . . no . . . the discordant orchestra was falling out of tune.

"*Cameriere*, water!"

6

She was slightly feverish.

"What a tiny room you have. . . . Yes, that's right; thank you very much. I shall lie down for a while. It is malaria, but then . . . I have a flat of my own. Don't leave me. It may come at any moment. Enrico!"

"Yes, darling."

"Why are you so silent? No, no, it is not necessary, better as it is. Ah, Enrico, I can't remember whether there was a morning today. Are they all still there?"

"What, Camilla?"

"The flowers."

"We'll have to take them away during the night. What a heavy perfume it is! How much must the perfume weigh? I shall have them taken away. What are you doing, Camilla?"

"I am getting up. By myself, thank you. It's all over now. I can stand on my own legs. . . . Yes, they must be taken away. But where can we take them? Wait a moment. I have a flat of my own in the Ariosto square. Surely you can see it from here!"

"It is dark already. A little cooler, perhaps."

"Why are there so few people in the street?"

"Shsh, they can hear every word."

"What are they speaking about?"

"I don't know, Camilla. Students, probably. Boasting, probably, perhaps about the same things that we. . . ."

"Let me see it. Now they are standing at the corner. Heavens, how he threw the boy over his head! Now it is quiet again. How oddly the light clings to the branches. But there are no street lamps to be seen. Are we the last?"

"The last what, Camilla?"

"Are there any floors above us?"

"Probably, Camilla."

Camilla leaned out of the window and peered over the cornice at the street below.

"No. . . ."—but Heine did not let her finish her speech. "There is nobody there at all," she repeated, as she disengaged herself from his embrace.

"What is the matter?"

"I thought there was a man there, a lamp in the window and he threw crumpled leaves and shadows into the street through the window. I wanted to turn my face there, to catch it on the cheeks, but there was no one. . . ."

"This is poetry, Camilla."

"Really? I don't know. There it is, near the theater. Where there is a lilac-colored glow."

"What is there, Camilla?"

"You are a queer fellow! Well, my house!"

"But it is all a kind of nervous paroxysm. I would like it if we had. . . ."

"A room has already been ordered for you."

"How terribly thoughtful of you! What time is it? We must go. We must go and have a look at my room. It's very interesting."

They left number eight, smiling and as excited as schoolboys laying siege to Troy in the courtyard.

7

Long before morning the churchbells were chattering garrulously about the approach of dawn, jerkily making their low and cold bows, leaping backward and forward on the tumbling beams. Only one of the hotel lamps was burning. It kindled when the telephone bell crackled corrosively, and it was not extinguished afterward. The lamp saw the porter, still half asleep as he left his pipe on the desk after a short quarrel with the man at the other end of the line; saw him as he lost himself in the depths of the corridor, emerging a short while later from the half-darkness of the hotel. "Yes, the signor is leaving in the morning. He will call you in half an hour if it is really urgent. Have the goodness to leave your number. And tell me, please, whom must he call?"

The lamp continued to burn while the man from number eight, who had been called to the telephone, came out of the side corridor into the main corridor in stockinged feet, on tiptoes and still dressing.

The lamp was opposite the room. The man from number eight, in order to reach the telephone, had to walk down the corridor, and the first step he made took place somewhere near room number eight. After a short conversation with the porter his features changed—nervous agitation gave place to sudden recklessness and curiosity, and he seized the telephone boldly and, after going through the whole technical ritual, began to speak with the editor of *Voce*.

"Listen, it's terrible. Who told you I was suffering from sleeplessness?"

. . . .

"I imagine you came to the telephone by mistake while you were climbing the steeple. What are they ringing the bells for? What is it all about?"

. . . .

"Yes, I remained a day longer."

. . . .

"The lackey was right. I did not give them my home address, and I have no intention of giving it to them."

. . . .

"For you? Not at all! I did not think of publishing it—at any rate not today, as you seem to have thought."

. . . .

"You won't need it at all."

. . . .

"Don't get into a temper, signor editor. I beg you to be cool."

. . . .

"Relinquimini will not have to make you the mediator."

. . . .

"Because he has no need of a mediator."

. . . .

"May I remind you once more of your incalculable worth when you are calm. Relinquimini has never lost a notebook in his life."

. . . .

"Excuse me. This is your first unequivocal statement. No, a thousand times no!"

. . . .

"Still talking about that? Good, I shall admit it. Within the limits of yesterday's issue of *Voce*, it is blackmail. But it is not blackmail at all outside these limits."

. . . .

"It was yesterday. At six o'clock."

. . . .

"If you could only guess what rose out of the yeast of this invention, you would call it by still harder names and they would be still further from the truth than the one you had the goodness to utter just now."

. . . .

"Willingly. Today I have no objections to saying it. Heinrich Heine."

. . . .

"Just so."

"Very pleased to hear it."

. . . .

"What are you saying? "

. . . .

"Very willingly. How to manage it? I am so sorry I have to leave today. Come to the station and we'll spend a short time together."

. . . .

"Nine thirty-five. Whatever the time—a chain of surprises. Better not come."

. . . .

"Come to the hotel. During the day. It will be better. Or to my flat. During the evening. In tails, and don't forget to bring the flowers."

. . . .

"Yes, yes, signor editor. You are—a prophet."

. . . .

"Or tomorrow, on the dueling square outside the town."

. . . .

"I don't know, perhaps it is quite serious."

. . . .

"Or if you are busy during the next two days, come to the *Campo Santo* the day after tomorrow."

. . . .

"You think so?"

. . . .

"You think so?"

. . . .

"What a strange conversation at the beginning of the day. Forgive me, I am tired, I must go back to my room."

. . . .

"I can't hear? Number eight? Oh, yes. Yes, yes, number eight. It is a marvelous room, signor editor—a climate entirely of its own, where there has been eternal spring for five hours. Good-bye, signor editor."

. . . .

Heine mechanically turned down the switch.

"Don't put it out, Enrico!"—a voice came from the darkness of the corridor.

"Camilla!"

1915

Aerial Tracks

Boris Pasternak

For Mikhail Alekseyevich Kuzmin

1

The nurse was asleep under the ancient mulberry tree, leaning against its trunk. When a huge lilac cloud, rising at the edge of the road, silenced also the grasshoppers that were chirping sultrily in the grass, and in the camps the drums sighed and ceased trembling, everything went dark before the earth's eyes, and life was no more in the universe.

"Back, back!" the crazy shepherdess gave a harelipped howl that was heard throughout the world. Preceded by a young bull-calf, she dragged an injured foot, and, brandishing a wild switch like forked lightning, she appeared in a cloud of rubbish from that edge of the garden where wilderness began: henbane, bricks, twisted wire, putrid murk.

And she vanished. The cloud took in at a glance the parched fields with their short stubble. They stretched as far as the horizon. The cloud reared effortlessly. The fields stretched even farther, beyond the camps. Descending, the cloud touched the ground with its forelegs and, crossing the road with a fluent motion, crawled noiselessly along the fourth rail of the switch. With the whole embankment, the bushes, partly uncovering their heads, followed it. They flowed, bowing to the cloud. It did not respond.

Berries and caterpillars were dropping from the tree. Overcome by the heat, they fell off and, sinking into the nurse's apron, ceased to think of anything.

The child crawled to the faucet. It had been crawling for a long time. It went on crawling.

When the shower finally comes, and both pairs of rails fly along the slanting fences to save themselves from the watery night that has been unchained to attack them; when, making an uproar, it will, as it runs, hastily shout at you not to be afraid of it, that it is called downpour, love, and something else, then I will tell you that the previous evening the parents of the boy who was being kidnapped had cleaned their piqué clothes and that it was still very early when, dressed completely in snow-white as for tennis, they walked through the garden, still dark, and reached the post with the name of the station at the very moment when the paunchy dish of the steam engine, rolling out from behind the kitchen gardens, enveloped the Turkish confectionery with clouds of stifling yellow smoke.

They were on their way to the harbor to meet the naval cadet who had once loved her, who was a friend of the husband's, and who that morning was expected in town after completing a training voyage around the world.

The husband was burning with impatience to initiate his

friend as soon as possible into the deep significance of fatherhood, of which he had not yet grown tired. That's what happens. A simple incident brings you in contact almost for the first time with the charm of a uniquely significant experience. This is so new to you that, chancing on a man who has gone round the world and seen everything and would seem to have much to tell, you imagine that at your meeting he will be the listener and you the chatterbox who will startle him.

In contrast to her husband, she was anxious to plunge, like an anchor into water, into the iron clamor of the harbor's hurly-burly, the carroty rust of the three-funneled giants, the streaming grain, the luminous splash of sky, sails, and sailor suits. Their motives were different.

It is raining, it is pouring, I start to carry out my promise. The branches of a nut tree crackle over the ditch. Two figures are running across the field. The man has a black beard. The woman's shaggy mane blows in the wind. The man wears a green caftan and silver earrings. In his arms he holds the ravished child. It is raining, raining torrents.

2

It turned out that he had been promoted to midshipman a long time ago.

Eleven o'clock at night. The last train from the city pulls into the station. Having cried its fill before, it had already cheered up going round the curve, and somehow began to bustle about. Now, having drawn in the air from the entire district, together with the leaves, sand, and dew that had poured into its bursting reservoirs, it stops, claps its hands, and grows silent, waiting for the answering rumble. Echo will have to flow toward it from all the paths. When the train hears it, the lady, the navy man, and the civilian, all in white, will turn off the road into the footpath, and the blinding disk of the dew-drenched roof will surface from behind the poplars straight in front of them. They will walk to the hedge, bang the wicket gate, and, dropping none of the gutters, ridges, and cornices which are swinging in its ears like tickling earrings, the iron planet will start setting as they approach it. The din of the departed train will unexpectedly spread out and, cheating itself and others, for a time will pretend to be silence, and then spill into a rain of small leavings of soap that die away. It will turn out, however, that it is not a train at all, but aquatic rockets, with which the sea is amusing itself. From behind the grove at the station the moon will walk out onto the road. And then, looking at this scene, it will seem to you that it was composed by an exceedingly well-known poet whose name you constantly forget and that it is something still given to children at Christmas. You will recall that you saw this very fence in a dream and that then it was called the end of the world.

A pail with paint gleamed white on the porch washed by the moon, and a house painter's brush leaned against the wall, bristles up. Then a window facing the garden was opened. "We had the painters today," a woman's voice said quietly. "Do you smell it? Let's go in to supper." Then silence again.

It did not last. The house was thrown into a turmoil. "What? What do you mean? Can't be found?!" a bass voice, husky as a relaxed string, and a woman's contralto sparkling with hysterics exclaimed simultaneously, "Under the tree? Under the tree? Get up this minute and talk sense. And don't wail. Let go of my hands, for Christ's sake! My God, it's not possible! My Tosha, Toshenka! Don't you dare! Don't you dare! To my face?! You good-for-nothing, you shameless, miserable hussy!" And the sounds, ceasing to be words, plaintively fused together, stopped short, and withdrew. They could no longer be heard.

The night was coming to an end, but dawn was distant. The earth was studded with shapes, stunned by silence, as with hayricks. They were resting. As if to permit them to rest better, the distances between them, compared with the daytime distances, widened; the shapes dispersed and moved away. In the spaces between them the chilly fields puffed and snorted at each other under thoroughly sweaty horsecloths. Only rarely did any of the shapes turn out to be a tree, a cloud, or something familiar. For the most part they were dim, nameless agglomerates. They were rather dizzy and, being in something of a faint, they could scarcely say if it had just rained, or if it was about to rain or to drizzle. They were constantly being tossed from the past into the future and from the future into the past, like sand in an hourglass that is frequently turned.

Far away, like linen torn at dawn from the fence by a gust and carried the devil knows where, three human figures dimly flickered at the farther edge of the field, and on the opposite side the eternally evaporating roar of the distant sea was tumbling. These four were borne solely from the past into the future, never in the opposite direction. People in white were running from place to place, stooping and straightening up, jumping into ditches and, having disappeared, emerging at the boundary at some altogether different place. Finding themselves far from one another, they hallooed and waved, and as these signals were constantly misinterpreted, they would begin to wave their hands in a different way, more impetuously, vexedly, and oftener, to indicate that the signals were not understood and were to be ignored, that the searchers should not turn back but continue to look where they had looked before. The harmonious storminess of these figures created the impression of people who were playing ball at night, who had lost the ball and were looking for it in ditches and, on finding it, would resume the game.

Among the resting shapes the air was calm, and already you believed in the impending dawn, but at the sight of these people who bristled above the ground like shaggy tufts of hair you could imagine that the glade had been whipped up and disheveled by wind, darkness, and anxiety, as by some black comb with three broken teeth.

There exists a law according to which what must quite often happen to others can never happen to us. This rule has been cited by writers more than once. That it is irrefutable follows from the fact that as long as friends recognize us we consider the misfortune remediable. But when we realize that it is beyond remedy, friends cease to recognize us and, as if to prove the rule, we ourselves become different—that is, we become people who are fated to have a fire, be ruined, be put on trial, or committed to a lunatic asylum.

While they were raking the nurse over the coals like normal people, they fancied that it depended on the vehemence of their outburst whether they would come into the nursery and with a sigh of relief find the boy there, restored to his place by the extent of their fright and anxiety. The sight of the empty bed skinned their voices. But even when, with their souls flayed, they rushed first to rummage in the garden, then moved farther and farther away from the house in their search, for a long time they were people of our sort—that is, they searched in order to find. However, hours passed, the night changed its countenance, they too changed, and now as the night was ending they were completely unrecognizable people who had ceased to understand for what sins and to what end cruel space was tossing them from spot to spot, without letting them catch their breath, on that earth on which they would never again see their son. And they had long since forgotten the midshipman, who transferred his search to the other side of the ravine.

Is it for the sake of this questionable observation that the author is concealing from the reader what he knows so well? Indeed, better than anyone else, he knows that as soon as the village bakeries open and the first trains pass each other, the news of the sad event will make the round of the summer cottages and finally indicate to the twin high-school boys from Olgina where they are to take their nameless acquaintance, the trophy of yesterday's victory.

Already from under the trees, as from under hoods pulled

down, the first beginnings of unawakened morning were showing. The day was dawning fitfully, with interruptions. Suddenly the roar of the sea seemed not to have been, and all grew quieter than before. Coming from nowhere, a mawkish tremor ran over the trees more and more frequently. Standing in a row, they took turns slapping the fence with their sweaty silver, and resumed for a long time the sleep that had just been interrupted. Two rare diamonds sparkled separately and independently in the deep nests of this blessed semidarkness: a bird and its chirping. Scared of its solitude and ashamed of its insignificance, with all its strength the little bird tried to dissolve completely in the immense sea of dew, too absentminded and sleepy to collect its thoughts. In this attempt the bird was nearly successful. Bending its head sideways and tightly screwing up its eyes, it silently reveled in the stupidity and melancholy of the newly born earth and rejoiced in its own disappearance. But its strength was insufficient. And suddenly, overcoming its resistance and betraying the bird, its ample twitter blazed: a cold star in an immutable pattern at an immutable height; a resilient tattoo scattered in needlelike spokes; the spray sounded, grew chilly and amazed, as though a saucer with a huge astonished eye were spilled.

But now day was dawning in earnest. The entire garden filled with damp white light. It clung most closely to the plastered wall, the graveled paths, and the trunks of the fruit trees smeared with some kind of vitriolic compound, white as lime. And with the same deathly film on her face, the child's mother, who had just returned from the field, dragged herself through the garden. Without stopping, her legs giving way under her, she walked straight to the back of the house, not noticing what her feet were trampling and into what they sank. The flower beds, rising and falling, tossed her up and down, as though her agitation needed shaking. Having crossed the kitchen garden, she went up to that part of the fence behind which you could see the road to the camps. The midshipman was making for that spot, intending to climb over the fence in order not to walk all the way round the garden. The yawning east bore him toward the fence as a badly listing boat is borne along by the wind in its white sail. She was waiting for him, holding onto the balustrade of the fence. It was obvious that she was about to speak and that she had prepared just what she was to say.

The same nearness of the expected or recently fallen rain was felt on the seashore as it was up above. Where could the din that had been heard all night long beyond the railroad track come from? The sea lay, growing chill, like the mercury-coated back of a mirror, and only at the rim it changed its mind and sobbed. Already the horizon showed yellow, morbidly and maliciously. This was forgivable on the part of the dawn that pressed against the back wall of the huge filthy sky, in which at any moment waves could become rabid and surge from all directions. Meanwhile they were crawling on their bellies and rubbing against each other almost imperceptibly, like an immense herd of black and slippery pigs. Emerging from behind a rock, the midshipman walked onto the seashore. He moved with quick, sprightly steps, sometimes jumping from stone to stone. He had just learned something stunning at the cottage. He picked up from the sand a flat fragment of a tile and skipped it along the surface of the water. The stone ricocheted slantingly as over spittle and emitted the same elusive childish sound as the entire shoal. But a moment before, when, despairing of his search, he had turned to the cottage and started to approach it from the glade, Lolya had run up to the fence and, letting him come close to it, had said hurriedly: "We can't go on. Save him. Find him. He is your son." When he seized her hand, she broke away and ran off, and when he climbed into the garden, he could not find her anywhere. He picked up stones one after another and went off skipping them as he walked away and disappeared back of the rock. Behind him his own footprints continued to live and stir. They too wanted to sleep. It was the disturbed gravel, crawling, crumbling, sighing, turning from side to side, rumbling as it tried to get into a comfortable position and then have a good sleep in peace.

3

More than fifteen years passed. Night was drawing on, indoors it was getting dark. Already for the third time an unknown lady was asking to see the member of the provincial Executive Committee, former naval officer Polivanov. A bored soldier stood before the lady. Through the window of the lobby one could see a yard cluttered with piles of snow-covered bricks. At its farther end, where there had once been a cesspool, a mountain of trash, which had long been accumulating, now loomed. Above it the sky looked like an unkempt thicket that had grown up on the slopes of this accumulation of cats' corpses and tin cans, which in a thaw rose from the dead and, catching their breath, started to reek of past springs and freedom, dripping, twittering, bumpily rumbling. But it was enough to take your eyes off this out-of-the- way spot and lift them aloft to be struck by the degree of this sky's newness.

Its present ability to spread all day long the din of cannon and rifle fire from the sea and the railroad station pushed its memory of 1905 into the remote past. Leveled from end to end by cannonade on a binge as by a steam roller, and now smoothed and crushed once and for all, it lowered silently and, without moving, led you somewhere, as is the nature of the monotonously unwinding ribbon of a railroad track in winter.

What sort of sky was it, then? Even by day it recalled the image of the night that we see in youth and when marching to war. Even by day it caught the eye and, immeasurably prominent, it was saturated with the devastated earth, it struck down the somnolent and roused the dreamers.

Those were aerial tracks, on which rolled daily, like trains, the rectilinear thoughts of Liebknecht, Lenin, and the few minds soaring as theirs did. They were tracks set at a level sufficient for crossing all frontiers, whatever their names. One of the lines built back in the war years retained its former strategic height, imposed upon the builders by the nature of the fronts over which it was constructed. This old military branch line—which at a certain place and time had intersected the frontiers first of Poland, then of Germany—here, at its start, before everyone's eyes, exceeded the limits of the understanding and the patience of mediocrity. It passed above the courtyard, which shied at the remoteness of its destination and its oppressive cumbersomeness, just as a suburb shies at a railway track and flees from it helter-skelter. It was the sky of the Third International.

The soldier told the lady that Polivanov had not yet returned. Three kinds of boredom were heard in his voice. It was the boredom of a being accustomed to liquid mud and finding himself in dry dust. It was the boredom of a man grown used, in antiprofiteering and requisitioning detachments, to asking questions that such ladies answered quailing and confused, and who was bored because the order of the model conversation was here reversed and undone. Finally, it was the feigned tedium with which people impart the appearance of complete ordinariness to something wholly unprecedented. Knowing perfectly well that the recent order of things must have seemed to the lady utterly unheard-of, he foolishly pretended that he had no inkling of her feelings and that he had never in his life breathed any other air than that of dictatorship.

Suddenly Lyovushka entered. Something like the strap of "giant strides," a gymnastic apparatus, swept him into the second floor from outdoors, whence came a gust of snow and unlit silence. Getting hold of the object, which turned out to be a briefcase, the soldier stopped him, as you stop a merry-go-round in full swing.

"There's this," he turned to the man who had just entered, "they came from the Prisoners and Refugees Office."

"Is that about the Hungarians again?"

"Why, yes."

"But they've already been told that documents alone won't get the group anywhere."

"Just what I said. I understand very well that it's a matter of steamers. I explained it to them."

"Well, and what happened?"

"'We don't need you to tell us that,' says he. 'Your job is to put the papers in order, as for embarkation, sort of. And then it'll be a routine matter, so to speak.' And they want lodgings."

"Well, and what else?"

"Nothing else. Just papers, lodgings, he says."

"No, no!" Polivanov interrupted. "Don't repeat yourself. That isn't what I was asking about."

"There's a package from Kanatnaya," the soldier named the street where the Cheka was located. Coming closer to Polivanov, he spoke under his breath, as in posting sentries.

"You don't say so! Well. Impossible." Polivanov murmured indifferently and absentmindedly.

The soldier stepped back again. For a moment they stood in silence.

"Did you bring bread?" the soldier asked suddenly with a sour air, because the shape of the briefcase made the answer unnecessary, and added:

"There's this citizen, too, waiting for you."

"Very well," Polivanov drawled in the same absentminded way.

The rope of the gymnastic apparatus shook and grew taut. The briefcase started moving.

"Please, comrade," he turned to the lady, inviting her into the study. He had not recognized her.

If the lobby was dim, this room was completely dark. She followed him and halted beyond the door.

Apparently the room was carpeted, because after he had taken two or three steps he disappeared, and then his steps were heard at the opposite end of the darkness. Then there were sounds that gradually set the table with shifting glasses, fragments of biscuits and pieces of sugar, parts of a revolver, hexagonal pencils. He moved his hand quietly over the table top, rolling and grinding something in search of matches. Her imagination was about to transfer the room, hung with pictures and furnished with wardrobes, palms, and bronzes, to one of the avenues of old Petersburg, and stood with a fistful of lights ready to fling them the length of the vista, when the telephone suddenly shrilled. Its gurgling rattle, tasting of a field or some out-of-the-way place, instantly reminded you that the wire had made its way here via the city plunged in complete darkness, and that all this was taking place in the provinces under the Bolsheviks.

"Yes," replied the sullen, impatient man, tired to death, probably shielding his eyes with his hand. "Yes. I know. I know. Nonsense. Check the line. Nonsense. I contacted the staff. Zhmerinka has been answered for about an hour. Is that all? Yes, I will, and I'll tell them. No, in about twenty minutes. Is that all?"

"Well, comrade," with a box in one hand and a blue drop of spitting sulphurous flame in the other, he turned to his visitor, and then almost simultaneously with the noise of the dropped and scattered matches came her broken, agitated whisper.

"Lolya!" Polivanov exclaimed, beside himself. "Impossible—forgive me—but no—Lolya?"

"Yes, yes, good eve—Let me get hold of myself . . . so we've met!" Lolya whispered, choking and crying in the same way.

Suddenly everything vanished. By the light of an oil lamp they faced each other: a man ravaged by lack of sleep, his short jacket unbuttoned, and a woman who had come straight from the station and had not washed for a long time. It was as though youth and the sea had never been. By the light of the oil lamp her arrival, the death of Dmitry and of her daughter, of whose existence he had not known, and, in a word, everything she had related before the lamp was lit turned out to be a compellingly depressing truth, which invited both of them into a grave, as long as his sympathy was not empty words. Looking at her by the light of the lamp, he immediately recalled the reason why they had not kissed at once when they met. And, with an involuntary smile, he wondered at the tenacity of such prejudices. In the lamp light all her hopes concerning the appointments of the room were shattered. As for this man, he seemed so alien to her that she could not attribute her feeling to the change in the room. All the more resolutely did she broach her own business, and again, as she had done once before, rushed to attend to it as she would a commission given her by strangers, acting blindly and as if she had learned her behavior by heart.

"If your child is dear to you," she began.

"Again!" Polivanov instantly flared up, and began to talk, talk, talk—quickly and without pause. He spoke as though he were composing an article, with *which*'s and commas. He paced the room, stopped sometimes, spreading his arms wide or shaking them. In the intervals, wrinkling the skin above the bridge of his nose and pinching it with three fingers, he rubbed and irritated this spot as the breeding ground of his indignation, which now died down, now blazed up. He implored her to stop thinking that people were not wise to her fictions and could be ordered about as she pleased. He charged her solemnly in the name of everything holy never again to talk such rot, particularly since she herself had admitted deception at the time. He said that even if one were to assume that this poppycock were true, the result would be the opposite of that intended. It is impossible to ram into a man's head the idea that the sudden appearance in his life of what had not been there a minute earlier is not a find but a loss. He recalled how lighthearted and free he had felt as soon as he came to believe her tale and that he had immediately lost the desire to continue ransacking the ditches and had wanted to go bathing. And if time were to flow backward, he attempted to taunt her, and it would be necessary to search for a member of her family again, in that case too he would take the trouble only for her sake or for the sake of Y or Z, but not for his own sake or for the sake of her ridiculous. . . .

"Have you finished?" she asked him, after allowing him to cool down. "You're right. I did take back what I said. Can it be that you don't understand? I agree that it was base and cowardly. I was beside myself with joy that the boy had been found —and how miraculously. Do you remember? After that could I have the heart to break my life and Dmitry's? So I recanted. But it isn't a question of me. He is yours. Oh, Lyova, Lyova, if you know in what danger he is now! I don't know how to begin. Let's take things in order. Since that day we haven't seen each other. You don't know him. He is so trustful. Some day this will ruin him. There is a scoundrel, an adventurer—let God be his judge, though—Neploshaev, Tosha's schoolmate. . . ."

Hearing these words, Polivanov, who had been pacing the room, became riveted to the spot and ceased to hear what she was saying. She had pronounced the name mentioned among other things by the soldier with whom he had just had a whispered conversation. He was familiar with the case. There was no hope for the accused, it was just a question of the hour.

"Did he act under an assumed name?"

She grew white when she heard this question. So he knew more about it than she did, and the situation was even worse than she had pictured it. She forgot in whose camp she was, and imagining that his only sin was that of using a fictitious name, she started pleading for her son on wholly unnecessary grounds:

"But, Lyova, he couldn't openly defend. . . ."

And again he ceased to hear her, having understood that her child could have concealed himself under any of the names he knew from the documents. He stood at the desk, made some telephone calls, obtained information, and with each successive connection he moved deeper and farther into the city and the night, until the abyss of the final, ultimate truth opened up before him.

He looked round. Lolya was not in the room. He felt a terrible ache in his eye sockets, and when he surveyed the room, it swam before him like streaming stalactites. He wanted to pinch the skin on the bridge of his nose, but instead he passed his hand over his eyes, and this movement made the stalactites dance and start melting. It would have been easier for him if their spasms had not been so frequent and noiseless. Then he discovered her. Like a huge doll, she lay, unbroken, between the cabinet next to the desk and the chair, on the layer of sawdust and rubbish which in the darkness she had mistaken for a carpet while she was conscious.

1924

On Gratitude

(From a diary for the year 1919)

Marina Tsvetaeva

When the five-year-old Mozart, scarcely risen from the clavichord, found himself sprawling on the slippery palace floor and when, of those present, only the seven-year-old Marie Antoinette ran to help him up, he said, "Celle-ci je l'épouserai," and when Marie Antoinette asked him why, he answered, "Par reconnaissance."

Of that great number whom, as Queen of France, she was later to raise from the floor—ever slippery for the flippant, the ambitious, the pleasure-loving—was there a single one who, *par reconnaissance*, would cry, "Vive la Reine!" as she passed on her way to the scaffold?

Reconnaissance: recognition. To recognize, through every mask and every wrinkle, recognize just once, in an enlightened flash, the true face.

Gratitude

I am never grateful to people for their actions, but only for their essence! Bread given me may appear to be an accident; a dream dreamed about me is always of the essence.

I take as I give, without discrimination, as indifferent to the hand that gives as I am to my own that takes.

My fellow man gives me bread. What do I do first? Return the gift. Return it so as not to be under an obligation. Gratitude is the giving of oneself in return for bounty received, that is, love that has been paid for.

I respect my fellow men too much to insult them with love that is paid for.

It insults me; consequently, it must insult others.

Good will with me as its object could never predetermine anything. The personal character of the gift (its being directed to me) does not exist in my mind. I am grateful neither in my own behalf nor in my neighbors': I am simply grateful.

I will not be bought. That is the crux of it all. I can be had only with what is essential. (Essential in me, that is.) In exchange for bread, you may get hypocrisy, false enthusiasm, amenability—all that is the scum of me, unless it is the dregs.

Buy—pay off. You'll not buy yourself from me.

I can be had only by what is of very Heaven. Of Heaven, where there may not even be a place for me.

I am grateful beyond the personal, which means only where, unknown to my fellow men and untouched by their good will, I can take myself.

Your mere attitude is not yet a judgment. I am tired of repeating this. Your giving me bread may have made me a better person, but it has not made you perfect.

An act is not an attitude; an attitude is not an evaluation; an evaluation (for example, an evaluation of Blok by his critics) is not the essence (of Blok himself). The essence is the intention, audible only to the ear.

A piece of bread from a repulsive individual is a lucky incident—no more.

I eat your bread and despise you. Yes. Only self-interest is grateful. Only self-interest measures the whole (the essence) of things by the piece it has received. Only an infantile blindness looks into the hand and affirms: "He gave me sugar, and so he is good." Sugar is good, certainly. But to evaluate the essence of a man by sugar and tips, by what is received from him, is pardonable only to children and servants: to an instinct. And even this is not true; we often see how dogs prefer the master who gives them nothing to the cook who feeds them.

To identify the source of bounty with the bounty itself (the cook with the meat, the uncle with sugar, the visitor with tips) indicates a complete lack of development in mind and soul: a being who has gone no further than his five senses.

A dog who loves because he is petted is superior to a cat who loves because she is petted; and a cat who loves because she is petted is superior to a child who loves because he is fed. The whole thing is a matter of degree.

And so from the simplest love in return for sugar, to the love in return for tenderness, to love through seeing, to love sight unseen (from afar),* to love no matter what (nonlove), from little love *because of* something, to great love *beyond* (myself), from love that gains (through another's will) and from love that takes (in spite of one's will, without one's awareness, against one's will!)—*to love in itself.*

The older we grow, the more we want: in childhood, it was only sugar; in adolescence, only love; in old age, only (!) what is of essence (of you beyond myself).

The less we appreciate external bounty, the more easily we give it and take it, the less we are grateful.

(In point of fact: only in silence will I allow gratitude for bread [the thing bestowed]. In gratitude made obvious there is a certain reproach that puts the giver to shame.)

The physical joy that is caused by bread—that is the best gratitude! Gratitude that ends as the last mouthful passes down the gullet.

Is it possible that such a little thing, a mere detail, a mere hint (as I see it) as *giving* must inevitably grow into a kind of mountain because of the increment added: *to me*?

Well, I certainly know how giving should be done: blindly. Moreover, would I permit anyone to thank me for bread? I won't even take thanks for verses. There you are!

*I am wholly at one with this idea.

Bread—is that me? Verse (an accident of the poetic gift)—is that me?

I stand alone under heaven. Keep your distance when you thank me.

I do not want to think of man as a low being. When I give bread to my fellow man, I give it to someone who is hungry, that is, to a gullet, *not to the man himself*. His soul is not involved. I can give to any man, and it is not I who gives, but any man. Bread gives itself. And I refuse to believe that anyone who has given to my gullet can demand my soul in return.

But the gullet is never the giver—the soul is! No, the hand is. These gifts are not personal. It is strange to prefer one stomach over another, but if it must be done, let it be for the hungriest stomach. As for today, mine (yours) is the hungriest. There's nothing I can do about it.

So, having sorted out the giver (the hand) from the receiver (the gullet), it would be strange that one lump of meat should demand from another lump of meat—gratitude.

Souls are grateful, but souls are grateful only for other souls. I thank you because you are.

Anything else—from me to my fellow man or from my fellow man to me—is an insult.

To give is not our activity. Nor is it our personality! Nor is it our passion! Nor our choice! It is something that belongs to everyone (bread) so (since I haven't any!), it being taken from me, returns (through you) to me (through me—to you).

Bread for the poor—the restitution of rights.

If we were to give to whomever *we* chose, we should be the lowest of scoundrels. We give to whoever *wants*. Hunger (will!) invokes our gesture (bread). Given, and forgotten. Taken, and forgotten. No ties, no connections. Once I have given, I have dissevered myself. Once I have taken, I have dissevered myself.

No Consequences

"Then why should you give anything?"
"So as not to be a scoundrel."

I remember in my high-school days—a beggar before the church. "Give, for the sake of Christ!" I went on by. "Give for the sake of Christ!" I walked on. And he, running after: "If you can't for the sake of Christ, at least for the sake of the Devil!"

Why did I give to him? Because he was enraged.

Bread. Gesture. Giving. Taking. Nothing of the sort *there*. That's why anything connected with giving and taking is a lie. The bread itself is a lie. Nothing based on bread will survive (even if mixed with yeast, it will not rise). The dough of our bread-emotions will surely fall in the cold temperature of immortality.

Not even worth the doing.

To take is a shameful thing: no, to give is a shameful thing. For the one who takes, it is clear, since he takes, that he does not have; for the one who gives, it is clear, since he gives, that he has. And so there comes a confrontation between having and not having.

Giving should be done on the knees, in the manner of the mendicant poor.

By a happy chance, the shame of giving is conferred only on the poor. (The tact with which gifts are made to them!) The rich limit themselves to a brief show of diffidence as they pay the doctor's fee.

Gratitude; it spans the whole distance from admiration to rejection.

I can show admiration only for the hand that gives the last piece; therefore I can never be grateful to the rich.

Perhaps only for their diffidence, their sense of guilt, that on the instant can make them look like innocents.

When the poor man gives, he says, "I'm afraid it's not much." The poor man's embarrassment comes from "I can't give more." When the rich man gives, he says nothing. The rich man's embarrassment comes from "I won't give more."

Giving is so much easier than taking—and so much easier than *being*.

The rich buy themselves off. Oh, the rich are deathly afraid—if not of the Revolution, then of the Last Judgment. I know one mother who buys milk for another's (sick) child. In saving the other's child from (certain) death, the rich mother has simply redeemed her own from possible death. (To influence Providence!)

I look into the source of the act, the intention behind it. In the Last Judgment this milk offering will cost the rich mother black pitch.

Bounty. The ring of Polycrates.

The poor man's gift (of his life's blood) is impersonal. "God-given." The rich man's gift (out of plenty, almost a left-over), bears a first name, a patronymic, a family name, rank, title, pedigree, day, hour, date. And—is remembered. The right hand has given, but both hands recall the giving.

The poor man, having given from one hand into another, forgets. The rich man, having sent his gift by a servant, remembers. And when you think about it, this is understandable: credit has thus been entered against his name for the Last Judgment.

A matter for conjecture.

1919

A little later, when I was six and in my first year of music in the Zograf-Plaksina School of Music in Merzlyakovsky Lane, there was a Christmas play, a public evening, as it used to be called in those days. They put on a scene from *Rusalka*, followed by *Rogneda*, and,

Now we'll flit over the garden
Where Tatyana encountered him. . . .*

A bench. On the bench, Tatyana. Then Onegin comes but does not sit down: *she* rises. Both are standing. And he alone speaks all the time, a long time, while she does not say a word. And here I realize that the red cat, Avgusta Ivanovna, and the dolls are not love, that *this* is love: when there is a bench, she is seated on the bench, then he comes and speaks all the time, while she does not say a word. Mother, after the performance: "Well, Musya, what did you like best?"

"Tatyana and Onegin."

"What? Not *Rusalka*, with the mill, and the prince, and the wood goblin? Not *Rogneda?*"

"Tatyana and Onegin."

"But how could it be? You did not understand anything in it. What could you understand?"

I am silent.

Mother, triumphantly: "You see, you did not understand a single word, just as I thought. A girl of six! What could you like in it?"

"Tatyana and Onegin."

"You are an absolute fool and more stubborn than ten asses!" Turning to the approaching director, A. L. Zograf:

"I know her: whatever I ask her, she will now repeat in the cab all the way home: 'Tatyana and Onegin.' I really regret bringing her. Not a single child in the world would have liked Tatyana and Onegin out of all the performance— everybody else would have preferred *Rusalka*, because it's a fairy tale, it's easy to understand. I really don't know what to do with her!"

The director, with great kindness: "But, Musenka, why Tatyana and Onegin?"

My unspoken reply in full:

"Because it is love."

"She must be seeing the seventh dream by now," says Nadezhda Yakovlevna Bryusova,† our best and oldest student, as she approaches us—and here I find out for the first time that

*The quotations from *Eugene Onegin* are taken from Vladimir Nabokov's translation in the Bollinger Series LXXII. (New York: Pantheon Books, 1964).

†Sister of Valery Bryusov.

there is a "seventh dream" that measures the depth of somnolence and night.

"And what is this, Musya," says the director, drawing out of my muff a mandarin orange he has placed there, replacing it inconspicuously (conspicuously!), and taking it out, again, and and again, and again. . . .

But I am already completely dumb, petrified, and none of his and Bryusova's mandarin smiles and no terrifying glares from my mother can elicit a smile of gratitude from me. On our way home (quiet streets, a late hour, a horse-drawn sleigh) mother scolds me: "You put me to shame. You did not say thank you for the mandarin orange. A girl of six, you fell in love with Onegin, like a fool!"

Mother was wrong. I fell in love, not with Onegin, but with Onegin and Tatyana (the more perhaps with Tatyana), with both of them, with love. And later I never wrote anything without first falling in love with the two simultaneously (the more with her than with him): not with the two of them, but rather with their love. With love.

The bench on which they did *not* sit proved to be a predestination. Neither then nor later did I ever love when the two were kissing, but always when they were parting. I never loved when they were sitting down together, but always when they were taking leave of each other. My first love scene was a nonlove scene: he did *not* love (I realized that), and that was why he did not sit down; *she* loved, and that was why she stood up. They had not been together for a single minute: they did nothing together; they did something quite opposite: he spoke, she was silent; he left, she stayed; so that if the curtain were raised, she would still be standing there, or perhaps sitting again, since she stood up only because *he* was standing, and afterward collapsed and would now be sitting like this forever.

This first love scene of mine predetermined all the rest, all the passion in me for the unfortunate, the unreciprocated, the impossible love. From that very minute I no longer wanted to be happy but condemned myself to *nonlove*.

The whole point was that he did not love her, and she had made such a choice, to the exclusion of any other, only because she secretly knew that he would be unable to love her. (I am telling this now, but I knew it even then; then I knew, and now I have learned how to tell it.) People with this fatal gift of unfortunate love, all of which they shoulder alone, without ever sharing, have a real genius for choosing unsuitable objects.

There was also another thing (not one thing but many) that *Eugene Onegin* had predetermined in me. If all my life to this very day I have always been the first to write, the first to stretch out my hand and my arms, braving judgment, it was only because at the dawn of my days Tatyana in the book, reclining by candlelight, the loose braid falling across her breast, had done so before my eyes. And if later, whenever I was being abandoned (as I always was), I never stretched out my arms to stop and never even so much as turned my head, it was only because then, in the garden, Tatyana stayed as motionless as a statue.

A lesson in courage. A lesson in pride. A lesson in faithfulness. A lesson in destiny. A lesson in loneliness.

What other nation has such an amorous heroine: brave yet dignified, enamored yet inexorable, clear-sighted yet loving?

There is not a shadow of vindictiveness in Tatyana's rebuff. This is why her vindication is complete; this is why Onegin stands "as if struck by thunder."

She had all the trumps in her hand so as to take vengeance, to drive him mad; all the trumps to humiliate him, trample him under foot, abase him to the parquet of that reception room. She did away with all that in a single slip of the tongue: "I love you (why dissimulate?)."

Why dissimulate? Surely, to be triumphant! But why be triumphant? To this question Tatyana truly can find no answer, at least no intelligible answer; and again she remains standing in the enchanted circle of the reception room, as once she stood in the enchanted circle of the garden—in the enchanted circle of her amorous loneliness: not needed then; coveted now; loving and unable to be loved, both then and now.

She had all the trumps, but she did not play them.

Yes, girls, yes! Be the first to declare love, then listen to rebuffs, then marry a distinguished wounded veteran, and then listen to his declaration of love yet concede nothing—and you will be a thousand times happier than that other heroine of ours, the one whose fulfilled desires left her no other choice but to lie down on the railroad track.*

My choice between the fullness of desire and the fulfillment of desires, between the fullness of suffering and the emptiness of happiness, was made the day I was born and even before then.

Because, before me, my mother had been influenced by Tatyana. When my grandfather, A. D. Mein, made her choose between himself and her beloved, she had chosen her father and not her beloved, and then she married in an even better fashion than Tatyana did, because "for poor Tanya all lots

* Anna Karenina.

were equal" whereas my mother drew the heaviest lot: a widower* twice her age, with two children, and still in love with the departed. She married to face someone else's children and the grief for someone else, while still loving, still continuing to love that *other* one, whom she never sought to meet later and whom, having met him for the first time and by chance at her husband's public lecture, she answered, when he asked how she was and whether she was happy: "My daughter is one year old; she is very big and clever; I am completely happy. . . ." (God, how she must have hated me—the big and clever one—at that moment because I was not *his* daughter.)

Thus, Tatyana had influenced not only my life but the very fact of my existence; had there been no Pushkin's Tatyana, I would not have come into being.

For this, and this alone, is the way women read poets.

It is significant, however, that mother did not name me Tatyana: she must have taken pity on the girl, for all that.

As far as I am concerned, the entire *Eugene Onegin* still consists today, as it did in my infancy, of three scenes: that candle, that bench, that parquet. Some of my contemporaries perceive in *Eugene Onegin* a brilliant joke, almost a satire. Perhaps they are right; perhaps, had I not read it before I was seven—but I read it at an age when there are neither jokes nor satires: there are dark gardens (as we had in Tarusa), there are crumpled bedclothes (as we had in our bedroom), and there is love (as I have in the hollow of my breast).

* Marina Tsvetaeva's father, Ivan Vladimirovich Tsvetaev (1846–1913), philologist and art historian, professor at the University of Moscow, director of the Rumyantsev Museum and founder of the Alexander III Museum of Fine Arts in Moscow, now the Pushkin Museum of Fine Arts.

The Cave

Evgeny Zamyatin

Glaciers, mammoths, wastes. Black, nocturnal cliffs, vaguely like houses; in the cliffs—caves. And there is no telling what creature trumpets at night on the rocky path among the cliffs and, sniffing the path, raises clouds of powdered snow. It may be a gray-trunked mammoth, it may be the wind, and it may be that the wind is nothing but the glacial roar of some super-mammoth. One thing is clear: it is winter. And you must clench your teeth tightly to keep them from chattering, and you must split wood with a stone ax, and each night carry your fire from cave to cave, deeper and deeper, and huddle closer in more of those shaggy hides.

At night among the cliffs where ages ago stood Petersburg, a gray-trunked mammoth was roaming. And muffled up in hides and coats and blankets and rags, the cave dwellers were constantly retreating from cave to cave. On the feast of the Intercession of the Holy Virgin Martin Martinych and Masha shut up the study; three weeks later they moved out of the dining room and entrenched themselves in the bedroom. They could retreat no farther: there they must withstand the siege or die.

In the troglodytic Petersburg bedroom all was as it had been in Noah's ark not long ago—the clean and the unclean in diluvial promiscuity: Martin Martinych's desk, books, stone-age cakes of ceramic appearance, Scriabin opus 74, a flatiron, five potatoes lovingly scrubbed white, nickel-plated bedsprings, an ax, a chiffonier, firewood. And in the center of this universe was its god, a short-legged, rusty-red, squat, greedy cave god: the iron stove.

The god roared mightily. In the dark cave the great miracle of fire was wrought. The humans, Martin Martinych and Masha, silently, gratefully, piously stretched out their arms to him. For one hour it was spring in the cave; for one hour hides, claws, tusks were shed, and through the frozen brain-crust sprang green shoots—thoughts:

"Mart, you have forgotten that tomorrow. . . . Yes, I see you *have* forgotten."

In October, when the leaves are already yellowed, withered, wilted, blue-eyed days may occur. If you tilt your head on such a day so as not to see the earth, you may believe that there is still joy, it is still summer. And it was the same with Masha: if you shut your eyes and only listened to her, you could believe that she was the same, that in a moment she was going to laugh, get up from her bed to hug you; and only an hour ago her voice had sounded like a knife on glass—not her voice at all, not she . . .

"Oh, Mart, Mart! How everything. . . . You didn't use to forget. The twenty-ninth: St. Mary's day. . . ."

The iron god was still roaring. There was no light: it wouldn't come until ten. The shaggy dark reaches of the cave were swaying. Martin Martinych, squatting (tie yourself in a knot, tightly—still more tightly!), his head tilted, kept looking at the October sky, so as not to see the withered, wilted lips. And Masha—

"You see, Mart, if we could start the stove in the morning tomorrow, so that all day it would be the way it is now! What do you say? How much is left? About a cord in the study?"

It was ages since Masha had been strong enough to make her way to the polar study, and she did not know that. . . . Tighten the knot, tighter!

"A cord? I think. . . ."

Suddenly it was light: it was exactly ten o'clock. And without saying any more, Martin Martinych screwed up his eyes and turned away: when it was light it was more difficult. You could see now that his face was crumpled and earthy. Many people have earthy faces now: reverting to Adam.

But Masha went on:

"And you know, Mart, perhaps I'll try and get up . . . if you start the stove early."

"Of course, Masha, of course. . . . On a day like that. . . . Of course, I'll start it early."

The cave god was quieting down, shrinking into himself. And now he was quite still, just crackling faintly. One could hear that downstairs at the Obertyshevs' someone was using a stone ax to split knotty logs, the remains of a barge—hewing Martin Martinych into pieces with a stone ax. One piece of Martin Martinych was smiling in a clayey way and grinding dried potato peelings in a coffee mill to make cakes with. Another piece of Martin Martinych was stupidly, blindly knocking against the ceiling, the windowpanes, the walls, like a bird that had flown into a room from outdoors: "Where find wood—where find wood—where find wood?"

Martin Martinych put on his coat and fastened it with a leather belt (the cave dwellers have a myth that this keeps you warmer). In the corner by the chiffonier he lifted the pail noisily.

"Where are you going, Mart?"

"I'll be back directly. To get water downstairs."

On the dark stairway, crusted with ice because of the water splashed on it, Martin Martinych stood awhile, swaying, sighing, and clanking the pail as if it were a prisoner's chain, went downstairs to the Obertyshevs': the water in their flat was still running. The door was opened by Obertyshev himself;

he wore a coat belted with a rope and was unshaven. His face was a waste overgrown with reddish dusty weeds. Through the weeds were visible yellow stone teeth and among the stones a lizard's instantaneous tail: a smile.

"Ah, Martin Martinych! Come to fetch water? Please, please, please."

The tiny cubicle between the outer and inner door was so narrow that one could scarcely turn around in it with a pail. Here Obertyshev kept his stack of wood. Clayey Martin Martinych knocked against the logs, and this made a deep dent in the clay. And there was even a deeper dent when he knocked against the corner of the chest of drawers in the dark passage. He made his way through the dining room; here were the Obertyshev dam and her three cubs. The dam hurriedly hid a dish under a napkin: a human had come from another cave, and—who knows?—he might fly at her and seize it.

In the kitchen, as he turned on the faucet, Obertyshev smiled a stone-toothed smile:

"Well, how's your wife? How's your wife? How's your wife?"

"What's there to say, Aleksey Ivanych? Just the same. It's a bad business. Tomorrow is her name day, and I haven't. . . ."

"No one has, Martin Martinych, no one has, no one. . . ."

The bird that had flown into the kitchen was rustling its wings and fluttering right, left, and suddenly it dashed its breast in despair against the wall.

"Aleksey Ivanych, I wanted . . . Aleksey Ivanych, couldn't I borrow at least five or six pieces of wood from you?"

Yellow stone teeth showed through the weeds; the eyes grew yellow teeth, all of Obertyshev sprouted teeth, which grew longer and longer.

"Good heavens, Martin Martinych! Good heavens! Good heavens! We ourselves are . . . You know very well how it is nowadays, you know very well, you know very well . . ."

Tighten the knot, tighter, still tighter! Martin Martinych gave himself a final twist, lifted the pail and made his way through the kitchen, the dark passage, the dining room. In the doorway of the dining room Obertyshev stuck out his lizard-nimble instantaneous hand:

"Well, so long . . . Only don't forget to slam the door, Martin Martinych, don't forget. Both doors, both, both—there is no keeping warm."

On the dark, ice-crusted landing Martin Martinych set down the pail, turned around, and shut the inner door tight. He listened, but heard only his own dry bony shivering and his jerking breaths forming a dotted line. In the narrow cubicle between the two doors he put out a hand and touched one log, and another, and another. . . . No! Quickly he shoved himself back onto the landing and closed the outer door, but not tightly. He needed only to slam it so that the lock would click.

But he could not bring himself to do it. He could not slam the door on Masha's tomorrow. And upon the dotted line made by Martin Martinych breathing, two Martin Martinyches engaged in a duel to the death: the old one, the Scriabin one, who knew "I may not," and the new one, the caveman, who knew "I must." The caveman, gnashing his teeth, knocked the other Martin Martinych down and throttled him, and Martin Martinych, breaking his nails, opened the door, plunged his hand into the stack of wood—one billet, another, the fourth, the fifth, thrust under his coat, stuck into his belt, dropped into the pail. Then he slammed the door and rushed upstairs with huge animal leaps. Halfway up the staircase, on one of the ice-coated steps, he suddenly stiffened and squeezed himself into the wall: downstairs the door clicked again and he heard Obertyshev's dust-clogged voice:

"Who's there? Who's there? Who's there?"

"It's me, Aleksey Ivanych. I forgot to slam the door. . . . I wanted . . . I went back—to slam it hard. . . . "

"You? Hm . . . How could you? One must be more careful, more careful. Everything gets stolen now, you know yourself, you know yourself. How could you?"

The twenty-ninth. All day long a low, cotton-batting sky, with holes, which let icy air through. But the cave god, his belly stuffed since morning, roared benevolently—and suppose there are holes, suppose Obertyshev, bristling with teeth all over, counts his billets—let him, it doesn't matter: only today matters; "tomorrow" makes no sense in a cave; centuries will pass before the words "tomorrow," "the day after tomorrow," will again assume meaning.

Masha got up, and swaying in an impalpable wind, did her hair in the old way: over the ears and parted in the middle. It was like a last dry leaf fluttering on a naked tree. From the middle drawer of his desk Martin Martinych took out papers, letters, a thermometer, a small blue medicine bottle (this he hurriedly thrust back, so that Masha should not see it); and finally from the furthest corner he drew a little black lacquered box. At the very bottom of it there was still some real—yes, yes, quite real–tea! They had real tea. Martin Martinych, his head tilted, listened to a voice which was almost as it used to be:

"Mart, do you remember: my blue room, and the piano with a cover on it, and on the piano an ash tray in the shape of a wooden horse, and I was playing, and you came up to me from behind. . . . "

Yes, that evening the universe was created, and the moon with its wonderful wise snout, and the nightingale trill of the bells in the hall.

"And do you remember, Mart: the window was open, a green sky—and below, from another world, an organ-grinder?"

Organ-grinder, wonderful organ-grinder, where are you?

"And on the embankment . . . the branches still bare, the water pink, and the last blue block of ice floating past, and looking like a coffin. And it was only funny, the coffin; because of course, we would never die. Remember?"

Downstairs they had started chopping wood. Suddenly, this stopped and there was the sound of running and shouting. Split in two , one half of Martin Martinych saw the immortal organ-grinder, the immortal wooden horse, the immortal block of ice, while the other half, breathing in a dotted line, counted the chunks of wood with Obertyshev. And now Obertyshev has finished counting; he is putting on his coat and, bristling with teeth, slams the door ferociously, and—

"Wait, Masha, I think, I think someone is knocking at the door."

No. No one. No one yet. One can still breathe; with head tilted one can still listen to that voice so like what it used to be.

Twilight. The twenty-ninth had grown old. Staring, dim, old woman's eyes, and everything shrinking, hunching under that fixed stare. The ceiling is caving in, the armchair, the desk, the beds, Martin Martinych himself—are all flattening out, and on the bed—Masha, perfectly flat, like paper.

It was evening when Selikhov came, the chairman of the house committee. He used to weigh some 250 pounds, but now half of him was gone and he rattled in his jacket like a nut in a gourd. But he had kept his rumbling laugh.

"Well, Martin Martinych, in the first place, in the second place, allow me to congratulate your spouse on her name day. Of course, of course! Obertyshev told me. . . ."

Martin Martinych was shot out of the armchair, and he jerked about, hurrying to speak, to say something, anything.

"Tea . . . right away, this very minute. We have real tea today. Real! Let me just. . . ."

"Tea? I'd prefer champagne, you know. You haven't any? You don't say. Haw-haw-haw! And the other day my friends and I made home-brew out of Hoffmann drops. It was a circus! Didn't we get soused. 'I am Zinoviev,' one fellow said; 'on your knees!' A circus! And when I was crossing the Field of Mars on my way home I met a man in nothing but a vest, I swear! 'What's wrong?' I asked. 'It's all right,' says he. 'I've just been robbed, I'm walking home, to Vasilyevsky Island.' A circus!"

Masha, a flattened, papery Masha, laughed in her bed. Tying himself in a tight knot, Martin Martinych laughed more and more loudly, in order to refuel Selikhov so that he might go on talking, only go on, and when he was finished with this, talk of something else. . . .

But Selikhov was petering out, and at last he was silent except for gentle snorts. He rolled to right and to left in the shell of his jacket and then got up.

"Well, let me kiss your little hand, birthday girl! AFF! What, you don't get it? A fond farewell—AFF, as *they* say. A circus!"

He was rumbling away in the passage, in the foyer. In a moment he would be gone, or. . . .

The floor was gently swaying and tossing under Martin Martinych. With a clayey smile he held onto the doorpost. Selikhov was panting with the effort of getting his feet into huge overshoes.

Mammothlike in overshoes and overcoat, he straightened and recovered his breath. Then he silently took Martin Martinych's arm, silently opened the door leading into the polar study, and silently sat down on the sofa.

The floor of the study was an ice floe, the ice floe cracked gently, broke off from the shore and floated Martin Martinych, spinning him around so that Selikhov's voice, coming from the farther shore, where the sofa stood, was scarcely audible.

"In the first place, in the second place, my dear sir, I must tell you: I would gladly squash this Obertyshev like a louse, by God. . . . But you understand, since he has made a formal declaration, since he says he'll go to the police. . . . What a louse! I can only give you this advice: go to him this very minute and stop his mouth with that wood."

The ice floe was spinning faster and faster. Tiny, flattened, hardly visible, a mere splinter, Martin Martinych replied to himself, speaking not of the wood, but of something quite different: "All right. Today. This very minute. . . ."

"Excellent, excellent. He is such a louse, such a louse, I tell you. . . ."

It was still dark in the cave. Clayey, cold, blind, Martin Martinych awkwardly stumbled against all the things that lay about there promiscuously. He started: a voice like Masha's, like what it used to be:

"What are you and Selikhov talking about? What? Ration books? And I was lying and thinking, Mart: if we could only pull ourselves together and go somewhere, South perhaps. . . . How noisy you are! Are you doing it on purpose? You know I can't stand it, I can't, I can't!"

A knife scratching glass. But now it didn't matter any more.

His arms and legs were mechanical contrivances. To lift and lower them, chains were required, a crane, a windlass, and to work the windlass one man was not enough: three were needed.

Working the windlass with an effort, Martin Martinych placed the teakettle and the pan on the stove and threw in the last of Obertyshev's billets.

"Do you hear me? Why don't you answer? Don't you hear?"

Of course, this wasn't Masha, no, it wasn't her voice. Martin Martinych moved more and more slowly, his feet stuck in the sand, it was getting increasingly difficult to work the crane. Suddenly a chain slid off a pulley, his arm dropped and stupidly knocked against the teakettle and the pan so that they went crashing down on the floor, while the cave god hissed like a snake.

And from over yonder, from the distant shore, from the bed, came a stranger's shrill voice:

"You are doing it on purpose! Go away! This minute! I don't want anyone, I want nothing, nothing! Go away!"

The twenty-ninth was dead, and dead the immortal organ-grinder and the block of ice in the water, pink with sunset, and Masha. And this was well. And there must be no incredible tomorrow, no Obertyshev, no Selikhov, no Martin Martinych; everything should die.

Mechanical, remote, Martin Martinych was still going through the motions of handling things. Perhaps he started that stove again and picked up the pan from the floor and set the teakettle to boil, and perhaps Masha was speaking. He did not hear: there were only the dully aching dents in the clay made by words and by the corners of the chiffonier, the chairs, the desk.

Martin Martinych was slowly extracting from the desk bundles of letters, a thermometer, sealing wax, the box of tea, more letters. And at last from the furthest recess came the little blue medicine bottle.

Ten o'clock: the light was on. Electric light, naked, hard, simple, cold, like cave life and death. And next to the flatiron, opus 74, the cakes—quite simply, the little blue medicine bottle.

The iron god roared benevolently, devouring the parchment-yellow, the bluish, the white paper of the letters. The teakettle gently called attention to itself—making a noise with its lid. Masha turned around:

"Is the tea boiling? Mart, darling, give me. . . ."

She saw. A moment shot through and through with clear, naked, cruel electric light: Martin Martinych squatting before the stove, a pink reflection, as on water at sunset, on the letters, and over yonder the little blue medicine bottle.

"Mart . . . should we already. . . ?"

Silence. Indifferently devouring the immortal words, bitter, tender, yellow, white, blue, the iron god was purring gently. And Masha, as simply as if she were asking for tea:

"Mart, darling! Give it to me!"

Martin Martinych smiled distantly.

"But you know, Masha, there's only enough for one."

"Mart, but as it is, I'm not living any more. This isn't me any more, anyhow, I'm going to . . . Mart you understand, don't you? Mart, have pity on me! Mart!"

Oh, that voice, the old voice . . . And if you tilted your head . . .

"Masha, I have deceived you: there isn't a single piece of wood in the study. And I went to the Obertyshevs' and there in the entry . . . I stole, and Selikhov came to . . . I must take it back at once, and I have burnt it all, every bit. . . ."

The iron god was unconcernedly dozing off. Dying down, the walls of the cave flickered gently and so did the houses, the cliffs, the mammoths, Masha.

"Mart, if you still love me. . . . Please, Mart, just remember."

The immortal wooden horse, the organ-grinder, the block of ice . . . Martin Martinych slowly rose from a kneeling position. Slowly working the crane with an effort, he took the blue little bottle from the desk and handed it to Masha.

She threw off the blanket, sat up in bed, pink, swift, immortal —like the water at sunset, then seized the little bottle, laughed:

"There, you see: not for nothing did I lie here and think of going away somewhere. Light another lamp—right here, on the table. So. Now throw something more into the stove."

Without looking, Martin Martinych fished some papers out of the drawer and tossed them into the stove.

"Now . . . Go and take a little walk. I think the moon is out, *my* moon: remember? Don't forget to take the key. You'll slam the door to, and without a key. . . . Who will let you in . . . ?"

No, there was no moon. Low, dark, thick clouds, like a vaulted ceiling, and the world one enormous silent cave. Narrow, endless passages between walls; and dark ice-coated cliffs resembling houses; in the cliffs—deep purple hollows; in the hollows, around the fire, humans, crouching. A light icy draught blows the powdery snow from under your feet, and over the white powder, the massive cliffs, the caves, the crouching humans, there moves, with inaudible, measured steps, some supermammoth.

1920

The Story of My Dovecote

Isaac Babel

When I was a boy I wanted badly to have my own dovecote. Never since have I wanted anything more. I was nine when my father promised to lay out the money for its construction and for a pair of doves. This was in 1904. I was studying to enter the preliminary class at the Nikolaev high school. My parents lived in the town of Nikolaev in the province of Kherson. That province no longer exists, for it has been absorbed into the Odessa district.

Being only nine, I dreaded examinations. In the two subjects set, Russian and arithmetic, I had to make a score of no less than five. At our high school the minority quota was strictly limited to five percent. Of the forty boys admitted only two might be Jewish. The masters would examine these two with special cunning; they never made the questions anything like as complicated except for us. This was why in promising to buy the doves my father required two five-pluses of me in return. Thus an excruciating martyrdom was imposed on me, like a waking dream without any end, a long, despairing child's dream, and in this dream I went to take the examination. Just the same, I passed with a higher mark than any of the others.

I had a talent for learning. For all their cunning, the masters could not belittle my intelligence and my omnivorous memory. Being quick to learn, I got five in both subjects. But then matters took an ill turn. Khariton Efrussi, a corn merchant and wheat exporter to Marseilles, greased somebody's palm with five hundred rubles on his son's behalf. I was given a five-minus, and Efrussi Junior went to the high school instead of me.

My father was terribly upset. From the time I was six he had taught me everything possible to teach. This slapping on of a minus reduced him to despair. He wanted to beat Efrussi out of his senses or pay a couple of longshoremen to do so, but my mother talked him out of it, and I began again working for admission the following year. I was not aware that my parents had wheedled a teacher into coaching me in both the preliminary and first-year classes within the one year. As we were used to expecting only the worst, I set to learning three books by heart: Smirnovsky's *Grammar*, Evtushevsky's *Collected Problems in Arithmetic*, and Putsykovich's *Elementary Manual of Russian History*. School children no longer use these books, but I learned them by heart, line for line, and the next year I won the coveted five-plus from the master, Karavaev.

This Karavaev was a red-cheeked, irate-looking man from the student circles of Moscow. He was barely thirty, and the color bloomed in his rugged features as it does in the cheeks of peasant children. On one side a mole sprouted hairs brindled like a cat's.

The other examiner besides Karavaev was the assistant principal, Pyatnitsky, who was looked up to not only in the school but also in the province. He began by questioning me on Peter the Great. A feeling of imminent annihilation came over me, a sense of my approaching end, of the abyss, the dry abyss, its walls encrusted with ecstasy and despair.

Regarding Peter the Great, I knew both Putsykovich's book and Pushkin's poem by heart. With sobs in my voice I began to recite it. At once the faces before me began to spin and shuffle like the cards in a newly opened pack. They went on shuffling on the retinas of my eyes while I, atremble, trying to sit up straight, hurried on shouting Pushkin's verses with all my might. I went on and on, yet no one interrupted my absurd declaiming. Meanwhile a new sense of freedom came to me through a crimson haze, and I saw old Pyatnitsky's face with its silvery beard bending toward me. He did not stop me. He merely turned to Karavaev (who was delighted with me and my Pushkin) and murmured, "What a race they are, those Jew boys of yours—there's the very devil in them."

When I broke off, he said to me, "All right, you can go, my young friend."

I went out of the classroom into the corridor. There, leaning against the unpainted wall, I little by little recovered from the clutch of my chimera. The Russian boys were playing about me; nearby the school bell hung in the well of the drab staircase; the janitor was dozing in his sagging chair. As I looked at him, I came to myself. The boys had been stealing up on me from every side. They may have wanted to rough me up a bit, or perhaps just have some fun with me, but just then Pyatnitsky appeared in the corridor. In passing me he stopped for a moment. I saw how his coat had ridden up his back in a great fold. As he moved on, I followed behind that broad baronial rear. "Boys," he said, "leave this youngster alone." His smooth, fine-boned hand rested on my shoulder. "My young friend, run and tell your father you've been admitted to the first class."

The splendid star shone on his chest, the decorations jingled. The big black-garbed body moved stiffly away between the gloomy walls. He sailed between the gloomy walls like a barge through a steep-walled canal and disappeared into the principal's office. A page boy took in a tea service with a ceremonious flourish. I ran home to the store.

In our store, scratching himself (being full of misgivings), sat a peasant customer. As soon as my father saw me, he abandoned the peasant. He accepted my story without a moment's hesitation. Calling to his assistant to close up shop, he rushed off to Sobornaya Street to buy me a cap with a shield on it. He was so beside himself my poor mother was hard put to it to keep him off me. My mother was pale: she was challenging destiny. By turns she caressed me, then pushed me away with aversion. She said that the papers usually published a list of all the successful candidates for high-school vacancies, she said that God would punish us, that everyone would laugh at us for buying a uniform ahead of time. My mother was pale: she gazed on me with bitter pity, as on a cripple, in my eyes she read destiny, for she alone fully understood how unfortunate our family was.

All the men in our family had trusted in human nature. They were all too apt to undertake ill-considered ventures. Nothing ever turned out lucky for us. My grandfather had once been a rabbi at Belaya Tserkov, but he had been kicked out of his office for blasphemy. He went on living in poverty for forty more tumultuous years, learning foreign languages, and, toward the last, beginning to lose his reason in his eightieth year. My uncle Lev, my father's brother, had studied at a Yeshiva school in Volozhin. In 1892 he had evaded the draft and ran away with the daughter of the army quartermaster then stationed in the Kiev military district. Uncle Lev took this girl to Los Angeles, deserted her there, and died in a penitentiary, among the blacks and the yellow skinned. After his death the Los Angeles police sent us a great trunk trussed with rusty iron straps. In it were some weights for lifting, locks of a woman's hair, a prayer shawl, whips with gilded hafts, and flower tea in a cheap canister studded with pearl beads.

By then only mad Uncle Simon, who lived in Odessa, my father, and myself remained of the entire family. But still my father went on trusting people. His effusiveness, like love at first sight, put them off. They could not forgive him for this, and they took to deceiving him. This was why my father believed his life was governed by an adverse fate, as if some inscrutable being unrelated to him were pursuing him. And so I was the only one of our family whom my mother trusted. Like other Jews, I was puny, frail, and a sufferer from headaches induced by eye strain. My mother saw all this, and was never for a moment deluded by my father and his beggar's pride, his incomprehensible faith that our family one day would become richer and more powerful than any on earth. She counted on no success for us. She was afraid of buying a uniform ahead of time. Her only concession was that I might go to the photographer's for a large studio portrait.

On September 20th, 1905, the list of those admitted to the first-year class was posted at the high school. My name was on the list. All our relations went to see it, even my granduncle

Joel. I liked the boastful old man because he sold fish in the market. His big hands were always damp, covered with fish scales, smelling of an exquisite world of cold. Joel was not of the ordinary run of men, for he told tall stories of the Polish uprising of 1831. In the old days Joel had been an innkeeper at Skvir. He had seen the troops of Nicholas I shoot down Count Godlevski and the others of the Polish insurrection. Or maybe he had not. Of course, I now know that Joel was just an old ignoramus and an artless liar, but I have never forgotten his tales. They were good ones. And here was foolish old Joel come to the high school to read the list with my name on it. That evening he tapped his foot and danced at our shabby little party.

To celebrate the joyous event, my father invited all his friends, corn merchants, real estate brokers, and commercial travelers selling agricultural machinery in our province. These travelers sold their machinery to everyone. The peasants and the landowners both feared them, for it was impossible to get rid of them without buying something. Of all Jews, the commercial travelers have the sharpest wits and the merriest natures. This evening they sang Hasidic chants based on only three words but sung at great length with a wealth of comic intonation. The charm of this is intelligible only to those who happen to have spent a Passover with the Hasidim or to have frequented their noisy synagogues at Volyn.

Besides the commercial travelers we had also invited old Lieberman, who taught me Hebrew and the Torah. He was always called "M'sieu Lieberman" in our house. He drank more Bessarabian wine than was good for him, the traditional silk cords hanging down below his red vest, and he proposed a toast in Hebrew in my honor. In it the old man congratulated my parents, saying that by my passing the examination I had overcome all my enemies, all the fat-cheeked Russian boys, and the sons of our brutish rich men. As in ancient times David, King of Judaea, had triumphed over Goliath, so I too had triumphed over Goliath, just as our people, through the might of their intellects, would triumph over the enemies surrounding us, thirsting for our blood. M'sieu Lieberman wept as he said this, and weeping he drank more wine, shouting, "Vivat!" The other guests drew him into a ring and began a square dance with him, as at a Jewish wedding. Everyone was in high spirits at our party. Even my mother sipped a little wine, though she did not care for vodka and could not see how anyone else could. This was why she thought all Russians were mad; she could not understand how Russian wives could bear to live with Russian husbands.

Our days of gladness were yet to come, however. They came for my mother when she began making my sandwiches before I left for school in the morning, and when we went to the store, happiness in our hearts, to buy my school supplies, a penholder, a coin purse, a book bag, new books with paper covers, and shiny covered notebooks. No one in the world has a stronger feeling for new things than children. Children quiver at the very scent, like hounds on the track of a hare, and are seized with the mad joy that later, when we reach maturity, is called inspiration. And the child's pure sense of the ownership of new things conveyed itself to my mother.

For a month we accustomed ourselves to the penholder in the early morning darkness, while I drank my tea at a corner of the large lighted table and filled my bag with my books; for a month we accustomed ourselves to our happy life, and it was only after the first quarter that I remembered the doves.

I had provided everything I needed for the doves (one ruble and fifty kopeks), and also the dovecote, made from a packing case by Granduncle Joel. The dovecote was painted brown. It would house twelve pairs of doves, and it had various perches on the roof and a special grid I had invented, the more to tempt visitors. By Sunday it was all ready. On October 20th I was all set for a visit to Okhotnitskaya Street, but on the way something unexpected happened.

The story I am telling (how I was admitted to the first year of the high school) took place in the fall of 1905. At that time Tsar Nicholas II had given the people of Russia a constitution, and orators in shabby overcoats climbed onto platforms outside the town hall and made speeches to the citizens. My mother did not want me to go to Okhotnitskaya Street because rifle shots were heard in the streets at night. That October 20th the neighborhood children had been flying kites since morning right outside the police station. Our water carrier had left his work to walk down the street, his hair oiled, his face pink. Then we saw that Kalistovs, the baker's sons, had brought out a leather horse and were doing acrobatics with it on the sidewalk. Nobody stopped them. Semyornikov, the patrolman, even urged them on to higher leaps. He was wearing a belt of roughspun silk, and that day his boots had been polished until they shone brighter than ever before. It was the patrolman's non-official costume that frightened my mother the most. It was because of him that she did not want me to go, but I slipped out into the street by the back yard and ran to Okhotnitskaya, which was nearby, beyond the railroad station.

Sitting in his usual place in the fowlers' market was Ivan Nikodimych, the dove vender. Besides doves he also sold rabbits and peacocks. One peacock sat on a perch, tail spread, darting his haughty head in every direction. One leg was tied to a wicker chair by a twisted string. As soon as I reached the old man, I bought a pair of plum-colored doves with superb tails and another pair of crested doves. Putting them in a bag, I hid them in the breast of my coat. I still had forty kopeks left, but the old man refused to sell me a pair of hook-billed pigeons for that amount. What I liked about such pigeons was their beaks, short, beaded, friendly. Forty kopeks was their actual price, but the fowler held out for more, turning away his yellow face lined by the fierce passions of fowling.

However, seeing at the close of business that he would find no other buyer, Ivan Nikodimych beckoned to me. It all turned out as I had wanted, but, as it later proved, for the worse.

At midday or a little after a man in felt boots crossed the square. His gait was light for all his stocky legs and the eyes in his worn face burned with intensity. "Ivan Nikodimych," he said as he passed the fowler, "put your gear away; in mid-town the noble sons of Jerusalem are getting the constitution. The people have killed that old man Babel at the fish market to celebrate."

This said, he went off among the cages, stepping lightly, like a barefoot farmhand following the tow path.

"For no reason," muttered Ivan Nikodimych, "for no reason," he cried on a higher note, gathering up the rabbits and the peacock and handing the pigeons over to me for the forty kopeks. I hid them in my bosom, staring at the market people running away. The peacock, perched on Ivan Nikodimych's shoulder, was last to go. He sat there like the sun in a damp autumn sky, he sat there like July on a reddish river bank, a July burning down on a long, cool expanse of green. No one remained in the market, and rifle shots sounded not far distant. I ran toward the station, across the station square, suddenly turned topsy-turvy, and into a deserted passage with a trampled yellow earth floor. In his wheelchair at the end of the passage sat legless Makarenko, who wheeled himself around the town peddling cigarets on a tray; the boys of our street bought from him, the children liked him. I dashed toward him. "Makarenko," I cried, out of breath from running, "have you seen Joel?"

No reply. His coarse face, molded of ruddy fat, fists, and iron, was alight. Excitedly he worked his wheelchair to and fro. His wife Katyusha, her padded back to him, was turning over some articles strewn on the ground. "What are you counting out there?" demanded Makarenko, recoiling from her as if expecting an answer that would be unbearable.

"Fourteen gaiters," said Katyusha, still bending over, "six sheets, and now I'm counting the caps."

"Caps!" screeched Makarenko, half choking with sobs, "Katerina, it seems as if God had ordained me to answer for everything. Here people are carrying off whole bolts of cloth, people being what they are, but as for us, we get the caps."

And indeed there was a woman with a pretty, bright face running through the passage. One arm was loaded with fezes, the other clutched a bolt of cloth. In a shrill, gay voice she called to her missing children, and a silk dress and sky-blue jacket billowed about her as she hurried. Makarenko, rolling after her, she ignored. The legless man could not catch up with her, his wheels churned as he worked them with all his might. "Hey, ma'am," he shouted, "where're you taking that striped cotton?"

But the flying dress and jacket were already gone, and the way was barred by a rickety cart that appeared from round the corner. In it a sturdy peasant youth stood upright. "Where's everybody running to?" he asked, pulling on the reins as his horses reared.

"They've all run to Sobornaya," said Makarenko coaxingly, "that's where they've gone, my lad. Anything you pick up, bring to me, I'll buy it all."

Leaning over the front board of his cart, the youth whipped his piebald team. The horses shook their soiled haunches, as calves do, and broke into a gallop. Once more the yellow passageway was yellow and empty. Then the legless man turned his disappointed gaze on me. "Seems I'm chosen by God," he commented apathetically, "am I really a son of man?"

Makarenko reached out his hand toward me, stained and spotted as if by leprosy. "What you got in that bag?" He snatched the bag that had been warming my heart. With his gross hand the cripple shook the lock open and drew a plum-colored dove into the light. She sat on his palm, her feet tucked up beneath her. "Doves," said Makarenko. With a grinding of his wheels he rolled up to me. "Doves," he repeated, and slapped me in the face. His fist squeezing the dove fetched me a backhand stroke. Katyusha's padded rear seemed to whirl. I fell to the ground in my new coat. "Stamp out their seed," said Katyusha, straightening up over her caps. "I hate their seed and their stinking filthy menfolk."

She said more about our seed, but I heard nothing. As I lay on the ground, the entrails of the crushed bird dripped on my temple, running down my cheek, spreading over me, blinding me. The dove's thin intestine trailed over my forehead. I closed my one unblinded eye so as not to see the world about me. A narrow, horrible world. A pebble lay before my eyes, a chipped pebble resembling an old woman's heavy jowled face, and beyond it lay a scrap of string and a still palpitating clump of feathers. I shut my eyes so as not to see it, pressing hard on the earth beneath me, mute and reassuring.

This trampled earth in no way resembled our life, nor the waiting for examinations in our life. Somewhere, far off, misfortune rode a tall horse, but the clatter of hoofs was dwindling and fading. Silence—the bitter silence that can take unhappy children by surprise—suddenly abolished what separated my body from the earth, the unmoving earth. It gave off a scent from its humid depths, a scent of the tomb, a scent of flowers. I breathed in this scent and unrestrainedly I began to weep. I walked along an alien street, blocked by white boxes, I walked adorned with bloodied feathers, alone, along the sidewalks swept clean as if on a Sunday, and I wept, as bitterly, fully, relievedly, as I was never to weep again in my life.

The gleaming wires buzzed over my head; a mongrel dog ran before me, on a side street a young peasant in his vest was smashing in a window frame in Khariton Efrussi's house. He flailed away with a mallet, his whole body swung with the blow, he was heaving and smiling, a happy smile of drunkenness, sweat, and wholesouled vehemence. The street resounded with a crashing and cracking, splinters flew about like a song. The peasant smashed on as if just to fling his body, drench himself with sweat, all the time shouting strange words in a tongue not Russian. He shouted and sang.

His blue eyes stared as he turned from the house to the street when a procession headed by a cross appeared, coming from the direction of the town hall. Old men in dyed beards bore the portrait of the Tsar, his hair combed and parted, banners displaying the Holy Sepulcher fluttered above the religious parade, headed by a scattering of excited old women. On seeing the marching column, the peasant in the vest clutched the mallet to his bosom and ran along with the banners. I waited for the marchers to pass, then I slipped away toward our house. It was empty. Its white doors were wide open. The grass about the dovecote was trampled. Only Kuzma had not fled the yard. Kuzma the janitor was in the shed laying out the dead Joel.

"The wind's blowing you about like a sliver of rotten wood," said the old man, seeing me. "You've been gone for ages. Just look how the people have done for our old granddad."

Kuzma sniffed, turned, and began to pull pike out of the holes in my granduncle's trousers. Two pike had been pushed into him, one into the fly of his trousers, the other into his mouth, and, though the old man was dead, one of the pike was still alive and quivering.

"They've done for our old granddad, just him," said Kuzma, throwing a pike to the cat. "He stood up to them, every mother's son of them, he cursed them good and dirty, he did, the good old man that he was. Will you get the five-kopek pieces for his eyes?"

Being only ten, I did not know why you had to have five-kopek pieces for the dead. "Kuzma," I whispered, "save us."

I huddled close to him, I clung to his bent old back with one shoulder higher than the other and from there stared at my granduncle. Joel was lying on sawdust, his chest crushed in, his beard upstanding, his feet bare in their coarse shoes. His spread-eagled legs were dirty, bluish-gray, dead. Kuzma busied himself with them; he bound the jaw and went on doing what remained to be done for the deceased, as busily as if the house were being redecorated. He let up only after he had combed the dead man's beard.

"Cursed 'em good and dirty, he did," he said, smiling affectionately at the corpse. "If it had been the Tartars he was facing, he'd have driven 'em off, but it was Russians, and their women folk with 'em, the katsaps*—the katsaps think it shameful to forgive. I know the katsaps."

He scattered some sawdust over the dead man, took off his carpenter's apron, and grasped my hand. "Let's go to your father," he muttered, gripping my hand tighter and tighter. "Your father's been looking for you since morning, he's about to die."

So Kuzma and I went off together to the tax inspector's, where my parents were hiding in their flight from the pogrom.

1925

*Ukrainian derogatory term for Russians.

The Widow

Isaac Babel

Shevelyov, the regimental commander, lies dying in the field cart. At his feet a woman is sitting. The vault of night is slashed with cannon fire. Lyovka, driver for the divisional commander, heats up food in a pot. As he leans over the fire his forelock drops. Nearby the tethered horses stamp in the crackling bushes. As he stirs the pot Lyovka talks to Shevelyov lying in the ambulance.

"I used to work in the town of Tyumrek, comrade. I was a show rider, and a first-rate athlete, too. Of course there's not much doing for women in a small town like Tyumrek. So the girls used to look me up and storm the walls. 'Lev Gavrilych, don't say No to a nice tidbit cooked to order. You won't regret living up a moment that comes but once. 'Well, so off I go with one of them to an eating house and we call for two plates of veal and half a bottle. We're sitting there, quietlike, having ourselves a drink, when I look up and see a well-dressed, decent-seeming gentleman, a respectable sort, but I notice there's something fancy about him, and he's had one too many. 'Pardon me,' he says, 'but I just wanted to know what nationality you are.'

"'What do you want to come and ask about my nationality for, mister?' I ask him. 'Can't you see I'm with a lady?'"

"So he says, 'What sort of a champ do you think you are?' he says. 'In the French style of fighting they knock fellows like you into a cocked hat, so just what is your nationality?'

"Well, I don't clobber him just yet.

"'Why,' I says, 'What, you (I don't know your father's name) want to create misunderstandings? Just go on like that and some one'll have to kick the bucket here and now, or, as they say, breathe his last.'"

"Breathe his last," repeats Lyovka excitedly, flinging his arms up and flailing the sky about his head like a nimbus. The untiring wind, the clean night wind, goes singing on, swelling with sound, stirring souls. The stars in the darkness blaze like betrothal rings, they fall on Lyovka, tangling in his hair, and are snuffed out in his shaggy mane.

Suddenly Shevelyov whispers through his blue lips, "Lev, come here. The gold, whatever there is, goes to Sashka," he says, "the rings and the harness, they all go to her. We lived as best we could, and I'm paying off my debts. The clothes, the linen, the decorations they gave me for valor beyond the call of duty, they all go to my mother, she lives on the Terek River. Send them to her with a letter. This is what you're to write: 'The Commander says good-bye. Don't weep. You'll have the cottage, old lady, so you go on living. If anyone wrongs you, go to Budyonny and say, "I'm Shevelyov's mother." 'My horse Abramka I'm leaving to the regiment, so that they'll pray for my soul."

"I get you about the horse," mutters Lyovka, waving his arms. "Sash," he shouts to the woman, "do you hear what he says? Swear to him: will you give the old woman what's hers or not?"

"You know what you can do with *her*!" retorts Sashka, and she goes off into the bushes, plunging straight ahead like a blind person.

"Will you give the orphan her share?" Lyovka runs after her and seizes her by the throat. "Swear it to him!"

"I will! Let me go!"

So, having got her promise, Lyovka takes the pot off the fire and begins spooning the soup into Shevelyov's stiffening mouth. The soup dribbles over the dying man, the spoon clicks on his already dead shining teeth, and through the vastness of the night the bullets went on whistling ever more poignantly.

"It's their rifle fire, the bastards," muttered Lyovka.

"Damn their impudence," answered Shevelyov, "cutting us to ribbons on the right flank with their machine guns."

Shevelyov, like a corpse on a table, closed his eyes with solemnity and gave himself up to listening to the battle with his huge waxen ears. Hunched beside him, Lyovka chomped on his meat, breathing hard as he ate. Once it was all down, he licked his lips and beckoned Sashka over to a hollow.

"Sash," he said, trembling. He wrung his hands, belching. "Sash, in the sight of God one sin's like another. We live but once, and we die but once. So you give in, Sash. I'll make it up to you if it takes my last drop of blood. His life is done for, Sash, but that don't mean God's days are numbered."

The place they were sitting was in the high grass. The loitering moon emerged, climbed the clouds, and fell on Sashka's bare knee.

"You may as well go and warm yourselves," muttered Shevelyov. "They've routed the fourteenth division, I'd guess."

Lyovka, still chewing, was breathing hard in the bushes. The cloud-girdled moon prowled the sky like a beggar. Puffs of rifle fire came from a distance. On the feathery grass of the uneasy earth the August meteors fell.

Sashka came back to her place. She began to change the wounded man's bandages, lifting the lantern high over the suppurating wound. "You'll be gone by tomorrow," she said, wiping away Shevelyov's cold sweat. "By tomorrow you'll be gone, it's got into your guts, death has."

At that moment a deafening thump hit the earth. The enemy had brought up four fresh bridges, and these had hurled their first shells onto the town of Busk; tearing through our communications, these had set the Bug watershed afire. On the horizon the heavy birds of bombardment lifted out of the flames. Busk was on fire. Lyovka catapulted into the forest on the swaying cart allotted to commander number 6 of the division. He pulled on the crimson reins; the varnished wheels grazed the stumps of trees. Behind him came the other field cart with Shevelyov inside, the horses rearing under Sashka's struggle with the reins.

Thus they reached the edge of the forest and the first-aid post. Lyovka unharnessed the horses, went to the post commander for a horse blanket. The forest was thick with carts. Under them the bodies of the medical orderlies protruded. The timorous dawn flitted over the sheepskins of the sleeping soldiers. Their boots were flung wide. Their eyes were rolled up. The dark holes of their mouths gaped awry.

The post commander had a horse blanket to spare. Lyovka returned to Shevelyov. He kissed his forehead. With the blanket he covered him from crown to toe. Then Sashka came up, untying her kerchief and shaking the straw from her skirt. "My darling Paul," she muttered, "my Jesus Christ," and she lay down beside the dead body, turning over him as if to shield him with her own ample self. Lyovka drove on toward Busk and the headquarters of the sixth cavalry division.

"She's grieving," said Lyovka. "Of course. You can't say they weren't well matched. Now she'll have to work up through the whole squadron again. It's her bad luck." And he drove on toward Busk and the headquarters of the sixth cavalry division.

Some ten vyorsts from the town the battle was going against the Savinkov Cossacks. Under the command of the Cossack captain, Yakovlev, who had gone over to the Poles, the traitors fought stubbornly. For the past forty-eight hours the divisional commander had stayed by his troops. So not finding him at the command post, Lyovka went to his own cottage, rubbed down the horses, swilled water over the wagon wheels, and lay down to sleep.

The place was full of fresh hay, as quick as perfume to catch fire. After a good sleep, Lyovka roused himself for the evening meal. His landlady had cooked him potatoes with curds. As he sat at the table, the bugles sounded the dirge, and there came the clatter of many hoofs. With its bugles and standards the squadron was passing along the winding Galician streets. Shevelyov's body had been laid on a gun carriage, covered with banners. Behind the coffin Sashka rode Shevelyov's stallion. From the ranks at the rear a Cossack song resounded.

Through the main street of the town the squadron passed,

then turned off toward the river. There, barefoot and bareheaded, his Cossack fur hat gone, Lyovka rushed out from behind the detachment as it moved away and seized the bridle of the squadron commander's horse. Neither the divisional commander, who had halted at the crossroads to salute the dead officer, nor any of his staff could hear what Lyovka was saying to the squadron commander.

"Underwear (the wind blew back a few unrelated words) . . . his mother on the Terek River (disconnected cries)." The squadron commander, ignoring all this, pulled his bridle free and waved in Sashka's direction. She shook her head and drove on. Lyovka vaulted onto her saddle, pulled her back by the hair, and smashed his fist into her face. Wiping off the blood with the hem of her skirt, Sashka drove on. Lyovka slid off, tossing back his forelock, and knotted a handsome red scarf about his hips. The bugles, sounding their sorrow, led the squadron toward the horizontal gleam of the Bug River.

Lyovka soon returned. Eyes blazing, he shouted: "After all, I've put her in her right place. 'I'll send them to his mother,' she says, 'when need be. I'll keep his memory alive,' she says, 'in my own way.' Ah, you do that, and don't you forget it, you slut. If you forget, we'll just remind you. And if you forget again, well, then, we'll have to remind you a second time."

1923

The Death of the Army Commander: A Tale of the Unextinguished Moon

Boris Pilnyak

1

As day broke over the city, the factory sirens sounded. In the side streets curled gray wisps of mist and night and frost, forerunners of the sad, gray, rimy dawn. At this hour the early editions had come off the press and soon boys from the delivery yards would scatter through the streets with batches of newspapers in their arms. One after another they would go through the deserted squares, clearing their throats before sounding the newsboy's cry they would yell all day: "Revolution in China! Gavrilov returns! Army Commander's illness!"

Just at this time a train came into the station serving the southern region, a special train, hooked onto a blue saloon car, shining and silent, with sentries posted on the running boards and shades lowered at the mirror-like windows. Out of the black night the train had come, from fields that had wasted the summer in high living against the winter, fields plundered in summer and left for winter to age. The train slipped noiselessly in under the station roof, pulling up on the track to the shed. Not a soul on the platform. Near the exits, probably not by chance, emergency groups of militia with their green stripes. Three men in army uniform with diamonds sewn on their sleeves walked toward the coach. Salutes were exchanged, the three standing on the running board, while the sentry called in a kind of whisper into the coach. Then the three mounted the steps and disappeared somewhere behind the curtains. An electric light was burning inside the coach. Two army electricians bustled around, working under the station roof to install telephone wires inside the car. Then another man came up; he wore a shabby spring overcoat and, incongruously, a fur cap with ear flaps. Giving no salute and getting none, this man said, "Tell Nikolay Ivanovich Popov's here.

The Red Army man slowly turned, scrutinized Popov, noticed his broken shoes, and just as slowly replied, "The Comrade Army Commander isn't up yet."

Popov gave the Red Army man an amiable smile and—for some reason using the familiar mode of address—told him, in a friendly way, "Never mind, brother, just go in and tell him Popov told you to say he's here."

The Red Army man disappeared, then came back. Popov climbed up into the coach. In the saloon—owing to the lowered shades and the light still burning—the night seemed permanent. On the table by the lamp lay an open book, and beside it an unfinished plate of semolina pudding, and beyond it an unfastened revolver holster with its shoulder strap trailing like a serpent. Opened bottles stood at the far end of the table. The three military men with diamonds on their sleeves were seated along one side of the table. They sat in leather chairs against the wall, self-effacing, straight-backed, not speaking, each holding a briefcase. Popov went around to the other side of the table, took off his overcoat and cap, laid them beside him, picked up the open book, glanced over it. A steward had now come in and, indifferent to everyone and everything, was busying himself with the table. He tidied the bottles away into a corner, swept the pomegranate skins off onto his tray, then, throwing a cloth over the table, put out a single glass in a holder, a plate of rusks, a small egg cup, and brought in a plate with two eggs on it, salt, some small bottles of medicine, lifted the corner of a shade and looked out at the morning. He pulled up the shades covering the windowpanes, the cords squeaking sadly, turned off the electric light—and now the gray morning with its air of autumnal frost slunk into the room. The faces of all present were yellow in that dull morning light—watery, diffuse light, like lymph. At the door next to the steward stood an orderly; the track switchboard was already operating, for the telephone rang.

At this moment the Army Commander came out of the sleeping compartment and into the saloon. He was not very tall, a fair, broad-shouldered man, his longish hair combed back from his forehead. His tunic—with four diamond shapes on the sleeve—hung on him awkwardly; it was cut out of green, creased army cloth. Though scrupulously polished, his spurred boots with their worn down heels, betrayed their extensive activity. This was a man whose very name bespoke the heroism of the civil war, the thousands and tens of thousands and hundreds of thousands of men that stood at his shoulder, the thousands and tens and hundreds of thousands of deaths, sufferings, mutilations, intense cold, icy roads, heat waves of the campaigns, thunder of cannons, whistling of bullets, winds of night, fires of the night watch, marches, victories and setbacks, and still more death. This was a man who had commanded armies, thousands of men—ordered them to victory, to death, through powder, smoke, shattered bones, torn flesh, to victory of the kind where red standards were raised by the hundreds among the massed multitudes, the kind that resounded all the way back to the rear, that radios had broadcast around the world, victories after which the living dug the sandy Russian soil to make deep ditches for the dead, ditches where thousands of human bodies had been hastily buried. This was a man whose name was steeped in legends of wars, of ingenious strategies, boundless acts of courage, boldness, and firm stands. A man who had the right, when he so willed it, to send men out to kill their fellowmen and to die.

Into the saloon car came the man—not very tall, broad-shouldered, his good-natured face somewhat drawn, like that of a seminarian. He walked quickly, his gait suggesting at once the horseman and the man of civil and not at all military demeanor. The three staff officers sprang to attention before him. The Army Commander paused, did not offer them his hand, but signaled to them to stand at ease. And, so standing before them, he received their reports. Each of the three took a step forward, came to attention, and reported: "By the office entrusted to me . . . in the service of the Revolution." The Army Commander clasped each one by the hand, in turn, as he reported—he had probably paid little heed to the reports themselves. Then he sat down before the single glass, and the steward hurried to his side to pour him tea from the brightly polished teapot. The Commander helped himself to an egg. "How're things going?" he asked, informally, not in the manner of one demanding a report.

One of the three spoke, gave him the news, and then asked, of his own accord, "How's your health, Comrade Gavrilov?"

For a second the Commander's face took on an alien expression, and he said moodily, "Oh, I've been in the Caucasus, had some treatment. I'm better now. (Pause.) I'm all right now. (Pause.) Just see to it there's no turn-outs or guards of honor, or anything of that sort. (Pause.) You may go, comrades."

The three staff officers made ready to leave. Without rising, the Army Commander gave his hand to each in turn. Noiselessly they left the car. When the Army Commander had first entered, Popov had not greeted him but had picked up the book and turned away from the Commander, leafing over the pages. The Army Commander had glanced at Popov out of the corner of his eye and had not greeted him either, as if not noticing he was there. Once the staff officers departed, the Commander turned without greeting him—as though they had last met only the evening before—and asked Popov, "Do you want tea, Alyoshka? Or wine?"

Before Popov had time to reply, the orderly came up ("Comrade Army Commander—") and reported that the motor had been taken off the unloading platform and dispatches had been left at the office—one package, marked *Secret*, had come from No. 1 House, brought by his secretary; rooms had been made ready at staff headquarters; a heap of telegrams and other messages of congratulation had come. The Army Commander gave the orderly leave to go, said he would go on living in the coach. Without waiting for Popov's reply, the steward put a glass of tea and a glass of wine on the table. Popov left his place and seated himself near the Army Commander. "How's your health, Nikolasha?" asked Popov with concern, as brother to brother.

"My health's all right, complete recovery, I'm well, but what's the use, you'll be one of my pallbearers, anyway," replied Gavrilov in a half-joking, half-teasing manner—in any case, not joyfully.

These two men, Popov and Gavrilov, were bound by an old friendship, by work they had done together in secret, by work they had done together in a factory, far back in their youth, when they had begun as weavers at Orekhovo-Zuevo; then, together, in Bogorodsk prison, and then the life of the professional revolutionary: deportation, escape, underground, temporary prison at Tagan, deportation, escape, emigration, Paris, Vienna, Chicago, and then the war clouds of 1914, Brindisi, Salonica, Romania, Kiev, Moscow, Petersburg, and then the storms of 1917, Smolny, the October Revolution, thunder of cannons over the Moscow Kremlin. Then the one, chief of staff of the Red Guard in Rostov, the other, "Marshal of Proletarian Nobility," to quote Rykov's witticism at Tula; the one geared to armies, victories, the command of artillery, of people, of death; the other given up to provincial commissions, executive committees, the VSNX, conferences, meetings, speeches. For these two men, everything, the whole of life, of thought, was dedicated to the greatest revolution in the world, to the greatest justice and truth in the world. But the one was always Nikolasha to the other and the other was always Aleksey (Alyoshka) to the first. They had always been friends and comrades, weavers, without rank or office.

"Tell me, Nikolasha, how's your health?" asked Popov.

"Well, I did have a stomach ulcer, perhaps I still have it. You know what that's like, pains, vomiting blood, awful heartburn—a dirty, rotten thing, however you look at it." The Army Commander spoke in low tones, leaning toward Aleksey. "They sent me to the Caucasus for a cure, the pains left off, I went back to work for half a year, then the pains and vomiting started up again, and they sent me back to the Caucasus. Now the pain's disappeared again, I've even drunk a bottle of wine to test it." The Army Commander broke off."Look Alyoshka, if you do want wine, there's some under the seat. I brought you a small case of it, open it up."

Popov sat leaning his head on his palm. He answered, "No, I don't drink so early in the morning. Go on with what you were saying."

"Yes, well, my health is back to normal." The Army Commander broke off. "Listen, Alyosha, why have I been called back here, d'you know? "

"No, I don't."

"Some paper or other came telling me to leave the Caucasus at once: couldn't even go and see my wife." The Army Commander paused. "The devil knows what it's all about, *I* don't; everything is OK in the Army, no meetings or anything like that."

The Army Commander spoke of the army and war, but probably he failed to notice that when he spoke of the army he ceased to be a weaver and became a strategist, a Red General of the Red Army. The Army Commander spoke of Orekhovo-Zuevo and Orekhovo-Zuevo times, and probably he failed to notice that he had become a weaver, a weaver who had fallen in love with the schoolteacher over the river, who cleaned his boots for her sake and went barefoot to school so his boots would not get dusty, putting them on only when he came to the little wood near the school; he bought a beribboned ornament and a jaunty style of hat, and even so there was no talking to that schoolteacher about anything but books—and certainly not romances at that—the schoolteacher simply turned away from him. The weaver-turned-Army Commander was an easy-going sort of man and a pleasant one, who could make jokes and see the funny side of things—and he made jokes as he talked to the other, yet now and again he would suddenly remember something and grow anxious, he would think of the enigma of his recall, stir uneasily in his chair and then, as the healthy young weaver would have spoken of the ailing Army Commander: "A high-ranking official, a field marshal and a senator as well, but I can't eat a plate of buckwheat porridge, yes, old man, the Committee likes to make sport of men—you can never take back a single word of anything," and he fell silent.

"Nikolasha, tell me, honestly, now, what is it you suspect?" asked Popov. "What's that you were mumbling about pall-bearers?"

The Army Commander took his time answering and then said slowly, "In Rostov I ran into Potap (using the Party nickname of a very eminent revolutionary of the 'glorious band' of 1918). Well, what he said was—he tried to persuade me to have an operation, have the ulcer taken out, or sewn up, or something, it was all rather suspicious, the way he tried to talk me into it. (Pause.) I feel all right, I'm just totally opposed to the idea of an operation, that's all, I don't need it—I can get better the way I'm going now. I don't even have any pain any more, I've put on weight—damned if I know what to make of it—an adult male, on his way to being an elder statesman, paying all this attention to his stomach. I'm ashamed. (The Army Commander broke off and picked up the open book.) Been reading old Tolstoy's *Childhood and Boyhood*. The old fellow certainly could write, he knew about life, and about blood. Blood I've seen a lot of, but I dread that operation like a child. I don't want it, they'll cut me up!" That old man knew a lot about a man's blood.

The orderly came in, stood at attention, and made his report: someone was there from staff headquarters to say that a motor had come for the Army Commander from No. 1 House, where his presence was requested; more telegrams had come; something from so-and-so about dispatches from the South. The orderly laid a pile of newspapers on the table. The Army Commander dismissed the orderly. The Army Commander ordered his greatcoat to be brought. The Army Commander opened one of the newspapers. In the column reserved for the most important events of the day, it said: "Army Commander Gavrilov's Arrival"—and on the third line down it announced that "Commander Gavrilov has left his armies temporarily and is coming today for a stomach ulcer operation." In the same column it said that "Commander Gavrilov's health has caused some concern," but that "the professors give their personal guarantee as to the success of the operation."

Gavrilov, old soldier of the Revolution, the army man, the Army Commander, the strategist who had sent thousands of men to death, the crowning achievement of the war machine that is designed to kill, to die, and to conquer by blood—Gavrilov threw himself back in his chair, drew his hand over his forehead, fixed his eyes on Popov, and said: "You hear, Alyosha? There's a motive behind all this! Ye-e-es! And what can I do about it?" Then he shouted: "Orderly, my greatcoat!"

2

The intersection of two main streets of the city, with motors, people, and wagons passing in endless succession, with railings, and behind these a columned mansion. The house bore no sign. On either side of the carriage entrance, on either side of those griffon-bearing gates, helmeted sentries. Past this house streamed people, motor horns, crowds, and time, streamed the gray daylight, newsboys, men with briefcases, women in skirts to the knee and stockings that deceived the beholder into thinking the legs were bare. Behind the griffon-bearing gates perturbation had quieted and ceased.

Just such another mansion stood at the other end of the city, built in the same classical style with a front of columns as well as wings that boasted a frieze of formidable mythological absurdities. A pair of gates gave access to this house, atop them fauns writhed and grimaced, beside them gatehouses had been set up and outside these, on benches along the walls, sat the gatekeepers in their felt boots, with brass discs on their aprons. A motor had pulled up before the gates—a black van with a red cross and the inscription "Ambulance."

On that particular day the editorial in one of the leading newspapers had discussed "the third year of stability of the gold *chervonets*," showing how a stable monetary unit can exist "only when the entire economic activity is founded on solid economic calculation, on a solid economic basis. Economic subsidies and the management of the people's economy in disproportion to the budget must infallibly disrupt a solid financial system." There were the large headlines: "China's Struggle against Imperialism." On the foreign page were cables from England, France, Germany, Czechoslovakia, Latvia, and the USA. In the middle section was a special article, "The Question of Revolutionary Violence." Then came two pages of announcements, among which, in large letters, could be read: "The Truth about Life: Syphilis" and "S. Broide's New Book, *In a Lunatic Asylum*."

At noon a closed Rolls Royce arrived at No. 1 House, the mansion where time stood still. The sentry opened the door and out of the limousine stepped the Army Commander.

In a private office at the far end of the house the curtains at the windows had been half-drawn, and outside the windows the street ran by. A fire had been lit in the fireplace. On the table, spread with a red cloth, three telephones emphasized the tranquility of the logs crackling on the hearth. The three telephones brought into the room three main arteries of the city, so that, out of that tranquility, the city could be commanded—commanded, that is to say, as regards the city itself and its arteries. On a desk in that private office stood a massive bronze desk set; the pen tray had been filled with red and blue pencils, a dozen or so. A radio receiver with two pairs of earphones had been fixed to the wall behind the desk, and the collection of electric buzzers ranged from "Reception" to "War Alert." In front of the desk, an easy chair; behind it, a wooden chair on which a man was sitting bolt upright. The curtains were half-drawn; an electric lamp with a green shade was burning on the desk, but the face of that straight-backed man was obscured by shadow.

The Army Commander crossed the room, treading on the rug, and sat down in the leather easy chair.

The first to speak was the straight-backed man. "Gavrilov, we aren't here to talk about the millstone of revolution. In the main, the wheel of history is made to turn by blood and death—unfortunately, I suppose. It's not for me or you to discuss blood and death. You remember how you and I led the half-naked soldiers of the Red Army at Ekaterinov. You had a rifle, so did I. A shell got your horse with you on it, and you went on, on foot. The Red Army was falling back, and you shot one soldier with your revolver to stop the others from running away. As Commander of the Army, you would have shot me, too, if I'd turned tail—and rightly, I'd say."

The second to speak was the Army Commander. "Well, what a layout you've got here! A proper Minister of State, no less! Can a fellow smoke in a place like this? Don't see any cigaret ends around."

"Don't smoke, it's not good for your health. I don't smoke myself."

The second, harshly, rapidly: "Look, straight out, now—what did you recall me for? No need to act the diplomat. Let's have it!"

The first: "I recalled you because you've got to have an operation. You're indispensable to the Revolution. I've called in the professors: they say in a month you'll be on your feet again. You must have it done for the Revolution's sake. The professors are expecting you, they'll check you over and get the whole picture. I've already given the order. Even brought in a German specialist."

The second: "I'll have a smoke whatever you say. My doctors told me there's no need for an operation. I can get well as I am. I feel absolutely fit, I don't need an operation, and, what's more, I won't have one."

The first man put his hand behind him, felt for the buzzer, and rang; a secretary slipped noiselessly in; the first man asked: "Is there anyone waiting in Reception?" The secretary replied that there was. The first man made no reply and dismissed the secretary.

The first man said: "Comrade Army Commander, you remember how we thrashed out between us whether or not to send four thousand men to certain death? You gave the order to dispatch them. And rightly. You'll be on your feet again in three weeks. Pardon me, but I've already given the order."

The telephone rang, not the city line, but the inside telephone that connected with thirty or forty others. The first man picked up the receiver, asked the caller to repeat the message, said: "The note to the French? Certainly, make it official, I said so yesterday. You know how we used to fish for trout: the French are slippery, too. What? Yes, that's it, clamp down on 'em! See you soon."

Then the first man said: "I trust you'll excuse me—there's nothing in it to discuss, Comrade Gavrilov."

The Army Commander finished his cigaret, stubbed it out among the red and blue pencils, and got up from the easy chair. The Army Commander said: "Good-bye."

The first man said: "See you soon."

The Army Commander crossed the red carpet and left the room. The Rolls Royce bore him away among the noises of the street. The straight-backed man stayed on in his office. No one else came in to see him. Unbending as ever, he pored over his papers, a thick red pencil in his hand. He rang, the secretary came, he said to the secretary: "Order them to take away the cigaret stub right here, from this holder!" Again he sat silent over his papers, red pencil in his hand.

An hour went by, then another, and still he went on working on the papers. At one moment the telephone rang, he picked up the receiver, listened, and said: "That's two million rubles' worth of galoshes and cloth for Turkestan— use up nonmarketable surplus? Yes, of course, obviously! Yes, go ahead! See you soon." The corridor attendant came in, making no noise, went to a little table near the window, on which he placed a tray with a glass of tea and a plate of cold meat covered with a napkin, and left the room. Then the straight-backed man again rang for his secretary and asked: "That secret communiqué ready?" The secretary replied that it was. "Bring it here." And again the straight-backed man spent a long while over a large sheet of paper headed with the names of the People's Commissar for Foreign Affairs, the Political and Economic Section of the OGPU, the People's Commissar of Internal Commerce, and the People's Commissar of Labor. Then the other two men of the Three who ruled came into the room.

At four o'clock the motors arriving at the far end of the city found No. 2 House plunged in darkness, as if this could warm the pervading dampness. Two men of the militia were posted, one on each side of the gates, in addition to the custodians in their aprons and boots. Two more militiamen stood at the door of the main entrance. Supple as a willow, the Red Army Commissar, wearing two decorations of the Order of the Red Banner, came in with two Red Army men. The Red Army Commissar and the two soldiers were received in the antechamber by a man in a white tunic. "Oh, yes, yes, indeed, don't you know!"

The room was large and bare. A table covered with white oilcloth had been placed in the middle; around this had been arranged a number of chairs with oilcloth covers and high backs, of a commonplace design such as is used on railroads. Against the wall stood a divan, covered with the same shiny oilcloth, over which a sheet had been thrown, and by the divan a wooden stool. On a glass shelf over the washbasin was an array of chemist's jars bearing various Latin names, a small bottle of disinfectant and a container with green soap in it. The yellowed towels that had not been soaked in laundry blueing hung at one side. The first motors to arrive brought professors, therapists, surgeons.

They came in, greeted one another, were received by the tall, bearded man, mild-faced, bald-headed, who acted as host.

Professor Lozovsky came toward him. He was a man of thirty-five, clean-shaven, wearing a jacket and pince-nez on a straight-bridged frame, his eyes deep set. "Oh, yes, yes, indeed, don't you know!"

The clean-shaven man handed the bearded one an envelope that had been sealed with wax and was torn open. The bearded man took a sheet of paper from it, settled his spectacles, and read. Again he adjusted his spectacles and with a perplexed air handed on the paper to a third.

The clean-shaven man said solemnly: "As you see, it's a paper of a secret nature, almost an order. I got it this morning. You follow me?"

The first, second, and third spoke disjointedly, in low, hurried tones:

"What's this consultation about?"

"I got an urgent summons to come here. A telegram addressed to the Rector of the University."

"Gavrilov, the Army Commander—you know, the one who. . . ."

"Yes, yes, don't you know—the Revolution, he's Army Commander, the title and all that, so it's 'Come!'"

"A consultation."

The light from the electric lamp fell so that it cut shadows sharp as a knife. One held on to the other by the breast-pocket button of his tunic; one hand-propelled the other into making a brief turn.

Then, at the doors, the rattle of rifles and the click of heels as the Red Army soldiers sprang to attention. A tall, willowy young man with the orders of the Red Banner pinned to his chest appeared and stood at attention before the entrance as the Army Commander came quickly into the room, brushing back has hand over his hair, tugging at the collar of his tunic, and said: "Greetings, comrades! Am I to get undressed?"

Then the professors taking their time, sat down on the shiny chairs behind the table, leaning their elbows on it, clasping and unclasping their hands, adjusting their spectacles and pince-nez. They asked the patient to be seated. The one who had handed over the sealed letter, whose eyes behind the pince-nez were deep set, addressed the bearded man: "Pavel Ivanovich, as you are *primus inter pares*, I imagine you wouldn't object to taking the chair?"

"Am I to get undressed?" asked the Army Commander, and put up his hand to his collar.

The chairman of the consultation, Pavel Ivanovich, pretended not to have heard the Army Commander's question and, sitting down in the presiding chair, said slowly: "I take it we're to ask the patient to tell us when it was he felt the onset of his illness and what the pathological symptoms were that proved to him he was ill. Then we shall proceed to examine the patient."

One sheet of paper, filled with illegible, professorial handwriting, was to remain of this discussion on the professorial level.

The proceedings of the consultation, at which the following were present: Professor Somebody, Professor Somebody, Professor Somebody (and so on: in all, seven names).

The patient, Citizen Nikolay Ivanovich Gavrilov, complained of pain in the epigastric region, accompanied by vomiting and pyrosis. He had been ill for two years without perceiving it. He had received occasional treatment as an outpatient and visited various watering-places: results negligible. At the patient's request, a consultation was arranged, attended by those named above.

Status praesens: The patient's general state of health is satisfactory. Lungs: negative. Heart: slight dilatation observed. Pulse: accelerated. Mild neurasthenia. Other organs (stomach excepted): no pathological condition observable. It was established that the patient is to all appearances suffering from *ulcus ventriculi* and should undergo an operation without delay. At this same consultation it was recommended that the operation be performed by Professor Anatoly Kozmich Lozovsky. Professor Pavel Ivanovich Kokosov agreed to be present at the operation.

City, date, seven professorial signatures.

Later—when the operation was already over and done with—it transpired from private talk that in fact not one of the professors had found the operation at all imperative, for each had presumed that the disorder was following a course making an operation unnecessary; only the German, a man of few words, had actually pointed to the unnecessariness of it: he did not dwell further on it following his colleagues' response. And it was also rumored that in the motor going back after the consultation to Scientists' House, Professor Kokosov, whose heavy brows overhung his eyes, had said to Professor Lozovsky: "You know, if my own brother had that illness, I—well, I wouldn't operate on it," to which Professor Lozovsky replied, "Yes, of course, but . . . but it isn't really a dangerous operation." The motorcar made a sound and started off.

The straight-backed man at No. 1 House was still sitting in his office. The windows were muffled by the drawn curtains. The fire yet burned in the hearth. The house was immersed in silence, as if that silence had been gathering for a century. The man sat on the same wooden chair. Now there were thick books open before him, in German and English—he wrote in Russian, in ink, in vertical handwriting, in a German lined notebook. The books lying open before him were works on affairs of state, questions of might and right. The light in the office fell from the ceiling, and now the man's face could be seen: it was a very ordinary face, just a little hard, perhaps—but its expression was one of concentration, not at all one of fatigue. The man sat over his books and notebooks like this for a long time. Then he rang for a stenotypist. He began to dictate. In broad outline his speech dealt with the USSR, the United States, Britain; the world as a whole and the USSR; British sterling and Russian wheat; heavy US industry; Chinese labor. The man spoke with a strong, harsh accent and uttered each sentence like a formula.

The moon passed over the city.

At this moment the Army Commander was sitting in Popov's room in a large hotel inhabited only by Communists. There were three present. Gavrilov was sitting at the table with Natashka fidgeting on his knee. Gavrilov was striking matches; wonderingly, as only children in this world can wonder about the mystery, Natashka watched the flame, made a tube of her lips, and breathed on it: she did not breathe hard enough to put it out at once, and it went out by itself—then there was such surprise, enchantment, and fear of the mystery in Natashka's blue eyes that he could not refuse to light another cigaret or to do homage to the mystery that Natashka had within her. Then Gavrilov laid Natashka down to sleep, sat down by her little bed, and said: "Close your eyes and I'll sing you a lullaby," and sang, never having sung a lullaby, knowing no lullabies, but making one up on the spot.

A stag came along and said,
"Sleep, sleep, sleep, sleepyhead."

He smiled, casting at Natashka and Popov a sly glance, and sang the first thing that came into his head to rhyme with "Sleep, sleepyhead," intoning:

A stag came along and said,
"Sleep, sleep, sleep, sleepyhead,
"But don't pipi in your bed."

Natashka opened her eyes and smiled, and Gavrilov went on singing the last two lines in an unmusical voice (true, he sang badly) until she fell asleep

Then Gavrilov and Popov drank tea together. Popov asked, "Nikolay, shall I make you a bowl of semolina?"

They were sitting facing each other, talking in low tones, not at all hurriedly, taking their time; they drank a good deal of tea. Gavrilov drank from his saucer, having unbuttoned the collar of his tunic. After chatting of this and that, they were half through the second pouring of tea before Popov pushed away his glass and after a pause said: "Nikolka, my Zina's left me, she's simply abandoned the child to my keeping and gone off with some engineer she was in love with before me or something—I don't know! I wouldn't set myself up as her judge, wouldn't demean myself with ugly words—but all the same, I mean to say, she ran off like a bitch, without a word, behind my back. I'm ashamed to think of it—I picked someone out of a trench at the front, I took care of her and loved her and cherished her like a fool—and a fine specimen she turned out to be! I hadn't even seen what sort of person she was, she'd been living with me hardly five years."

Down to the smallest detail Popov told of those differences that are always so painful, precisely because of their apparent triviality, petty details that screen off the larger issues behind them. Then their talk turned to the children, and Gavrilov spoke of his own family, his three sons, his wife, already grown old but still the only woman in all Gavrilov's life.

As he got up to go, the Army Commander said: "Give me something to read—only, *you* know, some rather simple kind of book about good people, true love, the same sort of thing as *Childhood and Boyhood*," said Gavrilov.

In every corner of Popov's apartment stood mountains of books; but a simple book about simple human love, simple relationships, a simple life, about the sun, people, and simple human joy—there was no such book in Popov's home.

"You and your revolutionary literature," Gavrilov teased him. "Well, all right, I'll read Tolstoy over again. There's a very nice description of some old dancing gloves." Gavrilov's face clouded; he was silent for a moment, then said in low tones: "I didn't tell you, Alyosha, so as not to waste our evening over what can't be helped. Today I went to the authorities and saw the professors at the hospital. I seem to have fired their professorial imagination. I don't want to be cut up, of course, I'm opposed to it. Tomorrow I'm to have the knife. So come to the hospital, don't forget your oldtime friend. But don't write anything about it to my wife and children. Farewell!" and Gavrilov went out of the room without shaking Popov's hand.

Near the hotel stood a closed car. Gavrilov got in and ordered, "Home, to the railroad car," and the car went off toward the station yard. The moon slipped across the rails that led to the shed; a dog ran howling by and was lost in the vast black silence over the tracks. By the coach steps stood a sentry who sprang to rigid attention as the Army Commander passed. The orderly ran out into the corridor, the steward put out his head, the electric light was switched on inside, and a wordless, blue, provincial calm prevailed in the car. The Army Commander went into his sleeping compartment, took off his boots, put on bedroom slippers, unbuttoned his collar, rang, ordered "Tea." He went into the saloon and sat down by the table lamp. The steward brought in the tea, but the Army Commander did not touch it; the Army Commander sat for a long time over his book *Childhood and Boyhood*, meditating. Then the Army Commander went into his sleeping compartment and came back with a large writing pad, rang, told his orderly, "Bring some ink, please," and began to write, slowly, thinking over every sentence. He wrote a letter, read it over, reflected on it, and sealed it in an envelope. He wrote a second letter, reflected, sealed it. He wrote a third letter, a very brief one, writing in haste—sealed it without rereading it. There was a dead calm in the coach. The sentry stood at attention in the corridor. Time seemed to stand at attention. For a long time the letters lay before the Army Commander in their white addressed envelopes. Then the Commander picked up a large envelope, sealed the three letters inside it, and wrote on the outside: "To be opened after my death."

3

The first snow fell on the day of Gavrilov's death. The city was stilled with a white stillness, it grew white, grew still, and outside the windows the snow on the trees was scattered by the tomtits who came along with the snow from beyond the city.

Professor Pavel Ivanovich Kokosov always awoke at seven in the morning, and it was at this hour that he awoke on the day of the operation.

The professor put out his head from under the blanket, hawked, stretched out his hairy hand toward the bedside table, felt around as he usually did for his spectacles, and saddled these on his nose, his heavy eyebrows roofing the lenses. Outside the window a tomtit was making the snow drop from a birch tree. The professor put on his robe. He pushed his feet into slippers and went to the bathroom.

All had been quiet in the house when the professor awoke, but when, grunting to himself, he came out of the bathroom, his wife, Ekaterina Pavlovna, was already making a clatter with a spoon as she insistently stirred the professor's sugar in his tea while the samovar was purring away in the dining room. The professor came in for his tea in his robe and slippers.

"Good morning, Pavel Ivanovich," said his wife.

"Good morning, Katerina Pavlovna," said her husband.

The professor kissed his wife's hand and sat down opposite her, adjusting his glasses to an easier position under the thatch of hair. The professor swallowed a mouthful of tea in silence as he sought for some commonplace thing to say. But the course of the morning tea ritual was broken by the telephone ringing. A call had not been expected. The professor shot a severe glance at the door of the study where the ringing was, then looked doubtfully at his wife, already aging, plump in her Japanese kimono, got up doubtfully and went to the telephone.

The professor's own words as they went down the instrument sounded querulous and senile. "Well, well, I'm listening. Who's calling and what's it about?"

Whoever it was replied that the call was coming from staff headquarters, where it was known that the time of the operation had been fixed for half-past eight, and that staff headquarters was inquiring whether it could be of any assistance: should a motor be sent for the professor? At this the professor suddenly grew angry, breathing hard down his nose, and rumbled: "My dear sir, I serve the community, don't you know, not any particular individual, my dear fellow, oh, yes, yes, indeed, and I always go down to my clinic by tram, my dear fellow, don't you know. I perform my duties, if I may say so, in accordance with my conscience. And I see no reason why I shouldn't go down there by tram today."

Cutting off further conversation, the professor noisily put down the receiver, snorted, and went back to table, wife, and tea. He sniffed, bit his moustache, his fit of anger fast disappearing. His eyes behind their lenses gleaming, intelligent and concentrated, the professor began tranquilly to speak: "Ivan the peasant falls ill in the village of Drakina Luzha, for three weeks he sleeps on hot coals, or so he feels, then he says his prayer, sighs to himself, and goes to his parents for advice, and then he pays a visit to Dr. Pyotr Ivanovich at the Zemstvo hospital. Pyotr Ivanovich has known Ivan for fifteen years, and during those years Ivan has brought Pyotr Ivanovich one and a half-dozen hens, he knows Pyotr Ivanovich's children, once he even pulled the ear of one of his boys. So Ivan goes to Pyotr Ivanovich and greets him, bringing one more little hen. Pyotr Ivanovich looks him over, auscultates, and, if need be, operates on him, calmly, unhurriedly, judiciously, and certainly not worse than I could do it myself. And if the operation isn't successful, if Ivan dies, they put a cross over him, and that's all. Or some bourgeois in a small line of business—Anatoly Yuryevich Svintsitsky—comes to see me. He goes over every detail till I'm dizzy. I examine him and reexamine him at least seven times, so I finally get to know him and can tell him, 'Come on, old man' I say, 'live with that ulcer, go carefully, and you can live with it for fifty years, and if you die—well, what's to be done, it'll be God's will, my dear fellow!' And if he says 'Operate,' I operate, and if he doesn't want an operation, nothing will make me perform one."

The professor did not speak for a while. "Today I'm assisting at an operation in my hospital on a Bolshevik, Army Commander Gavrilov."

"But he's the one who—" rejoined Ekaterina Pavlovna, "the one who . . . oh, you know, in the Bolshevik papers, a terrible name! And why aren't *you* doing the operation?"

"Oh, there's nothing very terrible in it, really," replied the professor, "and as for why Lozovsky's doing it—well, these days the youngsters are all in fashion, they must be pushed forward. But even so, no one really knows the patient well, after those consultations, even if all we celebrated doctors have felt his pulse, taken roentgen plates, opened his bowels, and examined him. What's more important, they don't know the man, haven't had anything to do with him, only with his title and image—a general of the umpteenth order gets written about in the papers every day to instill fear into people. And just try to deviate by so much as a hair's breadth from proper operative procedure, and there'll be no corner of Europe that can hold you, your life won't be worth living."

Professor Anatoly Kozmich Lozovsky's residence in no way resembled Kokosov's. If the Kokosov apartment preserved the spirit of the nineties, Lozovsky's had broken away to represent the years from 1907 to 1916. Here were heavy hangings, a wide divan, naked females in bronze bearing candles on a desk of solid oak, the walls were hung with rugs, and on these rugs small paintings had been put up, paintings of an inferior sort from the *Monde des Arts* exhibitions.

Lozovsky slept on the divan, not alone but with a pretty young woman—his starched shirt front lay on the carpet on the floor. Lozovsky awoke, placed a quiet kiss on the woman's shoulder, and rose briskly, pulled the curtain cord; the heavy curtain withdrew into the corner, and the snowy daylight came into the room. With the joyous gaze of those who love to feel the life within them, Lozovsky looked out on the street, the snow, the sky.

At that moment the telephone rang. The professor's telephone was over the divan behind the hangings. The professor lifted the receiver: "Yes. Yes, speaking." The call came from staff headquarters, inquiring whether a motor should be sent for the professor.

"Oh, yes, if you will, please! There's no cause for anxiety over the operation, it will all go off admirably, I'm sure. About the car—as soon as possible, if you will, as I've some business to attend to before the operation. Yes, that's right, at eight o'clock, please."

The morning of the operation Popov came to see Gavrilov before it took place. Again it was not yet dawn, and the lamps were still lit, but the two men had no opportunity to talk, because a special nurse came and took Gavrilov into the bathroom, Gavrilov said: "Alyosha, mind you, read *Boyhood* and see what Tolstoy says about what's *comme il faut* and what isn't. That old man knew about blood all right!" These were the last words Popov was to hear Gavrilov speak.

Before the operation people rushed, whispering, to and fro in the corridor leading from Gavrilov's room to the operating theater, bustling, but with minimum noise, about their business. The previous afternoon a rubber hose had been thrust down Gavrilov's esophagus, a siphon was used to pump up the digestive juices and wash out the stomach, a thing that brings on nausea and dejection, as if its function were to debase human dignity. The morning of the operation an enema had been ministered for the last time. Gavrilov entered the theater wearing a hospital robe over hospital shirt and trousers of coarse material (a shirt fastened with tapes instead of buttons), hospital slippers with a number, on his bare feet (that morning Gavrilov's own linen had been changed for the last time and replaced by sterilized linen). As he came into the operating theater, he looked pale, thinner, weary.

In the theater anteroom the spirit stove hissed, long nickel boxes boiled, and people in white overalls went about in silence. The operating theater was very large, entirely painted—floor, walls, and ceiling—in white. In the theater it was astonishingly light, for one of the walls was all window, looking out on a place somewhere across the river. In the middle of the room stood a long white operating table. Here Kokosov and Lozovsky came to encounter Gavrilov. And Kokosov and Lozovsky in their white overalls wore on their heads white caps, like those worn by kitchen workers, and Kokosov had covered his beard with a biblike mask that left his hair-framed eyes showing over the top. Some ten men, all wearing white, stood along the wall.

Gavrilov came in with a special nurse; he entered the theater quietly, gave the professors a silent greeting, and went up to the table to look through the window at the place across the river, his hands joined behind his back. A second nurse brought up a stand, on which was a boiling sterilizer containing instruments in a long nickel box.

Lozovsky whispered to Kokosov: "Shall we proceed, Pavel Ivanovich?"

"Oh, yes, indeed, don't you know," replied Kokosov.

And the professors went off to wash their hands, once and then again, pour sublimate on them and rub them with iodine. The anesthetist examined the mask, fingered the bottle.

"Comrade Gavrilov, we shall now begin," said Lozovsky. "Will you have the goodness to lie down on the table? Take off your slippers."

Looking in the nurse's direction with some embarrassment, Gavrilov pulled down his shirt—she saw Gavrilov as an object and smiled as one does at a baby. Gavrilov sat on the table, shook off one slipper, then another, and lay down on the table without more ado; having arranged the bolster under his head, he closed his eyes. Then, quickly, in the manner of one skilled and familiar with these things, the nurse fastened straps over his feet and tied the man to the table. The anesthetist placed a hand towel over the eyes, smoothed vaseline over the nose and mouth, and tied the mask over the face, picked up the patient's hand to feel his pulse, and dampened the mask with chloroform—and through the room floated the sweet, pungent smell of chloroform.

The anesthetist registered the time of the beginning of the operation. The professors drew back to the window in silence. The nurse picked up a pair of pincers and with them began to spread and arrange on a piece of sterilized guaze, sterilized cloth, scalpels, forceps, clamps, Pean's needles, silk threads. The anesthetist went on pouring chloroform. A glacial silence prevailed in the theater. Then the patient tossed his head and let out a groan. "I can't breathe at all, take this thing off my face," said Gavrilov, champing his teeth.

"Have patience a little longer, please," replied the anesthetist.

A few moments later the patient began to sing on one note, and talk:

The ice has gone, my golden one,
The Volga's on her way,
And I, the little river wave,
Have given my heart away,

sang the Army Commander, and then he whispered, "Sleep, sleep, sleepyhead." He was silent, then said severely: "Don't ever give me any more cranberry mush, I've had enough of it, it isn't *comme il faut*." He broke off, then gave a harsh cry, as he had probably done in battle: "Don't try to retreat! Not a step! I'll shoot you down!—Alyoshka, brother!—it's full speed ahead, the earth's far below us. I remember everything. I know what revolution is, what a might there is in it. And I'm not afraid of death.!" And again he intoned:

Over the Urals, my golden one,
A woodsman lives his life,
And there, my golden, golden. . . .

"How do you feel? Not sleepy?" the anesthetist asked Gavrilov in a low voice.

And in his normal tones, but speaking low as if to a fellow conspirator, Gavrilow answered: "Nothing special, I can't breathe at all."

"Patience, just a little longer," said the anesthetist and poured on more chloroform.

Kokosov looked at his watch with concern, bent over a pathological report, reading it through.

There is a physical constitution that reacts to anesthesia atypically. Twenty-seven minutes had already gone by in the attempt to put Gavrilov to sleep. Kokosov called a young assistant and pushed out his face toward him for the other to adjust the spectacles on the professor's nose. With a troubled air the anesthetist whispered to Lozovsky, "Suppose we stop the chloroform and try ether?"

"We'll keep on trying with chloroform. Otherwise, we'll have to postpone the operation. Things aren't done that way."

Kokosov looked around severely, then lowered his eyes with an expression of withdrawal. The anesthetist poured more chloroform. The professors were silent.

Gavrilov finally went to sleep at the forty-eighth minute. Then for the last time the professors rubbed their hands with surgical spirit. The nurse uncovered Gavrilov's abdomen; his thin ribs and his high belly were exposed to the light.

It was Kokosov who with bold strokes rubbed the operative field, the epigastric region, with alcohol, benzine, and iodine. The nurse poured half a bottle of iodine over Professor Lozovsky's hands. Lozovsky picked up the scalpel and drew it over the skin. The blood gushed out and the skin fell back on either side; from under the skin fat showed, yellow as mutton grease, arranged in layers, and streaked with blood vessels. Once again Lozovsky cut into human flesh, separating the brilliant white fascia interleaved with purplish muscle. Kokosov, with a skill surprising for his heaviness, stopped the bleeding vessels with tampons.

With another knife Lozovsky cut into the closed sac of the peritoneum. He put aside the knife, wiped away the blood with a sterilized cloth. On the inside of the cut: the intestines and the milky blue bag of the stomach. Lozovsky put his hand into the intestines, turned back the stomach, pressing it out.

On the gleaming flesh of the stomach, in the place where the ulcer should have been, there was—as if something like a dungbeetle's mask had been modeled in wax and placed there—a white scar, showing that the ulcer was cured, showing that the operation was uncalled for.

But at that moment, at that very moment when Gavrilov's stomach was in Professor Lozovsky's hands—

"Pulse! Pulse!" cried the anesthetist.

"Respiration!" Kokosov seemed to utter, mechanically, like an echo.

At that moment Kokosov's eyes started from behind their glasses and fringe of hair, so malevolent, so terribly malevolent—started and swiveled to the corners, while Lozovsky's eyes bulged from their orbits against the bridge of his nose, withdrew again to their depths and then became one single, dreadfully piercing eye.

There was no pulse in the patient, the heart no longer beat, respiration had ceased, and the legs were already cooling.

There had been heart failure: the constitution had opposed the chloroform and had been poisoned by it. This was the categorical sign that this man would never rise again alive, that this man was to die, even with artificial respiration, oxygen, camphor, saline solution, that death might be held back for one, ten, thirty hours, not more, that the patient would never regain consciousness, that in point of fact the patient was dead.

It was clear that Gavrilov had to die under the knife on the the operating table.

Professor Kokosov turned toward the nurse, pushed out his face at her so she might straighten his spectacles and cried: "Open the window! Bring camphor! Prepare a salt solution!"

The mute crowd of assistants grew muter still. As if nothing had happened, Kokosov leaned over the instruments on the trolley, looking at them, silent. Lozovsky also leaned next to Kokosov.

"Pavel Ivanovich?" said Lozovsky in a spiteful whisper.

"Well?" answered Kokosov aloud.

"Pavel Ivanovich" said Lozovsky in even lower tones, this time with no trace of spite.

"Well?" responded Kokosov aloud. "Go on with the operation."

The two professors straightened up, looked at each other. The eyes of one had molded into one single eye; the other's were starting out of their cavities. For a moment Lozovsky recoiled from Kokosov as if seized by a stroke, as if he sought perspective. His eyes became two again, then fused yet more sharply, piercingly, than before. Lozovsky whispered: "Pavel Ivanovich. . . .?"

And he lowered his hands to the wound; he did not sew but rather tacked the internal cavities together, he pinched the skin and began to darn it together, working only on the upper layer. He gave the order: "Free the arms—artificial respiration!"

The theater's enormous window stood open, and into the room stole the icy cold of the first snow. Camphor had already been injected into the man on the table. Aided by the anesthetist, Kokosov threw Gavrilov's arms back and then up, forcing artificial respiration. Lozovsky was busy stitching the wound. He cried: "Saline solution!"

And into the patient's chest the assistant thrust two thick needles, of almost a cigaret's thickness, through which a thousand cubic millimeters of saline solution would be poured into the dead man's blood, to relieve the vascular pressure. The patient's face was lifeless, blue, his lips had turned purple.

Then they lifted Gavrilov off the table, placed him on a stretcher, and rolled him back to his room. His heart was beating, and he was breathing, but he had not regained consciousness, and perhaps he did not regain it until the last minute before the camphor-treated, artificially salted heart ceased to beat, when after thirty-seven hours he had been abandoned by both camphor and doctors to die—perhaps because, up to the last minute, no one was allowed near him except the two professors and the nurses in charge—but, one hour before the official announcement of Gavrilov's death, the patient next door heard strange sounds as if the other men were exchanging signals by knocking on the wall, as those in prisons do. In that room a man was lying, full of camphor, both dead and alive, because in medicine it is an unwritten law that a patient should not be allowed to die under the operating knife.

The operation had begun at thirty-nine minutes after eight, and Gavrilov was wheeled out of the theater on a trolley at eleven minutes after eleven. Out in the corridor the janitor said that Professor Lozovsky had had two telephone calls from No. 1 House. The professor went up to the telephone desk by the window, hesitated, looking out at the first snow, biting his nails, then returned to the telephone, rang the number with thirty-four extensions, bowed before the receiver, and said that the operation had been successful, but that the patient was very weak and that the doctors admitted that his condition was serious, and excused himself for not being able to come over at once.

Gavrilov died, which is to say that Professor Lozovsky came out of his room with a sheet of white paper and, bowing his head, announced in solemn and sorrowful tones that to his infinite regret the patient, Army Commander Citizen Nikolay Ivanovich Gavrilov, had died that night at seventeen minutes past one.

Three-quarters of an hour later, at two o'clock in the morning, platoons of Red Army soldiers came in through the hospital doors, and sentries were stationed at all entrances and staircases. Now the clouds moved slowly across the sky, and behind them hastened the full moon, weary of haste. Now Professor Lozovsky in a covered Rolls Royce was urgently borne toward No. 1 House. The Rolls moved noiselessly through the griffon-mounted gates, past the sentries, and stopped by the entrance. A sentry opened the door, Lozovsky went into the office, where the three telephones stood on the red cloth covering the desk, and where a complex of buzzers was set at attention.

What the conversation was that Lozovsky had in that office is not known, but it lasted no more than three minutes. Lozovsky came out of the office, out of the main entrance, in a great hurry, carrying his hat and coat in his arms like a character in the *Tales of Hoffmann*; there was no more motor car. Lozovsky staggered along as if drunk—and in time with Lozovsky the streets swung under the moon in the motionless desert of night.

Like a Hoffmann character, Lozovsky had come out of the office at No. 1 House. The straight-backed man stayed on inside that office at No. 1 House. The man was standing behind the table, leaning forward on the table, on his fists. His head was lowered. He stood motionless for a long time. The man had been wrested from his papers and formulae. Then he began to move. His movements were angular and formulated, like the directives he dictated every night to the stenotypist. He moved very rapidly. He pressed the buzzer behind him, raised the telephone receiver. He told the attendant, "The motor—the open one." Into the telephone he said to the man who had probably been asleep, who was one of the Three—his voice sounded feeble: "Andrey, my dear friend! Another man has left us—Kolya Gavrilov is dead, our comrade-in-arms is no more. Call Potap, my friend."

To the chauffeur the straight-backed man said: "To the hospital!"

In the darkened passages sentries had been posted. The building was silent, as a house of death should be silent. The straight-backed man went through the dark corridors toward Army Commander Gavrilov's room. He went into the room—the Army Commander's body had been laid out on the bed, and the odor of camphor was stifling.

Everyone withdrew from the room except for the straight-backed man and Gavrilov's body. The man sat on the bed at the dead man's feet. Gavrilov's arms and hands lay straight beside him. For a long while the man remained seated near the body, his head bent, stockstill. Calm reigned in the room. The man took Gavrilov's hand, clasped it, and said: "Good-bye, comrade! Good-bye, brother!" and left the room with bowed head. Looking at no one, he said: "The fanlight should be opened in there, you can't breathe!" and quickly he went off along the dark corridor.

4

The night following the obsequies for Army Commander Gavrilov, when the brass instruments of the military bands had fallen silent, after the standards had been flown at half-mast, when the thousands of those attending the funeral had gone on their way, and the body of the man was growing cold in the earth along with the earth itself, Popov fell asleep in his room and awoke at his table, he could not make out at what o'clock. It was dark in the room and Natasha was quietly sobbing. Popov bent over his daughter, took her up in his arms, and carried her across the room.

Outside the window the moon scuttled along, weary of haste. Popov went to the window, looked out at the snow, the stillness of the night. Natasha got down from Popov's arms and took up a stance by the windowsill.

In Popov's pocket was Gavrilov's letter, that last brief letter he had written the night before he went to the hospital. The letter ran: "Alyosha, brother! I knew that I would surely die. Forgive me, but you're no longer very young. As I was holding your little girl in my arms, I thought things over. My wife is not very young, either, and you've known her twenty years. I've written to her. You write to her, too. Set up house and live out your lives together, get married, or something, you know what I mean. Bring up the children together. Forgive me, Alyosha!"

Natasha stood close to the windowsill, as Popov watched her: she puffed out her cheeks, made a tube of her lips, looked up at the moon, aimed at the moon, blew at it.

"What are you doing, Natasha?" asked her father.

"I want to puff out the moon," replied Natasha.

The full moon, like a peddler, fluttered behind the clouds, weary of her own haste.

It was the hour when the city machine awoke, when the sirens howled, they went on howling a long time, one, two, three, several of them fusing into one gray and undulating voice over the city. It was quite easy to hear, howling through these sirens, the soul of the city still frozen by the moon.

1926

The Child

Vsevolod Ivanov

1

Mongolia is a wild beast and a joyless one! Its rocky soil is a wild beast, its water, a wild beast; even the butterfly is only awaiting a chance to sting.

Who knows the heart of the man of Mongolia? He swathes himself in furs, he looks like a Chinese and he dwells a long way from the Russians, beyond the Nor-Kol Desert. They say he will go even farther, across China and down to India and the blue seven-shored lands no one knows.

Into Mongolia, fleeing from the Russian war, came the Khirghiz from the Irtysh River, close to the Russians. You know what their hearts are like, brittle as crystal with no good in them, you can see right through them. They've taken their time getting there, bringing with them their cattle, their children, and even their sick.

The Russians had been mercilessly driven here. That's how they came to be such sturdy peasants, sound in wind and limb. They had left their useless weakness behind on the rocky heights—some had died and some had been killed—and had abandoned their families and cattle to the White Russians. Mean as wolves in the spring time, that's those peasants for you. In the deep ravines, in their tents, they lay thinking of the steppe and the Irtysh River.

They numbered fifty or so. Their chief was Sergey Selivanov, so their detachment was called, "Comrade Selivanov's Red Guard Partisan Detachment."

Bored, that's what they were.

While on the run over the mountains, among the huge, dark rocks, their hearts had been filled with terror. Once they reached the steppe, boredom overwhelmed them. Because the steppe was like the steppe this side of the Irtysh: all sand, stiff grasses, and steel-forged sky. It was all alien, unlike their own, it had never known a plough; it was a wilderness.

And, what's more, it was hard on them that there were no women. At night they would tell the obscene stories soldiers tell about women, but when things got unbearable, they saddled their horses and rode out to catch Khirghiz women on the steppe. At the mere sight of the Russians, the Khirghiz women would obediently lie down flat on their backs. It made you feel bad, sick, to take them lying there, never moving and with their eyes tight shut. It was like sinning with beasts.

The Khirghiz men were afraid of the Russians and fled farther into the steppe. Whenever they caught sight of the Russians, they threatened them with their rifles and longbows, yelling and whooping, but they never fired. Might it have been they didn't know how?

2

Afanasy Petrovich, paymaster to the detachment, was apt to burst into tears, like a child. His face, too, was like a child's, small, hairless, pink. His legs, though, were long and sturdy, like a camel's. When mounted on a horse, however, he turned forbidding. His face wore a remote look, and he would sit, gray, wrathful, and terrifying.

On Trinity Day three men, Selivanov, Afanasy Petrovich, and Drevesinin, the clerk, were ordered to search the steppe for decent pasture.

The sands were smoking under the sun. Down from on high blew the wind. Up to the trembling sky rose the great heat from the earth. The bodies of the men and the beast were lethargic and heavy as stones. Misery.

Then Selivanov said hoarsely, "What are the pastures like over that way?"

They all knew it was the Irtysh he meant. But no word came from their thin beards. The hair of their faces had been singed by the sun, like the grass on the steppe. Their narrow eyes were reddened, like the gash left by a fishhook. Heat.

Only Afanasy Petrovich answered in his sorrowful way, "Can they be having a drought like this over there, boys?"

His voice was tearful, but his face was not. Only the horse beneath him, gasping with weariness, had complaining tears in its great staring eyes.

So, one behind the other, filing along the trails beaten by the wild goats, the partisans moved off into the steppe.

The grieving sands burned on. The stifling wind clung to their shoulders and heads. The sweat broiling inside them could not get out of their seared skin.

Toward evening, as they were riding out of a hollow, Selivanov said, pointing westward, "Riders, at full gallop."

And so it was. On the horizon the sands were sending up a rosy dust.

"Must be the Khirghiz."

They began to argue. Drevesinin said that the Khirghiz were a long way off and never came near Selivanov's ravine. Afanasy Petrovich said that they were surely Khirghiz: the very dust they raised was Khirghiz, thicklike. But when the dust rolled nearer, they all agreed: "Strangers."

The horses could sense in their master's voices that something odd was in the wind. They pricked up their ears and sank to the ground well before being given the order. In the ravine now, the recumbent bodies of horses lay, gray and yellow; they looked impotent and absurd, their legs thin as rails. Was it out of shame or the like that they closed their eyes, their breath coming in shallow gasps?

Selivanov and Afanasy Petrovich, the paymaster, were lying at the edge of the ravine. The paymaster had begun to snivel. To calm him down, Selivanov always had him lie at his side. The almost childish weeping made the peasant's tough heart gay and playful.

The trail spread its dust. Wheels rumbled fitfully. And whirled like the dust, long dark manes in halters.

Selivanov said with certainty: "Russians. Officers."

He summoned Drevesinin out of the hollow.

The new, wicker cart had two occupants wearing caps with red bands. Their faces were hidden because of the dust, as if the red-band wearers were flying in a yellow tornado. A gun stuck up whenever the hand with the whip emerged from the dust.

Drevesinin thought and said: "Officers, on business most likely. Reconnaissance—that's pretty clear."

Mischievously he winked his eye and twitched his mouth. "We'll give it to'em, Selivanov my boy."

The cart bore its passengers along, and bore them steadily. The horses! They were enjoying themselves with the cart, like a fox with its tail, sweeping the dust of Mongolia.

In a weepy voice, Afanasy Petrovich drawled, "We mustn't, boys. It's better to take prisoners. Wait before you finish them off."

"What about your own head, don't you care?"

Selivanov lost his temper, silently released the lock on his rifle, as if undoing a button, and said: "We don't need your weeping here, paymaster."

What annoyed them more than anything else was that the officers had shown up in the steppe alone, without an escort. As if they alone constituted a force of superior number, as if they were bringing death to the peasants. And just look, one of the officers stood bolt upright—he couldn't see properly. The dust; the evening wind blowing red on the burnt grass; on two boulders beside the hollow, that looked like the dead bodies of horses. But could they be boulders? Or the carcasses of horses?

In the red dust, the little cart, its wheels, its occupants and their thoughts—whirling.

They fired. Yelled. Fired again.

On the instant the red caps fell, tilting at each other, into the body of the cart.

The reins slackened—as if they had broken loose—the horses leapt away abruptly—they were about to break into a gallop, but all at once a milky foam came out on their withers. The bands of their powerful muscles quivering, they lowered their heads and stopped.

Afanasy Petrovich said: "They're dead."

They went up to look.

The red caps were dead. They were sitting shoulder to shoulder, their heads thrown back, and one of them was a woman. Her hair was a matted ruin from the dust, half yellow, half black, and her army tunic sat high above her bosom.

"That's odd," said Drevesinin. "It's your own fault, woman, you shouldn't have worn a service cap. Who'd knowingly kill a woman? Women are needed in society."

Afanasy Petrovich spat. "You're a cruel monster and a bourgeois. You've got no feeling or anything in you, you son of a bitch."

"Hold on," cut in Selivanov, "we're not bandits, it's our clear duty to make a list of the state's and the people's property. Give us some paper."

In the front of the cart, together with the "state's and the people's property," in a Chinese basket lay an infant with pale eyes and hair. He was clutching the end of a tan blanket in his fist. A suckling, tiny, and whimpering a little.

Afanasy Petrovich said tenderly: "He's here, too. I reckon he's got something to say about it, according to his own lights."

Once more they spared a woman and refrained from stripping her of her clothes, but they buried the man stark naked in the sand.

3

Afanasy Petrovich, returning in the captured cart, was holding the child in his arms and singing in a low voice:

Nightingale, nightingale, dear little bird,
Canary, canary, so little, so wee,
Sings sadder songs than ever were heard.

He was thinking of his native village of Lebyazhy, the herding of the cattle, his family, the younger children—and wept on a high note.

The child wept, too.

Moving, burning, the fluid sands ran, and running, they too wept on a high note.

The partisans, mounted on their sturdy, tough Mongolian horses, ran on. The partisans had seared faces and seared souls.

Along the trail the wormwood rambled, stifled by the sun. Like the sand, fine-grained, fugitive.

And the sands were wormwood, fine-grained and bitter.

You trails, trodden out by goats! You sands, bitter sands! Mongolia is a wild beast, and a joyless one.

They examined the officer's possessions. Books, a small chest of tobacco, instruments of shining steel. Among these objects, standing on three tall legs, was a small, square, segmented box.

The partisans drew near to look them over, feel them, and weigh them in their hands. They gave off a smell of sheep fat—they were eating a lot out of boredom—and their clothes were greasy. They had prominent cheekbones and soft, thin lips—those who came from the Cossack villages on the Don; black hair and cavernous faces—those who came from the chalk-mines. And they all had stunted bow legs and the guttural accents of the steppe.

Afanasy Petrovich picked up the brass-bound tripod and said: "A telescope!" He shut one eye. "And a good one. Costs about a million, this does. What they had when they looked at the moon and found the goldmines on her, lads. No need to pan it out; it was like flour, the cleanest gold ever. Just put it in your bag."

A young man from the city burst out laughing. "Listen to the leg-puller. Go on, pull the other one."

Afanasy Petrovich flared up. "A leg-puller, am I? You bastard! Just you wait."

"Who's waiting?"

Afanasy Petrovich drew his revolver.

"Shsh," said Selivanov.

They shared out the tobacco amongst them, but the instruments were handed over to Afanasy Petrovich: as paymaster, he could use them on occasion to trade with the Khirghiz. He set them out at the baby's feet. "Go on, enjoy yourself."

But he didn't see them, he was crying. Afanasy tried this and that way (sweating with the effort)—the child went on crying, he was not enjoying himself at all.

The cooks brought up the evening meal. There was an oppressive smell of oil, buckwheat, porridge, cabbage soup. They pulled their out-sized spoons out of their boot tops. The grass had been trampled down in the camp. From up on the crags the lookout called:

"What about me? Look sharp! I've got to eat too. Send up the relief."

Their meal finished, it occurred to them that the child must be fed. The child had gone on howling, nonstop.

Afanasy Petrovich chewed a piece of bread. He pushed the warm cud into the wet, open little mouth and chomped his teeth. "Yum, yum. Get it down, little cub. Lovely chow."

But the baby closed his little mouth and turned his head away: he wouldn't have any. He cried through his nose, a thin, strident crying.

The peasants came up and stood around him. Craning over

the other's heads, they gazed at the child. Nobody spoke. It was hot. Their cheeks and lips glistened with mutton fat. Their shirts were unbuttoned, their bare feet yellow, like the Mongolian soil. One suggested: "Try him with cabbage soup."

They let the soup cool a bit. Afanasy Petrovich dipped his finger into it, then put it in the baby's mouth. The good thick soup ran out of the small mouth onto the little pink shirt and the flannel blanket. No. He wouldn't take it. He went on howling.

"A puppy's cleverer—it'll lick it off your fingers."

"That's a dog; this is a human being."

"You don't say!"

There was no cow's milk anywhere in the detachment. They thought of giving him mare's milk—mares they did have. But, they decided, better not: koumiss would have made him tipsy, maybe sick.

They went off among their four-wheeled carts, swapping ideas, far from untroubled. Afanasy Petrovich skipped about in his Tartar tattered quilted jacket, flung over his shoulders. His narrow eyes looked tattered as well. His high, thin voice piped anxiously, like a child's, as if the baby himself were running about, complaining. "What's to be done? He won't eat, boys! And that won't do, will it? Suppose you good-for-nothings give him a bit of attention?"

They stood there, for all their broad shoulders and sturdy build, with a helpless look on their faces.

"That's a woman's work."

"That's sure."

"He'd eat up a ram, if a woman fed him."

"That's the truth."

Selivanov called a meeting, and declared: "We can't let a little Christian fellow die off like a beast. Even if his father was a bourgeois, the child, well, he's innocent, and who can say he isn't?"

The peasants all agreed. "It's not the child's doing. He's innocent."

Drevesinin burst out laughing:

"Keep on growing, little lad. He'll grow up with us. And then he'll fly to the moon, and the lands with all the gold."

The peasants, though, did not laugh. Afanasy Petrovich shook his fist and shouted: "You rotten dirty swine, the only cruel mocker in the detachment, that's you!"

He stamped his foot and waved his arms, and all of a sudden cried out, "A cow! That's what he needs, a cow!"

With one voice they responded: "No cow, and he's a goner."

"A cow he must have."

"He'll die if he don't have a cow."

Afanasy Petrovich said with resolution: "I'll go and get a cow, boys."

Drevesinin cut in, mischievously: "You mean, in Lebyazhy, on the Irtysh River?"

"I won't have to go to the Irtysh, you patented emetic. I'm going to the Khirghiz."

"What, and trade them the telescope for one? Go ahead, benefactor!"

Afanasy Petrovich was furious. In exasperation he yelled:

"You good-for-nothing bastard, how'd you a like a punch in the face?"

Seeing that they were starting a fight, contrary to good discipline, Selivanov as chairman of the meeting nipped it in the bud. "That's enough."

This is what they voted: Drevesinin, Afanasy Petrovich, and three more were to go to the Khirghiz settlement out on the steppe and bring back a cow, and if luck was with them, two or even five, for the cooks were coming to the end of their store of meat. They hung their rifles on their saddles and put on fox-fur caps, so as to look like the Khirghiz from a distance. "God go with you."

They wrapped the child in his blanket and laid him in the shade of a cart. One of the younger men sat down beside him and, to keep both the child and himself amused, fired his revolver every now and again at the wormwood bushes.

4

Alas, you sands of Mongolia, there's no joy to be had from you! Alas, you massed blue rocks, with your deep-digging, evil hands!

The Russians are riding over the sands. Night.

The sands smell of heat and of wormwood.

In the Khirghiz settlement the dogs are barking at wolves and at the darkness.

The Khirghiz are fleeing from death.

But can the cattle be led from death?

From the settlement comes a smell of dried manure, of *airan*, the Khirghiz name for soured milk. Sitting beside the yellow campfires are the young Khirghiz children, thin and famished-looking, and beside the children, the dogs, their ribs protruding, their muzzles sharpened. The nomads' tents, their *yurtas*, look like haystacks. Beyond the *yurtas* lies a lake, and reeds, and suddenly a shot rings out from the green reeds, winging its way toward the yellow fires: Oo-a-at!

On the instant the Khirghiz rushed out of their felt tents and cried in alarm: "Ui-boi! Ui-boi! Ak-kyzyl-urus. Ui-boi!"

They hurled themselves onto their horses, which always stood ready, saddled and bridled, day and night. The *yurtas* set up a trampling noise. The steppe followed suit. The reeds called out with a wild duck's voice: "Ai, ai, the Red-White Russians, ai-ai!"

A white-bearded Khirghiz fell off his horse headfirst into a cauldron and overturned it. Scalded, he roared in a deep bass. Beside him, a shaggy dog with its tail between its legs was timidly dipping its hungry muzzle into the warm milk.

The mares whinnied shrilly. Panicked, as if attacked by wolves, the sheep struggled in the pens. The cows breathed hard, in agitation.

Sighting the Russians, the submissive Khirghiz women lay down submissively on the felt rugs. Drevesinin broke into loud laughter. "Hey, what do you think we are, stallions? We don't always have time!"

He hastily filled a flat Austrian canteen with milk and by cracking his whip managed to drive a number of cows with their calves into a *yurta*. Freed from their tethers, the calves quickly nuzzled against their mothers' soft udders, joyfully seizing the teats with their long mobile lips.

"Just look at that! The great hungry lazy bones!" And Drevesinin emptied his revolver at the calves.

Afanasy Petrovich had gone round the settlement and was just about to leave with Drevesinin, but suddenly he remembered something. "What he wants is a teat. Goddamn it, we forgot the teat!"

He dashed into the *yurtas*, looking for a teat. The fires in the tents had gone out, so Afanasy Petrovich seized a brand, scattering the sparks, coughing from the smoke, in his search for a teat. In one hand he held the crackling brand, in the other his revolver. No teat to be found. On the felt rugs the submissive Khirghiz women lay stretched out with their heavy skirts thrown over their heads. Their babies were howling. Afanasy Petrovich lost his temper and shouted to a young woman in one *yurta*: "A teat, you platter-faced bitch, give us a teat here."

The Khirghiz woman burst into tears and began hastily unbuttoning her silk kaftan and pulling off her overblouse. "Ni kerek, al, al, take!" Beside her on the felt rug, a baby wrapped in rags lay howling. The Khirghiz woman was already spreading her legs. "Al, al! Go on!"

But Afanasy Petrovich grasped one of her breasts, squeezed it, and whistled with gratification. "There we are! That's what you'd call a teat! And a pretty full one at that!"

"Ni kerek, ni—What?"

"All right, stop squawking. Up with you! It's a good one!" And seizing the Khirghiz woman by the hand, he dragged her along after him. In the darkness he hoisted her onto the saddle, squeezing now and again at her breasts, and dashed off in the direction of the ravine Selivanov occupied, back to his detachment.

"I've found a good pair, I have," he told himself joyfully, and there were tears in his eyes. "I'll always be the one to find anything, brother; I'd dig it out of the earth if I had to."

5

But back in the camp, as it turned out—something Afanasy Petrovich had failed to notice—the Khirghiz woman had brought her own baby with her. "Let her be," said the peasants, "the milk'll be enough for both of 'em. We've got the cows, and she's a healthy woman."

She was one of those Khirghiz women of few words, austere, and she fed the babies when no one was looking. The two lay beside her in the tent, on a piece of felt, one a white little creature, the other yellow, and howled in unison.

A week later, at a general meeting, Afanasy Petrovich voiced a complaint: "Well, there's been some funny business here, comrades. That Khirghiz female, that bitch, I should say, cheats at feeding time: she lets her own child drain her dry and only gives ours the dregs. I've been watching her, brother. Just go and see for yourself."

The peasants went and looked. The babies were like all babies, one little creature white, the other yellow as a melon. But the Russian infant, it did seem, was thinner than the Khirghiz baby. Afanasy Petrovich raised his hands: "I've given him a name, Vaska. But there's been some funny business here, I'm sure of it."

Drevesinin said, but with no trace of his spiteful smile, "Well, Vaska, you do look like a poor little cuss, not long for this world."

They found a big stick and balanced it on the shaft of a cart, so that neither side weighed more than the other. They hung the babies at either end, to see which was the heavier. Suspended with ropes wrapped in their little rags, the children were howling. They gave off the penetrating odor of unwashed babies. The Khirghiz woman stood by the cart, and, understanding nothing, had fallen to weeping.

Silently the peasants surveyed the scene.

"Let go," ordered Selivanov. "Let go of the scales." Afanasy Petrovich took his hands from the stick and instantly the Russian baby shot upward.

"Will you look at the yellow-faced bastard," exclaimed Afanasy Petrovich, incensed, "he's certainly putting on weight."

He picked up a sheep's skull that happened to be lying on the ground and placed it on the Russian child. The two babies now balanced each other. The peasants began to protest, shouted, "She's fed him till he weighs a sheep-skull more, lads, ain't that so?"

"If she's not watched—"

"What an animal, look how she's fattened him."

"Who was to watch her?"

"We've got other work besides watching babies."

And some of them, the most respectable, confirmed this view:

"Get away with you! Who's going to turn nursemaid?"

"But then, she *is* his mother."

Afanasy Petrovich stamped and shouted, "So, by your lights, a Russian man must die because of some un-Christian bitch? Vaska must die, then? *My* Vaska?"

They stared at Vaska lying there pale and very thin. The sight sickened them.

Selivanov said to Afanasy Petrovich: "Here, you get rid of the other one—God be with him—leave him to die, the little Khirghiz; we'll not make up for the few we've killed with the one we'll save."

Glancing at Vaska, the peasants dispersed in silence. Afanasy Petrovich took the little Khirghiz and tied him up in a torn sack. The mother set up a wail. Afanasy Petrovich hit her, but lightly, in the teeth and left the camp for the open steppe.

6

Two days later the peasants were standing on tiptoe around a tent and peering over one another's shoulders, gazed inside where the Khirghiz woman, seated on a felt rug, was feeding the white child. The woman looked subdued, her eyes narrow as oat grains; she was wearing a kaftan of violet silk and soft leather boots. The child's face was turned to the breast. He was clutching the kaftan and his legs moved in a comical, clumsy way, as if trying to jump. Laughing hugely, the peasants looked on. More complacent than any, Afanasy Petrovich. He sniffed, and said, in his tearful voice: "See how he gobbles it down."

Outside and beyond the tent, were running—none knows where—the hollows, the rocks, the steppe of alien Mongolia.

No one knows where Mongolia is running, a wild beast, and a joyless one.

1922

Chocolate

Alexander
Tarasov-Rodyonov

1

Opening her eyes, she was again aware of the dark-bright enigma, like a dissolving gray net. A nervous shudder ran over her chilled limbs and settled as a rheumatic twinge in her feet. But then it suddenly pierced her heart, and everything became terrifyingly clear—the hard narrow bench, her fur coat slipping to the ground, the muff in place of a pillow, and the musty stillness disturbed by the same sound of nervous snoring. Somewhere behind the wall water was dripping slowly into a brass pan.

She was in such utter anguish that she felt she must weep again. During the long night, however, her eyes had been worn out by tears, and her throat was tightly constricted. Carefully, Elena moved her numb leg, pulled up her coat, and fell to listening with both ears.

"Just don't think—just don't think"—the words drilled into her brain.

But another small voice like a splinter of ice shot into the bright brown ringlets, disheveled and unruly, about her face. "How not to think? How not to think? What if they come today to take you out and shoot you?"

Again a cold, clammy shudder ran through Elena.

From the corridor behind the wall came the sound of footsteps. Like a cornered mouse trying to escape the cat, Elena pricked up her ears. Someone was walking with an even, unhurried tread, and each dull footfall tallied with the water dripping into the brass pan. The footsteps came close to the door, went past. The crisis of terror was over, but Elena's heart still beat shudderingly. The gray square of the window grew paler and paler; the men in the corner went on snoring.

"What beasts! How can they sleep so easily, so willingly?" thought Elena. "This very night they took five people away, and none have come back. Oh, God, what state are they in now?"

In her mind she saw an image of a muddy courtyard, its flagstones smeared with clotting blood, littered with shot bodies. Elena had never seen such horrors, not even in films, but someone had once described these things in vivid terms, and the memory had remained.

"That Latvian said that today they would decide the fate of us all." She shuddered. "Five already gone, now only four are left. Or even fewer?"

She got up and began feeling her way gingerly along the wall to count how many were left. By the window, wrapped in fur, the sturdy Gitanov lay like a huge black knot. Two steps further on, in the corner, a gray army cape covered the sleeping Kovalensky; his long legs were flung out straight. A little farther.

near the table, she made out the form of the stranger with the gray eyes that stared without any expression into the future.

"What an odd name he had," thought Elena, "Finikov—date palm! I've never heard such a name in my life. Like something sickly sweet, sticky, exotic. There's something altogether inscrutable about the man, something unapproachable. I wonder: could he have been the cause of this arrest?"

"Finikov!" he had growled when they were being charged, in such curt muffled tone that the Latvian taking down names demanded doubtfully: "Who? Who?"

"Fi-ni-kov!" repeated the stranger, stressing each syllable, so that the Latvian stopped short and threw an inquiring glance at Kovalensky.

"Or could it have been Kovalensky himself?" Elena asked herself. "How can anyone know? Nobody can get inside another's soul. An officer of the guards, an aristocrat, a gambler, a balletomane—could he suddenly have been so fired with civic duty that. . . ? O, poor man, oh, unfortunate man . . .Oh, how awful!" The shuddering went through her—"Whom was he struggling against who could make him the superfluous victim of a shooting?"

And what of Gitanov, that plump, splendid feather-bed of a man, always freshly shaven and smoothly combed, that stage-manager of souls, the darling of all the young girls? But how could any sympathy or genuine understanding really exist in this bloody human mousetrap of a place? All, all would be shot, and she, Elena Valtz, with them. "And for what reason, for what reason?" she reflected, pulling at her fingers, and, without realizing it, she wrung her hands. It grew colder. Limpidly, as if drowning, the moist, yellow morning of the North sank heavily and slowly into the well of the gloomy courtyard visible from the window. Terror again surged over her. Quickly, silently, Elena stole back to her bench and lay down, wrapping herself from head to foot in the soft folds of her coat.

"Just don't think! Just don't think!" Gritting her teeth, she fought down her thoughts. Even with eyes wide open she could see nothing from within the coat. She was pleasantly warmed by her own breath and the coat's softness caressing her nose and cheeks. There was a hint of perfume like new grass on a fragrant May morning.

Perhaps it came from the handkerchief wet with tears, tucked into the muff under her head. But she didn't even feel like reaching for it. Then, exhaustion had weighted her hands. How had this feeling of calm, lightness, and ease come about so suddenly? She remembered her soft bed—not the bed, but the path beneath the lime trees, the radiant sun in the green park, and the faint tickling of a grassy blade on her ear. Overhead in the infinite blue puffballs of clouds are scudding. No, not clouds, the spinning wheels of the landau, skimming the rough pavement of the driveway. Elena's legs have been wrapped in a rug by the attentive man beside her. He is charming. His hand wears a supple, brown leather glove. She wanted to lift her fringed lashes and send a gay, tender, caressing glance into his dear face. Her Edward, her Edward from the British embassy. Why hasn't he thought to bring her a bar of the Cailler chocolate she likes so much? She looked up. Dear God, how awful! Not Edward. A stranger, clean-shaven, with a huge face—fright shook Elena's curls. Yes, it was he, the Latvian! The Latvian who had arrested them. He made his way through them with a horrible, menacing laugh and brutally jerked the rug from her knees.

"Elena Valentinovna! Elena Valentinovna! My dear, don't be upset. It's for you."

Gitanov's spongy voice. He was standing like a lump of suet before her as she lay quivering in her fur coat. Gitanov had even had time to comb his hair, but he was wearing neither a collar nor a tie: both had been tossed onto the windowsill. Keeping his distance, his eyes blinking, Kovalensky was devouring her with his gaze, and close by was Finikov's calm, expressionless stare, indifferent. He would not entangle himself in words, or even gestures. It was all like an interval, a passing sideshow.

The brown-haired man was the matter. "Probably a Jew," went through her consciousness. He was hovering over her bench, and behind him, like a shadow, was a guard with a bayonet, a Red Army man. Springing up, Elena shook herself and gathered the coat around her shoulders.

"Bring them all with you!" said the brown-haired man and waved his hand at her bench.

"What does that mean, bring them all? So I'm not coming back again?!" Elena's heart froze. Hands trembling, she tied her silk scarf round her head, picked up her muff, slipped on her overshoes, and, without taking leave of anyone—ah, what was to come was to come—hastened with nervous, skittering steps out into the corridor in the wake of the brown-haired man. "What is to come, let it come, but come quickly!" Suddenly it was hot, so hot, her cheeks were on fire.

They went along the corridor and down some stairs; passing along a second, twisting corridor, they went up another flight of steps. Upstairs, passing by two rooms, they stopped outside a third.

"Wait here," said the brown-haired man to the guard and beckoned Elena forward.

A room with a dark red wallpaper—as if someone's blood, dropped in Elena's thoughts. A large window hung with cherry-colored drapes opened onto the street. There was a shelf by the window with papers on it and more papers on a table against the wall, near the door. Another immense table stood in the middle of the room. At this table sat a well-dressed, fair-haired man.

"This is Elena Valtz," said her escort. She was met with a look, weary, apathetic, expressionless.

"Sit down. Over here!" He pulled up a seat, and the light from the window fell on her face. The fair-haired man went on quietly, methodically, with his writing. Elena sat down beside the brown-haired man. Both were fast bound in silence, except that the hammering in Elena's temples did not cease.

"At last the fair man finished his writing, blotted it, and put it away. He took a fresh sheet of white paper, ruled it, and asked with a sad, low voice: "Your name, occupation, and address?"

"Elena Valentinovna Valtz. Ballerina. 38 Kapitanskaya Street, Apartment 4."

"What made you go to Gitanov's house, yesterday?"

"He's an old acquaintance of mine. There was a party at his house, a few of his old friends from the theater world. Nowadays, when people are hungry. . . . Truly. . . . " The tears came uninvited to Elena's eyes. The fair man's shape was hazy as he pushed the water carafe over toward her.

Yes. She would be calmer soon.

She would be in no danger if she spoke only the truth. Yes, she knew that.

"But what truth do you want of me? I know nothing. Truly—nothing at all."

The fair man took up an envelope and showed her the letter inside it.

No, she had never seen it before, was seeing it now for the first time.

How did that letter come to be under the carpet by the chair she had been sitting on at Gitanov's party?

But how was she to know?! It was as if he were binding her delicate little figure with an iron chain and fetters.

"I'm lost!" bored into her brain.

"Lost!" whispered the pallid lips.

Her muff fell to the floor; the sharp and sticky gaze of the two men—one quiet and fair, and the other brown-haired, restless—soaked deeper and deeper, right into her heart. Her hands, fluttering, sought the table edge, her throat contracted painfully, and everything began to reel and swim.

Again, the weary, drawling voice: "Calm yourself."

Her head was resting comfortably against the back of the armchair. Before her eyes an angle of the tiled stove—where was she? Ah, now she knew: still the same room and the same people tormenting her, only now the look in the fair man's eyes was rather softer.

"Tell us," he asked unexpectedly, hissing the words, "who was next to you, before the Cheka agent came into the room?"

"Oh, yes," she remembered. She would tell them directly. . . . Should she tell them? Betray?—a low-minded thing to do, criminal, abject.

"Consider," said the fair man, breaking the silence. "We know who it was. The testimony of the five we've already interrogated has revealed the facts. Your answer will only show us the degree of your own involvement in this affair. In any case, the facts themselves are as certain as my name is Deputy Investigator Horst."

So he was the terrible Horst! Elena again grasped for the tumbler of water, and the nervous chattering of her teeth was like a tattoo on the glass. No, she would conceal nothing from them, nothing. Next to her had been sitting—Kovalensky, the army officer, but he had not been holding anything in his hand, "nothing, believe me." She swore this by all she held sacred and dear in this world.

"And would you take an oath on your own life?" cut in the fair man. "Now, who sat next to him?"

"To him!"

"Yes, to him!"

"To him . . . no one . . . only a little way over—maybe one or two paces—over toward the window—what was his name?—was sitting . . . Finikov."

"And you'd never met him before?" The fair-haired man was smiling now.

"Oh, I swear to God I never in my life set eyes on him until last evening!"

"Very good. What else can you tell us?"

"Nothing."

"Nothing?"

"Nothing."

Soundlessly, the pen glided over the paper, swiftly, swiftly, it went minuetting over the lines.

"Now be careful and listen!"

She tried to listen, but scarcely heard him, thinking only: what now?

"Sign your name here!"

With trembling hands she took the pen, but the quill refused to write. Instead of Valtz, appeared the misnomer, "Valuy."

"Stay where you are."

The fair man picked up another paper and vanished through a side door.

With a flash of his diamond ring—how could she have failed to notice it before?—the brown-haired man had brought from his pocket a cigaret case with a solid gold monogram.

"You smoke?"

"No," lied Elena.

If only she could spring on him like a cat and bury her sharp claws in his face. . . . Heavens, how long since she had last had a manicure. . . . Then it occurred to her that today she had not even washed. "I certainly must look fine!"

A small blue cloud rose slowly above her. The brown-haired man fastened his lips on the cigaret and ran his eyes over Elena's neck. "If you please," the fair man abruptly summoned her, snapping open the door.

Again the spine-chilling smile. Gooseflesh came up on her arms. With a look of terror, Elena walked submissively behind the fair-haired man's dark back toward the tobacco-brown, silk drapery. Before her lay a deep-blue room decorated in Gothic style. At the window loomed a tall dark shadow that now stirred and took a place at the table.

"Very well, Comrade Horst, leave me alone with her and tell Comrade Lipshaevich to let no one in here. No one—tell the courier as well."

The hateful question, "What does he want?" flashed through Elena's brain.

But the voice was deep, sympathetic.

Horst went out.

"I am the head of the Cheka for this region, Citizeness Valtz, my name is Zudin," said the stranger. At once Elena's fear vanished, as if an old acquaintance at a chance encounter had told her an interesting anecdote. The dark blue of the walls was a background to the gold silk of the window hangings. The casements soared as though unbarred by windowpanes. It was as if the deep-lying husk of the street with its motor fumes had burst freely into the room. And here at the table, within earshot of the busy tramway, sat an unknown acquaintance.

Oh, what had he been saying at such length? Now Elena could make out his face: haggard, pale, the eyes enlarged, a colorless moustache, and a sparse wedge of a beard. Beneath his ill-shaven chin was the collar of a dark shirt, and over this a dark jacket.

"From worker to official," thought Elena. So this was what he looked like, this Zudin. Why had he sounded so awful before, in the stories her friends had told her? And why had she been brought to see him? Was it so serious? Oh yes, that disastrous, ill-fated letter! Perhaps he had even forged it himself! To have them all shot at will? But what was this Zudin talking of now?

"You must tell everything and hide nothing from me."

"What is it I must tell you?"

"What I tell you to tell me: which of these men have you been on intimate terms with, and when?"

Like a whiplash in the face. The color flared in Elena's cheeks.

Absolutely not! Never! What could he have in his mind? Just because she was a ballerina . . .

And a mighty current, a rushing storm of tears, enveloped her thoughts and emotions. The mountain that had been weighing on Elena's heart melted swiftly away in that flood of weeping.

Where was the carafe? Nobody offered her any water. Zudin sat on, unmoving. "You misunderstand me, Citizeness Valtz. It was by no means my intention to offend you by my questions or to cast aspersions on your character. I only wish to clarify your role, the role you have played in this affair."

Ah, how fast his voice grew in awfulness!

"Not your role at the theater, but the role you have played as a woman among these men. Politics is a nasty business, Citizeness Ballerina. The letter found under the carpet where you were sitting contains a mention of murder—the political murder of some of our most prominent comrades. And among the papers belonging to the persons arrested with you were found letters, written by you. I hope you now understand why I expect from you a full and truthful answer, without any false modesty whatever."

Elena said nothing.

"Ah, how terrible it is, how exquisitely terrible!" she thought. "And how do they contrive to ferret out every last thing? Letters I wrote—in whose possession did you find them?"

But Zudin no longer had his eyes fixed on her; he had gone over to the window. Perhaps it was better not to see the eyes when these things were spoken of Why wasn't a woman examining her? On second thought, no, better not a woman. A woman could not understand about *that*.

"How terrible!" Elena thought aloud.

"Passion is a natural thing—we're none of us saints, and to err is human. There's no shame in it!" Zudin tried to encourage her with sympathetic words. "Don't worry. Your secret will be buried here in this room forever, not even put down on paper. I gave the express order that all doors were to be closed."

But what answer was she to give? With which of them had

she been on intimate terms? Well, yes, there was Kovalensky, the officer, but that was a long, long time ago, at the beginning of the war. He used to call for her at the theater, come to her lodgings—and then—then they had not met again for a long time. He was at the front. But wait . . . wait . . . yes, once he had sought her out. She had never been to his rooms.

"With whom else?"

"Daryalovsky, the comic actor, who once stood trial with you. Theater life throws people together, but we don't take it seriously. The same for that man, Gitanov. He had been pestering me for a long time, and it was hard to turn him away. He was very likable, good-hearted, and he made me laugh . . . and he had helped me a great deal—"

"Who else? No one of the arrest . . . I don't think. . . ."

"And what about Finikov?"

"Finikov! No! I've already told you: it was the first time I'd seen him. We were introduced by Gitanov. He was extremely polite, but not talkative. I hardly exchanged a word with him."

Had she taken money from these men?

Again she reddened, and her eyes filled with tears.

"What? Even that you want to know?! Is there nothing, nothing sacred for you, even a woman's secrets?"

Had she taken money?

"Ye-e-es . . . I did . . . quite a lot . . . from them all. Oh, if you only knew, Comrade Zudin!"

Ah, dear God, what had she said? Come to your senses, Elena —you called him comrade?

"No, no, no!" screamed Elena in utter despair.

"If you only knew, Comrade Zudin"—from Elena's mouth and eyes it all flowed out onto her breast—"if you only knew what a ballerina's whole existence can be, when she has been forced from fifteen years of age, yes, forced—the ballet tradition is unshakable—forced to sell herself to filthy, sweating men—dear Zudin, Comrade Zudin! No, it wasn't you who flung filth at me, but this vile life, this vile life, that dirtied us—there's no hope of salvation for such lost, loathsome creatures as we are! . . . If I ever get—I get the chance to earn a loaf of bread, honest bread, I would. Oh, why tell you the rest? You can never know the whole truth of it! What Gitanov invited me for was to set me up with this—what's his name?—Finikov. He said he would pay me—a lot of money! And I was so hungry, yes, hungry. Oh, hunger! I sold my entire wardrobe. Only my coat and muff and a few other clothes were left. Dear, good C-C-Comrade Zudin! Before all this began, I was a girl in high school—fifth class! Just a living, not slavery, but a living, an honest living—not much to ask—I beg of you—I'm ready, I want to work! Must I sell myself again?! A wretched little prostitute—that's how I've been branded!"

Moans followed close upon one another, Elena, beside herself with grief, groveled on the floor. Her scarf fell off, her coat also. Her curls stuck to her temples. Only the chestnut gleam of her hair and the rosiness of her soft little ear told the aloof gray sky outside the clear window of that blue, Gothic room that here was a woman grieving, deeply unhappy.

Suddenly, Elena's pitiful little hand was taken into a strong, male grasp. "Now, enough, Comrade Valtz, get up, set yourself to rights, and calm down!"

Zudin was speaking. How eagerly she would have gone on listening to his dear voice.

"We Communists are fighting this bloody struggle precisely for the good of all those crushed by the capitalist yoke, and so for the good of people like you. Get up and compose yourself now! And if you want work, here's what you can do: come back here again, say, the day after tomorrow, around one o'clock and ask for me. I'll be a friend to you and help you. So come along, stand up and put on your wraps, and off with you. You're free."

Zudin pressed a button, and behind the door a high, shrill ring was heard.

2

The air was filled with sunlight. It merrily whirled the dust around in a gay waltz. It pressed against one's cheeks and its warm, affectionate paws stroked the eyelids. In silent spring ecstasy the sun scattered its brightness as if entranced.

"What was that name? Valtz? What case was this? *I* told her to come? I don't remember it. All right, I'll see her."

He is terribly sleepy—hands dropping, eyes closing, thoughts flagging. Time to go home and sleep. And in the evening—to work again.

"Call Comrade Katzmann. Valtz? Let her wait!"

"Comrade Plastov, Comrade Plastov! Just a second! Have you heard from Dynin about that naval officer, what's his name? The one who went to Finland? You haven't? Very strange. Have the inquiry rated 'urgent.' They still have it on the schedule? Excellent. Those French airmen should be committed for a hearing here as quickly as possible. Too late? A great pity! Anyway, you undertake the inquiry yourself, so that navy man doesn't give us the slip."

"Ah, there you are, Abram!"

"I've no more need of you, Comrade Plastov, and be sure to come to me early tomorrow morning with a full report on that naval officer."

"Well, now, Abram! Close the door carefully. Now, where've we got to in this affair? Did you find the Englishman? Those British bulldogs are sly bastards! Now, they're not going to lie low for too long—they're certainly going to make an appearance somewhere. What information was Planchette able to give us? What's his name? Heckey? Mr Heckey? Very well. We're putting the heat on him now, not Lockhart—if only we can bring him in! Well, now, next, Abram, my friend, Pavlov has been explaining his actions to me in that gambling-house affair. He says there's been something about discharging some con man with a name like Bocharkin. It's not at all clear to me. You look into the case yourself; mind you're unobtrusive. That's all! I'll probably be back around six. When Horst has had his rest, he's to brief me on the Kvashinin case. I'll probably sound out the young one myself. Oh, yes! Has Dagnis made his report to you? What's he done with Finikov? Liquidated? When? This morning? Excellent. Get a telegram out to Moscow in my name. Mark it 'urgent.' Nothing else for the present. So please look into this Bocharkin business. Understood? So long for now, see you this evening. . . ."

"Hallo, Miss, get me 22–48."

"One moment, comrade! I'll soon have finished with the phone, then you bring her in."

"Is that 22–48? Thanks. Is that you, Comrade Ignatyev? This is Zudin. And good day to you! Thank you, very well. I wanted to let you know that things have turned out exactly as we thought. Yes, to be sure, in that affair—Savinkov's, I mean! We picked up the entire ring, all through a woman. It was quite an affair! Executed this morning. Yes? Yes? Good! So good-bye for now. I'll be here this evening. During the day I'll be at home. Must get some rest. Good-bye!"

He fell back wearily in his chair. His eyes closed of their own accord. And, on top of it all, this sunshine! Like spring! With the dazzling caprice of a jester, it beat and cried insistently at the window, casting its glittering powder into the darkest corner. By its golden haze all was made invisible. And through eyelids cleaving together bloomed the color-bright rainbows.

"Is the motor there? I'm coming. Oh, yes, Valtz, let her in!"

Like a picture: dazzling in a purple and beige mantle. Too bright and gay a color. And even more so in the sunlight! In a halo made by the shafts of gilded dust. The hair like fire.

"Please sit down! What a lovely day, isn't it? You'll pardon me, I'm very tired. You want to work? That's splendid, splendid."

How annoying not to have a shade to pull down over that window. We must get one this spring, because it's blinding one with red spots in the eyes.

"Good, then, we'll find you some work. Do you know what it means to keep a file? Well, that's splendid!"

Oh, the hell with these bells and their jingling—like a shower bath.

"Listen here, Comrade Lipshaevich, we're going to take on Comrade Valtz as a clerk. We'll try her out by putting her in charge of the file on closed cases—numbering and entering names. Snegireva can take on the current cases for Shalenko. So that's settled. Where shall she sit? She can sit here, in the corner office with the gray paint. She can keep the records on the side. We-e-ll, that's that! Now I'll let you go. And you, comrade, will show her the work. So, to keep the records in order. We-e-ll, good-bye for now. I wish you well!"

Scattering the golden sheaf of sunny beams, he raced out like a whirlwind. Below, the motor roared once, then faded into the distance.

And what about this room? It hardly corresponded to the underground stronghold of some Grand Inquisitor. And this sunshine! This sunshine! Strewing its drops of amber . . . .

"Good. Let's go. Will you kindly show me the way? Your name's Lipshaevich, isn't it? Comrade Lipshaevich? Mine's Elena Valentinovna Valtz. Oh, I'm forgetting you know that already!"

The motor swung down into the petted and uneven streets to dump its load. Zudin's hat had fallen off, and his briefcase had come open. On either side of him the glass of the windows flew like gleaming hedges. The roofs were dripping, the streets muddy. And the shadows were quite purple—in a painting not to be believed. Even people's faces were purple. There was actually a haze of violet. And so warm! So warm! Only the ice on the river was gray.

The car stopped before a gray house all in shadow, blue and crimson shadow.

"Come back for me at six!" He shut the door. Ran up the staircase lit by windows opening onto a courtyard. Pealed loudly on the bell.

"I'm home, Lisa! Do you know, I think I'll just go and lie down for a bit. No, can't wait a minute. My head's splitting. I've only fifteen minutes for supper. Wake me when you're ready. What've you got today? Pea soup? Oh, good! Rubbish, it doesn't need any butter. Lisa, please, let be, we'll talk about it later. Let me get some sleep now . . . .

"Well, it's certainly been spring today. There's no shade at all in this bedroom. Well, never mind: the sleep will refresh me. If I can only get my boots off . . . .

"No, I'm careful: I won't dirty the covers. Mitya darling, you and Masha go into the other room. I must have a little rest. Lisanka, take Masha away, will you? Only for a little while. When I'm asleep, they can make all the row they want and shoot off their cannons. All right, come and give me a kiss, only not too much noise. Your shoes all worn out? I'll get you new ones—at Easter."

"Ts-s-s!"

"He's asleep."

"Mitenka, leave that shade down. Take your book into the dining room, let Papa sleep. He's been working very hard. Take Masha with you: show her the pictures. And I'll be laying the table. Dinner will soon be ready."

Slowly, audibly, the clock, keeper of time, ticked on.

It was three o'clock.

"Lyosha, get up!"

"But . . . ? Who . . . ? Get going!"

"Lyosha? Get up now, we're ready to eat! Masha, pull on Papa's leg. Mitya, don't jump!"

"It 's not at all pleasant getting up! Br-r-r . . . . Chilly!"

"It *is* rather cold. Or is it after your nap that you feel it? Now, let's go, shall we?"

"Here, Masha, you little mischief, leave my spoon alone!"

"Well! It seems it's a holiday in this house: meat in the soup!"

"Well, you see, I was afraid the horsemeat was going bad in the window. It's so warm today, the snow's melting and running off the roofs."

"So you cooked it all! But I'm afraid we can't ask for more rations, Lisok. Well, it doesn't matter, let's eat. Is there any mustard?"

"Go on, you bourgeois!"

"So now I'm a bourgeois?"

"Did you ever get mustard with it in the factory canteen?"

"At that time it was bitter enough without it!"

"So now are you all right?"

"Well, better than before."

"Mustard or not, it did taste better in the old days. There was butter in everything. And now . . . ."

"Now we're getting out of hand. I believe you're a Communist, aren't you?"

"What do you mean, Communist? An idea is an idea. I'm saying nothing, mind you. Only, Lyosha dear, don't be a bear. It's no good without butter. Butter is good for Mitya and Masha, too. Only look how pale they are, skin and bone! Isn't it nourishing for them? And what about us? We need it, too. We used to eat much better in the old days. Now my heart's ready to burst. They're our own children! But I mustn't talk of heartache to you."

"You'd have the rivers flowing milk right away?"

"There you are! It's difficult to talk to you!"

"Mitya, don't play with your fork!"

"Whether they flow milk or not, you could phone Ignatyev. Or even just his secretary. A big deal! Everybody gets something more than the ration. Just consider your own situation. You were better off even in exile, weren't you? Working like a beast of burden, night and day, and what food do you get? Not enough to feed a bird, and peas, peas, peas. And this is what's called proletarian rule! And you can't even mention milk pudding, or they call you a milksop!"

"Whew! What a play on words! Wipe Masha's nose, she's got it all smeared with your proletarian rule. But compared to reality, all your emotion is just so much rubbish! We're not the only ones to live like this. Hundreds of thousands of people don't even have this much. What would they say to your cooking with butter? People in the factories complain anyway: 'The commissars take everything.' There isn't a stick of wood in the city, yet look at us!"

"There's no talking to you. We haven't had a piece of soap in the house for two months, we keep on piling up washing. And when you're able to get a pound or so, you hear me . . ."

"You hear me, you hear me. We had a young woman in the office today, a ballet dancer. Just for a piece of bread she had to sell herself to the first man to come along. Now she's got herself mixed up in a spy case. And all for nothing, for a mere piece of bread. She showed me what my own attitude should be: philanthropical. Why are you looking at me like that? I mean it!"

"Just see that she doesn't make any trouble for you over there."

"She certainly won't make any trouble! Mitya, you scamp, get me a cigaret out of my jacket pocket. No, leave it, I'll get it myself."

The sunbeams, curving, crept off the bed and up the wall, twisted about the window frame and the painted brass window fastener.

"Who took the receiver off the hook? Ah, you little ones are a torment. Someone may have wanted to call us here, and we couldn't have heard."

"Don't be upset, Lyosha, it's my fault, I took it off. People must let a man rest. Shall I start the samovar?"

"Go ahead. Only, you know, I'd like another little nap: there's a lot of work for tonight. And wake me when the motor comes. Oh, Masha, Masha, you again! Get away! Her felt boots are certainly worn through, and she's not wearing stockings."

"I've been telling you for a long time: the children have no stockings to wear."

"Yes, indeed you have, but what's to be done about it, Lisa? Just wait till we break the blockade. Eh-eh-a-ah!"

"There, have your nap. I'll come and wake you."

"Mommy, what's a blockade?"

"Don't talk! Papa's asleep."

Papa was asleep; the children crept noiselessly to the window and looked out at the disappearing red ball that crouched on the roof, at the sky tinting itself pink. The little courtyard, the muddy ground, shone red as they reflected the setting sun, its smile of farewell. A breeze blew through the window. The wind gathered strength and sent feathers of cloud high into the sky. In a small, thin voice the samovar began to sing in the kitchen.

The sky grew dark, a wavering star glittered overhead, delicately, exquisitely hanging, like a diamond drop from a slender wand. It gazed down on Mitya and Masha, who open-mouthed stood glued to the breath-clouded window.

Valtz had arranged the papers, put on her coat, and was going down the stairs. Lipshaevich was waiting for her on the landing.

"Don't we take the same direction? Where do you live? Kapitanskaya? That's right in my neighborhood. If I'm not in your way?"

Matching their steps, they went through the quiet streets in the cool of the evening. Playing with his sparkling ring and splendid in the tailored cut of his jacket, Lipshaevich began to discourse on the theater, drama, the ballet. At one corner, as Valtz lost her footing, he took her arm and did not release it till they reached her lodging, all the time breathing heavily in her ear; his small eyes seemed to grow oilier than ever. He finally took his leave of her at her house door. Valtz disappeared through the entrance, ran across the muddy yard, gazing at the stars in the greenish sky. She hastened up the familiar steps, knocked, and answered the shuffling footsteps behind the door: "It's I!"

Her cigaret glowing in the dark, "An old friend came to see you," the lodging-house keeper told her.

"And old friend?" At once the bright legend of the escaping day vanished.

"The one who used to come a lot a year ago; he left a package and a letter; he seemed very interested in hearing about you; I told him all I could."

Quickly she snatched the key from the lodging-house

keeper's hand, scarcely heeding what she said, and ran into her room. There on the table lay a large, paper-wrapped package and a letter in a pale gray envelope. Hastily she lit the candle and, hands trembling, opened the string-tied package.

Good Heavens! Chocolate! There must be twenty pounds of it here!

She tore open the envelope.

My dear Nelly,

I came here on the off chance, with something for you. Of course, I shan't soon forget how much my kitten liked to nibble chocolate and how long it must be since she has had any. But I find that my little creature has gone into the service of the tiger: is this so? Good luck to you!

Even if this is true and irrevocable, my chocolate shall remain here as a farewell gift.

If, though, it should be a fleeting whim, a bold flirtation with danger, and should my kitten still be the careless little creature she once was, you might (as you read this I am watching you unnoticed from the court) give me a sign. Take the candle over to the window and snuff it right out; then go slowly to the back door and let me in. The landlady must suspect nothing. Au revoir; I am waiting—one way or the other; with the tiger against me, or with me.

Your affectionate Edward.

P.S. I shall not wait long for my answer and shall disappear for good.—E.H.

The paper fell from Elena's hands.

What should she do? And with so little time to decide? Outside the window, Edward—well-shaven, clean-cut and elegant, pleasant, amiable, and so tenderly solicitous. On the table before her lay his chocolate. What should she do? Give the signal? And there *he* was in his big, dark blue room, the master of her new spirit—so mindful of her welfare, so formidable to everyone—Zudin. Which was it to be?

"I shall not wait long for my answer and shall disappear for good."

Oh, let anything happen that was to happen. She would not be too permissive, she was sure, but she would not deny herself the right to say just a word to Edward—otherwise it would be too impolite and ungrateful.

Dear, thoughtful Edward! On her account, he was risking his life outside this very window, while she . . .?!

The flame made its butterfly flight from the table to the window. Two seconds passed—and all went dark.

3

Snow was falling. Gone the mild sunshine. The sky had covered itself with cold cotton wool. The snow fell in jagged, fungus-like flakes over the earth. In the entrance the scrape of an iron heel was heard as it knocked off the icy wetness. The orchestra fell silent. Through the veil of snow the black crowd pressed on, hundreds of feet driving obstinately through the wet of the crumbly snow. They stumbled, but always came upright again.

The flags hung in rags, savaged by the white paws of the storm.

"But to what purpose?" the timidly confident question came murmuring, like warm mists.

The cold snowflakes of the hard answer dispelled the warmth.

"To what purpose? To conquer!"

"And later?"

"Later will not come soon."

"Is the enemy so strong then?"

"But do you know who our enemies are?"

Valtz keenly felt the contempt behind the question and whispered hesitatingly: "The White Guard, the factory owners, the property owners, Finns, Poles."

"They're all no-accounts! Our enemies are far more serious!"

"More serious? Then it's true what they say: your mission is to conquer the world?"

But, instead of a reply, there came back the riddle: "And what do you consider to be the world?"

"I haven't forgotten my geography: France, England, Germany, America, China—all the countries, in short!"

Decidedly, he was in a bad mood today.

"Even if we conquered it, we wouldn't be the whole world."

Valtz was disconcerted. She was silent, but her thoughts were clothing themselves more and more in words.

"It would be good to know for sure that we—Russia—have conquered the whole world!"

"Rubbish, we don't need to conquer in that sense."

"But what sense, then, Aleksey Ivanovich, what sense?"

Zudin reflected in silence. Did it pay to hand out clumsy propaganda? These matters should be spoken of as they had been in the past, in a gloomy, half-darkened hall, before the grimy countenances, the attentive gaze, the open mouths of earnest workmen sitting erect, such as he was himself, such as he had always been. They were kindred souls who understood the words in their inner selves. But who was this? And he threw a wondering look at the elegant, dainty girl gliding swiftly along beside him in the snowy white of the streets. Valtz's eyes drowned in their darkness behind lowered lids. Only the lips, opening buds, showed the row of gleaming jasmine blossoms that were her teeth. She was a tender creature, alluring because of her warmth, this Valtz in furs, Valtz in perfume.

"So you want to know where our archenemy is? I will tell you: in ourselves!"

For an answer he received a faintly quizzical glance, teasing and confident, from her velvety, chocolate-brown eyes.

"Yes, in ourselves!" Zudin was beginning to lose his temper. "In our inward harking back to the old times, the old order of things, old rags, old habits. There you have our enemy! If people could only see the world from a new viewpoint, the world would at once become a new and better place."

"You sound like the Holy Writ."

"Holy Writ has nothing at all to do with it. We don't expect any help from Heaven! We are our own gods!"

His words hissed like swords against whatever was fragile, sentimental, and dear. Zudin longed to slash, excruciatingly, ever more fiercely, to slash with piercing, implacable words.

"Are you angry?" she asked softly and submissively. Zudin felt her warm little hand's soft touch upon his own cold hand.

"Why are you angry, Aleksey Ivanovich? I'm so foolish and ignorant, that's why I asked you."

Zudin felt ashamed. What had he really been in such a fury about? How idiotic! On whom had he been revenging himself? Against whom had he been raging?

He realized how deep was this unexplainable feeling that now glowed so heatedly within him. And at the same time shame at himself and at his emotion came over him. He felt embarrassed before the people he had encountered, that in the snow and the dim streets he should have lost his temper with a woman, tripping anxiously along beside him,—Valtz wearing furs, Valtz wearing perfume.

"To start with, I shouldn't have come back with her from the demonstration. Yet I did so with pleasure. And now I've been feeling prejudice, false shame." Zudin laughed to himself scornfully.

"It seems to me," Valtz was saying, "that your words contain the same idea of perfection in human existence as the Gospel: the enemy within. How is man to attain perfection?"

This was no foolish little woman, marveled Zudin; she had gone straight to the crux of the matter. "Perfection will come only when we have attained a new order of society, when we have shaken off the yoke of slavery and capitalist exploitation."

"Yes, and in the meantime?"

"What do you mean, 'in the meantime'?"

"What are we to do with our inner hidden enemy?"

"We almost do not have it any more, and we'll tear it out of whoever still has it inside him," retorted Zudin harshly, raising his clenched fist.

Valtz was silent, thinking. Then: "I don't believe that's very likely to come about, Aleksey Ivanovich," she said decisively, with a rebellious toss of her head. "If all men would only look the truth squarely and openly in the face, they would long ago have realized that this appetite for self-indulgence, this inclination toward different—let's say, comfortable ways of life, has been our legacy for thousands of generations; anyhow, this whole culture is based on the comfort you despise so much—now don't deny it and shake your head, I can feel that you despise it—and is a part of us, a part of our constitution, and to kill it off is—well, it's impossible! And so," she stopped in her tracks and cast a deep glance into his eyes, "I bow to you and your holy ideals, but I don't for a moment believe in your communism, no, not for a moment."

His gaze fell slowly to the sidewalk.

"And can't you realize, even for a moment, that all these selfish interests and demands and prejudices are in you, too? Frankly, don't they make life beautiful? I'd be sorry for the man who hasn't anything at all. He would be like an empty husk, a shell without a kernel. And it's just that kernel which is most sacred in man, in me, and in you. Now take your family, for example,"—with a colder note in her voice—" your wife, Elizaveta Vasilyevna, such a lovable woman, your children—aren't they your personal responsibility, and can it be otherwise? This feeling of what is ours is part of us, and much more than we imagine, but for some reason or other it's considered an outrage to take up a stand on it. I know you're going to assure me, aren't you, that it wouldn't affect you at all if any hooligan that came along offered to barter his filthy cap for your Persian lamb one?"

"We do not reject personal property," answered Zudin, rather at a loss. It disturbed him that Valtz should have mentioned his wife by name. In his heart he was unpleasantly occupied by that enigma he had puzzled over a thousand times: how is it that women become friends so easily? His Lisa and this Valtz woman, what could they have in common? Ever since that time Valtz had brought some official papers to his home, she had got into the habit of often calling on Lisa when he was out. What attracted Valtz in Lisa? And, what was more, Lisa herself had quite altered: there was now in her manner an unfamiliar tone that had been noticeable more and more frequently of late. And what about Valtz? She was blooming as she walked beside him in her furry coat, in sheer, transparent stockings, in the fragrance that so much attracted him. Yet again it was disagreeable to him that he should let himself be seen with her. Soon he would have to mount the stairs to his office under the thousand watchful eyes that were so obsequious and flattering to his face and so keen and insolent behind his back. There would undoubtedly be gossip about their being together.

And here, already, was the familiar gray corner of the frightened street. There were no passers-by, but a sentry was on duty here and a second at the entrance further on. Zudin scowled. But—what luck!—in front of the building a motor had pulled up.

"Elena Valentinovna, tell them upstairs that I'm just going home for a moment; I'll stay only to eat and be right back."

"Panteleev, drive me home!"

All covered with melting snow, the driver Panteleev sounded the horn, and at this the attendant, in a shabby fur coat, a cap with ear muffs, and clumsy fur gloves blundered hastily out. He brushed the snow off the seat with his sleeve. Zudin got in. The attendant cranked the engine. Nervously, the heart of the machine began to flutter. The doors were slammed. A sharp jerk, and they were away.

The snow went on falling in rounded flakes, beating into faces, blowing into eyes, and chasing thought after thought around in the mind, like snowflakes that grow out of nowhere and perish into nowhere.

"Wait for me, I'll be back in twenty minutes."

For heaven's sake, Lisa's all decked out in her best dress. She's sleeked down her fair hair smooth as cream.

"What's the occasion?"

With a happy smile: "The occasion is victory!"

"Ah, that's true, and in spite of having had no sleep last night, I had to hurry off duty this morning and go to the demonstration. I walked with the main column as far as Zarev Square. All our crowd was there. I didn't get to the grand session of the assembly, as a matter of fact, too many urgent things to attend to; I walked along with Valtz on the way back. And now give me something to eat, quick; the car's waiting downstairs."

"Do you know, Lyosha, Valtz and I sat up together till late last night. I wanted her to spend the night, but she wouldn't. She really is a most likable woman."

She spoke so gaily as she bustled about, rattling the plates. Mitya and Masha climbed onto their father's knees.

"Smeary little mouths they've got. What's made them like that?"

"Papa, do you know what Auntie gave us yesterday? Chocolate!" shouted the children, and as they laughed in their excitement, great lumps of it could be seen dissolving in their mouths.

Lisa turned red, the spoon slipped from her hand. "Lyosha, don't be angry. Elena Valentinovna is so kind and good; she brought us a lot of gifts—about two pounds of chocolate, real, imported chocolate, just taste it—for the children, and she brought them each a pair of first-quality lisle stockings, long ones, just look! And do you know what she brought me?" Her gaze fell to the table. "I didn't want to take them, but I couldn't put her off, she was really so determined. She gave me two pairs of silk stockings, so sheer, best quality, well, just see!"

Somewhat flushed and embarrassed, Liza took a step backward, lifted the heavy hem of her dress, and coyly showed her legs covered in transparent silk, then suddenly, as if ashamed, she threw her arms round her husband's neck.

"This is most distressing!" Zudin drew away. "Yes, distressing *and* improper, too: you know she's under me. It would have been far better if you'd accepted nothing from her, Liza. It smells of bribery!" A wave of nausea went over him.

"Whatever are you saying, Lyosha? You should be ashamed of yourself, you should indeed! Look me in the eye and ask forgiveness. You won't? Then say over to yourself: how could Valtz and bribery go together? How could they? So we mustn't make friends with anyone who's under you? Even exchange a word? Or do you think I didn't try to refuse? But she kept on saying, 'Please try to understand, I'm a dancer, an artist! I've got some old silk things, old stuff, things I haven't even worn, trunks full of them, and now I'm working, what am I to do with it all? Before, I was selling them—or does it really disgrace you to accept these little things as a gift?'"

"*Little* things! What can it all have cost?"

"She didn't buy them herself, Lyosha, she assured me of that. She had a whole drawerful of silk stockings from before the war. The children's stockings belonged to her sister, who has one child; they went abroad a long time ago. The chocolate was brought her, she says, by a well-known actor, who has just come back from Archangel with his troupe. She assured me we'd commandeered a lot from the British: there was no end of fine things they had. Her friend the actor brought back half a hundredweight for himself. So, can you really be angry about little trivial things like this? Can you, Lyosha? I offered to pay for it all, but she very firmly refused and got quite offended, she went all red."

"She had more pride than you have, then!" cried Zudin.

"Oh, Lyosha, Lyosha, can this really be you? So this is what you call your love for me! Another man would be glad of his wife's getting a present, and for his children to get stockings—at last!—and taste a piece of candy! But you! Masha, Mitya, give your father the chocolate! Since it makes him so miserable, let him take it. Like a dog in the manger, not letting anyone else. . . ."

With a look of complete astonishment, Mitya laid the rest of his chocolate on the table, while Masha blew out her cheeks, went as red as a little turkey, and split the silence with a loud howl. Brown specks flew out of her rounded little open mouth, sweat stood out on her little brow.

"Child, child, don't be upset, my darling!" said Zudin hastily to her. He bundled her up in his arms, held her close to him; thus cradling her, he walked back and forth across the room, laughing nervously. Tenderly he patted the child's shoulder; her face was screwed up as children do when they are unhappy, her chocolaty tears dirtying his collar roused pangs of remorse in him.

"Mitya, take back your chocolate and see that you enjoy it! It's not the children's fault," he mumbled, vexed, as his wife wearing a morose, angry look brought in a plate of steaming soup.

"It seems we mustn't accept a gift for the children that's offered in friendship," she said, spoiling for a fight.

"Friendship?" he repeated, drawling the word in a sneering tone. "Since when this sudden friendship?"

"Since she entered your service at the Cheka!" she parried swiftly and, spurred on by her effective response, added gratuitously: "Or are you hiring the good-for-nothings now over there?"

He set the child down, now quiet at last, on the stool beside him, stroked the woebegone Mitya affectionately, and began to drink the scalding hot soup.

He ate hastily, not looking at his wife. After the soup he had a little bread—without butter—and salt, got up, and opened the kitchen door. Here he found the china teapot on the table, its spout chipped, the legend "Grand Hotel" written on it in blue; he drank a mere mouthful of the thin, lukewarm tea and, wiping his mouth, looked around him at the cockroaches running hither and thither. In deep thought, without seeking out his wife, he took his coat off the hook and hurried out.

The first thing he noticed was that it was not snowing now and that dusk was falling. Here and there solitary lights were already grinning. The lamps began to dissect the darkening streets as the motor bore its load forward. In the desire to divert his spirits, Zudin felt he would enjoy a puff or two at a cigaret. For something, some unpleasant, apathetic burden, was sitting on his heart. Somewhere something had rung false. Where and what it was he did not know himself.

In point of fact: someone had given the children some chocolate—wasn't he pleased, in any event, for their sakes? The light in their faces, and the rapture in their eyes! His wife had received the gift of a pair of stockings from a woman friend.

I wouldn't have taken them, thought Zudin. But *she*?

How many long, painful years had they lived and struggled together, without work and outlawed, in Siberia! How much unhappiness and sorrow had they endured in the hard fight for the future of the worker! Had not his dear wife Lisa always been his true and sure support, a constant, lasting friend? If she had not resisted the temptation to accept a gift from a friend, vanities in which women find so much consolation—for all women are the same, he reflected—why was it he had treated her so harshly? And he had never wanted anything but to be good to her, he told himself, scornfully.

He recalled how Lisa, blushing, had stepped back, coyly lifting the hem of her dress to show him her present.

The way she looked at it, you could quite well make a silk purse from a proletarian ear, he thought, still a little disgruntled. But that meant she was not ready to carry the proletarian banner to the end; no sooner had she been offered the lure of silk stockings than she had fallen for it. All women seemed to be made to the same pattern. And his heart ached. He saw now how she was taking off a fine new stocking. He himself was lying in bed, while she, wearing only a chemise, sat on the edge of the bed taking off her stockings. Her dull yellow hair fell like a mop over her face with its green eyes and her thick-set shoulders. There was a smell of sweat. And a bedbug crawled over the wall.

All this shook Zudin to the core, he flung his cigaret away. With angry resentment he remembered his wife's trying to get the last word with the spiteful phrase: "Or maybe you're employing the no-goods at the Cheka, now?"

He? "No-goods?"

At this point, with a soft hiss, the motor halted, as if at the pull of reins, before the entrance to the building where the sentry stood.

"What about Valtz?" thought Zudin as he unhurriedly climbed the broad steps. One small and solitary electric bulb shed scanty light on the dirty marble of the steps, the withered, dusty palm in the corner of the spacious landing, the attendant's endless stream of cigaret ends.

Zudin took the key from old Agafya, the woman orderly, and unlocked his room. "Who's on duty this evening?"

"You know, that little lady, what's her name now? Valtz!"

Zudin entered in a bad temper and turned on the glaring center light. He pulled the curtain over the blue-black window and sat himself down at his desk. The wallpaper gave back the familiar blue-gray color that contrasted with the golden amber of the hangings, like warm patches on the pilasters rising from the patterned floor to form a Gothic arch above. After running through several files, he selected a thick one and zealously leafed through the contents, his brows knit, his forehead furrowed also in a Gothic arch.

The heavy white light fell on papers, wallpapers, files, and the many various objects strewn about in the corner on the floor: here a heap of rifles and sabers sent in from somewhere or other, there bundles of papers and letters; near some trunks and boxes of different sizes stood about a dozen dusty bottles of confiscated wine.

Zudin sat for a long time plunged in his work, he turned over pages, read, made notes in the margin, until he yawned, stretched, and stood up in gloomy silence.

He did not recall ever having been so distressed and without a clear reason as he had been today—as if someone, say, himself, was bound to go far off somewhere and with no inclination to go. Or as if he had been ordered to spend the night alone in an abandoned fortress somewhere at the front.

"I'm tired," he thought. "It would be good to take a rest; soon it would be spring." Perhaps he could even take a leave of absence and get away to the country, where it smelled of grass and hay and chickens, where you could sleep pleasantly on a wide peasant mattress in a shady cabin or, dozing, listen to the laughter and song of the country lasses. And when you awoke, drive swiftly out of the farm, past the herb and vegetable garden, through the shady valley to the river, where, by the level of transparent water, at the edge of the grass, the leeches wriggled like tapeworms.

Zudin got undressed and walked slowly over the feather-soft, sloping sand into the glittering, sunny water. The waves and the warming sun played with his limbs like eager, merry, laughing eyes—Valtz's eyes.

Why was he shaking? Why should this foolish idea have galvanized his imagination like an electric current?

Coughing, old Agafya entered, letting a cold draught into the room, and noisily threw an apronful of firewood by the stove. Opening the iron door with a clatter, she put in the wood and set it alight with a burning splinter. The fire began to crackle and spit, rattling the oven door, while all around the stove there danced a rosy glow. Groaning, Agafya got to her feet and went out of the room.

"I can't get down to work this evening; or was it that I got an unusual amount of fresh air today?" the nonplussed Zudin asked himself. "Or did that unpleasantness tire me? Oh, this indomitable wish to lie down and dream and sleep!"

He went over the soft carpet to the stove and sat down on the sofa there, after first turning out the center light, so that only the dim white flare of the table lamp shone at a distance from him. The red half-light issued from the stove and covered the carpet, the sofa, with a frolicsome glimmer that came through its chinks.

"The one on duty, should she bring you in the telegrams herself or should she wait for your secretary to come back?" asked Agafya, appearing at the door.

"She can bring them."

Reluctantly, Zudin stood up and went uncertainly back to his desk.

Her entry unnoticed, she suddenly emerged from the darkness, graceful in her rustling dress, Valtz wearing silk, Valtz wearing perfume.

The red-gold glow from the stove played on her little feet. Chocolate brown was the color of the dark-bright flowing hair that framed her face—tender, delicate, and winsome as a squirrel's. As if keeping a secret, the capricious little mouth concealed the shy, flashing smile. And all at once, Zudin found himself snared in the friendly attentiveness that shone through the thick lashes from her brown eyes, Valtz's eyes.

Again came the image of the dream village in fresh air and sunlight, the rushing water grateful to the weary body. And all at once it became warm, burningly pleasurable, burningly painful.

"Six telegrams," she whispered.

"Good. Please sit down."

She seated herself quietly at the desk, directly across from him. He could clearly hear the beat of her heart and the rustle of silk on the chair.

Inexplicably, his hand tearing open the telegrams began to shake. Two from Moscow, the others from the front: two from Pskov, one from Archangel, and one from Smolensk. His eyes ran quickly over the lines: the conclusion of the Girot case; an inquiry concerning Finnish bandits; a line on the Savinkov intrigue—the name of a Pole, Stefanitski—and much else, mere inquiries.

"This is for Horst to see to, this for Plastov, this for Katzmann, and these two for Fomin. Now it's only for Petrova to enter them in the diary early tomorrow morning; then file these for me under the Rosenblatt case—I've looked them through, we'll have the decision at the meeting of the Commission tomorrow."

He was speaking jerkily like this when he realized that she did not want to leave. With a dissatisfied air, she was unhurriedly putting the papers back into the file. Her breast rose and fell spasmodically, and the sapphire pendant tossed between these waves.

"You have been so kind as to hand a package to my wife. I want to thank you truly and sincerely. My wife was very pleased indeed. But I hope you will not do us the wrong of making us a gift of something we have not paid for. Allow me, please, to reimburse you for however much it cost."

Valtz stood gazing sadly at the floor. "If you consider it an act of kindness to pay me for something that came from my heart, then I deserve no better. But I really don't know the price of those little things: I didn't buy them."

Her cheeks began to flame. The chocolate-colored eyes widened, their sorrowful look cut Zudin to the heart. Her lips tightened, showing the white line of her teeth. With a sudden rustling movement, Valtz turned to the door.

She's not a woman, she's a devil, thought Zudin. He suddenly felt the urge to spring with a youth's litheness, seize her, and bury his face in the softness of her throat.

"I was wrong to come in to work tonight; I'm a much-married man"—Zudin rebuked himself. But in vain. The calm and the downy softness of the sofa drew him like a viscous fluid. Passing the dusty chests with their papers and sundry rubbish, the weapons and the bottles, he went over to the stove, opened the iron door, and with every pore of his body breathed in the heat from the burning coals that penetrated even his clothing.

It would be a good idea to poke the fire and make it burn even brighter. He pressed the bell to call Agafya. Unaccountably, Valtz appeared in the doorway. "You rang—Agafya will only be a moment."

"It doesn't matter—I can wait. When she comes, please tell her I'd like a poker."

"I'll bring it at once!"

Before he could reply, she had flown off like a bird and was soon back again with the poker. "Don't bother—I'll poke it for you!"

Quickly and efficiently she crouched before the stove and, spreading her skirts, began to poke at the fading fire. The stillness and the warmth, the half-light, the soft, comfortable sofa, an elegant woman—like a vision in a dream. His will overcome, Zudin surrendered to the moment.

"It's cozy in your office," said Valtz, musingly. She got up and stood the poker in the corner.

"Will it do like that?" she asked, pointing to the stove's open door and smiling with open tenderness.

Zudin nodded in silence, wanting it all to stay like that forever, stove, half-light, fire, warmth, and Valtz, tender, flower-like, alluring Valtz, like a picture inspired by a naive legend, like part of a living dream.

"Why don't you stay?" he said in an undertone. "Sit down, here, on the sofa, or the armchair, if you like!"

"May I?" Her dress rustling, she sat down beside him.

Leaning back onto the cushions, he considered himself and wondered at what he saw. There was a hammering in his temples, something strong and painfully sweet was pressing on his heart. Powerful waves drew him, like a pack of she-wolves, like an electric current, to Valtz, sweet, desirable, alluring Valtz. Stirring, he happened to touch her warm hand and a thrill of delight pierced him. Like a man bewitched, his nerves quivering, he was aware of Valtz's tender fingers cautiously stroking his hand.

"Alik, my dear, my love, why did you insult me so?" he heard her hot, passionate murmur. In the shadows he glimpsed her face, familiar, caressing, inscrutable, with the dark pools of her eyes and her confident, open, moistly inviting, eager mouth, like dark-shining leaves of jasmine.

"Alik, I love you dearly, madly!"

Convulsively she pressed his hand in a transport of ecstasy. "You are my god, my idol, my only love, my master! Oh, don't be afraid, I'll make no demands on you. You'll keep your family, your comrades, your work, your position, your revolution, you'll keep everything in your own life. I need so little, so little: a trusting look, a little affection, and love. Only you in all the world understand me. Alik, I'm so hopelessly alone without you—I was always alone until you came. Only you have ever understood me, only you, my terrible one, my true knight. And you—aren't you lonely? I know you're like a storm, what with the revolution, the party, your cases. But, secretly, in your heart of hearts, are you really happy? Does anyone show you even a spark of sympathy? Not so much to Comrade Zudin, to Aleksey Ivanovich, not even to 'Lyosha,' out of habit, the husband and father, but to Alik the beloved, with all his natural superiority and with his weaknesses too, his failings and sins, with all his doubts and sorrows? Only give me permission to love you as you are, love you, never making any claims on you! You see how little I'm asking and how much that little means in my life. Only don't send me away, Alik! I couldn't bear the biting whiplash of your rejecting me. When I took those little things to your family, believe me, I only wanted to give a couple of seconds' pleasure to your pure-hearted children and your wife and to you, through them, to you above all else. But you! 'Pay!' How terrible! Now let me hear you speak, my dearest Alik, my only one, I'm all yours now, say something, please!"

It seemed to Zudin that the words of this amorous Valtz, Elena Valtz, who now laid her hot lips on his hand—that her words went dancing and frolicking into his brain and melted away there, like wax. It seemed to Zudin that a soft, warm, fragrant, sticky lava had enveloped him in an effusion tasting of milk chocolate, filling his mouth and choking his throat. It was not so much Valtz's insinuating whisper as that same growing inner misgiving, beating like hammers, that sent a cold shiver trickling down his legs, hands, and back, as if Valtz were floating before him, whirling on tiptoe. Then it seemed to Zudin—the conviction was like the growing rumble of a storm—that this was not Valtz, but a fearful, alien dynamo, a machine designed to quiver with passion, impelled by a noisy, fast driving belt. He sat at her side, fascinated by the whirring and humming—a machine that in addition could pipe and call and entice. It called and enticed: leave the dirty, soot-begrimed factory and come over to me; look into the untamed blue dance of the fire that leaps, stronger and stronger, wilder and wilder, in my throat!

"Careful, Aleksey!" Someone shook him heavily by the shoulder. It was Comrade Danila, the oiler. "Careful, don't let the machine go rusty. Hey, what are you gawking at?"

Alarmed, Zudin passed a shaking hand over his hair, turned carefully away, slowly stood up, and began to pace up and down the room, while Valtz abandoned herself to pitiful weeping.

He brought the cool leather armchair over to the sofa, slowly lit a cigaret, and said: "I don't know whether you're making a mistake, I don't know, but I want to caution you against making one. I will readily believe you have acted with high and sincere intentions, but you must also believe me: I simply am not in a position to give in to any careless feelings of passion, indeed I am not, it's quite impossible. I am sorry from the bottom of my heart, but you must believe this: love is not for us!"

Valtz leaped up like an arrow, took two steps across the carpet, then sat down, as if strength failed her, on the studded top of one of the chests.

"Far be it from me to want to offend you, I only want you not to make a foolish mistake. Of course, I'm no saint, I have the same feelings as everyone else. Whatever is peculiar to men is also not alien to me. But there is in me something that you hardly understand, Elena Valentinovna, it's—how can I put it?—class consciousness. That glorious, eternal, mighty stigma! From this fact, I draw sustenance and drink of the highest personal happiness. How I came by it I don't know myself, only, whenever I looked out of the window—my mother (she was a washerwoman) and I lived in a dirty, dark cellar—when I watched the legs of the people going by, I understood as clearly as a ragged urchin can that there are fine folk in the world with shiny, new galoshes but with horrible, dirty souls, and that there are many,

many people who go barefoot and dirty but whose souls are full of glory! And as surely as the factory has been master of my life from the moment the sirens sounded early every morning, I saw that one day happiness in this world would come for us dirty urchins, too, and soon I discovered for myself the way that led to this happiness, the happiness of us all. Oh, it isn't easy for us to follow along that way. We have to face many obstacles and pitfalls. Yes, and many sacrifices and failures, and doubts and waverings, as well as weariness and indolence. And often the desire to lie down and forget overwhelms us. But the thunderous voice of the working class flashes through the clouds and wakes us. It confers on us the reward of that same happiness, beside which individual dreams of hearts and flowers and women are just— rubbish. It fills our hearts with the keenest pathos; its strong, peace-loving might is thought and feeling to us. And should we repress it and change it and forget it, in exchange for what? Affection, the love of women! Chocolate can only be had elsewhere, so it is unknown to us. And as for me, I am not used to it; we don't miss it. I hope you understand me now and will not be upset any more. It is impossible for me to be your lover. That is why we will control ourselves now and not part on bad terms, but remain friends as before."

Her head bowed to her knee, Valtz was plucking mutely at her handkerchief, but in her heart a bitter ball of fire was growing, to melt at last in tears. She got up slowly, saying not a word, and slipped quietly out, biting her lips; the door closed soundlessly. There was a stillness in the room, and little by little utter weariness began to take possession of Zudin. He rolled up his coat, put it under his head, and stretched out on the sofa to doze for a while. Later, through his slumbering ears, he heard Agafya making up the already extinguished fire.

4

Rumor slunk drowsily through the city. It humped along with the gnarled old women on the dirty pavement by the church door. There it lay hidden in the bosom of a degenerate who not long before had been a stout and sturdy fellow, but now his scrawny throat was sunk deep in a beaver fur collar and he zealously crossed the yellow creases of his wrinkles. The once stout and sturdy fellow had suddenly felt an itch in his back; he turned to his neighbor's shoulder and whispered, "Have you heard?"

Go-o o-o-nn! Go-o o-o-nn! Go-o o-o-nn! chimed the bells above.

The deacon chanted in hoarse, monotonous tones while the scowling, shaggy-haired priest swung the incense burner, its lilac-tinged globules of incense pouring out clouds of smoke.

"Have you heard that the Mexican emperor Belinder has declared war on the Bolsheviks?" . . .

"What's going to happen to us?"

"We stay in our basements, so as not to breathe the gases. . . ."

"Have you heard? Shu-shu-shu. . . ."

"The Communists are on the run—running like mice before the . . . shu-shu. . . ."

"Trotsky hacked off Lenin's head—did it himself. My goodness, I wouldn't like to be in his shoes.—Shu-shu.—My nephew arrived from Moscow yesterday, saw it himself, he did—works in the Kremlin, Narkomprod."

"Is he a Communist, then?" A salvo of scornful and hostile looks were fired at the old gossip. . . .

"Yesterday the Cheka shot eight hundred people. One thousand arrested and eight hundred shot. That means two hundred were able to buy themselves off. Shu-shu."

"Who were they?"

"Those who could pay. Some paid a hundred thousand, and some handed over their gold or flour. Those hangmen take it all!"

"They say Vanka Krasavin had to offer them four Persian rugs, some diamond earrings, and two hundred thousand into the bargain before they'd let him go. The elder of the church, Thomas Ignatyev, is his godfather. . . ."

The rumor crawled on, serpentlike, into the outskirts of the town where the factories stood with doused fires. It tagged onto the end of a line of workers on early call, as they waited for bread at the canteen. A rotting black rope, it wound itself around them: old women with packs on their backs, children with their father's coat thrown over their heads, unhealthy-looking, yellow-faced women, laborers with caps pulled down over their eyes. Hands thrust into pockets. Eyes smarting and shot with red, like marbles. Mouths tight shut.

Caps were pulled further down. Hands were thrust deeper into pockets. Eyes cold and bloodshot. Like marbles.

In the gray building with the sentry at the entrance, the work is going on. . . . Brows knit, fingers running through glistening hair, Zudin was listening to Katzmann's report. Katzmann was sitting, round-shouldered, his pince-nez astride his hooked nose, and sucking back the disobedient saliva.

"Yes, Aleksey Ivanovich, Foreign Service Agents Sokol and Zvonky were able to identify Mr. Heckey—yes, it was the same man, they got up close to him. He slipped into a courtyard and began to run. They fired, but then he was too far away. Unfortunately the courtyard was full of angles and it was dark, too.

They searched for him, but he'd completely disappeared. Later the whole courtyard was searched thoroughly. Heckey had climbed over the wall and gone through a small alley, all that was found of him was an overshoe. It's a pity we haven't a photograph of the gentleman, otherwise we'd have alerted all agents and soon caught him. Now we'll have to wait our chances—Sokol may come across him again. I've sent him to patrol the neighborhood. That's all about Heckey, he hasn't been caught yet, but he is in the city. Now, then, it's my idea, more than ever, that we ought to remove Pavlov. Those little tricks he pulled off in the Bocharkin case were very suspicious, as you know. And then that diamond affair—without my knowledge he contrived to get them away from Fomin. And now he's trying to hide them. I think it's clear we must get Dukhonin from headquarters to keep Pavlov under surveillance." A thin, crooked smile appeared on Katzmann's hook-nosed face.

"All right, Abram, do as you think best." Zudin was preoccupied with his thoughts.

"Then there's another thing, Aleksey Ivanovich," said Katzmann in a low tone, keeping his eyes turned away. "Along with Pavlov, it might be a good idea if we were to keep a more watchful eye on our personnel here. I don't know about you, but I don't care for Lipshaevich at all."

"Yes, yes," nodded Zudin. "That's what I wanted to tell *you*."

"And then, you know, this Valtz. . . ." And thereupon, as if ashamed, he raised his eyes to Zudin's.

"Valtz? Oh, no, I don't believe that," Zudin reddened, forcing a smile.

"There, you see, you have too much faith in her. Take care you're not deceiving yourself." Katzmann dropped his gaze.

"Never mind, Abram! I know what you mean, but I assure you there's no substance in it. Of course she's a bit coquettish when I'm there, but it cuts no ice with me. That's one thing. Then she's as grateful to me as a dog for taking her out of that den of iniquity she'd got herself into and giving her a position. She'd go through fire and water for us. Just look how many new slants she's got out of those old 'closed' cases!" Zudin smiled triumphantly.

"Well, just as you think best," said Katzmann, moving his head to show obedience, "only. . . ."

Fomin appeared in the doorway.

"Good day, Aleksey Ivanovich, and good day to you, Abram Moiseich. I come directly from Ignatyev. He wanted you to be fetched for an affair he couldn't discuss on the telephone, and now he's commissioned me to perform the task, brothers—it's quite a thing. Today he received dispatches from Moscow to say they had got a line there on a fighting unit of the SR—the whole crew is supposed to be here in our area! About ten kilometers north of town in Osennikov village there's been a neat little band of them lying low and making their preparations as calmly as you please, under our all-seeing eye, too! Wait, wait, it gets better! That robbery at the People's Bank—that's their doing. And their organization, friends, is nothing short of fantastic. And if we want to catch them, one, or preferably two of us will have to go and carry out a thorough survey of their terrain and then lay hold of 'em, if and when they all get together in the same place. Anyway, here, read it for yourselves!" And with a self-satisfied smile, he threw himself into an armchair, leaving his colleagues to read the document.

"Whom to send? Who can get out there?" Zudin, in some agitation, was thinking aloud. He thrust his hands into his pockets and stared at Fomin. "What if we sent Kulikov?"

"Shall I tell you what? I'll go myself!" Katzmann got up abruptly.

There was a silence.

"All right, you say yourself, then go yourself, if you're inclined. It's a case of serious and absorbing interest. Only, you know, brother, you should take someone along to help, say, Kulikov or Dagnis. And at the next station send us a communiqué without fail. Then things will be splendid," Zudin decided.

"Yes, indeed," approved Fomin.

And at the prospect of the important job before him, Katzmann's eyes beamed gaily with excitement.

"I'll take Dagnis along as my assistant, that boy's as clever as a fox!"

In the small gray office Valtz was poring over a document with the closest attention. She even stood up, then kneeled on the stool. Her modest white dress of simple material hung in airy folds, chastely covering her arms and throat.

"Petya Chotkin, my friend! You here?" she smiled, amused and surprised.

The image of Petya Chotkin stood vividly before her, tall and gangling, with large protruding ears, in brand new evening dress of an extravagant design and a much-wrinkled, low-cut vest. His hands were always sweating.

Yes, there was no mistake. "Pyotr Ivanovich Chotkin; father's profession: merchant."

She recalled his loud, resonant laugh, his gross manners. In the flower of his idle, golden youth, but, like an obscure pain, he was tolerated and accepted, for he was the sole heir to the millions of a well-known jeweler.

Who didn't know Pyotr Ivanovich Chotkin?

Valtz remembered how once he had filled her bodice to the top with twenty-ruble notes. As she was delightedly picking them out, the joke went round, "Daddy's going to give Petichka a whipping! Ha, ha, ha!"

Valtz quickly turned to the records: arrested; held in custody for the last three months. She exclaimed in curiosity. But why? What for?

An old friend and familiar of his, an officer and an agent of Denikin, had once spent the night at his house and had declared this at the hearing. That was all. There was certainly not much evidence against him. The investigation had long been concluded—the officer, incidentally, had been shot. The records also showed the judge's decision: case closed; Chotkin to be released. Although the decision had been entered in the records, it had still not been put into effect officially. It had also happened that Verekhleev, the investigator on the case, had had an urgent call to Moscow, the case had been filed, and Petya still sat on in prison, forgotten by all.

Valtz jumped up and went straight to Shalenko in the next room. "Where's the file of persons in custody?" Yes, here were the C's: Chotkin, Pyotr Ivanovich; Cell No. 45; Investigator Verekhleev.

She returned to her place, pleased with herself, and turning over Chotkin's predicament in her mind.

"Never fear, brother, I'll help you for old time's sake. Tomorrow you'll be free. Tomorrow you'll jump like a giraffe to please your mamma and papa! I'll take the records straight to Zudin and get him to give the order." She smiled brightly and contentedly to herself.

Suddenly an afterthought occurred to her and she stood communing with herself. Then without haste she laid the papers among the other dossiers, looking about her uneasily: no, no one had seen. She breathed again and went directly into Katzmann's office.

"Abram Moiseich, I really feel quite ill today. May I go home? If I'm better, I'll come in again this evening, but now I feel so bad. I can hardly keep upright. May I?"

Had Abram paid attention to Valtz?

"Very well, you can go."

Like a schoolgirl cowering under the stern eye of her teacher, her gaze artlessly cast down to her moving feet, repressing her bubbling gaiety, throwing shy glances to right and left, Valtz went downstairs, stepping carefully, as if she were seriously ill.

Outside, the sky was a length of azure silk. The emerald breezes blew limpid and gentle; there was not a cloud in the sky.

Once in the street, Elena bent and ran as fast as she could. Stealthily, she glanced around her, stopping before the bulletin on the wall and again at the corner, then hurried on. Her pounding heels cracked the brittle crystal crusts, the thin ice on the puddles.

Here was the stone house, humped, like an immense black castle: the Chotkin residence. Valtz knew it well. She went toward the imposing steps—they were still boarded up. Then she went to the lower entrance and read on the roster: "I. Chotkin Apartment 17." She looked around the courtyard for the number. It must be here: 13, 14, 15, 16, 17—aha! Then 18, and so on. Up the stone stairs with the wrought iron balustrade, past doorways lacking their doors, she at last came to the third floor. It smelled of slops and frying and cats. She rapped gently with the door knocker, but no one appeared; she knocked again, more loudly, boldly. In tones of alarm, someone demanded through the door: "Who's there?"

"I must speak to Ivan Petrovich Chotkin on an urgent personal matter."

"They're not at home. Ivan Petrovich is out."

A pregnant silence.

"What was it you wanted to speak to him about?"

"I've come on behalf of your son, Pyotr Ivanovich." Valtz simulated the woman's accent. "It's very important. Don't be alarmed. Can't you hear by my voice that I'm a woman, not a housebreaker?"

The bolt rattled, the door opened a slit, and then was flung open.

"Please step in."

"I'm an acquaintance of Pyotr Ivanovich's, and I've heard something very urgent about him, only I must first speak to his father, Ivan Petrovich."

"Has something happened for the worse?"

"Oh, no, there's no worse, in fact, I heard that Pyotr Ivanovich will soon be released: that's why I came."

"God be praised! Please be seated. Ivan Petrovich should have been back a long time ago. Please come into the dining room," said the lady in the lace shawl with some animation and opened a door leading off the passage.

It was gloomy in the dining room. The windows opened onto a tiled area. The linen shades had been raised. Behind them hung a birdcage in which a canary was hopping about, scattering grain over the sill. Before the ikon a small lamp of dark green glass flickered. A clock with heavy black weights hung on the wall. On the table, spread with dark oilcloth, was a plate of candy. The oaken seats ranged against the walls stood guard over the great, heavy, shapeless breakfront. On the dresser, also of oak, lay a kind of bag from which something wet was oozing forth.

That'll be raisins or dried plums, thought Valtz, it smells very nice. They are very well off, but it's as dark as the tomb. I wouldn't live here for worlds.

Suddenly voices came from behind the door. (That leads to the kitchen. They've come back, then.) And indeed in walked, excitedly, still wearing his fur coat, the stout, wrinkled Chotkin, gray and unshaven, like a porcupine. On his arm, waddling like a goose, was a round ball of a woman, the lady of the house.

"You've come about our son?" Excitedly, "What's happened? You say he's to be released?"

"Released, yes. Will you grant me a few words in private?"

There was a distressed silence. The women's gaze ran beseechingly over Ivan Petrovich's lead-colored eyes, imploring help from under his beetling gray brows.

"If it is secret," he said in slow, hollow tones, "I'll ask you to come into my study."

He looked round the room and opened a door that had a mat against drafts. "Only, you must excuse us, the room is not heated. We sit in the dining room or the bedroom or the servant's room."

A huge room that probably looked out onto the street. The shades were drawn and the furniture was in dust covers, themselves covered with dust. The pictures had sheets of paper pasted over them. The parquet floor had been polished and shone coldly.

Completely disorder reigned in the study. Many ill-assorted pieces of furniture stood massed against the wall; beneath these thick rugs were rolled. On the wall, in a gangrenous gold frame, a penitent Magdalene lay in a gloomy cave. She seemed sunk in apathetic meditation, a book held close to her pendulous breasts. Below the Magdalene stood a small chest covered with canvas. On the floor were the vestiges of a meal, smelling faintly of herring.

A large, heavy desk draped with a dark-red cloth bore various writing materials. The ink stand was decorated with two massive bears.

Chotkin brought up a semicircular morocco-leather armchair for Valtz. He himself sat on a plain wooden chair, with carved arms, and waited silently.

"Now, I'm an old acquaintance of your son's—that is, I used to meet him often with some friends we had in common. I used to be in the theater and came across him there," said Valtz incoherently. "Well, anyway, I've known your son for a long time and wish him well." She suddenly felt the piercing cold in that damp room.

"You see, I've just now discovered that he is in grave danger. I have some reliable contacts at the Cheka, and that's what they told me."

His eyes blinking, Chotkin hung trembling on Elena's carmined carefree lips.

"Don't be alarmed, though he is in grave danger. You see, he could either be shot or set free. His case will be decided tomorrow, and the decision depends on one man alone, whom you may be able to influence."

"Who is this man?"

"The Chief of the Cheka himself, Zudin."

Chotkin collapsed, his forearms slid under the table. His whole body seemed to recede into his fur coat. Only his closely shorn gray head and protruding lower lip trembled and the tears ran down his stubby chin.

"What can I do?" came his almost inaudible whisper.

"Don't be silly! I am telling you: your son's fate lies in your hands alone, thank God. You can certainly save him from the firing squad. Only by noon tomorrow you must have a certain something ready."

"Yes, what?"

"Twenty pounds in gold."

The old man stood up, his mouth fell open. To keep from falling, he pressed his hands on the table. His breath gasped and bubbled in his wrinkled throat.

"Twenty pounds, twenty pounds—twenty pounds," he muttered thickly. "In gold? Where am I to get it? My God, it's quite impossible."

"Your son's head is caught in a very terrible trap. I have gone over all the possible ways of saving him, but there is no other. But, naturally, if you can't, you must resign yourself to your grief, and I wish you well. You can't blame me—I've warned you."

Valtz moved as if to rise with her nose in the air.

"Oh, but wait! My God, what is happening to us today?" Quite unnerved Chotkin caught Valtz by the coat and held on to it. Then, letting his head drop to the table, he began sobbing jerkily.

"Petya, my beloved son! What's happened to you, in Christ's name, my child, my only child!"

Through the doorway waddled the old woman, short, round, and all in gray, like a real goose. She had already taken off her wraps.

"What's wrong, Ivan Petrovich?" she flung at her husband. "What's happened to Petichka?" She turned to Valtz, clinging to her husband's arm.

"Anyuta, my love, ou-our Petichka is to be sh-shot tomorrow!" Chotkin moaned, sobbing.

Still clinging to her husband's arm, she slumped to the floor with long wails of lamentation.

Valtz shrugged. "I really cannot understand how rich people, who used to own gold by the hundredweight, can moan and wail now at giving a few pounds to save their son's life! Well, good-bye!" She tore her coat away from the old man's weakening hand.

"Wait, wait, for the love of Christ!" whimpered Chotkin hoarsely and hobbled after her. Behind him, the old woman, wailing, shaking, dissolved in tears.

"Well, what now?" queried Valtz haughtily, stopping.

"Where are you running off to? At least give us time to think things over and collect ourselves."

"I really have no time." She pressed her lips together and lowered her thick eyelashes over the chocolate of her eyes. "Besides, it's a delicate matter, and I wouldn't like it to get to the ears of any outsiders."

Leaning on her and in tears, the old man drew her back into the room with the repentant Magdalene.

"Can't it be done for less?" Ivan Petrovich's streaming eyes appealed to Elena. "They demand twenty pounds in gold by tomorrow morning, Anyuta," he informed his wife in a drained voice. She wiped her eyes and nose with her handkerchief and waited with an imploring gaze for Valtz's answer.

"You really are a funny man, Ivan Petrovich. You're not in a store now. Does one bargain over such things? Since you've been blessed with the chance of saving your son's life, you should be grateful you haven't been asked for more."

"At least, not all at once. Where can I get so much?" He threw out his hands helplessly.

"It must be all there by noon tomorrow," she said, emphasizing each syllable.

"Ivan Petrovich," the old woman cried, "take all my bracelets, rings, and earrings, take my pendant and your watch and chain. Our son is worth more to us," and again she shook with long, convulsive sobs.

"It isn't enough, it isn't enough, my dear!" Chotkin's brow furrowed in thought. "Perhaps I could try to borrow from friends? But who will give it me? In God's name, make it less!"

"I've told you, there can be no bargaining."

"But to whom must it be paid? Supposing it never got to him?"

"Have no fear on that score. I'll take it upon myself to guarantee that."

(But how? Valtz asked herself. Why didn't I think of that before?)

"Have the gold ready," she said slowly, "by twelve noon tomorrow and at that time Pyotr will be freed and all will be well."

"So it's to be paid *when* he's released?" was Chotkin's careful question.

"No, why, 'when he's released?'" Valtz got the better of him. "An order for his release will be sent from the Cheka, and then you pay." Valtz swallowed, and babbled, "It will be on that order that he is to be released."

"I must tell you, miss, or madam—pardon me, I'm ignorant in such matters, an old man," puffed Chotkin hastily, "but living here in this house, just over us, there's an old friend of mine, Counsellor Vunsh. Oh, don't worry," he said seeing Valtz's gesture of refusal. "I have no secrets from him, I talk to him as to my father confessor. And, believe me, he's as secret as the grave and as devoted to me as to a brother, so permit me to ask his advice. I shall return at once." The old man slipped away cautiously, as if he were frightened lest Valtz change her mind and leave.

Anna Zakharyevna dried her tears and stared before her with dim, vacant eyes, like a jackdaw, while Valtz sat down in the armchair, her thoughts undetermined, pulling her coat about her. The canary's song came to them from the dining room, rousing in Valtz a sense of the ferment of verdant spring. And it vexed her to think of birds and fresh buds, here among the dusty litter in this gloomy, cold tomb of a room, spinning out this unpleasant commercial discussion.

But to what end! To what end! She roused herself with the thought. What a lot of real sun-bright living I can buy myself with this dirty gold! Her heart leaped with joy. Only let's put an end to this hard problem that jarred on Valtz's dream of the future.

From somewhere came the sound of a door closing, hasty, heavy footsteps, a muttering. The canary fluttered, scattering grain. The steps were coming through the large room; the tread of one, the man of the house, was soft and massive, the other's steps clicked across the polished floor. From behind the fold of the door curtain there appeared beside Chotkin a hunched, bald little man with small gray eyes behind gold-rimmed spectacles and a narrow little muzzle like a hamster's.

"Vunsh," he said obsequiously, bowing with one leg behind the other.

"Ivan Petrovich has informed me of the matter," and from behind his spectacles he looked respectfully toward the exhausted Chotkin, as though waving a dusty gray scarf at him. "However, what exactly is the transaction you propose regarding their son?" Again the gray scarf waved.

"Their son, Pyotr Ivanovich," Valtz replied quietly, "is in custody at the Cheka. Tomorrow he will be shot." The old woman winced and her scarcely dried eyes clouded with fresh tears. Chotkin choked and withdrew into his fur coat. "Or rather, he will be shot if he isn't saved," amended Valtz. "Saving him is a simple matter of bribing a high official, then Pyotr Ivanovich will come home a free man tomorrow."

Vunsh's eyes were twinkling like those of a tiny mouse, his finger tracing circles on his knee.

"How much is needed?"

"Twenty pounds in gold, either in coin or in kind."

"Oho!" The gray dust of his eyes ran to the disheveled Chotkin, then again he turned courteously to Valtz.

"Such cases—forgive me—as you can very well understand, demand very careful consideration. Exactly who are you? Might we see your papers? What you are proposing is too important to be settled merely with talk. As you will understand, a serious conversation requires serious conduct."

His eyes were quite disguised by the glassy shine of his spectacles.

Valtz colored, her upper lip curling in disdain, took a paper from an inner pocket, and showed it to Vunsh. "I'm an employee of the Cheka for this region, secretary to the Chief."

Her chocolate eyes modestly withdrew beneath her eyelashes. "I hope you are now convinced and can appreciate what a very delicate and risky matter this is. Or would you rather have the Chief come here himself?" she ended arrogantly.

"Oh, yes, indeed, we understand." Politely, and as though embarrassed, Vunsh interrupted her, handed her back the paper with the photograph attached.

"What's to be done now?" Vunsh turned to Chotkin.

"I don't know," answered the other despairingly. "You know I haven't got so much."

"When must you have it?" Vunsh turned back to Valtz.

"At twelve noon tomorrow you must bring me the whole amount, and the same evening Pyotr Chotkin will be free. Otherwise you'll never see him again. In actual fact," she awkwardly tried to cover herself, "he has acted so rashly that he should really pay the extreme penalty for what he did, and if I, an old acquaintance of his, had not had the chance to persuade an important person, you would never, even by the greatest sacrifice, have the chance to save him." She shot a sly glance at Vunsh.

"But—pardon me—what guarantee have we that you'll release him after you have the gold?"

"Well, I ask you, who would be so foolish as to make every effort to save him from death without being certain of a reward?" Valtz's words came out with a rush; she pouted sulkily.

"You'll excuse me," his spectacles gleaming, Vunsh dwelt deliberately on his words, "but you are in the position to rearrest him if we don't fulfill our part of the obligation. There is no risk in it for you: we are all in your hands, as he is." Without taking his eyes off the blushing Valtz, he rocked backward and forward in his chair.

"That is a false representation of the Cheka." She spoke slowly, clumsily. Trying to conceal her confusion, she mentally ran over a thousand ways of escaping the noose that Vunsh had thrown about her.

"The Chief hasn't the right to release a prisoner one day and rearrest him the next. He has to justify his actions to the High Commission, which doesn't always agree with him—or the amount of gold asked for would be five times greater than now," Valtz pertly ended the sentence, delighted at her own ingenuity. Triumphantly she met Vunsh's eyes. "The need for this whole conversation in general is beyond me. The terms of my proposal are clear and definite. If you can't, or won't, accept it," she turned to Chotkin with an abrupt movement as though she were about to rise, "then I can only get on my way."

Anna Zakharyevna's gray mouth again squared itself. She raised her handkerchief to her eyes. Chotkin, bereft of strength, his lower lip drooping, threw Valtz a beseeching look of utter despair, but she was looking at Vunsh, who, chattering with exaggerated politeness, again bent his head toward her.

"No need to go, no need to go. We are agreed. We shall make every effort to have the entire amount ready; only, we most respectfully ask you to be patient for a while, should we not be able to raise quite all of it before tomorrow. Ivan Petrovich is very far from possessing such assets; all his valuables were confiscated from the safe-deposit. He must make the rounds of his old acquaintances to beg from whoever is able to give him anything at all."

He looked deferentially at Chotkin, who nodded his gray head at Vunsh's tactfulness.

"I hope you will not be too demanding," Vunsh looked obsequiously through his spectacles. "And now I have to ask: when and where is the sum to be handed over to you? The thing is not at all without danger, it can have grievous consequences both for us and for you."

"Then this is what we'll do," decided Valtz. "You have the

gold ready, and tomorrow I'll come here with a duplicate of the order for Pyotr Ivanovich's release, which you will hold as an insurance and guarantee that we are fulfilling our part of the agreement. And the same evening, or the next day at the latest, Pyotr Ivanovich will be here himself."

"Very well," chirped Vunsh.

"Very well," whispered Chotkin.

"Very well," murmured Anna Zakharyevna.

"Then good-bye till tomorrow at twelve!" Valtz got up energetically. "Only, please see you observe one important condition: not a word of this to Pyotr Ivanovich or to anyone else."

"Oh, mercy, you can be sure of that." Again Vunsh made his foot-scraping little bow.

Valtz shook hands with each of them and with a silky-soft rustle went out, brightening the long-undisturbed dust of that gloomy room with the shine of her fiery hair, like a splendor amid rubble. Behind her, gray and withered, Vunsh shuffled over the parquet floor and behind him came the swaying, melancholy figures of the grizzled Chotkins.

She passed through the upholstered room, then the large drawing room, and the dining room with the canary and the green glass oil lamp for the icon. She heard the clatter of utensils in the kitchen, and then the ordeal was at an end. She ran down the stairs, across the courtyard and, once in the street, the joy of liberation came over her. Now Valtz walked more slowly, drew in a deep breath, and audibly expelled it: "Ooff!"

All night long, however, she could not sleep. A sense of dreadfulness lay deep in her mind. Nor could she bury the insistent feeling under multitudes of trivial, humdrum considerations. In the morning she awoke, with wandering and confused thoughts. The weather was cloudy. She had a vague awareness of an immense load weighing on her. By making a special effort of will, she managed to restore order and clarity to her mind.

Now, quick! Put an end to this affair!

She was not aware how swiftly she made the journey to her office to take out the now notorious records. It was only agreeable to think that it was not all a dream and that there was only one obstacle now before Chotkin went free and she got the gold, and so much of it. She was seized with a fit of trembling as, the file held tight under her arm, she knocked timidly on Zudin's door: "May I come in?"

Zudin leaned back exhausted, with an unquiet expression in his half-closed eyes.

"I've come about a very unusual matter, Aleksey Ivanovich. Good morning."

"Good morning."

"This is the file on the Chotkin case. There's an order entered in the records: 'To be released,' but–Chotkin is *still* in custody."

"Who's in custody?" he queried absently, his thoughts elsewhere.

"Here's the order to Investigator Verekhleev that the prisoner is to be released and the case closed. Somehow or other it came to my notice that the prisoner is still in custody, and it will soon be more than three months since the order was given."

"That's right," said Zudin, scarcely disturbed. "Very well, leave it here. I'll look into the matter." He ran his fingers through his hair and made as if to bury himself once more in his papers.

Valtz shuddered as with sudden cold. Her shoes squeaked as she crossed the carpet. "It would only need a second Aleksey Ivanovich. Won't you look into it now? The order is here, right enough, you certainly have read it, only you forgot to endorse it. Isn't it a shame that the man should have had to stay in custody so long and nobody noticed?"

How friendly, candid, and at the same time insinuating her voice was. Valtz was astonished at herself: who else could speak to him like that? Her lashes lowered their delicate lace over her eyes. She's as pretty as a picture, thought Zudin. Reluctantly, he left his own work and turned to Valtz standing beside him.

"There! You see?" The document lay before him.

A rosy, enameled finger, like a thin flute of precious china, ran over the paper.

Yes, it was written: "To be released. Investigator Verekhleev."

Zudin sighed wearily and wrote with a freshly sharpened quill at the top of the paper: "This case is closed."

"What's his name?"

"Chotkin."

Yes, Chotkin, he saw it himself.

"Chotkin is to be released. Zudin."

Why this eagerness on Valtz's part? He looked searchingly into her eyes. He riffled through the file; the case was a brief one; he again scrutinized the italicized portions, comments, and dates. There was nothing suspicious. The case had been satisfactorily closed. He found no grounds for uneasiness. Chotkin had been kept in custody through an oversight. Or was he, Zudin, tired now, should he once more check through the matter, dropping it now for the time being? He wondered doubtfully.

Horst burst into the room. "Aleksey Ivanovich!" His hands were trembling, his blue eyes staring. "Katzmann's been killed!

Dagnis has been wounded and Katzmann killed. They're being brought here at once."

"How's that—killed?" The room swam before him. He cried out like a wounded beast. A shaft of thoughts, piercing and sharp, flashed in an electric storm behind his eyes. The file he had taken from the desk dropped onto one of the overturned bottles in the corner; it began to roll over and over as he stared at Horst. "How killed, where?"

"The Section Chief Kuntsevich just phoned from the station. Katzmann was killed this morning in an exchange of fire with a Social Revolutionary unit in Osennikov. Dagnis was wounded. One S.R. was shot down. The rest got away. We've put cordons around the place."

"Oh, the scoundrels!" In his rage Zudin spat copiously. "The villains! Now tell me if those Judases shouldn't be exterminated! Katzmann killed. Oh, there's no Abram any more." Zudin gave a deep, weary groan. "He took the risk too soon, he attempted too much," he muttered to himself. "Oh, what a shame, what a shame, Horst, that this should happen to Katzmann! No more Abram!" Zudin could not smother his distress.

Horst was silent, biting his lips.

"Just wait! They'll regret the day! I'll go to the station myself at once, and you send off a telegram right away to Moscow and a copy to the Central Committee, I'll sign it at once. Yes, and we must call Ignatyev—where's Fomin? And bring me a list of persons in custody. I'll have a hundred shot—I'll make a funeral pyre. Poor Abram! Those devils'll find out what it is to murder one of our head workers! There are some files here. . . ."

Mad with rage, Zudin swept the files off the desk. "Don't spare any of them! We answer terror with terror; for one individual we strike the whole class!"

Valtz's heart turned cold. Katzmann's murder and Zudin's sudden uncontrolled rage appalled her. And then the files swept onto the floor in utter disorder, with Chotkin's papers among them!

Can this be pure coincidence? Through a simple accident? When it was all so nearly over? Valtz's teeth chattered audibly.

Like a raging whirlwind Zudin stormed out of the room. In silent distress Horst began to assemble the files. Their order abolished, they lay strewn in every direction.

"This is one of mine," said Valtz, and swooped down on the edge of the familiar file.

"He said to leave none!"

"Yes, but this is an order he signed himself! This is a closed case. It really isn't right to rearrest and shoot a man who's innocent and has already been released, just because of an unforeseen accident!"

She snatched the file out of Horst's hand and went out of the room. Only quick now, in case anything else happens to keep the order back. She ran straight in to Shalenko.

"Konstantin Konstantinovich! Write me out this judgment quickly: Zudin's order's on it. But please let me have a copy. The released man's old mother is waiting downstairs, I want to make her happy!"

"What do you want a copy for? It isn't necessary. He's free, that's all there is to it."

"Now, really, what does it matter to you? Don't want to waste a small piece of paper, is that it? You *are* tough! I asked Aleksey Ivanovich and he approved it." She was red to the tips of her ears with agitation.

"Oh, all right, all right," yielded Shalenko, "I'll do it, wait a moment. Only, you're wrong to show this case so much sympathy, Elena Valentinovna, when Abram Moiseich has just been killed. Poor man, what a shame! He was a good and noble human being. And how he worked!"

But Elena could hardly bear the impatience that was needling her; oh, quick, quick, it's almost one o'clock!

At last it was done. She raced, gasping and stumbling, past boarded-up windows, their glass shattered, past peeling paint-work, men's clothing stores. Empty store windows stared like the eye sockets of fleshless skulls.

Here was the house at last, protected by the stillness of that dying street of unconsidered people who crept about like worms. She went flying up the wet, slippery stairs to the third floor. Chotkin himself opened the door and, his eyes blinking under their shaggy brows, asked her: "Now what's been done?"

"It's all ready. Here's the order, and the copy I hand over to you. He'll be freed this evening. Then he should get away, to the country somewhere, and at once; who knows what can happen?"

The old woman crossed herself piously.

The first thing Elena noticed were Ivan Petrovich's withered cheeks, haggard and sunken, and the masked and turgid gray gaze of the fidgety Vunsh.

Hands trembling, Chotkin brought a canvas bag out of the bedroom and placed it before Valtz on the table. "There are nineteen pounds here, please be so good as to weigh it." He pulled forward a pair of kitchen scales.

"You must believe us, we could not raise more, and to get this my wife and I had to spend the whole night on our knees before our acquaintances. It is hard for people to understand another's misery. Ah, very hard! There is one gram short of nineteen pounds. We crawled on our knees to get it. Indeed, to get three pounds we had to make twenty-seven attempts."

The old woman's eyes were wet and red-rimmed with weeping, she was wrinkled, hugely fat, tottering, a fountain of tears.

"Have pity on us, have pity, in Christ's name!"

Valtz made a grimace of distaste. Only to be gone, to be done with her part in this silly farce. Hastily she shook out the jingling gold onto the table.

Great God! What riches: bracelets, rings, pendants, chains, watches, and round gold coins leaping forth as though alive, and so much, so much. Like firebirds, they streamed before her.

"That's all right, the one I give it to will check it. And as for the remainder, you must get it as soon as possible, in a very few days. Otherwise, he won't show any leniency. And if he finds you've offered him anything of inferior value, you'll have to make up for it. What's agreed is agreed." Her hasty fingers quivering with joy, she carefully put the mass of gold back in the little bag, fastened it, and stuffed it inside her coat.

How heavy it was!

She had left the copy of the order lying carelessly on the table; as a token guarantee she handed it over to the Chotkins. Vunsh pounced on it and carefully examined the seal. She was put to it to parry their questions.

"When will they let Petitchka out?"

"Is there any chance they will let us down?"

"Is Petitchka alive?"

"Is he well?"

"How long before he'll be here?"

"He'll come home today!"

In a frenzy of haste she got away. Hurriedly but carefully, so as not to trip. The little bag was stuffed under her coat. She turned the corner.

People coming across an acquaintance in the street would silently look deep into each other's eyes, look cautiously around them.

"Have you heard they've killed one of the Cheka higher-ups over in Osennikov?"

"What's that you say?"

"It's true!" Joyfully, "It's the last of the New Era!" And again, secretively, "and did you know that a Moravian king, Belinder, has landed with a terrible submarine to fight them with? No? It's true! Now you can be certain: in a week the Bolshevik supremacy will be over and done with! I have it from a very reliable source."

5

In Zudin's office the window was open. From the street came the rumble of wheels, and from the gutter, the splash of dripping water.

The blue room, where for a long time now the stove had not been lit, smelled of mildew. Beyond the open window stretched the fresh, sunny skies of spring.

Zudin's jaw was covered with stubble. He was in a ratlike rage as he sat at his desk, chewing his pencil. This vile hunting of him was getting too much. He would not endure it any longer. He thumped the desk with such force that the inkstand jingled and the penholder fell to the floor. He raised his clenched fist at some invisible foe—no one else was there with him in the room.

It was all clear now. Fomin wanted to entrench himself behind him. Through Ignatyev, he was plotting against Zudin. Zudin was sensitive to the veiled hints and oblique glances thrown him by the comrades of the Party Committee. He would show them! Everything must be brought out into the open.

"Pull yourself together, Alik," he told himself aloud in a broken, exhausted voice. "Pull yourself together and show you're a match for any of them!"

This thought so assuaged him that he got up and took a turn back and forth across the soft unswept carpet.

How slyly these scoundrels conduct their campaigns, he thought, his anger rising. Friendly cooperation to his face, secrets and underhandedness behind his back. Was this then, the hostility, competition, and crafty, mean-minded ambition that had prevailed in the old social order, was this what he, Zudin, had so fervently fought, and continued to fight against? Zudin shook himself and raised his clenched fist. Was this accursed rule truly so powerful that it could corrode what was most sacred and mighty in Zudin's understanding: the Communist Party? A troubled expression crept to his face.

Zudin could remember how once during his exile he had been laid low with severe chills in a Siberian village and had asked for tea. Sokov, his morose, bitter companion, had refused to warm some up for him. Zudin had had to get up, though feverish, teeth chattering, and run several times into the forest for wood to make a fire. He could hold up his feverish head only with the thought that soon he would be drinking hot tea. But when he came back with his last load of wood, it turned out that Sokov had profited by his absence to drink all the brewed tea himself. It was a bitter thing, a wounding thing. Besides, that Sokov, jeering at Zudin, had later boasted about this and, in the presence of others, called Zudin a yokel and a boor.

That had happened, though, in the years of failure, when their common concerns and common hopes had grown rusty with defeatism. But now, when they had won such a fabulous victory, when, by having taken those first steps of national revolution, they had made a beginning on the noble edifice of world revolution—where, now, was the comradely cohesion, the brotherly self-sacrifice, and the deep sincerity? They now have many more enemies, thirsty for their blood, stronger and more cunning than ever. Did not he, the Chief of the all-powerful Cheka in a large city, often see himself as a great green grasshopper sitting on the limb of a tree from which he could be cast down by any wild outcropping of capitalism? Should they not all stand together as one? And yet—envy, Communist pride, revolutionary hypocrisy! That red fox Fomin was an example of it. Rage boiled and surged in Zudin's breast.

"Enough!" he shouted. "Enough! I'll put an end to all this!"

There was a knock at the door and Lipshaevich slunk into the room.

"May I have a moment of your time, Aleksey Ivanovich? I have something to tell you." He darted an uneasy eye around the room.

"I have to warn you." He drew up close to Zudin and hurriedly whispered in his ear: "They're setting a trap for you, they're determined to get you somehow. I swear to God I'm thinking only of your good: without you, we're all done for. Beware of Fomin: he's up to something; this evening Pavolv and Valtz were arrested, nobody knows by whom."

This revolted Zudin. He had no faith in Lipshaevich. He was repelled by the other's eyes, at once insolent and unctuous, in which he had found only compliance or obsequiousness, and by his gangster's dirty tone of complicity. Besides, he knew that Pavlov had never been trustworthy, and that he should long have been kicked out of the Cheka. The effect of Lipshaevich's words was to fill him with bitter rage.

Arrested! On what grounds, where? And above all, without his—Zudin's—knowledge? That meant he was no longer trusted. Very well, then, let that be the last drop that brought the mass of his passions to overflowing. After the information Lipshaevich had brought him, it was no longer possible to play any game of concealment. Very well, then, very well! he roared inwardly, hunching his shoulders and rubbing his hands, grown cold—from an inner nervous chill, or from a fresh breeze blown in through the open window?

"I don't understand what's bothering you." He turned on Lipshaevich with contempt. "I'm not afraid of intrigue: my conscience is calm and clear." Scornfully, he observed Lipshaevich's disconcerted air as he crept out of the room.

He hurled himself onto the telephone and called Ignatyev. "I'd like to speak to you on an urgent matter. May I come and see you at once?"

"Please do, this is most opportune; I'm expecting you."

"Very well."

He drew a breath of relief, taking strength from the knowledge that he had done no wrong. He called for a motor, then took a sheet of paper, smoothed it, and wrote out a telegram:

Moscow. To Chief of Soviet Commission for Extraordinary Affairs. Copy to the Central Committee of the Soviet Communist Party. Secret. Urgent. Please relieve me of my duties. Am tired of intrigues. Zudin.

He folded the paper, put it in the pocket of his worn and shabby coat, and went out. His heart was gay and sturdy.

Once in the street, he heard the rumble of a fierce bombardment in the far distance. Passers-by stopped timorously, listening with keen ears, murmuring among themselves.

Splashing through the slush, frowning, in small groups, bearing rifles, wearing caps and capes, workers were passing on their way to somewhere. Sailors in pea jackets crossed the street, their bell-bottomed trousers flapping. In the distance, across the bridge, a long, gray, swarming mass of soldiers crept along.

Reinforcements, thought Zudin. We should be talking things over today with the Head of the Special Department. But, he recalled, all this now had been unnecessarily aborted and ruined. He, Zudin, was not needed any more.

At the street corners, like black heaps of cockroaches, the bystanders stood glued to the newspapers pasted on the walls.

Yes, the enemy is near. The enemy is at the gates.

Sending up spray from a puddle, the motor drew up in front of the Central Committee building, a great yellow edifice with a columned front. Zudin went quietly up the spiral staircase, its walls decorated with flags and portraits of the leaders of the Party. He went past the sentries, along the corridor, through the waiting room and the secretary's office to Ignatyev's room.

"One second, I'll announce you!" The secretary leaped up and rushing to the door, shut it in Zudin's face.

This unusual reception wounded Zudin still further and roused afresh his anger at Fomin, at Ignatyev, at the whole world, which seemed to have agreed to conspire against Zudin, simple and trustworthy though he had always been.

"This way, please!" The secretary darted out. Ignatyev was sitting as always in his armchair at the desk. Near him, on a small leather sofa, sat Comrade Shustry, a little man in a raincoat, who looked at Zudin with dark, searching eyes.

"Back from Moscow? When?"

"Day before yesterday."

"Anything happening up there?"

"Nothing in particular."

No further conversation. In any case, Zudin had little appetite for one. He had come for another reason. And since Ignatyev, his chin in his hand, made no move to get Shustry to leave, it might be a trick to avoid his giving Zudin an explanation of Fomin's actions. Zudin would stand for it no longer. Enough lies! Hot and angry, he sat down in an armchair by the desk.

"I've come to see you, Comrade Ignatyev," he said in a distinct dry tone, so that Shustry should hear, "to let you know I am giving up my post!" He moved his hand to his pocket to take out the telegram.

"We know," said Ignatyev, quietly.

"*We know?*" stammered Zudin, and looked at both in inquiring astonishment.

"All the better for that. Since your comrades are so ingenious and calculating in their work that they can foresee events, somebody's going to be the recipient of it all." He laughed caustically. "I telegraphed the Party and asked the Organization Bureau for an investigation."

"The Organization Bureau also knows about the case, Comrade Zudin," shrilled Ignatyev's high voice. "They've already appointed Comrade Shustry here to carry out the investigation."

The latter, clearly enjoying the effect these words were having, handed Zudin his letter of appointment. Signed by a personage of high standing, it ordered Shustry to investigate Zudin's case. Zudin gave a nervous start. So his enemies had really got down to work: now they had contrived to make out "a case" against him. And he, like a fool, had unfalteringly placed his trust in the brotherliness of his Party comrades. So the maxim applied here, too: war is war!

Suddenly, somewhere, that old habit, that powerful, trusty structure, Zudin's understanding of the world, emitted a deep groan and toppled. And after the collapse, all that remained was gray rubble and clouds of dust. "I'm ready!" he said contemptuously to Shustry. "I should like to bring to your notice the fact that certain acts of insubordination have been carried out in the Cheka without my knowledge. This evening, two of my workers were arrested. This isn't the first time Fomin has taken it on himself to . . . ."

"Fomin had nothing to do with that; your workers were

arrested at my order!" interrupted Shustry. "Comrade Ingatyev, is there a free room we might use where we might, as it were, speak openly?" Shustry whinnied slyly.

"There is such a room." Ignatyev pressed a bell. "The secretary will show you the way."

"By the way," Shustry turned to Zudin as the latter stood gazing at Ignatyev, "may I have your revolver?" Zudin handed him the revolver. Shustry pushed it into his trouser pocket.

"Would you have another one on your person?"

"No."

Having taken Zudin to the door, he turned back to Ignatyev and whispered something in his ear; the other nodded.

How loathsome all this is! Zudin shuddered with repugnance. "This pathetic conspiring right in front of me—how guilefully it's all being carried out. That man Ignatyev. Just you wait, my friend, we'll see how the cards fall."

They went up to a remote room on the third floor, where there stood only a table and three stools. The window gave out onto the river and revealed a watch tower standing in the sun.

Shustry closed the door and locked it carefully with a key he had been given. He sat down at the table and spread out before him a great sheaf of papers he had taken from his briefcase. He made a show of assiduously searching for something among the papers. Black eyebrows knit, black eyes protruding noticeably from the yellow of the face, and the gray of the close-cropped head with the short-cropped silvery moustache.

"The Cheka hereby brings an accusation against you," he began familiarly, like a slinking tomcat, and his eyes roamed over the table and the papers and came to rest on Zudin's sleeve, as if he were afraid to meet his eye. "An accusation, the gist of which you must already be quite aware."

"I don't care to fuss with deciphering sordid gossip."

"We shall soon decipher whether it is gossip or something else," chirped Shustry, as if jesting on Zudin's account. "And therefore, will you kindly tell me, *Comrade* Zudin—"the word "comrade" rang deliberately false, as if someone in greeting had pushed a toad into your hand. Zudin perceived all this, conscious of the rage mounting inside him. "Tell me, Comrade Zudin: when, from whom, and in what amount, have you accepted bribes?"

If a cannon had been abruptly let off in front of Zudin, the shock of the report could not have been more shattering. All the muscles of his face began working, his nostrils flared, his eyes widened in hatred and disdain, his teeth burrowed into his lower lip.

"Now, which is it to be, Comrade Zudin?" mocked Shustry

with feigned good humor. "Will you answer the question at once, or would you like to think about it?"

"I consider your question a shameful attempt to wrong me." Zudin brought out the words in a strange, falling tone.

"All right, all right!" Shustry gave a friendly laugh. "I'd forgotten what an experienced man you are. Who would be such a fool as to take a bribe when there's such an institution as a secretary, particularly a lady secretary, to do it for him? A convenient arrangement: a pretty young woman to perform all these transactions in all security, and be a bedfellow into the bargain; but the best of it all is, it's so easy with her assistance to fill one's pockets. Isn't it so, Comrade Zudin?"

He laughed, and the black of his eyes flickered over Zudin's frozen mind as he sat there motionless.

"I have no woman secretary, and I do not understand your allusions. If you are in possession of concrete evidence, it is your duty to pass it on to me. That would be much better than speaking in riddles," said Zudin, and he thought: can all this be some senseless dream?

"Oh, that's how it is! Anyone as composed as that is no thief. Then we shall have to proceed in another way," says Shustry, smacking his lips at the pleasurable prospect. "You are no boy, and by no means new to the Party, not to be able to understand that your lack of sincerity and your denials somewhat qualify your standing in the eyes of the Cheka and cause your actions to appear in a special light."

"What has the Cheka to do with it?" Zudin broke in angrily, in a fresh surge of rage. The desire overtook him to smash this addle-pated idiot's skull.

"I am investigating the circumstances by order of the Cheka!" said Shustry, bridling with self-satisfaction.

Once more Zudin felt his world disintegrating. Fishing in his briefcase, Shustry pulled out a sheet of paper and addressed himself to Zudin with the easy solicitude of an undertaker measuring a corpse and asking the customary questions—age, social position, and so on—writing down the answers on the paper before him.

"Can you recall any occasion on which you received any kind of gift in any shape or form from your subordinates?"

"No, I cannot."

"Splendid. We'll put that down: 'Cannot recall.' Not from Valtz, for example?"

Bright red spread over Zudin's face. He thought, how could he have forgotten that? How the devil will this look to them?

"One should not receive bribes in person: it is much more prudent to do so through one's relatives," sneered Shustry.

"I am aware that once, without my knowledge, my wife allowed herself to accept some trifling gift from Valtz."

"'Without my knowledge'—excellent! Then why didn't you take the trouble to return that 'trifling gift?' But that's only by the way. Now tell me, Comrade Zudin, what would you call a 'trifling gift?' Would you consider twenty pounds in gold a 'trifling gift,' for example?" Shustry's little eyes buried themselves in the papers.

Zudin's hands began to quake, as if he were in a rattling wagon, his thoughts dispersed. He felt distinctly the nearness of danger, he made a motion to stand up, but his legs seemed to fold. With his remaining strength he took off his coat and seated himself, feeling somewhat easier.

"I'm only just beginning to realize that there has been some drastic misunderstanding here that someone has made use of to provide the grounds in this ridiculous case." Zudin clearly had trouble in bringing out his words. "Who it was that made use of it, and to what purpose, is what has to be found out. I would not be an old Party member—a loyal member since 1903—and I would not have suffered exile and prison if I did not believe in the justness and the discernment of the Party."

Shustry uttered an evil laugh. "Perhaps you would be so good as to give a straight answer to the question: do you know yourself to be guilty of taking gifts of any sort at all from Valtz and others?"

"Set your mind at rest. I shall reply openly and honestly."

"That may very well be. Only, your future hangs on the degree of sincerity with which you reply."

"My own future is of little interest to me. *Our* future is all that concerns me."

"That's good. I'll make a note of it in your favor. Well?"

"Well, I am aware that my wife accepted a pair of silk stockings from Valtz, in fact, I believe, two pairs—I don't exactly know. Besides that, she accepted two pairs of children's stockings and a few bars of chocolate for the children, also from Valtz. That is all. There was no other gift from Valtz, nor from anyone else, to the best of my knowledge and belief."

"Splendid. First, from nobody at all, then from Valtz through your wife; first, it's one pair of stockings, then, maybe two, and then it's two. A slow-working memory. (That's just by the way.)"

"I know this, Comrade Yuzhanin!" Shustry's prerevolutionary name suddenly came back to Zudin. "I am a Bolshevik of old standing; I have never been, nor will I be, anything else, and I declare to you as a comrade and as a Cheka official that I am telling you the complete truth. If you want to believe me, that is your affair."

In an insulting manner, Shustry drummed his fingers on the table.

"On the other hand, I myself was once a Menshevik, as you know, but never, either then or now, have I or my relatives for me accepted bribes, whether stockings, candy, or gold. That's all by the way. But what about the gold? Did you think it proper to take it or not?"

"I tell you yet again: I have taken no gold and. . . . "

"And your wife?"

Out of nowhere the mocking face of insinuation suddenly grinned at Zudin. Supposing his wife had really . . . ? Lisa? No, that's out of the question, it couldn't be, said Zudin, like a lost man, to himself.

"You wouldn't guarantee it?"

If he would guarantee it? His shoulders jerked convulsively as he looked in vain for help from the cold, dismal walls.

"So you won't guarantee it? Sensible of you!"

Shustry wrote something.

You artful journalist, thought Zudin, and his head swam with a sharp, vile scent that, as it seemed, emanated from Shustry. That steel-hardened brow could not relate to pathos.

"Now, how much do you know about Pavlov? How much did he share with you, or—pardon—with your wife? Or has your memory left you in the lurch again?"

Biting his lips till they bled, Zudin was silent a few seconds. "I repeat that, beside the instance I have already spoken about, I have absolutely no knowledge of my wife's ever having taken any sort of gift, whether in kind or cash, from any person, and I consider it to be absolutely out of the question, inasmuch as I know and trust her. I ask you to make a note of that, too."

"Do you recall that Katzmann tried to impress upon you the necessity for immediately dismissing Pavlov and Valtz, and that you put him off?"

Zudin racked his brains in the effort to recall this.

"You don't remember? Comrade Fomin very definitely affirms that this was so; indeed, Katzmann himself told him about it. Why should they both have lied?"

"In connection with Pavlov, I remember that my suspicions were the first to have been roused, particularly after the Bocharkin case, and I apprised Katzmann of this. I believe I spoke of it at length to Katzmann some time later, and he said he considered it imperative that Pavlov and, I believe, Valtz should be discharged."

"What does that mean, 'And, you believe, Valtz?'"

"And, I believe, Valtz." Zudin reddened. "I told him that I was in complete agreement with him over Pavlov, as at that time certain other machinations of Pavlov's over that diamond affair were known to us, but as concerning Valtz, I considered his argument groundless, and he then said he agreed with me."

"Obviously, it was going to be 'groundless,' after the nice gifts she had given your wife. Anyhow, that's all by the way, not pertinent to the case. So, concerning Valtz, you were not in agreement, whereas, concerning Pavlov, you were entirely of one mind? We'll write that down. Now can you tell me why you didn't dismiss Pavlov on the spot? At least, Pavlov?"

Why didn't I dismiss him? thought Zudin, but could find no answer.

"It was a mistake on my part, an oversight," he muttered in distress. "I didn't think of doing it then because of the pressure of work; when Katzmann was killed, I was very much occupied with other matters."

"Splendid! Now, Comrade Zudin, will you kindly tell me what your relations were with Valtz? I mean, of course, your intimate relations?"

"I fail to see what possible connection—"

"Ah, you 'fail to see'! Very well, we'll make a note of that. All the same, I must categorically insist on an answer to my question."

"There were no relations between Valtz and myself."

"You call your being found next to each other on the sofa at night, 'no relations?' Have I understood you correctly?"

"This is really too vile to be borne!" Zudin, red with indignation and embarrassment, could hardly control himself. "I have said what I have to say and will say nothing further on the subject."

"Very good, very good! Now, as to the confiscated wine in your office: do you recall having drunk it yourself or having given it to someone else? Pavlov testified that the wine found in his apartment came from your office. What do you have to say to that?"

"Confiscated wine and other objects often come into my office. I neither drank it nor gave it to anybody. No, wait, I do remember once having drunk a bottle of light wine when I was very tired. How the wine got to Pavlov's apartment, I have no idea; my office is always locked, and the key is kept by the attendant."

Shustry wrote rapidly. "Now, that's enough for me. Would you be so kind as to read this all through and sign it?" He laid the document before Zudin and stretched himself wearily. Then he ran to the door and called to someone in the corridor.

"You are an excellent man, Comrade Zudin, and yet at the start you tried to play hide-and-go-seek with me."

"*I*? *Play* with you?"

"Well, never mind, never mind. In any event, that was only my personal impression. The case will come before an Extraordinary Commission, which is to meet in a few days. My duty was only to make a report. My part is a small one. I have to be absolutely objective. You saw for yourself that I noted everything down, not only things that go against you, but also things in your favor. I have been altogether objective. Now allow me to have you placed under arrest."

Though Zudin had felt that all this coming, yet the sense of insult and bitterness overwhelmed him. "I shan't run away anywhere. Aren't you going to allow me to see my family?"

"Absolutely out of the question! You may write, but must remain here in this room, under guard. Don't excite yourself. Your case will be decided upon in two or three days at the most. What the decision is will depend on the Commission's conclusions. My business is only to be an impartial observer. And should anything occur to you that might exonerate you, write it down and send it to me through Ignatyev's secretary; I'll tell them to send you paper and pencil. Your food will be brought to you from the Executive's Commissary."

Shustry disappeared. Zudin sat and looked dully out onto the river's wide sunlit bank. The square of the window gave this spacious, empty room the plain charm of a country sitting room. The ice floes breaking up on the river's surface were like jagged teeth. And farther, beyond the river, workers' cottages spread, like series of boxes in the sun. All at once, the dreadfulness of what had happened vanished, it forcibly withdrew into the depths of the soul, to be replaced on surface by a youthful feeling of liberation, as though the iron works, where he had hastened daily to his work, had suddenly been closed down, and he might romp and frolic to his heart's content without a second thought. He was seized with a soft, warm sense of airiness and space, of freedom.

This feeling did not stay with him for long. Boots clumping, a guard strode in, scrutinized both him and the room in an unfriendly, searching fashion, went to the window, tested the bolt, and went straight out again to stand directly in front of the door, hitting the floor with his rifle butt.

Then two young women in white aprons came in from the Commissary, the double doors were both flung open, and an iron bedstead with a straw-filled pillow and a rough cover was brought in. They asked him if he wanted anything to eat. No, he wanted nothing, only to be brought pencil and paper.

Pencil and paper were soon brought by Ignatyev's secretary himself, with a look of harassment and discomfort in his eyes that embittered Zudin's resentment all the more.

"I want to write to my wife, and I should like it taken to my home as soon as possible. Can it be done?"

"Yes, Comrade Shustry will come at six o'clock; he'll read it through, and I'm sure he'll send it on at once."

"Thank you."

Zudin wished only to be left alone with his swelling impressions of what had occurred; rounding and tightening into lumps of lead, they pressed upon his aching heart. He sat down on the creaking bed with its bristly straw filling and pressed his temples with both hands. He must keep calm, pull himself together. Of precisely what was he being accused? One thing was certain: Pavlov and Valtz had been taken in the act. What was the gold they were said to have taken? Who had taken it? Pavlov? Yes, there had been negligence. But what had he, Zudin, to do with it? Was it the fact that he had not dismissed him? Or was it that Valtz had taken the amount of gold? Could she have shared it with Lisa? Would Lisa have accepted it?

A succession of shocks went over him. He twisted convulsively, his breath caught painfully in his chest. Vividly he could imagine what would be done to Lisa, if it had really happened. Oh, if only he knew it had not! If only it could turn out to be an idle suspicion. Had Lisa not been able, then, to see through all that?

He rooted for an answer in her soul. No, Lisa could never have done such a thing, no; whatever might come, she stood firmly by the proletarian convictions, her consciousness of the proletarian class conflict. She was a Communist, in spite of everything.

He smiled indulgently: he knew her frailties, her faltering constancy. She had never engaged in any active struggle. She was a true daughter of her class, but also a wife and a mother. If both sides of her existence were to be placed on the scales, they would come down on the side of the wife and mother. She was therefore not to be condemned; it was the eternal stipulation that women bound to primitive emotions and instincts had to submit to the yoke of the husband and provider. It was hard to change all that from one moment to the next, thought Zudin.

But will she be shot for it? His hair stood on end at the thought. He saw Lisa and her calm smile, Lisa as a girl, Lisa, her head tied in a scarf, with dimples in her round cheeks. It was spring, as it was now, when, full of awkward zeal and unshed tears of happiness, he had taken her rough, workworn fingers in his hand,—but tenderly, as he would a little flower in bloom—and looking into her misty gray eyes had said:

"Lisochka! We'll live together, and fight together, and suffer together, and love together, as man and wife."

How long, ah, how long ago that was! Zudin's shoulders drooped at the remembrance of past emotions. And afterward? Had he been able to keep his word? No, he had to admit he had not. Lisa had shown herself to be as true and as loving a wife as there ever was. He had forgotten that behind her lay a thousand years of unprotesting slavery and, furthermore, that she was the wife of a domineering, masterful man. And was she, then, capable of understanding all his feelings, the joys and sorrows of his struggles, caged as she was with cooking and screaming children, while the storm of life raged outside?

He swam in the flood of emotion. He had fought, sleeves rolled back, with the steel of his gray eyes. He came to Lisa only to take a breather, to eat, to drink, and to see his children, who turned their round, innocent children's eyes on their papa and reached up their little hands to him. He had drawn farther and farther away from her, but Lisa had stayed constantly alone in that dead, putrid place. Her cheeks had faded, the light in her eyes had gone out, and her back was bent from hard work. He had let her down, and the farther he went, the deeper became his betrayal of her. How was it he had only now been able to see clearly and distinctly that he had used her cruelly, shamefully, that he had taken a mean advantage of her helplessness, her wifely simplicity, her wifely love? The symphony of miraculous love he had dreamed of had become nothing more than a street-organ tune.

And if she was now to be taken out and shot, he, and only he, would be her murderer.

His throat contracted with pity and sorrow.

But could he have behaved otherwise? Could he have given up his struggle, his suffering, for the happiness of all mankind, to avoid the sorrows of a loving wife? Besides, had he not paid too dearly for having bound himself to a family? Had he not often let his arm fall because of the whimpers of hungry children—no child should take the place of a worker—having raised his hand to strike a blow, only to let it fall, shamefaced; had he not, with downcast eyes, raised the hammer in work, feeling on him the mocking grin of necessity? Who was to blame? The insatiable, inflated Moloch, who sat enthroned in the blood and the brain? Oh, if only he could dwindle to the size of—a bee? a bullet?—no: to a scarcely visible needle, that would go unnoticed and strike the triumphant Colossus in the middle of his forehead, which on the instant would burst, with a hiss like a gas-filled balloon, to the accompaniment of joyous laughter from free men. Childish fancies! This was the most serious matter of all. Lisa was all but lost.

Yet, supposing she had not taken any gold? Joyfully, Zudin jumped to his feet and went over to the window. Was it right that she should be so cruelly punished, simply for taking stockings or chocolate, because she understood nothing of politics and had acted like a devoted mother and wife who had wanted to please her husband? That cursed, vicious, unescapable circle!

"Without my knowledge"—how the words had resounded at the questioning! What did they imply? That if he had known and complied with it, it would have been he who had taken the things, and not his wife? How could he have spoken so thoughtlessly? Had he been anxious about himself? He must write to her at once, so that she would know about this mistake and correct it at the hearing.

He remembered, though, that the letter must pass through Shustry's hands. How irritating to have to use guile and pretense. Guile against whom? Against the comrades he had worked beside? His gaze dropped as he studied the dust on the floor. Then he again looked out of the window at the pure blue sky, the ice floes swimming soft and white on the river, the little houses on the opposite banks, gilded, their windows kissed by the setting sun. He glanced at his watch.

The devil, it was already six! Shustry might quite well have come and gone away again. He must hurry with the letter to Lisa.

What should he write, and how should he write it? Or should he write nothing at all? If only all this could flow as calmly and strongly as that ever-rolling river that knew no law and no boundary. Warmed by the sun, it unfolded its turbid floods, and in the dark blue of the night, it lay quiet and motionless, withdrawn.

He would not go home again soon, perhaps never. What would she think, poor woman, alone with her children? Supposing slanderous tongues should spit the venom of gold, wine, mistresses, into her face? What lay before her, what thoughts, what experiences? What was the purpose of this persistent overwhelming torment that would be so easily wrung from her tender heart?

Zudin sat down at the table and wrote:

Dearest Lisa,

Because of a foolish accident and an inquiry concerning certain misdeeds on the part of Pavlov and Valtz, I shall be kept at the Executive Committee building under house arrest for a very few days. Don't distress yourself and don't worry! There is a mass of absurd accusations, involving wine, money, and love affairs, but these will blow over like smoke. It needs patience and vigilance. So don't be upset, keep your chin up, and kiss the children for me! Valtz has dragged in the stockings and the chocolate we accepted. It is all pure nonsense, of course. A fond embrace and kisses—I'll be seeing you soon.

your Alik.

You have to lie, and lie boldly, he decided, as he finished the letter. He folded it into an envelope and asked the guard at the door to call the secretary. The guard, in a few clumsy strides, knocked at a door. After a long, exasperating wait, a messenger at last appeared.

"Please give this letter to Comrade Ignatyev's secretary. It's urgent."

The messenger nooded and withdrew. Zudin stood like a signpost at a crossroad, looking out indifferently at the red wings of the sunset rising over the blue-gray mists of the river.

6

Zudin stayed in solitary confinement for five days. No one asked for him, no one came. It often occurred to him that, in the restless haste of everyday concerns and the confusion of civil war, he had been forgotten. Somewhere, perhaps even very near, now attacking, now retreating, generals in dusty uniforms with gold braid marched from one village to the next. Some led through the fields from horizon to horizon, hiding naively behind translucent hay stacks or throwing themselves flat on the ground before the invisible missiles, lying with knees pressed together, with clutching knotted fingers.

Zudin did not see a newspaper. Every day he was brought food, which for the most part he left untouched. He grew thin, pallid, his cheeks and eyes, hollow and dull. He fell into a completely disoriented way of life. He barely got up, he slept for as long as it suited him, he woke fortuitously, and waking, did not know whether it was early morning or late at night. Then he would go to the window and try—if the sun was shining—to guess by the light what time it was. Sun-gilded houses or dimly lit barges, it was indifferent to him what he saw through the window. Sitting in the broad, low window embrasure, he could make out a small patch of garden in the courtyard, the lopped black boughs of gray poplars, the narrow cinder paths, the crumpled rotting grass of former years, and withered leaves. The garden was surrounded by a yellow stone wall, along which a sentry with a rifle patrolled back and forth, beneath the window. This meant that Zudin had been not completely forgotten. He often tried to glean some knowledge of the outside world. Once, when his door opened, he sensed a muffled alarm run through the corridor in a succession of waves.

"It's a Soviet assembly," said the woman-servant who had brought in his evening meal. "The Mensheviks and S.R.s are making a big fuss. They're asking for the abolition of the Cheka. There's been an uproar in the city; they're asking for increased rations and are threatening a strike. The workers have refused to go to the front. Krastilitsy is already taken. The communists are all mobilized. And how many new ones came! All for the front!" And she added in a whisper: "They say the workers are preparing a revolt. Maybe they'll free you then. . . ."

Zudin sighed hoarsely.

On the fifth day, quite unexpectedly, when the light was already switched on, the door suddenly opened, and Shustry, wearing his raincoat, darted in and cried, "Come with me!" Escorted by the sentry, they went along the corridor and into a room close by, where some men were already seated at a table. Zudin had known them all for a long time; their faces were now as if painted with expressions of gravity. Zudin's eyes fell first on Tkacheev, an old Party worker, whom he knew only a little and in the past had most often met at assemblies; his expression was calm and venerable, like that of a country priest, pulling with visible pride at his thick, well-tended beard that fell over his chest and his paunch. Tkacheev raised his round eyes as he entered, then dropped them again. At the opposite side of the table sat Zudin's old friend, Vasya Shcheglov, a metal worker. He looked exactly like a bird, small, snub-nosed, with a shock of white hair, his Adam's apple running up and down his long, thin throat. In the central seat sat the dread Comrade Stepan. His long predatory nose was forever snuffing the air around him, his cheeks were sunken, right up to the eyes; the sparse little beard on his crooked chin and the scant hair on his head completed the picture. There was an ominousness about the three silent men sitting there. Only one man, a secretary, young and colorless, bending over his papers, disturbed the mystic holiness of this council of wise men with the prosaic rustling of documents.

Zudin was about to hold up his hand to his comrades in greeting, but the idea no sooner occurred to him than he saw it might be considered compromising, as he thought, so he only nodded and awkwardly sat down on the stool to which all eyes consigned him. Opposite, at the short side of the table, portfolio spread out before him, sat the bellicose Shustry.

Not looking at anyone, Stepan was doodling on a sheet of paper, but Shcheglov made an effort to keep a painfully inappropriate smile on his face, as if very glad to see his old friend Zudin again, yet anxious at the role he might have to play in a friend's fate. Stepan abruptly left off doodling and turned on Shustry eyes that never left him while he spoke. On the other hand, Shcheglov, timid and perplexed, sent his boyish gaze to and fro from Shustry to Zudin. Only Tkacheev sat on unmoving, like a Buddha, his eyes fixed on the table before him.

"The case before us, comrades," began Shustry, shifting in his seat and sending a scathing look at Zudin, "is in no way a usual one in the annals of our Party and in our struggle in the cause of the revolution." He was holding several sheets of written paper; from time to time he would turn these over, bending low over them awhile, then flash the pitch-black fire of his compelling eyes now at Stepan, now at Zudin. His voice resounded in the empty corners of the room like a bell over wasteland.

"There sits before us no average Party member, no inexperienced youth, but one of the oldest workers in our Party, a revolutionary since 1903"—Shustry dwelt on the words—"and this famous person, at the most serious and responsible moment of the revolution, has sunk so low that he, occupying an important position in Soviet Russia and the Party—for to be chief of the Regional Cheka is indeed important—has for the foulest and most grossly selfish motives betrayed the trust of the working classes and brought corruption and demoralization to the office of the watchful eye of proletarian rule entrusted to him; that he has set his subordinates the villainous example of corruptibility, negligence, and drunkenness; that he has surrounded himself with co-workers—oh, worthy indeed!—in the service of our bitterest counterrevolutionary enemies. Investigation has yet to bring to light many of Citizen Zudin's deeds, but what it has so far discovered is enough to show that in the cause of revolutionary justice you should not defer your decision.

"I ask your forgiveness if I have inadvertently forgotten myself and my duty to act as an objective reporter," said he, somewhat awkwardly, as if in response to something in Stepan's look, "but, comrades, who can restrain himself when speaking of such vile acts?

"From the actual details that I have been able to assemble concerning Zudin's accomplice and Zudin himself, it appears indisputable that Zudin used his unlimited authority as Chief of the Cheka to procure a place in his service for Citizenness Elena Valtz, an open and active counterrevolutionary, and to keep her by him as his secretary; this same woman had previously been arrested by the Cheka and, having been convicted, was to have been shot. Since he was having an affair and had entered into every kind of relation with her, he could not have been unaware that she was associated with the dangerous

British spy, Edward Heckey, the organizer of the White Guard raids, for whom the Soviet Commission for Extraordinary Affairs has been searching throughout the country, while he was cozily spending the nights with Valtz. She herself confessed that he had spent at least two nights with her. Heckey managed to escape, and consequently these last days there have transpired a whole series of assassinations of our best comrades, including Comrade Katzmann, a deed for which—to put it delicately—Citizen Zudin is indirectly responsible. Such monstrous insolence has never been seen. But Citizen Zudin did not long content himself with that. In betraying the Party and the revolution, in being himself an accessory to the death of his old comrade, who had trusted him unwaveringly, he has proved that he did not act out of political motives alone, though these clearly played a large part. The chief factor in his entire criminal activity was his greed for personal gain. As an absolutely objective reporter, I must further state that Zudin was not content to accept bribes through his female accomplice, who was a convenient tool to him in all these intrigues—yes, in his association with her he certainly acted with cunning and circumspection—bribes that met domestic needs, which Valtz used to advantage and shared with her lover and accomplice, an example of which is the silk stockings for his wife, but also she often used to give him presents *in natura* that she had received from the White Guard, as, for example, the chocolate she received (something like half a hundredweight) from the aforementioned British spy, Heckey. In Zudin's behalf, she blackmailed the family of a merchant named Chotkin, whose son had been arrested at Zudin's order, without any grounds whatsoever, and kept in custody at the Cheka for about four months. She threatened Chotkin's aged parents with the execution of their son and extorted twenty pounds in gold and valuables from them. Although Valtz now denies Zudin's part in this affair, she finds it impossible to contest it, because, first, Chotkin was released on the very day Katzmann was killed, after Valtz had come to terms with Chotkin's parents; second, at Zudin's order, the Head of Chancery at the Cheka got out a duplicate—which is most irregular—of the order for Chotkin's release, this being ancillary to the extortion; and third, that he took the gold from Valtz and thought he had hidden it well, for it was not found in Valtz's rooms; according to her, it was stolen in her absence, though in the final analysis her testimony is unclear. Above all, it will appear to any unprejudiced person logical and natural to conclude that Zudin cannot have contented himself with taking only stockings and chocolate. Thanks to Valtz's talkativeness, all the Cheka employees knew about these so-called gifts, but, terrorized by Zudin, they dared say nothing. Of this we shall speak further.

"At his first hearing, Zudin began by denying everything, but then, in the face of irrefutable evidence, he admitted accepting, in person or through his wife, the stockings, the chocolate, and the gold as 'gifts,' as he calls them, from Valtz. Zudin's plan consists in laying the blame on his wife, since he can no longer deny the receipt of the stockings, the chocolate, and the gold."

"Gold?" echoed Zudin, with quivering lips.

"Oh, yes, I ask your pardon, it was a slip of the tongue: of course, chocolate; Zudin obstinately denies that he accepted gold."

What was in Zudin's thoughts? A blank. His mouth wore a sad smile of confusion and hopelessness. In his subconscious mind he felt that he, who had gone on his arduous way with such firm and sure steps, had now stumbled suddenly; a gigantic unforeseen whirlpool was bearing him along, dragging him relentlessly on to some terrible chasm; bewildered by the howling and turbulence of the elements, he did not once attempt to seek salvation on the rocks against which he was thrown, but then saw them too late, after they had gone by. Now there was nothing in his thoughts. He was conscious only of a complete despair and an anguish, he scarcely thought of the clear conscience he had left somewhere behind, only half aware that he was on his way to the fearful abyss of death.

He had more than once had the feeling that the look in the other men's eyes was burning into him: the searching eyes of Comrade Stepan, or perhaps the bewildered expression of Shcheglov, his friend, who sat there, flushed and wretched. Or, as he sat there with his pen, had the secretary, whose round, sleepy eyes had been opened in ordinary curiosity, been sending him stealthy looks? But Zudin had no time to assemble his thoughts. The whirling stream of Shustry's words carried him still further and deeper.

"Yes, comrades, as a reporter who has been at pains to remain objective, I must categorically affirm that Citizen Zudin is a most profoundly mendacious and deceitful individual. It is for you to see whether my opinion holds good."

"As what? As deceitful?" echoed Stepan, who had lost the thread of Shustry's discourse.

"Most profoundly deceitful!" emphasized Shustry loudly, and Zudin saw the edgy look again come over Comrade Stepan's features.

"I have already expressed to Zudin's face the conviction that he won't be able to deny it. It wasn't enough for him to take Valtz into his service, though, as a supporter of the White

Guard, she was an adequate accomplice. But that was not enough for him. He managed to recruit all kinds of rabble into the Cheka under his wing, extortionists and other potential swindlers, who naturally hindered the work of the honest comrades who had the misfortune to work with Zudin. To illustrate this, we adduce the example of Pavlov, an open extortionist, who repeatedly blackmailed those whose arrest he had been ordered to investigate and who had received from them immense sums which he evidently shared with Zudin. He, like Valtz, has now been arrested. Zudin was properly warned about Pavlov by Comrade Katzmann, as Comrade Fomin testifies, and as Zudin himself does not deny; on the contrary, he asserts that he, Zudin, had drawn Katzmann's attention to Pavlov. This blatant lie on Zudin's part can be disproved by the single fact that he did not dismiss Pavlov from the Cheka, which became easier at Katzmann's death because Katzmann had insisted on Pavlov's dismissal. After Valtz and Pavlov were taken into custody, Zudin tried to protest against the arrest of these two splendid specimens and do you know what he called it? 'Cheka insubordination!' That is what he said to Ignatyev in my presence. There is testimony by Ignatyev about this, which I hardly think Zudin will deny.

"Comrades, the greed and perfidy in Zudin's character is further shown in his terrifying implacability. The fact that he himself was indirectly the instigator in Comrade Katzmann's murder did not deter him from taking rapacious advantage of the Cheka Commission to put through the order that a hundred of the most distinguished citizens arrested by the Cheka (who in most cases if not all were innocent) were to be shot. It is superfluous to point out that this act was the real cause of the stirring up of the populace against Soviet rule."

"What is it you're driving at now?" said Zudin aloud.

"I'm driving at the victory of revolutionary justice, and nothing else."

"Is there any chance of it?"

"That remains to be seen! But I fear I have tired the comrades unnecessarily with my long speech, since the case lies clear and simple before them. The most monstrous thing in this matter is that the accused should have held an outstandingly responsible post and, as a former Party comrade, enjoyed especial confidence. I will not supplement my report with the mention of orgies in which confiscated wine was drunk. That evil was constantly in Zudin's office. Pavlov had access to it, although, according to Zudin, the office was invariably locked. Neither will I mention the love intrigue between Zudin and Valtz, which the stove attendant Agafya happened to know of, when she heard a part of their conversation through the door on one occasion. These are only details of small importance beside the main accusation."

A heavy, pervasive silence fell. All looked at Zudin.

"Will you make a declaration with respect to this?" asked Stepan at last.

"Yes . . ..yes, naturally I will!" declared Zudin, as if he had just awakened.

"Zudin's declaration positively must not be carried over, I propose, in order to save time," exploded Shustry.

"Oh, yes, yes, we'll see about that." Stepan made an ill-tempered gesture in Shustry's direction, and turned to Zudin. "We're listening."

His mind, once so vivid and clear, was in tatters, however. Where to begin? "Comrades," he said, "you may believe me or not, I am an honest man, as I have always been. Are all my years of work in the underground no evidence to you of my honesty?"

Zudin was aware that what he was saying was inadmissible as evidence, and not what, while waiting for his hearing, he had intended to say. Shustry's malicious look was putting him out of countenance.

"We would ask you not to rake up the past. We all know it well enough. We ask you only to make a brief, clear declaration as to the accusation made in the report. Do you know yourself to be guilty or not?" Comrade Stepan interrupted in a cold, firm voice.

"Yes, yes, at once. At once." Zudin's control of himself became still weaker; panic now seized him—not fear of the final calamity which, like a tram out of control, with its flaring eyes came ever nearer and brighter, so much as fear that, standing alone, he would not be able to defend his rights.

Zudin realized that he must at once, and unhesitatingly, assemble what strength he had left, that he must now set all the thoughts he had ever had in his life to work in order to keep a firm hold on this utterly intolerable, hateful situation, he must put to use the sufferings of all his lifetime, since he was a little uncommitted child up to this very day, when he stood threatened with annihilation. But which of these wrongs was he to redress? Was he not surrounded by his true, devoted comrades, even the vindictive Shustry? Was he then to perish without a sound, without one scream of pain, to go through the whole world without a hope that somewhere the faintest echo of that would be heard?

"I am not guilty," said Zudin firmly. "Not guilty," he repeated; his voice rang out more positively and clearly, and his words seared his listeners' ears like sharp, fiery tongs. "It is not true that Valtz is my mistress, it is not ture that she was to have been shot and that I saved her out of some lecherous passion for her. All that is untrue. She was arrested by chance in the case of the Savinkov agent, Finikov, and I was absolutely convinced she had nothing at all to do with it. I was sorry for her and believed that honest work would free her from the slime of the capitalistic way of life. It seems I was mistaken. The power of chocolate was stronger."

"What was stronger?" they all asked in one voice.

"Chocolate," said Shustry, with an ironic smile.

"Yes, chocolate. It proved to be the stronger. This is the first time I have heard that Valtz had relations with Heckey. I find myself unable to explain it on the spur of the moment. It is true that Valtz gave my wife stockings, and chocolate for the children that she brought to my house. She told my wife she still had many fine things of the sort left from when she was in the theater—she was once a ballerina—and, besides, a former colleague of hers had brought her the chocolate from the front. I must say frankly that I believed this. Had I been there when she brought the things to my house, we should certainly have sent her away; however, my wife accepted the things without suspecting anything; when she told me about it later, it was hard for me to give them back. I did not want to hurt my wife's feelings. In my stupidity I took it all as being without importance. Again, I have heard for the first time today that Valtz extorted twenty pounds in gold from Chotkin's parents. I only recall that she was unusually persistent about freeing the son, which made me somewhat suspicious, but it was true that Chotkin had been kept on in prison without grounds and in error, and should have been released a long time before; he might have stayed in custody indefinitely because of the remissness of the investigator, who had suddenly been called away, if Valtz had not chanced to find his records in the file of a case that had already been closed."

"You mean that Valtz was justified in taking the bribe?" interjected Shustry, with a sneer.

"Never mind," Stepan warned him with a gesture of the hand.

"Also, I never gave the order for any sort of duplicate to be made. In a word, to suspect me of having been in some sort of association with Heckey, of knowing anything at all about the gold, and of entering into immoral relations with Valtz is pure and concentrated rubbish. She did indeed sit next to me one evening on the sofa and began speaking of love—I was then of the opinion that it was genuine—but then, too, I immediately sent her away. If old Agafya was actually eavesdropping, she must be able to confirm this. It is also nonsensical to accuse me with reference to Pavlov. I had always looked on him with suspicion. I spoke with Katzmann about this, and we decided to dismiss him. But then I got so involved with events that I simply did not think any more about this. That is all. It was painful, comrades, to realize the extent to which Comrade Yuzhanin has transformed all this in his objective report." Zudin imbued these words with caustic fastidiousness.

"As for the so-called orgies," he went on emphatically, "what orgies? What kind of orgies? If the confiscated wine has been carried off and its disappearance unnoticed by us, it is vexatious and shameful, if you will. But what has that to do with this pathetic orgy talk that Yuzhanin has brought up? I'm still Zudin, and not a bartender!" He turned on Shustry with hostility.

"So much the worse!" screamed Shustry, jumping to his feet.

"Never mind," again Stepan warned him.

"Still more ridiculous is the accusation that I deliberately instigated a reign of terror, which, I believe, is how Yuzhanin qualifies my activities. I, acting out of spite, to have a hundred innocent citizens shot like common criminals?! Allow me to say, comrades, that this accusation is beyond my comprehension. Above all, this was no personal decree of my own but a special decree of the Commission's at a meeting at which Fomin and Ignatyev were both present. Would I actually have gone through with the executions if anyone had seriously opposed me?"

"You terrorized them all," said Shustry.

"Or did someone feel obliged to beat a retreat out of repentance for sins committed and, in trying to wash his hands of the guilt, throw the entire responsibility onto me? Does this mean that the time may soon come when we shall set ourselves up to judge our comrades for having tried tc be efficient in carrying out our own directives and stipulations? But I am not afraid of responsibility, and, if this situation should repeat itself, I should do just so much and no more."

"Of course it's ridiculous!" muttered Stepan almost inaudibly, and the motionless Tkacheev raised his eyes to Zudin's.

"I may have arrested a hundred people." Zudin's voice had the ring of steel. "I was not long in establishing their guilt. What possible guilt could there have been? Is it a crime of the bourgeois that he's a bourgeois? Or a crime of the crocodile that he's crocodile? Do we not admit into our ranks dozens of our former bitterest enemies from the counterrevolutionary camp, and, if they succeed in changing their feelings and ideas through the power of conviction, do we not take them in as brothers in the common fight? Have we not at other times put behind bars many brave fellows who once did so much for the revolution and are still even now devoted to her cause, but who, out of stupidity and obstinacy, have opposed us as bitter enemies and formed the capitalist avant-garde? Can you say this isn't so?"

"Would you care to classify yourself under that heading?" Again the mocking smile played about Shustry's mouth.

"Myself?" said Zudin, bewildered. "No, I'm saying this to show that I was right to proceed with these executions without looking for guilt. For me it is a question of whether they were guilty or not in your own commonplace mind. Only don't believe, Comrade Yuzhanin, that I would allow myself to proceed against this deplorable pack of dogs we call our enemies in a spirit of revenge. Revenge motivates me least. This ridiculous bias may be a comfort to some who could assault the table they fall against, or attack the sea because a boat with their next of kin in it was sunk. Revenge is an unrewarding self-betrayal. And still I had the—if you will—unguilty shot!"

"What monstrous logic!" Shustry said agitatedly.

Tkacheev seemed to come alive, looking Zudin straight in the eye, while Shcheglov, red in the face, stared at him, open-mouthed; only Stepan went on tranquilly scribbling with his pencil on a sheet of paper.

"It was the capitalist organization that killed Katzmann. It hardly matters if a few foolish Social Revolutionaries consider themselves enemies of capitalism. This is of small importance. In reality they are conscientious upholders of the bourgeoisie. Their personal convictions do not alter the case. We continue to conduct class warfare on a grand international scale. We must answer attack with counterattack. They direct their blows against individuals because they do not understand the socialist way of life and its commandments. But I strike my blows against a whole class. I have executed the foremost of them in order, as I came across them, no more and no fewer, because that was the inevitable consequence of their deeds. 'Are you dear fellows going to repeat the attack?' That is what they have to consider now, for they know that if they do, they'll pay dearly for it."

"You were not charged with that," Stepan interrupted him. "That we know: somehow or somewhere terror in class warfare is inevitable and necessary. Only, in the final analysis, we try always to annihilate those same agents and organizers who perform acts of enmity against our class. Well, let the talkers mourn over that. But now, would you be so good as to answer the one or two questions I have written down here?" He handed Zudin a scrap of paper.

"Why was Valtz not placed under surveillance?"

"What impression has this case produced on the limited number of Cheka employees and in particular on the wider circle of workers who have spread rumors that Zudin accepted bribes through his wife?"

"Yes, that was a lapse on my part," said Zudin, distressed. "What impression? The worst!" he muttered with drooping head. Now for the first time he knew the torture of shame; he would have sunk through the floor if he could.

"Has anyone else a question?" He turned to the others. Shustry was about to say something then noticed that he was the only one and closed his mouth again.

Stepan whispered inaudibly, first to Tkacheev, then to Shcheglov. Both nodded agreement.

"Comrade Shustry, please make arrangements for Comrade Zudin to be taken back at once to the same place.

"The Commission will summon you to acquaint you of its decisions as soon as it has met," he said, turning to Zudin, and looked at his watch.

Again, an alarming weight of anxiety fell upon Zudin. Confusedly, he sought for his coat, until he remembered he had had none with him. Shustry conducting him, he went, perspiring and red-faced, through the door, crushed, exhausted, with shuddering heart. With a hostile gaze on Zudin's back, the same sentry escorted him back to the room with the dark window in its square embrasure. Zudin shrank into himself. The distant sky at the horizon was lit by flashes of gunfire. The city, a blackness beyond the window, grew cold.

7

Zudin lay down. Now what was in store for him? How was he to know? His head would not think.

His heart beat with burning shame: how had it happened that he, Zudin, the ever cautious, ever watchful, had made such a mess of everything: the common cause of world revolution, the Party, the trust of the working classes? Was it all really a dream?

With trembling hands he covered his eyes, and before him appeared old, long-dead pictures, only now there was quite another light upon them. A dirty, broken, scurrying sky. A wide, crusted, ploughed field, drenched with autumn rain. A gigantic rough-hewn peasant in a ragged coat stumbled on tired, shambling legs along the wet and muddy road. His face was tanned with sun and wind and furrowed with lines. He went his way with bowed shoulders, his back humped toward the sky. With submission in his eye, he stomped, coughing, through the maze of moisture.

"What a hero," mused Zudin. "Who could fail beside such a fellow traveler? Lord of the earth, why is your look so sad?"

The peasant slowed his steps and turned on Zudin a friendly, sharp-eyed stare of appraisal.

"I'm hungry, man, hungry!"

"But who has the power to take your bread from you, an honest workman?"

The giant stood still; his eyes fell on the thick mire of the way.

"No one took it from me, man. I myself gave it to the landowner. Dues, friend, dues." He sighed heavily.

"Have you really nothing left? Something must be left to you. What have you done with the rest?"

"A-ah, dear man, well may you ask. It's the taxes that destroy us. We have to buy our wheels, and our wood, and a few nails—my house is in ruins, as you see—and so I have to take everything I have to the tax collector at the countinghouse."

"My friend," Zudin told him, "shake off your bonds! Together we shall take arms against landowner and tax collector! Come, we shall plough up the whole world, for others and for ourselves. Then life will begin for us! Your bread will be yours to the last mouthful. Will you come? Brother, we shall begin a new life, a fairy-tale existence: a wonder-horse of copper with a fiery mane will plough your fields and seek neither food nor reward. All we need is time, and we shall accomplish all."

"You speak so strangely." The peasant looked about him with a bright, crafty eye. "Attack the landowner—why not? All will go well if only the whole community declares itself to be on our side. Then, certainly, things would be easier. But, about the fiery horse—there, dear man, you go too far. What should we do with fire when a mere nag would be enough for us? But tell me the truth, brother, the whole truth, will no one then take our bread from us, truly?"

"Do you think that nuts shell themselves and fall from heaven into our mouths? Will you not, for the sake of the wonder-horse, to escape from the landowner, suffer hunger a while longer, and, when expedient, share your last piece of bread with others, in return for which you shall live without landowners and merchants? Think of it!"

The peasant cringed, breathed heavily, and then waved his hand.

"Well, brother, if it's only for a short while, why not? We don't need to accustom ourselves to hunger, we are past masters at it: you see how slack my belly is. It is as you say: this can no longer be borne. But take you, brother, are you not deceiving us?"

"You need have no fear for me. I have suffered hunger not less than you. We shall fight side by side and share all between us. Maybe you can share a morsel of bread with me now; come, follow me, only step lively, not so slow!"

Reluctantly, the peasant took a small crust of bread from his bosom, broke it in two, and spent a long time considering which was the larger piece, so as to give Zudin the other; but then, aware that Zudin was looking at him, he handed him the larger piece forthwith, then followed Zudin at a clumsy jog-trot through the filthy mire. Zudin stepped out lustily, his legs rising high out of the softened loam. The peasant could hardly keep pace with him. Gasping for breath, he came to a standstill, then halted yet again to wipe the pouring sweat from his face with his hand.

"Ah, dear man, don't go so fast; a little slower, please. There's no keeping up with you. I am so lean from hunger; that bread I gave you was the last I had, I've kept it by me this long while for when I should grow weak from lack of food."

"Never mind, pull yourself together: we must make haste or we cannot win. I am no less emaciated than you, for didn't I ask you for bread? And just see how I go! We must keep our heads in all things." Zudin tried to push the bread he was holding into his pocket, but it would not go, something was stopping it—what was it? Zudin put his hand in his pocket and pulled out—a bar of chocolate. The peasant's look grew hostile.

"What's that? Have you been deceiving me? You took my last piece of bread, with candy in your pocket?"

"Comrade, it got there I don't know how."

"LIAR!!"

Zudin trembled helplessly. I can't prove it. I can never prove it! My cause is lost!

He began to run, fell in the mire, got to his feet, ran on, and fell again. He was covered from head to foot in foul, brown slime. Was it clay? Or chocolate? He could not tell. Would he ever arrive, would he ever get out of this net of endless autumn rain? His legs were growing feebler, encumbered by the thick mud of the softened earth. The peasant's breath sounded nearer and nearer. No, he could not escape.

"No, I can't escape!" said Zudin, aloud, and opened his eyes. The room was still and empty, only an electric lamp went on monotonously burning. Zudin suppressed a slight shiver.

How had it all happened? What had he done? In what did his offense consist? Why were they discussing so long in there? And what would their decision be? Would they execute him pitilessly, execute him for an oversight, a lapse of attention? He suddenly thought of Shustry and his "revolutionary justice."

Still fully dressed, he lay down again on his back and pressed his hands over his closed eyes.

Had all this come about because of that cursed bar of chocolate that pursued him so relentlessly? His mind began to fill with an increasing tumult that both quieted and disquieted him, like the rushing of a waterfall or the stirring of trees in a forest. Oh, that sound had been well known to Zudin since childhood, so congenial to him, as the clinking of chains is congenial to the convict grown gray in prison. Zudin knew every one of its finer tones, its nuances, such as were not perceptible to another. . . .

8

Was it the effervescing of an acid? No, it was the caustic poison of anxiety burning the heart of Vasily Shcheglov, eating into its very core. His sweet, vanished childhood shone at him, as the shards of broken glass shine on a dump. The mild years of childhood flickered in his eyes as through the tender green foliage of a richly fragrant elder tree. Beneath the elder, children's calloused feet flashed in and out of the circle, where plump and gold-colored jacks tossed up and down. There was a frown on sun-tanned Alyosha's large-eyed little face. And Vasya's heart was beating in hard throbs, like a single two-kopek coin in the loosely hanging pocket of a worn pair of trousers. He clutched a fragment of iron tiling—it was heavy and could only be grasped with difficulty by his straining palm.

"Ah, those slickers! Are they going to pick up more than us? Are they going to beat us hollow?" But Alyosha's little arm nudged Vasya in the side, and he heard Alyosha's playful whisper: "Hold them, Vasya, you can do better than the slickers. . . ."

And although now it is as if there were, not one, but a whole mass of Shustrys, waving their tentacles, like spiders in a dark corner, Vasya is not going to let Alyosha down. Keeping before him that faraway youth, the elder tree and the dump, Vasya feels his heart grow strong inside him until it is a lump of steel.

Stepan's cold tenor voiced a swift question, his slitlike eyes raised over his pencil. Quickly, nervously, Vasya answered back as if ready to spring, then one after the other the issues transpired, like tomcats tucking in their back legs prior to jumping on terrified mice.

Suddenly, and quite out of turn, Shustry blurted out: "Allow me to. . . ."

"No, we've had enough!" Vasya went red all over. "Enough from you. You've planted us with too many of your nasty fleas. Do you think I don't know Zudin? But I do know Alyosha, comrades. Known him since childhood. And he's the sincerest of men, stands with us on every front . . . in a word—"

"Are you implying I'm capable of libel?" blustered Shustry.

"One at a time!" frowned Stepan. "We'll give Shustry another five minutes, but no more. Are you getting all this down?" He suddenly turned on the open-mouthed secretary.

The secretary hastily rubbed his sweating hands on his trousers; his pen went on skipping and spluttering listlessly over the unfeeling paper. Shustry puffed himself out like a sparrow and chirped at length about how Alyosha constantly missed the meetings of a cell, how "metal worker" Zudin had forgotten his factory days, how people were getting restless in the workers' quarter.

"It's just like a running sore to hear him," cut in Vasily.

"Now see here. . . !"

"Don't interrupt!" Stepan intervened. Thus encouraged, Shustry shed a smile of victory over his portfolio and fell to adjusting its papers with an affectation of care only to be found in a country doctor's assistant at a postmortem, when the doctor himself has gone to wash his hands: then the assistant digs about assiduously inside the belly, prodding at the bowels. And he thinks: Now, mind what you're doing: don't pull out the heart and put it back under the gut. In the same sense nothing was going to divert Shustry from his goal. He exposed all the guile and all the deviousness in Zudin's perfidious character. He, Shustry, was proud of the confidence that had been placed in him. He knew how much envy there was among the workers, that there were those who would like to climb up in the Party and there render as much service as lice, defiling the Party organization, bringing in every scoundrel and knave in the business. But leave it to Shustry—he'll clean things up.

"Comrade?! Party member?!" he jeered. "But he's never paid his monthly dues for over half a year. That was at the root of it all: Pavlov, then Valtz, and the Socialist Revolutionaries at Osennikov—that was no chance affair. Nor was it by chance that our Chief of the Cheka reduced the whole organization to a dump!" And Shustry wiped his well-trimmed moustache in disgust.

Vasya Shcheglov heard the words "dump" and at once the warm brightness of the fires from the broken tile as it gaily flirted with the sun called at him and softened his heart with the affection of their elder-tree childhood.

And Shustry shot covert, infuriated looks at Shcheglov and his wet, parted lips, and thought how little he dreamed what was lying at that very moment like an impenetrable iron wall in the Party's way. And Shustry thrust, pressed, and stabbed at the flabby block of sympathy with the steely chisel of his sharp words.

"Does anyone suppose the White Guard are such fools as to be satisfied with wine and candy and not make it their business to find out from the same Heckey, whom Valtz and Zudin contrived to hide, what the secrets of the Cheka are, down to the smallest detail? Zudin entrusted everything to Valtz! Zudin handed secrets over to the enemy! For that alone shooting would be too good for him! And this is what you call—" and Shustry's black eyes like bullets darted their fire at Shcheglov—"'the sincerest of men on all fronts'! When we entrusted him with the sword of responsibility, he dishonored it by accepting bribes and taking criminals into his confidence—he is guilty of all that. Guilty on all counts! And guilty of those mangled corpses!" Shustry rolled his eyes at the dimmed black windows of the city. "And what about those other corpses—the bloodless corpses of heroes, those stoical fighting comrades of ours, who are selflessly perishing at this very moment because of Zudin and lying in great piles at the gates of our city not twenty-five versts from here. Yes, Zudin alone is to blame for this. He was never in evidence at any rebellion! I am not even sure"—and with a dexterous movement Shustry closed his portfolio—"I am not even sure if we'll still be here by morning. The reinforcements are proving worthless. And are we to surrender the city?" He shook his closed fists in the air, revealing the hairy, emaciated backs of his hands. "Without delay, or mercy, Zudin must be shot!!"

The red pile of the tablecloth smoothly sucked in even the sharpest words; that was why they all sat silently looking at it, by a kind of tacit agreement.

"You have the floor, Shcheglov."

"Well, here's what I have to say—" his voice broke. He got up nervously; one hand felt tremblingly for the tuft of hair on his head, the other aimlessly pulled at the black rope belt. "Here's what I have to say: a more villainous flood of gossip—" But at Stepan's compelling, knife-sharp look, Vasya was forced to lower his voice from its shout of protest. "Never in my life have I witnessed such treatment of one of our oldest comrades. Zudin took bribes, you say? Has it been proved? I'll answer with my own life that it isn't so. I've known Alyosha since childhood, and he's the same fellow he always was. And then you say he didn't come to the meetings of the cell: how extraordinary, you think! But wasn't his work at the Cheka even more important? And then, as Chief of the Cheka for this region, he had to be present at every meeting of the Committee. Why did Comrade

Shustry, that 'objective reporter,' never say a word about that? And since when have the activities of the Cheka ceased to be Party activities, and the most responsible part of them, what's more! But we must bend our minds to the question of the cell! And what was he playing at, there in the Cheka? Jacks?"

"Jills, more likely. He went about with women," put in Tkacheev, clearly and calmly.

"With women? With *women*? Ah, comrades, it's an obscure affair, this woman business . . . a bad business. The devil induced him to take pity on that bitch. How she was able to stir him to pity, I am simply unable to understand. If we judge them by our own lights, clearly such fine ladies are not good for us. They're a kind of lace frill, not human beings at all. And only the devil knows if he met her by chance or if it was all predestined. As I see it, we shouldn't even touch on this business. It belongs to them. Bitches will always be bitches, as we know. For, of course, he took pity on her for nothing. In fact, she did him an evil turn. But Alyosha is guilty in absolutely nothing toward us. It's true he is guilty of a tiny error, he was caught off guard. Who among us is never tempted? But he has always been our faithful fighter and scout to the very end. And a scout always goes on in front, he is a lonely figure. In so doing he may even sometimes make a mistake. But is he to be branded with guilt? Is it possible to shoot him for it? The strength of the revolution is as mighty as a mountain in him. And Shustry calls on us to shoot a man like that! No, comrades, I am sure we are not going to do that. We Bolsheviks are going to do no such thing. If we decided to transfer him to another town, to do another kind of work, to be on closer terms with the workers, I would concur. But as for what Shustry demands"—and Shustry dug his nails hard into the tablecloth—I would as soon hand Shustry himself over to the Party tribunal right away because of his erroneous juggling with the facts!"

"Beg leave to speak!" Shustry was on his feet.

"I shall not allow any personal quarreling," cut in Stepan decisively. "Your own fault. . . ."

Shustry's eyebrows flew up with surprise and stayed there.

"Of course your duties were not easy, unearthing every kind of meanness. So you have got into the habit of seeing everyone either as an inveterate scoundrel or a godlike hero. Hence all this talk of 'evil intent,' 'injustice,' and other Philistine rubbish. About terrorizing the masses, I think you go too far. It would be more profitable if the Central Committee were to transfer you to another job. In your own interest. . . ."

Stepan looked thoughtfully at the others.

"What do you say?"

Just at this point, slowly and wearily, Tkacheev raised his eyelids. And then a terrible cold ran over Shcheglov, as though he had seen a storm approaching like gray, swirling smoke. As the cloud crept nearer, it filled the sky with an evil omen, and no one could say whether it would water the still cornfields with a pelting shower or silence the greed of the fields with crackling, leaping hail. And it seemed to Shcheglov that he was caught in that storm and must bow before it, and that there was nowhere he could hide while the confident, unyielding hail of Tkacheev's words beat and danced on his head.

"Both are wrong: Shcheglov as well as Shustry; both have failed to grasp the essence of the affair. Shcheglov himself has admitted that Zudin blundered over a woman of the town, a venomous creature in frills and furbelows. And Zudin took pity on her. He took pity on the hothouse parasite that is feeding on our blood and sweat. He took pity on her because he knew she would perish, a delicate, charming thing, under the heel of our peasants' boots. He felt pity for her in spite of us, and contrary to us, and he was ruined. These are the basic facts."

Tkacheev tore off the edge of a piece of paper lying before him, rolled it into a tube, poured shag tobacco into it from his pouch and, lighting it with the brimstone-smelling blue flame of a match, went on:

"All these last days Stepan and I have been going around the factories." He wrapped himself in dense puffs of smoke, like a steamer. "They didn't let us speak. They ganged up on us and shouted, 'Hey, Commissars! You treat us factory workers like a military governor treats a town. Where have you been till now? Gorging yourselves on chocolate? Where's your Zudin? Hand him over to us, we'll deal with him. We get two ounces of tea a day, and he—gets chocolate! Our children are dying of hunger and cold, and he goes out with ballerinas dressed in silk! What are you hiding him for? Unless you root out that weed of a fellow in our presence, we shan't trust you any more. And we shan't go anywhere for you. You can go gobble your chocolate!' And this is what all the workers are saying. You can call it demagogy, or say they're only the backward masses. If you ask me, they're right. Did he take chocolate, or didn't he? He did. Now prove it wasn't a bribe from one of the White Guard, but a gift from one of our own people, a Bolshevik girl. You think you can get away with it? The whole town knows about it: the Red Army, the factories, everybody. Just you try now, Shcheglov, try and explain to them that it's all been a mistake, there's nothing in it. Just try and speak to the workers. Persuade them to go to the front or else the city will fall. But let's leave out the workers. Even try to explain to our Party in general that Zudin never took gold. And where did it go to? That's why the Socialist Revolutionaries and Mensheviks have got the upper hand. Only to think that in *our* Soviet there should suddenly arise a question of the corruption of the Cheka! And at what a moment, too, just think of it! And do you know, Shcheglov, that the better part of our Communist Party voted for that institution, not to mention all the non-Party men! What do you say to that? Was it for this we became Bolsheviks—to give explanations and change things around? Tell us where, tell us when, they say, and then you try to make them understand that Zudin isn't guilty, that he's a lonely fighter, and a scout. You harp on one string: 'He isn't guilty.' And then the question arises: 'Who is? Who is guilty in general?' Nobody is guilty of anything. Not you, not me, not Kolchak, not Denikin. And what will be the result? In our 'innocence,' we perform shady acts, and the factories as well as the Red Army say nothing about it: we are innocent, you see. No, my dear fellow, it can't be done. We may not care a straw for the Mensheviks and the Social Revolutionaries and all that pack of Philistines. But not to care what our workers and soldiers think!—no, old fellow, excuse me. We can't separate ourselves from them. You can say what you like about them: they lack culture, they descend from the petty bourgeois, they don't understand politics. We can slander everything about them, but stand apart from them we cannot. It's as if we were world-tugs pulling a world-class behind us. And it's not for nothing they're all aroused against Zudin. None of your tricks with the working masses, no, there can be no yearning for silk stockings, as the worker sees it. It's as if they had you and your work under a microscope. Setting a fine example is much better than all your propaganda."

"So what do you suggest?" whispered Vasya Shcheglov.

"What do I suggest? First of all, no harking back to a time that no longer exists. Now you can't pull the wool over anybody's eyes. And you never will be able to do so again. All the comrades are fighting at the fronts. The enemy is pressing hard. This is the moment to rouse all the workers and move them to battle—otherwise the city will be lost. And so this is no time for long-drawn-out deliberations. There's no taking into consideration the fact that he was once a good comrade. Supposing he stumbled again, and brought corruption into our ranks, and ruined our cohesion with the working masses? No, there is only one way out. The blood of the working class is more precious for us all than the blood of one individual."

Shustry was nodding staunchly. And Vasya Shcheglov shook himself like an autumn bird that has got its feathers wet, and his sharp little nose became more pointed still. With protruding lip, Stepan hastily wrote on a small piece of paper, folded it and, beckoning to Shustry, handed it to him, whispering in his ear. The other scurried out with an air of concern and, as the door opened, a current of damp air penetrated the room. Vasya shivered with the sudden chill.

"Yes, he has fallen into a terrible difficulty," he sighed, "but there must be a way out of this without killing him. I'll tell you how— "

"How do you mean, how?" Stepan had not been following.

"Well, we could hold him up as an example and say we'd shot him, but really smuggle him out of the country to do secret work somewhere a long way off— America or some place like that."

"Are you asking us to deceive the Party?" Stepan smiled maliciously, ironically. "No, Comrade Vasily, we don't deal in political intrigue. We must hide nothing, but instruct the Party openly on what we have decided."

"So all we care about is 'what Auntie will say'?" mumbled Vasya Shcheglov.

Stepan stood stock still, his face suffused, and smashed his fist down on the table with such force that the pencil flew headlong to the floor.

"Ah, don't provoke me, brother! It's no 'Auntie,' it's the Party! Yes! Our Party! We don't allow jokes here. We'll have to retail this vivid example to the Party, just as it is, show them where your idealistic approach is leading! 'Lonely figures!' That may be, but don't forget the relation they bear to the rest of our class. Because then they will start aspiring to 'decency' and 'critical reason' and forget the workers' miserable stolen kopek."

It seemed to Vasya Shcheglov that the falling leaves of September were floating and spiraling before him, rows of countless workers' stolen kopeks.

It seemed as if Vasya Shcheglov had been in this reverie since the beginning of time, but it was only for a moment. The window panes quivered dully. Unbidden, the dark blue dawn was already creeping over the black windows, and Stepan still kept on slashing at the air with the pencil tightly grasped in his hand.

"And if any one of us can go so far as to allow himself to be softened by the beauty and sweetness of those blood-stained kopeks that the parasites turn into luxury, it can only mean that he is decadent. Then, if there is time, save him, plunge him into the lowest stratum of the working class. If there isn't time, cut him down. Otherwise, all our work, all our great struggle, will go for nothing."

"But I feel so terribly sorry for Zudin," sighed Shcheglov in utter weariness. "Oh, if only you knew, comrades, how sorry I feel." And his voice stopped short in his throat.

From inside Stepan's grip a brittle snap was heard. And Tkacheev suddenly stood up and tugged at his shirt collar. The button flew off and clicked along the floor.

"'Sorry'? But do you imagine we aren't sorry, too?" And he included everyone in his quick, comprehensive glance. "*Sorry*?! You know Shcheglov—" Speaking in a hoarse quaver, Tkacheev abruptly knocked over a stool as he took a heavy step toward the other man and seized him by his dejected shoulders. His beard moved like a dark cloud pierced by the lightening shaft of his yellow teeth. His heavy eyelids lifted like hatches, revealing a glare as glassy bright as a red-hot furnace. "Ah, Shcheglov, anyone of us would stand up against the wall, and be glad to do it, for a comrade. But would it be of any use if we did? And would you save our cause from the White Guard by it? Is this the way you would free the workers in their hovels from the bloodiness of unjust punishment? And can you really be sorry only for him? Aren't you sorry for the rest? What will happen to them if we neglect them?"

And in that second Shcheglov's vision of the sunny warmth of the elder tree melted away. Before him now was the buckling of girders, the jangle of breaking glass, the muffled screams of violated women. It was enough to make you grind your teeth, chill your blood, set the dogs howling.

The blue window panes tinkled again.

"It seems it has begun," said Stepan, rousing himself. "We must make haste because the battle has started. If we can only hang on till tomorrow, we'll show them a thing or two."

The door creaked open and Shustry darted into the room, out of breath. He was breathless.

"Things are going badly." He hoisted himself up on a stool. "During the night we surrendered Osennikov and Steglitsy. The enemy has been bringing British tanks in. Fomin has just arrested eleven officers out of the regiment that came in: they were getting ready to cross over with a whole unit. Our reinforcements are still holding the edge of the forest by Krastilitsy."

Quickly Stepan unrolled a crackling, crumpled map and bent over it diligently.

"Yes," he murmured.

"Ignatyev is talking direct with Moscow. He promised to follow me here, if nothing happens to delay him."

"So what are we to say?" Stepan shook his head. "What's there to write? Quite plainly, there is no time. I'm referring to the one who neglected the matter of the kopek. We must move all the workers to the front at once. And precisely *on* that occasion, and not *because of* anything else, Zudin will be shot."

Silence. The rustling of the map as they smoothed it out, and the tick of the watch on the secretary's wrist.

"But suppose," Shcheglov got out at last; his face was gray, his eyes dejected, and his Adam's apple moved up and down. He sighed. "Suppose," he said, "we could tell future generations all about this struggle of ours. . . ."

"There will be no occasion to do so, man," interrupted Stepan, rising swiftly to his feet, "and they might not believe it even then."

"And then again they might," said Tkacheev in a strained voice, "but, to be sure, not everyone will understand. And the grumblers will certainly have something to say about sacrifice and cruelty. But the devil with them!—it's not they who bring the revolution." He got out his tobacco again and smoked.

"Well, now, here you are," said Stepan, once more making slits of his eyes and addressing the secretary, "write out a resolution to read something like this: 'Subsequent to the alienation from the working and the Party masses of the former Chief of the Provincial Cheka Zudin, and further, in consequence of his admission to employment at the Cheka of the White Guard spy and extortionist, the former ballerina, Citizenness Valtz—from whom Zudin accepted on behalf of his family stockings and chocolate, and for his insufficient supervision of the duties entrusted to the said Zudin as Chief of the Cheka for this region, following which . . . there transpired the bribery of his co-worker, Citizen Pavlov, and others, the results of whose operations are still in evidence. . . .' Have you got that? Now take this down: 'Whereas, by these and similar crimes, Zudin has undermined the confidence of the working masses in Soviet rule, and has at a critical moment in the White Guard offensive brought disruption within the hitherto united front of the working class, the above-mentioned Zudin, the former Chief of the Cheka for this region, and similarly, his co-workers, Pavlov and the former ballerina Valtz—are to be shot.' Period. 'Sentence to be carried out immediately. Signed, The member of the responsible Commission. . . .' Ready?"

He took the written record of the proceedings, squinting as he read it through, and signed it with a flourish. Tkacheev also signed it. Then Shcheglov added his own signature. His eyes had a staring, anxious look.

Shustry was pacing the room to and fro, from corner to corner, looking at the empty walls with his small troubled eyes. Outside the window the blue was now complete, and they all could hear distinctly now the incessant tinkling of the windowpanes at the thundering of distant artillery.

"Now," Stepan addressed the secretary, "please tell Ignatyev's secretary to type out our resolution. One of the copies is to be marked 'Urgent' and sent to the Cheka. The other must be taken to the printer's at once: in three hours' time it must be posted at all street corners and taken round all of the factories. Then it must be sent to the newspapers at once. Ignatyev and I are going out to the front, right away, that is." He looked at his watch.

"Only someone absolutely must go and see Fomin. I don't know what he could have pulled off in one single night at the Cheka, but however—weren't you going to drop in on him, Tkacheev?"

"No, I'd better take control of the factories as soon as I can. By lunch time I shall have been around them all and recruited strong troops from among the workers. By this evening they'll all be at the front. That would be best, I think."

"Yes, yes, you're right! But you stay here, Shcheglov," Stepan flung at him as he stood there buttoning the coat he had just put on. "You stay here and keep in touch with Moscow and with us."

"Oh," Shustry sucked in his lips with displeasure, "and I too was just getting ready to go to the factories."

"No, you'll have to spend the day here in Ispolkom. Tkacheev will do the rounds of the factories, and he'll pick up some local people here and there who are left in town. You wait here till we get back. You'll be in direct contact with the Cheka. But, there—I nearly forget! The brigadier sent me an urgent wire yesterday evening: he's in desperate need of sixteen machine guns. I gave the order at once, so they must be ready by now. They must be dispatched to Shklyaev at once, by car. Talk to Lavrukhin about it. I would have taken them myself, only I think we should go to Krastilitsy first and have a look at what's happening with those boys of ours."

Everyone was already in outdoor clothes; Shustry was pulling on his raincoat. The secretary picked up the report and turned off the light. The walls turned bluish gray. Outside a thin mist was spreading. The windowpanes were still quivering.

"You will allow me—" Shustry stepped to one side before Stepan. "You will allow me to get those machine guns from Lavrukhin and take them to Shklyaev. In fact, I could stay there with him for as long as the situation remains serious. In any case, I have absolutely nothing more to do here." And he lowered his eyes.

"Very well, then," answered Stepan. "That's an excellent suggestion."

They went toward the doors.

"Yes, but someone will have to acquaint Zudin with our decision. What about you, Shcheglov? Do you want to do it?"

"No, please, Stepan, I couldn't, I wouldn't know how. . . ."

"Well, I haven't got time now. It seems to rest with you, Tkacheev, to go and see him a minute."

They all went out at the same time, crowded together in a manner both quick and businesslike. The room at once went gloomy and dull. The floor was strewn with cigaret stubs and scraps of paper. On the tablecloth lay the remains of the pencil Stepan had snapped in two. And the stool used by Shustry and his tightly buckled black portfolio suddenly looked abandoned and redundant. There was a smell of tobacco smoke; indeed, it hung in the air like a thick, bluish shroud reminiscent of the boom of the battle nearby and the abrupt report of the coming execution.

9

A long heavy chain was pulling on Zudin's arm, and he had no more strength to oppose it. He groaned, turned, and opened his eyes. The gray morning shone soberly into the room, beside the bed stood Tkacheev. Zudin leaped up. It was suddenly so hot, so oppressive, that his heart beat against the walls of his breast like a machine gun.

"I woke you, comrade?" His words had a soft and friendly ring. Zudin's skin was burning with anxiety, he was drenched with sweat. "But I could't wait. I had to hurry and inform you of our decision."

He sat down next to Zudin, on the hard, prickly mattress. Zudin eagerly searched his sunken eyes.

"Yes! You're to be shot." Softly and sadly he answered Zudin's unspoken question, without raising his eyes.

"I knew it," whispered Zudin, and took Tkacheev's hand. "I knew it."

Tkacheev sighed.

"They wanted to send Shcheglov to you, and then Stepan wanted to come, but they've known you for too long. They said, 'A good comrade, what a pity,' and they couldn't bring themselves to come. I don't know you so well, so I had to be the one to tell you of the verdict. It is a hard task, Comrade Zudin. Please believe only that we did not decide out of hate or revenge: there was no other way!" And now for the first time, he raised his deep-sunk, tormented eyes to Zudin.

"The nonsense Shustry talked disgusted us all. But he's a good fellow, honest, of sound and morally upright principles, perhaps a little narrow-minded, but one can't encompass everything in one's head. Of course, we were not in agreement with him."

"And I thought . . ." ventured Zudin, nervously, fearfully.

"No, we simply reasoned from the start that you were guilty. You had aggravated the mistrust of the workers, which might ruin our cause. Not us, you understand, but our cause. The devil drove you to take pity on that terrible woman. How many of that miserable scum we still have! But you, an old revolutionary! You should have fixed your attention only on the facts of the matter and, as for anything else, passed on, passed on! But it goes without saying that this old mud is very sticky. If one examines oneself, one sees that that is the way things go, with very few exceptions. If we are so audacious as to want, as we do, to raze a mountain, we'll be disgusted at the amount of mud that will fall on us. All this would not, of course, be of importance if we were our own subjects. Man is as man is. There's no making a black horse white. But we are the leaders. Often, at a meeting, one can stand somewhere and count nothing but heads, heads, heads, a whole sea of them. And you know, the revolution, the shifting of the world onto new foundations, is done by those heads, and not by us. Comrade, it is only self-deception and illusion to think that it is our will that will be imposed on those heads. Only a fool would think that. We only hammer a united will out of their elemental needs. We are authorizing the unproductive expenditure of thousands of those heads as targets in the struggle that signify our class strength. We don't, and can't do otherwise, other than what affects the simplest and most basic interest of those heads. The most lofty ideals must be founded on and harmonized with the urgent and limited interests of the masses.

"'Children, would you like some fresh white rolls? Like these?' And you throw them one to taste. First, they begin to whoop with enthusiasm, then they foam at the mouth. 'I'll tell you how you can get them. Follow me! Knock down this! Grab that!' And then fall the walls of reinforced concrete, the cast-iron girders crack like rotten wood, and it is the masses who do this, the masses who know nothing, to be sure, but believe they will get the longed-for bread.

"And now the walls have fallen, but there are no rolls. They throw you distrustful looks from their weary eyes. Have you deceived them? Didn't you yourself believe that this was the way to fresh white rolls? And you look them frankly and honestly in the eye, because you know that right is on your side, and that you have not deceived them. You have stayed true to the interests of the masses at large. This calms them. 'Comrades, be patient! You have overcome only the first obstacle. Arm yourselves with hatred and endurance, so as to strike a fresh blow at the enemy. Don't you see that you are getting nearer to your crisp white bread?'

"'We see, we certainly do see,' they cry in their enthusiasm, though they see, and can see, nothing, yet they steadfastly believe that they see.

"You lead them, and they are blindly devoted to you, they make a god of you. You are their hero, their idol, their dictator, their good witch doctor, in short, you are their all. With them, you surmount the obstacles that bar your way. And these masses are happy, every one of them, to give their lives for you. And the white bread rolls? At times they forget them completely. They are bewitched by the noble spell of the struggle. But don't believe for one moment that you can lead them forward on enthusiasm alone. The beacon of that fresh white bread, on account of which they were roused to arms, will shine still nearer and more dazzling. Only then is the continuation of the fight for a better world order assured. Only then are the masses ready to follow you, ready to give their lives for your ideal, for an ideal that is probably not clear to them, not understood, but which they feel in their unconscious mind to be good. They feel it in you, in your heart, in your whole bearing, in your open, honest love for those suffering masses, love for which you are ready at any second to die for them, for those in chains. Then you become the pulse, the heart, and the mind of those great sacred masses. And then, through them, you can accomplish marvels of the sort that occur in fairy tales, marvels the world has not yet seen, marvels that leave the heavens gaping with wonder. Only, see that you yourself betray no weakness. Think, consider, go over every step of everything you do, for what is personal behavior becomes general. Fix your mind on the essentials of any situation, so as not to be confused later by any fresh obstacle, except the kind where you can stay smiling and steadfast in bearing, and say, 'And now, what?'

"Only look at yourself and your gleaming eyes as you eagerly follow my every word! And now picture to yourself one of these mighty leaders who has led the hungry suffering masses from their first uprising to the last resolute battles—led them to glory, you understand—suddenly, and without stopping to think, stooping to pick up some chip of a bygone luxury and put it in his pocket. And they all see him do it. Only think of that!" Tkacheev sighed again and slowly shook his head.

"We are placed too high, comrade, we may not stoop. How could we? The struggle is too crucial to take any chances. One false step, and mistrust raises its ugly head. Every day a friend notices something about another friend. Every day you can observe some common unrest. Mistrust of us, mistrust of Shustry, mistrust of you. They do not waver. I saw how you looked at us on the Commission, and how narrow-minded the proceedings appeared to you. Yes, that is how *we* felt. But the masses have suddenly come to a standstill and have raised a whole forest of even stronger fists.

"Liars and traitors! Can that be true? Yes, indeed, you may all be such! All are tarred with the same brush! 'Strike them down!' cries a single, bold voice. So then what happens? Another moment's delay, and we shall all be torn to pieces. It's too late to try to explain, and impossible. The masses can never grasp any attempt at justification. The masses understand only yes or no. Our whole cause, you understand, our great struggle for the happiness of millions, everything we've attained with so many sacrifices, with so much hardship, suffering, and blood on the part of many generations, can vanish like smoke, like a soap bubble, because a good comrade allowed himself to be negligent out of kindness, or because he was tired and was caught off guard. Now tell me, what should be done with him in order to save the great cause?"

"Cut him down!" rapped out Zudin, in tones both hollow and sharp.

"Yes, cut him down," echoed Tkacheev. "So we are cutting you down to save our cause and, in departing, we press your honest hand."

He gripped Zudin's hand hard and stood up.

"Yes, it is frightful if you look at it long enough. Shcheglov tried to pass a motion not to execute you but to pretend that we had, and send you into perpetual exile where you could work under another name. But it would be hard—impossible—to conduct yourself in such a way as always to go unrecognized and unknown. We are all too much in view, the eyes of the world are on us. Besides, we are a Party, a great Party. And is that all we are? We do not wish to speak of things we have already dwelt on: of how their eyes go everywhere, and we must always keep very careful watch. How many honest and righteous men are there who have gone forward hand in hand with us, but who have strayed from our ranks because of some petty misunderstanding and lost their footing, so that they grasp at every straw that comes their way. And if we were to tell these sincere and upright masses now that Zudin is not guilty but wasn't conscious of what he was doing, do you think they would understand? Or believe it? Maybe, in time to come, when the long struggle for a better social order will have brought them to a maturer mind. But now, in the present state of things, they'll never understand. No one will believe it. Take

Shustry, for only one! And do you know what they *will* say?" Tkacheev made an embittered gesture. "The devil knows what they'll say!

"And think how great those risks were that took the form of chocolate, silk, dancers, music, wine, and all the rest of it, things that are not at all mean or contemptible in themselves—quite the contrary!—but things that are still unattainable by the masses and to which they are not accustomed, for these are things that belong to the still glittering ruins that are reminders—however slight—of the sovereign lords of a past world. Are there not too many of these risks in our path? Tell me! In our path and in the Party workers' path. Or is a man to believe that the temptation is not too great? Certainly, there are many among us who have been reared in the monastic asceticism of the Party's underground movement. But even so!" Tkacheev was pulling wrathfully at his beard. "What will they say when it all comes out that even Zudin, who seemed to be the most honest of men, has vilely betrayed us all—this is the kind of thing they'll say, brother—taken bribes of chocolate, silk, and gold. There will be no excuse we can make to them, for the deprivations of centuries have made them mistrustful, and men will say, 'That bandit Zudin, who they said had been shot, has really been hidden by our leaders! That's our leaders for you!'

"Zudin, you will understand that this would be like a warm shower of blessed spring rain on the seed sown by those self-seeking hypocrites and other scum, whose only thought is how to bring shame on our cause: 'If Zudin can do it and they cover up for him, so can we.' So we must wipe out this scandal with a sharp and bloody retort, effective for ourselves and for others.

"Merciless terror! Blood-stained horror! On the heads of all those who forget, who grow weary, all those who have had the naive temerity to place themselves in the foremost rank of the revolution, in full view of the millions of eyes of the whole world, without considering their own strength. And only see how we shall use this to drive forward, like a chisel of steel into the wedge. What though shivers of our steel armorhead fall away at the impact? The struggle demands sacrifice. Think of that gigantic wave of universal proportions that we have raised for ourselves against this obstacle, and how we must press through a swell made up of the generality of mankind, a swell grown hard through centuries of exploitation of man by man. And you know that we shall achieve our goal only when we can remain honest and severe with others and, in the sight of others, with ourselves.

"That is the fate of us all and, Zudin, your fate, too!

"I still have something to tell you of minor importance. We have resolved not to delay, but to execute judgment tonight. Then, what else?"—and again Tkacheev clasped his hand. "Valtz and Pavlov were shot this morning." He was silent a while. "And something else: your wife and children asked for permission to visit you. We refused up till today. But today—well, it's as you like. They must now be downstairs in the commandant's office. Will you see them, or had you rather we refuse again?"

Utterly broken, Zudin sucked in air through clenched teeth.

"Let them come," he said wearily.

"So, now, good-bye!"

"Good-bye!"

"Brother, don't be angry. Face it bravely!"

But Zudin could no longer stand on his feet. Strength leaving him, he fell back, his face upturned.

In his earliest youth he had been in the habit of stretching out flat on his back, as he was now, and staring at the blue, boundless sky that suddenly seemed to come nearer. He would push his hands into the earth around him, to get a hold. The thin silver cobwebs hovered in the air, stirring at the slightest breeze, and in the hollow nearby, for the most part overgrown with dry prickly burdocks, there flew and chattered swarms of colored goldfinches. It was gay and friendly, and at the same time sad and melancholy. Beyond this was a stretch of barren grass, warmed by the setting sun, and a flow of water, over which great green and golden flies whirled and played. So lying, he liked to forget that nearby, at the rear of the dirty courtyard, his mother might be impatiently waiting for him in her squalid, musty cellar, with rags covering her faded bosom, with fingers shriveled and raw from washing, waiting for him to come back from the store with the laundry blueing she had sent him to bring. He felt sad now as he had then, yet he knew no more why he felt this now than he did before.

From the corridor loud, familiar voices came to his ears. Zudin jumped to his feet, tidied his bed, and forced a smile to his lips as, the sentry standing close by, a white and trembling Lisa appeared in the doorway with Mitya and Masha clinging to her in fear.

The thought, "Still the same old, worn-out shoes," flew through Zudin's mind, and with a lack of restraint and a gaiety unnatural to him, he stretched out his hands to them.

"Well, hallo! You missed me, did you? You were really worried?" He looked searchingly at Lisa, who sank abruptly onto the stool.

"Lyosha, my dear! Whatever's happened? Whatever's happened?" She burst into tears.

"But, Lisa, what is there to cry about? What's so out of the ordinary? That I was placed under arrest for a few days? You should be used to that by now."

"Yes, when it was the gendarmes. But now—our own people! And everyone said—everyone said that we were ruined, that you'd been shot, and they'd found gold, chocolate . . . Lyosha, dear, it was torture, torture, imagine!" And again she started to quiver with hysterical spasms that went through her whole body, gulping out words that were stifled with her fast-flowing tears.

"'Everyone said!' Don't you yourself know best what the truth is? What frightened you then? Old wives' chatter! Now be a good girl and leave off crying, calm yourself. It's all over, and there's nothing more to cry about. Now, smile!"

"Mitya, Masha, come and sit on Father's knee. I'll show you how the Cossacks ride. Don't be afraid, that's right! Now, hold on tight to my neck. 'This is the way the Cossack rides. . . .'"

After a while he set the children down again.

"Now, Lisa, do stop howling. Or have you made up your mind to sit there crying till the stool comes unglued? Now, what's there to cry about?"

"Oh, Lyosha, my dear, my darling, I'm so afraid. I don't understand or know what to think: what, how, why?!"

"There's nothing to understand. The White Guard used the fact that we accepted those stockings and chocolate and made a whole business out of it. So I was arrested until the case could be proved. And now it's all been threshed out that it was a trumped-up business, and the affair is over and done with."

"Oh, Lyosha, Lyosha, I was so frightened. I was arrested, too, that day, and they came to search the house, and turned everything upside down—for two days I couldn't move out of the house—they posted a sentry at the door. The people flocked into our courtyard—oh, they must have come from all over the city; someone threatened to smash our windows. They were bourgeois, and also there were our own people.

"Then a quick little man with short hair came with a briefcase and kept on asking if I'd ever accepted gold. Everyone said you must be dead. Then the sentry moved away from the house and told me I could go out. But they wouldn't let me come to you. I was afraid to leave the house, but it was terrible there, too. . . . And then, you know, they said all sorts of vile things about you, that you had lived with Valtz. . . ." She reddened with embarrassment as she said this. "Lyosha, can that really be true? Have you? Have you been unfaithful to me?"

"Oh, Lisa! What nonsense! I'm your faithful old Alik, always true, never changing."

She uttered a sigh of relief.

"But what's to happen now? You say the case is over? So will you be released? Otherwise, we're lost without you! Dear Heaven, how thin you've got. Haven't they fed you here?"

"What? . . . What did you say? . . . Oh, *food*! . . . Don't worry, they've fed me very well. Perhaps I'm thinner because I had a cold. But that's all over now. Tomorrow I'll be out. Only, Lisa, you should know this has been a very unpleasant case. The word's got out that Valtz was nothing but a White Guard spy and a thief. Remember what I told you then? Chocolate and stockings don't make a brother. And how right I was! She has compromised me so that it's impossible for me to stay in Russia. The Cheka is sending me abroad, to Australia. It's very, very far away and the mission will take at least a year, if not longer. The worst part is that I won't be able to write. I may even have to stay away for a few years, and even as much as ten. But there's nothing to be done about it; the revolution and the happiness of the international proletariat is worth it. Don't you think I'm right? . . ." And he looked into her eyes that had again filled with tears.

"Lyosha, how terrible! For us to be deserted again, without you, and alone in the world! Lyosha, my dearest, talk yourself out of it somehow. Oh, my darling, don't go away!"

"What sort of rubbish is this? You're the wife of a revolutionary! So be proud that your husband has left his family and home, perhaps for a long time or even for ever, to go to the other end of the world and break the chains that bind us. Lisochka, dear, think of the glory: doesn't it make you terribly proud?"

A long silence fell, broken only by the woman's stifled sobbing.

"You and the children will be taken care of; you won't be deserted. In case of need, call Shcheglov—Vasily Prokofich. He is here from Moscow now. You could work at a factory. You should certainly go and work at a factory. The children could go and live with your sister in the country. Besides, you're completely free. There is a possibility I may not come back. I shouldn't be offended if you had a companion you wanted to marry, as long as he's an honest man, like me. In fact, that would be far more natural for you than to stay on like a nun and live out the rest of your life, remembering. Of course, you must always think of the children. They must grow up to be good and strong people and know how to take life by the throat and never bow their heads in slavery!"

"Lyosha, I'm afraid. You speak so strangely, as if you were really going away for ever. Or are you hiding something from me, something dreadful?"

"You're a silly! What should I be hiding? There's nothing dreadful: would I be behaving like this if there were? No, I'm only taking the long view of the matter: I must soon go very far away, and who knows if and when I'll come back, maybe we shan't see each other again.

"I'll probably have to leave tomorrow morning. So, without our wanting it to be, this will be our last meeting today. I'll tell you what: let's take each other's departure as being for ever, so we'll be even happier to see each other again, that's all!"

They embraced each other tenderly. He stepped back to stroke the frightened children's hair. Lisa went on spasmodically sobbing.

"Oh, Lyosha, if you knew how hard this is. What an awful affliction it is to have our whole lives suddenly wiped out like this! Of course, I'm proud of you, terribly proud! You're my only pride and joy! You're not like anyone else. That's why I love you so very much. But living without you and knowing that, somewhere in the world, you're trying to manage all alone, or may be ill, or dying, and I don't know it and can never get there—can any torment be worse than that? Ah, Lyosha, Lyosha, I haven't any strength left. My whole life is going. From the moment I met you I've been heartsick for you—and now! . . ."

In hopeless pain, this pale, unprepossessing woman lowered her transparent, tear-washed gaze, as if she were seeking for something in the depths below, but could not find it.

"Lisa, it's the rule here that visits shouldn't last longer than ten minutes: we've gone a long way over. You'll have to leave, my dearest. Come again tomorrow. But telephone first to see if I haven't gone."

Lisa drew a deep, painful breath and began to prepare for departure, tying her warm scarf about her head.

"Oh, yes, another thing—I nearly forgot to tell you the most important part: what I told you about my journey is a great Party secret. No one must hear about it, do you understand? You must swear to me that you won't ever breathe a word of it to a soul, otherwise it would mean death for me. Do you understand? Outside yourself and three members of the Central Committee, no one knows about it. For anyone else it will be openly passed around that Zudin was shot for being in league with the White Guard. But it's all untrue. You know the truth now: I'm alive and have gone on a long journey, that's all it is. Now, farewell, Lisochka! Bear up, and be worthy of your husband!"

He hastily kissed the children. Leaning his forearms on the table and forcing his lips, as if with tongs, into a smile, he saw how his wife went bowed with grief through the door, and how the children anxiously clung to her, and then, in the distance, he again caught the sound of their familiar, strident, beloved little voices.

Now Zudin could resist no longer. He threw himself on the bed. He began to weep soundlessly, with sobs that shook his whole body. He bit into the pillow.

It was all past and done with. There remained to him only a poor little long-drawn-out empty second, and then—death. What's past is past, thought Zudin, there is nothing more, nothing, not even death, because I'll not sense it. There may be a sharp physical pain probably lasting for one or two seconds, a sense of taking leave of life for the last time. But of death itself I shall have no sensation, because there is no death. For an alive man there is no death. And a dead man doesn't sense it.

It vexes me that they will not only execute me but sully my name as well, and everyone will believe that Zudin, the head of the regional Cheka, allowed himself to take bribes, and that shooting me was a victory over capitalism.

Ah, if you could only live it over again, even a little of it, if only you could work again . . . you'd go straight to the front. What a fresh and joyful aspect that would give to life. You would turn your energies to completely fresh fields.

It will be bitter shame for the children, when they grow up, to discover what a slur there is on your name. They will find out the details and curse their father. Couldn't something have been done to avoid that? What a pity he had not brought up the matter when he talked with Tkacheev. It had not even occurred to him then.

He thrust his hands into his pockets, went to the window, and looked out at the river. He could see the ice moving in defiance and beauty, where before there had been only gloom and mist over everything. Below, beyond the yellow stone wall, children played on the stone-paved quay; he could hear their voices, though not clearly, and see their gestures. A little girl with thin braids in a short velvet coat hopped on one leg from one white-chalked square to the next, her braids flapping as she went. Zudin thought of his own little Masha, and again something struggled in his throat. But he overcame it and sat down quietly at the table.

Perhaps no other solution was possible. The only important thing is the cause—that the cause should not suffer. That alone matters, and all the rest . . . Zudin pondered deeply.

Now what if, when they'd shot you, they then said they'd shot an honest man? But that would be foolish. Nobody would understand or believe it. People would say, "If he was innocent, why did you shoot him? That sort of thing isn't done, you know!

So you're not as steel-infallible as you were thought to be."

And there would be some who chuckle craftily and prick up their ears and greedily drag their tasty morsels into the corner to the sound of their "lady secretaries'" gay laughter. Or don't such people exist?

But how many honest comrades are there, how many of them would wish a pure idealism to sweep away the fragments of chocolate, ballerinas, and other rubble of the past, things that adhere to past luxury? Such persons must be borne in mind so that, at every opportunity, people could cry, "*Remember Zudin!* He was a poor wretch who for one moment betrayed the future to the past. We shot him down like a dangerous beast, like a dog. Are you tempted by his fate? Then drop all the mud of the past, however glittering and enticing it seems, and think of the future. The future and the present!"

But it may be, thought Zudin, that lone beings will arise who wrench themselves entirely away from the masses in their work and their mode of life, who begin to philosophize and think about the obverse: how to save the revolution—from the masses, from the workers, from mutiny—and even go as far as ballerinas and chocolate, and smoking Havana cigars, blowing on their chocolate in fine china cups, toying with massive watch chains that dangle from their vests, they may mumble in refined tones from shaven lips: "We are Communists."

What? What about Zudin? Have you forgotten how he was punished for your sake?

No, may the name of that pitiful wretch burn itself into the minds of all men and be a reminder of treachery and baseness and transgression in the face of that most pure and noble cause, the Revolution. For on this steadfastness, on this eternal movement forward, on this life in the future and the happiness of mankind, that Communism for which it is rewarding to live and die is founded.

Zudin straightened in gladness and pride, his eyes shone with courage, he took a pace up and down the room, sat down at the table and began impatiently to drum on it with his fingers.

Far in the distance, beyond the river, the black ripples of endless columns of workers were already streaming onward, and above them, the spring air swung and vibrated deeply with the noble strains of the mighty "*International.*"

1922

Fro

Andrey Platonov

He had gone far off, and for a long time. He might never return. The express train had drawn away, and now in the open country began to sing a song of parting. Those who had come onto the platform to see the passengers off returned to their sedentary lives. A porter came up with a broom and began to sweep the platform, now resembling the deck of a deserted ship.

"Move aside, citizeness," said the porter to the two sturdy legs that remained.

The young woman moved over to the wall by the letter box and began to read the collection times printed on it. The collections were frequent. You could write letters every day. She ran her finger over the iron casing of the box. It was strong. Your very soul could go into a letter and not be lost.

Beyond the station lay a new railroad town; on the white walls of the houses quivered shadows cast by the leaves of trees, the summer evening sun spread its light, clear and sad, over nature and dwellings alike, as if through a transparent emptiness without any air to breathe. At the hour when night was about to descend on the world, everything was far too distinctly outlined, dazzling to the point of illusion, as if unreal.

The young woman halted, startled at the strangeness of the light. In all her twenty years she could not remember such a deserted, shining, silent vacuum of space; her heart felt faint with the rarity of the air, with the longing for the man she loved to return. She caught sight of her reflection in the hairdresser's window: a commonplace appearance, her hair arranged in puffs and loops (in the style of the last century), two deep gray eyes looking out with a kind of tenderness so intense as to seem artificial—it had become second nature to love the man who had gone away, she wanted him to love her, continuously, unceasingly, so that deep in her body, inside her ordinary, dull soul, there might linger and grow a second cherished life. But she could not love as she wished to love, strongly and unfailingly; sometimes when wearied she wept that her heart had not proved itself unquenchable.

She lived in a new three-room apartment. One room was occupied by her widowed father, a locomotive engineer; the other two belonged to her and her husband, who had just left for the Far East to install and put into operation certain incomprehensible electrical apparatus. He was always busy with mysterious machines, hoping that machines would transform the world to the greater welfare and delight of mankind, or for some such reason. His wife did not know what exactly.

Aging now, her father took a train out only rarely. He was called on as substitute engineer if one of the others fell ill. He would test machines returned from the repair shop, or he might run a light train on local service. The year before they had thought of pensioning him off. Not knowing what this would mean, the old man at first agreed but after four days at liberty, on the fifth he went out to the semaphore and seated himself on a rise in the yard and stayed there till late at night, his eyes bright with tears, watching the engines lumbering at the head of the trains. Since then he had gone daily to the rise to watch the engines, living in imagination and compassion for them. Each evening he would turn up at home, worn out, as if he had himself been handling an engine in heavy traffic. Once home, he would wash his hands, sighing, telling how the brake block had dropped out of a train on Hill 9,000 or something of the sort. He would ask his daughter shyly for some vaseline to grease his left palm, as if it had grown calloused pulling on the stiff governor valve. Then he would sit down to his supper and soon would fall asleep in sheer content.

Next morning he would again go down to the yard and spend the day watching, tears in his eyes, carried away by imagination, compassion, and the frenzy of his lonely enthusiasm. If he thought some locomotive on the track showed a defect or that an engineer was driving a particularly well-tuned engine, he would shout words of blame or caution from his elevated post: "Draw off the water, open that faucet, you good-for-nothing! Blow through it! . . . Tip off that sand: you'll never get up the slope! What the hell're you wasting it like that for? . . . Screw that cap down tighter, don't let your steam off; what d'you think you're driving, an engine or a stove?" If the train had come out badly assembled, with the lighter cars at the head or in the middle, where they could be crushed by a too sudden braking, the retired engineer up on his rise would shake his fist at the guard in the caboose. Again, when his old locomotive happened by, with his one-time fireman, Benjamin, at the controls, the old man would always find some obvious fault with the engine—it was different in his time—and call out to the fireman about what to do to the engineer: "Hi, Benjamin, spit in his eye, Benjamin, old lad," the old man would call from his lonely stand on the rise.

When the weather was overcast, he would take an umbrella, and his only daughter would take his lunch to the rise, for she felt sorry for him when he came back at night, haggard, hungry, and out of sorts because of his unquenched longing for work. But recently, while the old man was standing at his usual vantage point, keeping his eye on the traffic and hurling blasphemies, the party organizer from the depot, Comrade Piskunov, came up to him. He took the old man by the arm and led him back to the depot. The clerk in the depot office re-

registered the old man for active service. The old man climbed up to the cabin of a cold locomotive, sat down, and hugged the boiler, as if he had been reunited with the entire working class.

When his daughter returned from seeing her husband off to work, he would call to her, "Frossy, give me a bite of what you've got in the oven, I may get called out tonight."

He was always expecting to be called at any moment to take out a train, but in fact this happened only once every three or four days, when freight trains were being assembled out of lightweight cars, or for some other easy task. Even so, the father was afraid of having to go out on an empty stomach, unfueled and in a bad humor. Consequently, he was always careful of his health, his strength, and his digestion, for in his own estimation he was the mainstay of the railroad, a steel-hardened cadre. "Citizen engineer," the old man would address himself with great dignity and precise articulation, and his response to this was an important silence, as if hearing a distant ovation.

Now Frossy opened the oven door, took out a hot dish, and gave her father a helping. The evening sun lit up every corner of the apartment, even penetrating Frossy's body to where her heart was beating, an engine that continually tuned the coursing blood and the sense of vitality. She went to her own room. On her table stood a photograph of her husband as a boy; he had never had his photograph taken since childhood, for he was completely uninterested in himself and indifferent to his own face. The yellowing photograph showed a little boy with an infant's large head and wearing a poor shirt and cheap trousers, with no shoes on his feet. Behind him was a magical background of trees with a fountain and a palace in the distance. The little boy looked out attentively on a world as yet little known to him, without seeming to notice the beautiful existence in the photographer's backcloth. The beautiful existence was in the boy himself, the wide-faced, alert, shy little boy, who held a green sprig instead of a toy and whose bare feet confidently stood on the earth.

Night had already fallen. The local herder had brought the cows in from the steppe. They were mooing their demands to rest beside their masters; the women of the house led them into the yard. The long day grew chilly as it changed to night. Frossy sat in the dark, content with love and remembrance of the man who had gone. Outside the window the pine trees rose straight up to the serene vastness of the skies, the tiny voice of tiny birds sang their late songs, chorusing sleepily, while the crickets, those guardians of darkness, chorused their sweet assurance that all was well, that they would not sleep but keep watch.

The father asked Frossy whether she was going to the social

club. There was to be novel entertainment there that evening: a battle of flowers and a comic turn by members of the conductors' reserve.

"No, I'm not," said Frossy, "I'll be longing for my husband here at home."

"Longing for Fedka?" said the engineer, "he'll be back; he'll be here before the year is up. But never mind, long for him. I used to be away for only a day or two, but your poor dear mother hardly knew what to do with herself, the little bourgeois housewife."

"Well, I'm not a bourgeois housewife, and I don't know what to do with myself either," returned Frossy, surprised at herself. "No, that's not right, surely I'm a bourgeois, too."

Her father said soothingly, "*You're* not a bourgeois housewife! They don't exist any more, they're all dead and gone long since. To be a bourgeois, you'll have to live and learn a long time yet; they were all right, those women."

"If you'll go to your room, papa," said Frossy, "I'll bring you your supper directly, but just now I'd like to be alone."

"It *is* suppertime," he concurred, "but I shouldn't be surprised if they sent for me from the depot. Someone may fall ill, or go off on a binge, or maybe a death in the family—anything can happen. So then *I* have to turn out—the railroad must run. Ah, your Fedka's well away by this time in that express—green lights flashing to let her by. You know, they clear the track now for forty kilometers ahead. The engineer can see a long distance, and he's got electricity to tend the engine by—everything just so!"

The old man delayed leaving. He went out, then came back, mumbling. He liked to be with his daughter or to be with someone when a locomotive was not possessing all his thoughts and feelings.

"Papa, go and get ready for supper!" His daughter bade him; she wanted to listen to the crickets, gaze at the pine trees outside the window, and think about her husband.

"Well, you're a strange one," muttered her father as he went off.

When she had given her father his meal, Frossy left the house. Entertainment night at the club was in full swing, with music and singing by a group of comedians from the conductors' reserve: "Oh, pine tree, what a pine tree, and what pine cones on the pine tree! Toot-toot-toot (a locomotive) rrearrr (an airplane) phew-phew-phew (an ice breaker). Now do what we do and bend over, do as we do and get up, say toot-toot, rrearrr, wake up every coffin, more art, more culture, more output, that's our goal!"

The audience stirred itself, mumbled timidly, and was hard put to follow the comedians' example and keep up the tenor of the entertainment.

Frossy went past the club to the point, now deserted, where the mountings protecting the main line began. A fast train came in from the Far East. The locomotive cut off steam, and the engine strained forward, casting its brilliant searchlight ahead. Somewhere along the line this train would have met the express rushing on toward the Far East carrying off her dear one. Intently she stared at the fast train that had passed her husband. She went back to the station, but on her way the train, having come to a halt, left again. The tail coach disappeared into the darkness, indifferent to the melancholy of people who came and went. There was no one Frossy did not know on the platform or in the station; none of the passengers had got off the train, so there was no one she could ask about the express train or about her husband. Still, perhaps someone had seen it and would know something.

At the station, however, there were only two old women sitting and waiting for the midnight local, and the peasant who came daily to clean was as usual sweeping around their feet. They always come and sweep when you simply want to stand there and think, as if they were against people.

Frossy moved out of the cleaner's way, but he pursued her with his broom. "You wouldn't have heard anything about the No. 2 express, would you?" she asked him. "Is it all right? It came through here today. Have there been any announcements about it?"

"You can go on the platform when the train comes in," said the cleaner, "but there aren't any trains expected now. Go inside the station, citizeness. The public are always hanging around here. Better at home in bed, reading the papers. But no, they must hang around, dirtying up the place."

Frossy crossed the tracks, past the points, toward the other side of the station. Here was the circular loading yard for the freight trains, the coaling yard, the slag pit, and a turntable for the locomotives. The area was brightly lit, and clouds of steam and smoke floated in the upper air. Some of the engines were throbbing, getting up steam, while others were letting off steam or cooling as they were washed down. Four women carrying iron shovels passed close to Frossy, and behind them came a man, perhaps an official in charge of works or a crew foreman.

"Who're you looking for out here, my pretty?" he asked. "You've lost him, you won't get him back: they don't come back once they've gone. What about lending us a hand with the rolling stock?"

Frossy hesitated. "Give me a shovel."

"Here's mine." The foreman handed it to her. "You women," he ordered the others, "go over to the third pit; I'll be at the first."

He led Frossy to the clinker pit, where the locomotives were emptying their furnaces, put her to work, and left. Two other women were working in the pit, throwing the hot clinkers out. Frossy got down beside them and began to shovel, glad that the others were strangers. There was a smell of burning and of gas: breathing was not easy; it was a heavy, tiring job heaving the clinkers up, for the pit was narrow and oppressively hot. But it was just this that made Frossy feel better, it was something for her to do, in company with her workmates, under the huge, free night, lit by stars and electric lamps. In her heart her love slept in peace. The express was now well on its way. Lying on a plank in an upper berth of a comfortless coach, her man slept with Siberia all around him. Let him sleep untroubled and may the engineer see far ahead and keep clear of accidents.

Before long Frossy and one of the other women came out of the pit. The clinkers had to be loaded onto a flatcar now. As they tossed up the hot cinders, they glanced at each other and now and then exchanged a few words when they stopped to rest and breathe in the fresh air.

Frossy's workmate was about thirty. Hot as it was, she kept shivering and tugging her shabby coat about her. She had just come out of jail, having spent four days in custody on a charge brought by a mean man. Her husband was a nightwatchman. It was his job, armed with a rifle, to patrol the cooperative storehouse all night, for which he was paid sixty rubles a month. When his wife was arrested, the nightwatchman went in tears to the prison authorities to beg for her release; until her arrest, she had been living with another man, who carelessly, on impulse (perhaps out of weariness or fear), had told her of some fraud he had committed. But then, it seems, getting frightened, he had tried to ruin her to prevent her from reporting him. Now he himself had been arrested and, she hoped, was suffering. Now that she was freed, she would again be living with her husband. There was work to be had now, bread they could buy, and clothing that together they would find somehow or other.

Frossy told her of her own sorrow and of her husband's having gone off on a long trip.

"He's only gone on a trip, he's not dead, he'll come back," the woman comforted her. "But in that jail I got really downhearted, I felt so blue, I'd never been in jail before, I wasn't used to it; I wouldn't have felt so bad if I had been. I was always so innocent, the law never had laid a hand on me. When I came out and went home, my husband was so happy to see me he cried, but he wouldn't kiss me: he thinks I'm a prisoner, an important person! But, really, like always, I'm easy to get along with. That night he had to go out to work. That was hard on us both. He takes his gun. 'Come on, I'll buy you a drink,' he says. All I had was twelve kopeks, though, only enough for one glass, so we could have had half a glass each. But I was feeling so blue, it just wouldn't pass. I told him to go ahead and have his own glass, and then when we'd more money and my heart didn't feel so heavy, we'd go out together and have a whole bottle. So that's what I told him to do, and I came on down here to work. I was pretty sure they'd be loading timber, or changing rails, or something. Even at night there's always some job going. I felt, if I could get down here with other people, I'd get over the blues and feel better. And honest, since I've been talking to you, I feel as if you might be a cousin of mine. Well now, let's finish with the flatcar, they'll give us our money at the office, and I'll be able to go out and buy bread tomorrow. Frossy!" she called over to the slag pit where a namesake of Frossy's was working, "is there much left to do?"

"No," answered the other Frossy, "not much at all, only a few lumps."

"Climb up here," said the nightwatchman's wife, "We'll get done faster, and go get what's owing to us, together."

Around them locomotives were being stoked for long journeys, or else were cooling off letting their breath out into the air. The crew foreman came up. "Well, how's it going, you women? Finished in the pit? Aha! Quick march, off you all go to the office, I'll be along in a jiffy. That's where you get your pay, and then we'll see who's going dancing at the club and who's going home to raise a family. You'll have plenty to do."

At the office the women signed their names: Efrosinya Evstafyeva, Natalya Bukova, and three letters that looked like Eva, followed by the hammer-and-sickle, instead of another Efrosinya, for the owner of the name had fallen back into illiteracy. They each got three rubles and twenty kopeks and set off for home. Frossy Evstafyeva and Natasha, the nightwatchman's wife, walked together. Frossy invited her new friend home to wash and freshen up.

The old man lay asleep on the trunk in the kitchen. He was fully dressed, with even a winter jacket and a cap with the engineer's badge on it. He was ready for any sudden call about some technical breakdown, for in that event he would have to present himself on the instant at the scene of the mishap.

Noiselessly, the women freshened themselves, powdered

their noses, smiled at each other, and went out again. It was already quite late, probably the dance and certainly the battle of flowers had begun at the club. As long as Frossy's husband lay sleeping in the uncomfortable coach, his heart felt nothing, had no recollection of her, and no love for her. She was as if alone in the world, free from either happiness or depression and she wanted now to dance a little, hear music, hold others by the hand. In the morning, when he would wake alone and the thought of her would abruptly return to him, she would perhaps let the tears fall.

The two women ran at top speed to the club. The local train went by. It was midnight, then, not yet too late. An amateur jazz band was playing at the club, and Frossy Evstafyeva was at once invited by an assistant mechanic to dance to the strains of "Rio Rita."

Frossy went on dancing with a happy face; she liked music; in her mind the music of sorrow and gladness were inseparable, as in real life, as in her own soul. While dancing she had only a dim recollection of herself. She moved as if in a slight trance, bemused, her body making the right steps of its own accord, her blood roused by the tune.

"Have they had the battle of flowers yet?" she murmured to her partner, her breathing coming fast.

"It's just finished. Why did you get here so late?" he answered tenderly, as if he had always been in love with Frossy, always pining for her.

"Oh, what a pity," said Frossy.

"You like it here?" asked her partner.

"I certainly do," she replied. "It's lovely."

Natasha Bukova did not know how to dance. She stood by the wall holding her workmate's hat.

While the band was resting, Frossy and Natasha shared two bottles of cider. Natasha had been in the club only once before, and that a long time ago. She gazed at her surroundings, the cleanness and the decorations, with a kind of gentle joy.

"Fross, hey, Fross!" she whispered. "Is it true—with socialism here now—all the rooms will be like this?"

"I'd say so, they certainly will," said Frossy. "Well, maybe just a little better."

"Imagine that!" Natasha exclaimed.

After the musicians had rested, Frossy danced again. This time it was the dispatcher who asked her. The band was playing a foxtrot, "My Baby." The dispatcher pressed his partner against him with his cheek on Frossy's hair, but this did not disturb her, she loved her distant man, her poor body was deaf and withheld.

"What's your name?" asked her partner in her ear as they danced. "I know you by sight, but I don't seem to remember who your father is."

"Fro!" she answered.

"Fro? Aren't you Russian?"

"Certainly not, why should I be?"

"Why shouldn't you be? I've got it, your father's a Russian, Evstafyev!"

"It doesn't matter," murmured Frossy. "They call me Fro."

They danced on in silence. The onlookers stood against the wall, observing the dancers. There were in all three couples dancing, the others being too shy or else ignorant of the steps. Frossy bent her head closer to the dispatcher's chest. Her abundant hair, done in an old-fashioned style, was on a level with his eyes, and this tiny show of confidence pleased him. He felt proud in the sight of the onlookers. He longed to stroke her hair, but was afraid of provoking a scandal. Furthermore, his fiancée was among the crowd and might very well create a scene later about this Fro. So the dispatcher drew back a trifle from his partner for the sake of decorum, but Frossy leaned close to him, her head pushing his tie to one side. The pressure opened his shirt showing the flesh. Somewhat uneasily, he went on dancing till the music should end. But the music rose on a crescendo, and the girl did not shift from her partner's arms. Suddenly drops of moisture tickled his skin with its curly hair under the tie.

"Are you crying?" he asked in dismay.

"Just a little," said Fro in a low voice. "Take me over to the door. I can't dance any more."

Frossy's partner danced her toward the exit, and she went into the corridor, where there were few people. Natasha handed back her friend's hat. Frossy went on home, while Natasha went over to the cooperative storehouse, where her husband was on duty. Next to the storehouse was a building contractor's yard, watched over by a pleasant-mannered woman. Natasha wanted to find out whether there was any affection or sympathy between this woman and her husband.

Next morning Frossy got a telegram her husband had wired from a station in Siberia beyond the Urals. He had written: "Dear Fro I love you and I see you in my dreams."

Her father was not at home. He had gone off to the depot to chat for a while in the Red Corner, read *The Whistle,* and hear about the night's events in the hauling sector. Later he would have a beer in the refreshment room with a workmate and a friendly talk about their common concerns.

Frossy did not brush her teeth, she hardly washed, merely

dashing a little water on her face, troubling no more than this about her appearance. She had no time for anything but the emotion of love, for she lacked the feminine zeal women now have for their grooming. From the third floor overhead came the sound of a harmonica. The tune would stop, only to begin again. Frossy had first waked that morning when it was still dark and had gone back to sleep. Then she heard the modest little tune coming from upstairs like the song of a small gray bird on the steppe, spending his strength on his work, so that little breath remained for singing. Upstairs there lived a little boy, the son of a screw cutter at the depot; his father would surely have gone to work, the mother was washing clothes, and so he was trying to amuse himself.

Without stopping for food, Frossy went about her work on her courses in railroad communications and signals. Frossy had not been attending these courses for the past four days, and certainly her classmates had missed her, but she went only listlessly to join them. She was forgiven a great deal at these courses because of her capacity to learn and because of her clear perception of the aims of technical science; but she did not clearly understand how she came by this facility. For the most part she was imitating her husband, a graduate of two technical colleges, who understood the intricacies of machines as intimately as he did his own flesh.

At the start Frossy had been a bad student. Nothing attracted her in Pupin cells, rail-coupling, or calculating the resistance of grid wire. But then her husband had pronounced these names wholeheartedly, imaginatively, entering into the very essence of the abstruse, inanimate mechanisms, telling her how the lifeless matter of her study became animate in operation and how there was a hidden quality in meticulous calculation by virtue of which machines became alive. He had the faculty of actually feeling the degree of intensity of an electric current, as if it were a secret passion of his own. Everything that came into contact with his hands or his thoughts was brought to life, and so he had acquired a true conception of the forces at work in any mechanical setup and an immediate insight into the strength or endurance of the basic metal in any machine.

From then on reels, Wheatstone bridges, contactors, candle-power became sacred objects for Frossy, as if they were living parts of her man; she began to understand them and to cherish them in her mind as in her soul. When in difficulty Frossy would come home, sighing, "Fyodor, all that about microfarads and eddy currents is so boring." But as he embraced his wife after their day's separation, Fyodor changed himself into a microfarad or an eddy current. Frossy could almost see what before she had only wanted to understand and could not. It was a matter of objects as simple, natural, and disarming as the many-colored grasses on the plain.

At night Frossy was often sad at the thought that she was only a woman and could not feel like a microfarad, or a locomotive, or electricity as Fyodor could—and she drew her finger cautiously over his warm back; he was sound asleep and did not wake. For some mysterious reason he was always warm, strange, uncannily able to sleep amid noise, to eat any food with complete indifference to whether it was tasty or tasteless, never to feel ill; he liked to spend money on little things; he had volunteered as a soldier to serve in Soviet South China.

When Frossy now attended the course, her thoughts would stray, taking nothing in of the day's lessons. She made desultory copies in her notebook from the drawings on the blackboard of the vector diagram of current resonance and sadly listened to the institute lecturer's discourse on the influence of iron saturation on harmonics. Since Fyodor was not here, communications and signals held no attraction for her, while electricity itself had become alien to her. Pupin coils, microfarads, Wheatstone bridges, iron cores had grown sore and barren in her heart; as for the upper harmonics of currents, she could make nothing of them. In her head the monotonous little song piped by the boy on his harmonica played itself over and over again: "Mother's washing, father's working, when'll they come again? To be alone and lonely is a thing of pain, of pain."

Frossy took her eyes off the lecturer and wrote down her thoughts in her notebook: "I'm a silly, hopeless girl, Fyodor, come back sooner, I may be learning about communications, but I'll die, you can bury me and go back to China."

At home her father was sitting with his boots, his outdoor clothes, and his cap on. He was certain he would be called out on a trip that day. "Are you home?" he called to his daughter; he was glad when someone was in the apartment; he constantly listened for footsteps on the stairs, as if expecting a caller, come unannounced, with happiness stuck in his hatband.

"Would you like me to warm you up some buckwheat grits and butter?" asked the father. "They'll be ready in no time."

The daughter declined.

"Well, fry you some sausages, then?"

"No," said Frossy.

The father was silent for a while, then asked again, but more hesitantly, "What about some tea and crackers? I can get it for you quick."

His daughter made no reply. "Or some of yesterday's macaroni? It hasn't been touched, I left it for you."

"Oh, let me alone, can't you!" cried Frossy. "If they'd only sent *you* out to the Far East—"

"I've asked them to, often, but they won't, they say I'm too old and my eyesight's failing," her father sighed.

He was aware that our children are our enemies, and he was not angry with the enemy; but he was afraid that Frossy would shut herself up in her room, whereas he wanted her to stay with him and talk, so the old man looked for any way of keeping Frossy with him. "Why haven't you put on any lipstick today?" he asked. "Maybe you've run out of it, have you? I can go and buy some for you right away."

Tears sprang into Frossy's gray eyes, and she went off to her own room. Her father was left alone; he busied himself tidying the kitchen and sweeping up, then, squatting on his heels, he opened the oven door, put his head inside, weeping into the dish of macaroni.

There was a knock on the door. Frossy did not stir. The old man took his head out of the oven—the kitchen cloths hung dirty all around, so he wiped his face with the mop and went to the door. A messenger had come from the depot. "Sign here, Nefed Stepanovich: you're on at eight o'clock, you're to take out the cold engine for heavy repairs. It'll be pulling the No. 310 mixed-traffic train. Take some food and clothes with you, you won't be back for a week."

Nefed Stepanovich signed the book and the messenger left. The old man opened his metal lunchbox: it still had the bread he had put there the day before, an onion, and a piece of sugar. To this he added an ounce or two of millet, two apples. He thought for a moment, and then closed the little chest with an enormous padlock. Then he knocked cautiously on Frossy's door. "Daughter! Shut the door behind me, I'm going off, I'll be gone a week or two. I'm taking out that gray locomotive, the ZH, she's cold, but never mind."

Frossy waited until her father had left, then she came out and closed the door of the apartment.

"Go on playing! Why don't you play?" muttered Frossy to the apartment upstairs, where the boy with the harmonica lived. He had probably gone out for a walk. It was summer time, with its long days; toward evening the wind died down among the sleeping pines. The harmonica player was still too young to have chosen the one being in the entire world as the object of his undying love. She lost herself gazing at the sky with the traces of the setting sun, telling herself that happiness must surely be found in that firmament. . . .

Between the two pillows Frossy found a short hair that could only be Fyodor's. Holding it up to the light, she saw it was white.

Fyodor was now in his twenty-ninth year, and some twenty white hairs had appeared on his head. Her father's hair was also white, but he never came near their bed. Frossy put her nose against the pillow where Fyodor had slept: it still smelled of his body; the pillowcase had not been washed since he left. Frossy sank her head into Fyodor's pillow and was somewhat comforted.

Upstairs on the third floor the little boy had come back and was playing on his harmonica the same tune as before. Frossy got up and put the hair into a little box on her table. The boy had stopped playing. Perhaps is was his bedtime, or else, now that his father had returned from work, he was sitting on his knee.

That evening Frossy walked along the railroad tracks to a little wood close by and to the rye fields. She passed the slag pit where she had worked. It was full to the top with clinkers, but no one was there. Frossy did not know where Natasha Bukova lived. She had not asked her the night before; but she did not want to visit friends; for some reason she was ashamed to face anybody: she could not talk to other people of her love, and the rest of living held no vital interest for her. She went past the cooperative storehouse where Natasha's husband was pacing up and down, alone with his gun. Frossy wanted to give him a few rubles to buy a bottle for himself and his wife the next day, but she had not the courage.

"Move on, citizeness! You can't loiter here, it's the cooperative storehouse, state property," the nightwatchman said as Frossy halted and felt in her jacket for her money.

Beyond the storehouse lay wasteland, unused and abandoned, where a kind of grass grew, stubby, stiff, poisonous, Having come this far, in anguish of spirit Frossy tarried amid these evil weeds from whose mean sphere there seemed to stretch a distance of two kilometers to the stars.

"Oh, Fro, Fro, if only you had somebody to cherish you!" she said to herself.

Once home again, Frossy went straight to bed. The little boy had gone off to sleep long before, and the crickets had ceased to chirrup. But something kept her from sleeping. She looked around her in the darkness and sniffed: it was the pillow that was disturbing her, Fyodor's pillow. It still gave forth the sharp, earthy odor of a warm, familiar body, and this odor depressed her spirits all the more. She wrapped the pillow in a sheet and pushed it into a closet. Then she fell asleep alone, like an orphan.

Frossy no longer went to her communications courses. In any event they had become incomprehensible. She stayed at home and waited for a letter or a telegram from Fyodor, fearing the mailman might bring a letter and find no one at home. But four days went by, then six, but Fyodor sent no further news.

The father returned from his assignment on the cold locomotive. It was good to have been away and to have tired himself working. He had passed through many distant stations, had encountered various incidents; he now had enough for thought, talk, and reminiscence to last a long time. As Frossy put no questions to him, her father began to tell her everything himself, how the cold locomotive had functioned, and how he had gone sleepless at night so that the fitters at stations along the way would not take the engine parts, at what places fruit was sold cheaply, but also where the spring frosts had spoiled the crops. Frossy made no response; even when Nefed Stepanovich told her of the cotton voile and the synthetic silk they were making at Sverdlovsk, his daughter showed absolutely no interest. "Is she a fascist or what?" mused her father. "How she came to be born to me and my good woman, I don't know."

When neither letter nor telegram came from Fyodor, Frossy sought a job with the letter carriers at the post office. She suspected that letters could be lost, and so she herself would deliver the whole lot to the addresses. What was more, she would receive Fyodor's letters sooner than if they were brought by some apathetic, unknown mailman, and they would not get lost if she had the handling of them. She arrived at the delivery section earlier than the other letter carriers—even before the boy played his harmonica on the upper floor—and volunteered her help in the sorting and packaging of the mail. She read the addresses on all the envelopes—none from Fyodor. All the envelopes were addressed to other people, and so their contents had no interest. Even so, Frossy diligently went out twice a day from house to house, carrying the letters, which she hoped bore only good tidings. Very early in the morning she went quickly along the streets of the residential part of the town carrying the heavy bag on her belly like a pregnant woman, knocking at doors, giving letters and rolls of printed matter to men in underpants, women still undressed, and little children who had waked before the grown-ups.

The dark blue sky still stretched over the earth when Frossy was already at work, seeking in fatigue to exhaust the anguish in her heart. Several of the addressees inquired about her life as they took in their mail, asking her questions about everyday affairs. "Do they pay you eighty rubles a month?" "Yes, they do," Frossy would answer, "after income tax deductions." "Do you still go out when you have your period, or do they give you sick leave?" "Sick leave," Frossy declared," they provide us with a belt, but I haven't had mine yet." "You'll get it all right," promised the other woman, "you'll get it anyway." A man who took in the paper *Red Virginlands* proposed marriage to her on an experimental basis; it might result in happiness, he argued, and it would certainly be a useful experience. "What's *your* reaction?" he asked her. "I'll think about it," answered Frossy. "Don't think," he advised her, "come and visit to start with, you'll see what sort of a man I am: I'm kind, well read, cultured —you can see that from the papers I subscribe to. This periodical is edited by a committee— many intelligent people, as you can see,—and then there won't be one of us any more but two. It's a very respectable arrangement, and as a married woman you'll have more authority. But an unmarried girl is— how shall I put it?— a lonely creature, you might almost say antisocial."

Frossy came to know a good many people, standing with a letter or a package at strangers' doors. Some even offered her wine or a bite to eat and complained to her of their daily lives. Life was never empty or uneventful.

When he left, Fyodor had promised Frossy to tell her at once where he would be working, for he himself did not exactly know then. But now two weeks had gone by, there was still no word from him, and she had no idea where to write. In trying to bear this separation, Frossy did the rounds faster and faster delivering the mail, breathing faster and faster in her attempt to sink her feelings in work and so wear out her depression.

One day, quite unexpectedly, she cried out in the presence of others while making the second delivery of the day. Frossy was unaware of how her chest had suddenly contracted, how her breathing stopped and her heart was skipping. She cried out on a high, singing note. The passers-by stared at her. When she came to herself, she ran off into the fields, still carrying the mailbag, for she could not bear her shallow breathing. She threw herself to the ground and cried until her heart recovered its normal pace.

Frossy sat up, straightened her clothes, and smiled. Now she felt better, she did not feel like crying any more. After completing her deliveries, Frossy looked in at the telegraph office. A telegram from Fyodor, containing his address and kisses, was handed her. Returning home at once without stopping to eat, she began a letter to her husband. She did not see the day ending outside the window, she did not hear the boy piping on his harmonica. Her father knocked on her door and brought his daughter a glass of tea and a slice of bread with butter. He switched on the light so that Frossy should not strain her eyes in the dark.

That night Nefed Stepanovich lay asleep on his trunk in the

kitchen. Six days had passed since he had last been called to the depot; tonight, he thought, they must call him again, and he listened for the messenger's footstep on the stairs. At one o'clock at night Frossy came into the kitchen with a folded piece of paper in her hand. "Papa!"

"What is it, daughter?" The old man had been sleeping lightly and fitfully.

"Will you take this telegram to the telegraph office? I'm too tired to go."

"But supposing the messenger comes while I'm out?" said the father, alarmed.

"I'll get him to wait," promised Frossy. "You haven't far to go, anyway. Only don't read the telegram yourself, just hand it to the clerk."

"I won't read it, but you were writing a letter, let me take that, too."

"It's no concern of yours, if I was. Have you any money on you?"

He had. He took the telegram and set off. When he got to the telegraph office, the old man did read the telegram; his daughter might have got something wrong, he told himself, so he ought to take a glance at it.

The telegram was addressed to Fyodor in the Far East: "Return by first train your wife my daughter Frossy dying respiratory disorder Nefed Evstafyev father."

"Young peoples' doings," thought Nefed Stepanovich and handed the telegram in at the window.

"But I saw Frossy today!" said the clerk. "Can she really be sick?"

"She got sick after, that's what," declared the engineer.

Next morning Frossy asked her father to go again to the post office, this time to hand in her voluntary resignation because of her failing state of health. The old man went again; in any case he wanted to go to the depot.

Frossy did some sewing, darned socks, washed the floors, and tidied the apartment, never stirring out of doors.

Two days later an urgent telegram came: "Leaving for home very upset distressed hold funeral till my return Fyodor."

Frossy worked it out exactly how long it would take her husband to come. On the seventh day after the arrival of his telegram she was walking the station platfrom, tremulous and gay. The trans-Siberian express from the East was never late. Frossy's father too was on the platform, but he kept away from his daughter not to disturb her.

The express engineer brought the train into the station at a fine clip and gently, lovingly put on the brake. Nefed Stepanovich stood watching with tear-bright eyes, even forgetting the reason why he had come.

Only one passenger got off the train. He was wearing a hat and a long blue raincoat. His deep-set eyes gleamed expectantly. The girl ran toward him.

"Fro!" exclaimed the man and threw down his suitcase onto the platform. The father picked up the case and followed his daughter and son-in-law. Halfway home the daughter turned to her father. "Papa, go down to the depot and ask for an assignment. You get so bored staying at home all the time."

"It *is* dull," admitted the old man, "I'll go now. You take the suitcase."

His son-in-law turned to the old engineer. "Greetings, Nefed Stepanovich!"

"Hallo, Fedka, welcome home!"

"Thank you, Nefed Stepanovich."

"I've spring-cleaned the whole apartment, dear," said Frossy, "I wasn't dying at all."

"I guessed that on the way—that you weren't about to die," her husband answered. "After a while I didn't believe your telegram."

"Why did you come then?" asked Fro, surprised.

"I love you, I was lost without you," he replied sadly.

Frossy was distressed. "I'm afraid you'll stop loving me one day, and then I really will die."

Fyodor kissed her on the cheek as he walked beside her. "If you died, you would forget everything, and me as well."

Frossy had quite recovered from her distress. "No, there's no point in dying. It's pure inertia."

"Oh, inertia, of course," smiled Fyodor; he liked her superior, erudite words. Fro had even asked him specially to teach her some cleverly worded sentences, and he had filled a whole notebook with empty but intelligent-sounding phrases: "Whoever says 'A', must say 'B'." "A stone is placed at the vertex of an angle." "If it is thus, it is precisely so," and so on. But Fro saw through them herself. She asked: "But why does it follow that anyone should say 'B' after saying 'A'? What if it doesn't follow, or I don't want it to?"

At the apartment they lay down to rest and fell asleep. Three hours had gone by when the father knocked at the door. Frossy went to open it and waited while the old man put food and clothing into his little metal chest and left again. He must have been given an assignment. Frossy closed the door and lay down to sleep again.

It was night when they woke. They talked for a little, then Fyodor took Fro in his arms, and they were silent until morning.

Next morning Frossy quickly got breakfast, fed her husband and ate something herself. She now did everything in a slapdash way, sleepily, careless of the taste, but it was of no consequence to them what they ate or drank, so long as they did not lose a moment of their love for secondary matters.

Frossy told Fyodor that she would now begin studying hard and assiduously, learn a lot, and give of her strength so that everyone in the country should have a better life.

Fyodor listened to Fro, then explained his own thoughts and plans to her in detail, about the transmission of energy by using a driving force, not a conductor but ionized air, about increasing the strength of all metals by treating their supersonic waves, about the stratosphere, a hundred kilometers high, where there were special conditions of light, heat, and electricity capable of ensuring man eternal life—thus the ancient dream of heaven might now be realized—and there were many other things that Fyodor vowed to study and accomplish for Fro and for all humankind.

Frossy listened to her husband's words, her yearning lips parted in rapture. After talking they went into each other's arms—they wanted their happiness at once, that very moment, before their concentrated application to the future should yield results affecting both their own and the common happiness. No heart can bear postponement, its suffering is such that it loses faith. After having slept out of sheer exhaustion from all the thinking, talking, and pleasure, they woke refreshed and ready to go on with life. Frossy wanted to have children, she would raise them to carry on the task begun by their father, by communism, and by science. With all the passion of his imaginativeness, Fyodor whispered to Frossy about the mysterious force of nature that provides humanity with abundance, the radical transformation of man's poor soul. Then they kissed and embraced, and their noble dream took on the form of pleasure, as if it had suddenly come into reality.

In the evenings Frossy would leave the house briefly to shop for herself and her husband: now both their appetites were growing. They had spent four days without leaving each other's side. The father had not yet come back from his trip; he must have been driving a cold locomotive on another long journey.

After another two days Frossy told Fyodor that they could stay together a little longer, but then they would have to go back to working and earning their bread. "So tomorrow, or the day after, you and I will begin living in earnest," said Fyodor, holding Frossy tightly to him.

"The day after," Fro murmured.

On the eighth day, Fyodor woke up sad. "Fro! Now let's go back to work and live as we ought. You must go on with your communications courses."

"Tomorrow!" whispered Fro, taking her husband's head in her hands. He smiled at her resignedly.

"But when, Fro?" Fyodor asked the next day.

"Soon, soon," she answered drowsily, gently; she was holding his hand, he kissed her on the forehead.

One morning Frossy awoke late. Outside, the day had long since grown warm. She was alone in her room, for the eleventh or twelfth day of unbroken reunion with her husband. Frossy got out of bed at once, threw the windows wide open, and heard the strains of the harmonica she had completely forgotten. This time the sounds were not coming from upstairs. She peered out of the window. A log lay near the woodshed, and on it sat the barefoot little boy with a child's large head, playing on his mouth organ.

All the house was quiet and somehow strange: Fyodor had gone off somewhere. Frossy went into the kitchen. There her father was sitting on a stool, dozing, with his head, still wearing the cap, on the kitchen table. Frossy woke him.

"When did you get back?"

"Eh?" the old man ejaculated. "This morning, very early."

"Who opened the door for you? Fyodor?"

"No one," said her father, "it was open. Fyodor came and found me at the station. I was sleeping on one of the benches."

"What were you sleeping at the station for, haven't you got a place of your own?" protested Frossy angrily.

"Why not? I'm used to it," returned her father. "I thought I'd be in your way."

"What silly nonsense! And where is Fyodor, when's he coming back?"

The father seemed embarrassed.

"He's not coming," said the old man. "He's gone."

Fro stood in silence, staring at her father. The father fixed his eyes on the dish cloth and went on: "There was an express this morning, he got on it and went back to the East. 'I might even go on into China,' he said. 'I don't know yet.'"

"What else did he say?" asked Fro.

"Nothing,"—answered her father. "He told me to go back home to you and look after you. As soon as he gets through all his work, he told me, he'll come back here, or he'll send for you to go there."

"What work?" Frossy wanted to know.

"I don't know," declared her father. "He said you'd know all about it: communism—wasn't it?—or something like that—whatever comes up!"

Fro left her father, went into her own room, lay down with her stomach pressed against the windowsill, watching the boy outside as he played his harmonica.

"Little boy!" she called. "Come and visit me."

"Just a moment," he replied.

He got down from the log, wiped his harmonica on the hem of his shirt, and came toward the house.

Fro stood in her nightdress in the middle of the large room. She smiled as she awaited her visitor.

"Good-bye, Fyodor!"

Perhaps she was foolish, perhaps her own life was not worth two kopeks, not worth her cherishing, but it was at least true that she alone knew how to turn two kopeks into two rubles.

"Good-bye, Fyodor! You'll come back to me, and I'll be waiting for you."

The little visitor knocked shyly on the apartment door. Frossy let him in; she crouched down and took the child's hands in hers, and praised the little musician. For he was surely a man, a member of that humanity Fyodor had spoken of to her with such loving kindness.

1936

The Watercolor

Alexander Grin

Clisson awoke in a sour mood. The night before, Betsy had reproached him vehemently for hanging like a millstone round her neck, while Wilson had signed on the river boat "Dennem."

Clisson had meant to sail on the "Dennem" as a stoker, but in the end he missed the train on purpose, so that the boat had already set out on her trip. The laundress made a fair living. Clisson deliberately encouraged her drinking, for when she was in her cups she freely gave him money. She was known to be good at her job, and this always assured her plenty of work.

Stretched out on the bed with a heavy head and a case of heartburn, Clisson smoked a cigaret and tried to think how he could get hold of a crown or so. It was a public holiday: the day before, the stoker had arranged to meet some of his mates at Fuchs's Tavern.

A joyous green morning was rustling the leaves of the ivy outside his window. Fragrant shrubs grew against the house walls. Gazing at the white and yellow flowers, Clisson imagined them to be gold and silver coins. He counted forty such coins and sighed.

Betsy brought in a metal teapot. Yawning, she began to set the table. There was no other furniture in the room but a stool or so, two beds, and an old stuffed armchair. The dust and fluff of one whole week had accumulated in the corners and behind the door. On the windowsill there were remnants of food, while the floor was strewn with cucumber and apple peel. Against the wall, several enormous laundry baskets gave off a smell of mildew and damp.

As the laundress moved around the table, her foot hit an empty bottle, and it rolled away so that Clisson knew that a pick-me-up was what he needed. But Betsy's sullenness did not encourage optimism. Regretting that he had not been foresighted enough to have wheedled the money out of her the day before, Clisson gloomily got dressed. Fearing that she might repeat the tirade of the previous evening, he was in no hurry to start a conversation.

They drank their tea in silence. When Betsy snatched the knife he was using to cut the bread out of his hand, Clisson was lugubriously certain that her mind was still on the "Dennem." Thinking that he had nothing to lose, Clisson said: "All right, so I missed the train. D'you think I did it on purpose? It was an accident, that's all. Can you let me have a shilling?"

"I'll be damned if I give you anything," answered Betsy quietly. "I've done the wash for five houses this week. I'm going to give up working and start to booze, like you."

The quarrel flared and flickered out again. Disgusted, Clisson made himself swallow the mugful of tea, envying Betsy, who never had a headache. As if in self-vindication, "You drink quite a bit yourself," he said. "You got tight yesterday and started to sing. Then you put on someone's lace-trimmed blouse and showed yourself off."

"What you should've done was not to give me anything to drink. I never drank so much before, but now I will, and I'll go on doing it, but money I will not give you!"

Just as the fight was about to break out, a neighbor knocked on the window for Betsy. She went out, tossing a glance at one of the laundry baskets. The moment his wife was out of sight, Clisson threw himself on the basket and searched in the linen Betsy had eyed as she left the room. There was a cigaretbox in it with money inside. Clisson took out a crown, put the linen as it was before, and sat down again at the table.

Returning instantly, Betsy looked with hard suspicion at Clisson, but guessed nothing of the theft. Sighing, she took up a blanket and shook it out of the window, while Clisson pushed his cap into an inner pocket of his jacket. He made his way through some rooms standing empty, waiting for lodgers, and opened a window. He jumped out and skirted the washhouse where Betsy worked in the summer. Then he put his cap on and, having made sure she was not pursuing him, hurried off to the tram stop. Once in the crowded tram, Clisson was able to catch his breath.

Half an hour later he was in the city, gloating over his stolen crown on his way to Fuchs's tavern. As he passed from one side of the street to the other, he happened to turn his head, and his heart leaped into his mouth: Betsy was running straight to him, her eyes fixed on him. As she approached, she nodded at him ominously, and halting in spite of himself, he hunched his shoulders.

The coming quarrel weighed so heavily on Clisson that he could not find the courage to face the storm. The sight of the black skirt and checkered kerchief, coming straight at him at top speed through the passers-by, impelled him to take flight. He darted off, searching every doorway, every opening, for a safe place to hide in. The cry, "You won't get away with this, you rotter!" behind his back made him bolt around the corner. Here was a deeply recessed, imposing entrance with a revolving door. Spurred on by fear, Clisson had just enough time to read the legend on an oval shield, "Spring Exhibition by Watercolor Artists," and run up the flight of sunlit steps that led into the hall. Here a stern young woman stopped him, demanding his ticket. As he took his change from the stolen coin, he felt a certain satisfaction that at least part of the money had been spent on himself and that Betsy must have lost sight of him as he fled.

Clisson passed on into the hall, where many faces looked down at him from high up on the walls. He was not of a mind to view Smiles or Deshry with the eye of a critic; he simply wanted to stay a while and then leave. He saw the other visitors, pensively exchanging comments in low tones, and then, unmistakably, he spotted Betsy, a cold smile on her lips, drawing closer to him. Her eyes were narrowed, seeing no one but Clisson, who had taken her money.

"So you didn't escape?" said Betsy icily. "Now we can have a little chat."

"Not here," said Clisson, hastening ahead. "This is an exhibition, I wanted to go to an exhibition, where were you? I didn't see you on the tram."

"I was in the next one. I want to know how long things're going to go on like this, you rotter!"

"You haven't got me on a leash," snarled Clisson, hastening faster and faster through the crowd.

Trying to keep their voices low, they swore and cursed at each other, and Betsy began to cry. The role of thief became unbearable to Clisson. He could see the visitors looking at him and the laundress; he caught their raised eyebrows and their smiles. Not knowing what to do, he turned into one doorway and out the next, with Betsy following like a drill through wood. Suddenly he hit on the ruse of stopping before a picture—though one looked at the moment very much like another—choosing those with the greatest number of visitors in front of them. Then Betsy had to be silent, but no sooner did he move on than he heard her stifled whisper: "Idler! Swindler! Drunkard!" or else, "Get away from here this minute and give me my money back!"

"Hold your tongue," said Clisson so audibly that she, not wishing to be involved in a public scene, fell silent. Following close behind him, she stopped before the picture Clisson was now gazing at, as at a smiling enemy. There were some ten other people looking at it. A garden walk with rays of light passing through the leaves and falling on the ivied walls of a brick house with steps leading up to it; on a wooden bench close by stood an empty cage: it seemed familiar to Clisson. "That looks like our house," he said in a conciliatory tone, as if to subdue the tortue he was suffering.

"What's up—you off your head?"

But the more closely Betsy stared at the picture, the more certain she was that it was the same house from which the unlucky crown had been stolen. She recognized the windows, the bench, the trunks of the maple and the oak, between which she had hung her washing, the pit amid the bushes, the turn of the wall at the corner, the angle of the roof, even the empty jam jar lying on the ground below—there was no doubt of it in her mind. In sight and in memory, Betsy and Clisson were looking at their own house. Delighted and also taken aback, the one interrupting the other with remarks on the details, they eagerly set about proving to each other that there was no mistaking the house.

"That slop bucket behind the steps—you can't see it!" Betsy declared joyfully.

"Yes, but what about the inside? If you'd only cleaned *that* up a bit," Clisson retorted bitterly.

They withdrew into a corner, whispering, trying to understand how the likeness of their house had come to be here. Clisson advanced the theory that the picture was in reality a colored photograph. But then Betsy recalled that some six weeks before she had seen a man with a box and a folded stool.

"I thought at once: I had never seen anyone like him," she said. "He paid no mind to anything or anybody. I wanted to go back into the house—it seemed kind of queer that he should be there. And as for you, you'd been gone for three whole days. I'd been looking for you for two days." When they had talked enough, they went back to the painting: the hostility between them had fallen away unaccountably. Several people were now standing before the picture. It was a strange sensation to Clisson to see them as if they had come to the house to inspect the life they were living. One of them, a lady, said: "The most exquisite thing of the season. How beautiful the light is! And just look at the ivy!"

Hearing this, Clisson and Betsy took heart and went closer. They were troubled lest the visitors catch sight of the empty bottles and knotted bundles of dirty linen. The painting impressed them more and more; they were struck with delight at the overgrown greenery wreathing the brick house on the morning when the man with the folding chair had come along that light-flecked path.

They gazed at it proudly, sorry that they could not decide to declare to everyone present that the house was theirs. "It's been two years since we've been renting it," they thought privately. Clisson drew himself up. Betsy held her kerchief to her hard-worn self.

"All the same, they no longer send any washing to that Reyben slut," said Betsy, "because I know my job too well. I don't throw in piles of soda—I don't spare my hands. Well, seeing as you've flown the coop, you may as well go on to the tavern, I suppose— but don't spend all the money."

But Clisson was silent for a moment; then he whispered:

"Come, I'm ready for a drink. When I say something, I mean it. Tomorrow I'll make it my business to go and talk to Hobson. He promised to get me a job, if Sneck won't."

"You're sure they're not putting you on?"

"Never mind, we'll go and have a drink, anyway, and talk it over with Hobson."

Once more they walked past the watercolor, looking at it out of the corners of their eyes, then they went out into the street, surprised to be returning to that house, of which strangers had talked with sympathy and tenderness.

1928

Second Lieutenant Likewise

Yury Tynyanov

1

Emperor Paul was dozing near the open window. During the postprandial hour, when food wages its slow fight with the body, any upsetting matters were forbidden. He dozed, seated on a lofty chair, partitioned in at the back and on either side with a glass screen. Paul Petrovich was dreaming his usual postprandial dream.

He was (in this dream) in Gatchina, sitting in his small topiary garden, and a well-rounded Cupid was peeping at him from around a corner as he, Paul, dined with his family. Then a creaking noise arose far off. It came bumping along over an uneven road, monotonously and jouncingly. Paul Petrovich, from afar, caught sight of a cocked hat, a horse galloping along, the shafts of a cabriolet, dust. He ducked under a table, since the cocked hat was that of a courier. They were coming for him post haste from St. Petersburg.

"*Nous sommes perdus!* We are lost!" he shouted hoarsely to his wife from under the table, so that she too might duck under it. There wasn't too much air under the table, and by now the creaking noise was right there; the shafts of the cabriolet were heading straight at him.

The courier peered under the table, came upon Paul Petrovich there, and said to him: "Your Majesty! Her Majesty, your mother has passed away."

But no sooner had Paul Petrovich started to crawl out from under the table than the courier dealt him a fillip on the forehead and shouted: "Help! Guards!"

Paul Petrovich brushed the courier away . . . and caught a fly. Thus did he sit, his gray eyes goggling through one of the windows of the Pavlovsky Palace, as he gasped from food and ennui, with a fly buzzing in his fist, and cocked up his ears.

Someone, under his window, was shouting: "Help! Guards!"

2

The clerk of the Regiment of Transfiguration had been sent off to Siberia, after a flogging.

The new clerk, so young that he was hardly more than a boy, was seated at a table, writing. His hand shook; he was behind time.

He had to finish transcribing a regimental order by the stroke of six, so that the adjutant on duty might carry it off to the palace, where another adjutant, after adding this order to others just like it, was to present it to the Emperor at nine. Lateness was a criminal offense. The regimental clerk had got up ahead of time, but had botched the order and was now at work on a new transcript. He had, in the first copy, made two errors; he had written down Lieutenant Sinukhaev as dead, because Sinukhaev's name came right after that of Major Sokolov, deceased, and had permitted himself such an absurd slip of the pen as: "Second Lieutenants Likewise, Steven, Rybin, and Azancheev are hereby designated . . ." instead of: "Likewise, Second Lieutenants Steven, Rybin, and Azancheev are hereby designated. . . ." Just as he had been about to write the names of the second lieutenants an officer had entered and he had drawn himself up to attention before him, and then, when he had sat down to his regimental order again, he had become confused and thus created a Second Lieutenant Likewise.

He knew that if by six the regimental order were not ready, the adjutant would call out: "Take him away!" And take him they would. For that reason his hand refused to move; he wrote more and more slowly and suddenly let a blot splash, as big and beautiful as a fountain, right on the regimental order.

He had ten minutes left, all in all.

Throwing himself back in his chair the clerk eyed the clock, as if it were a living person; then his fingers, as if they were detached from his body and acting of their own volition, began rummaging among the papers for a fresh sheet, although there were no fresh sheets there, since they were neatly stacked in a closet.

But, rummaging thus in despair, and solely as a face-saving device for his own self, he became petrified a second time.

Another and no less important paper had been written incorrectly.

In accordance with Imperial Directive No. 940, *review* was to be avoided and *inspect* used instead; *fulfill* was to be used instead of *carry out*; one had to write *guard*, not *watch*; and in no case was it permitted to write *detail*: the correct expression was *detachment*.

There was a supplementary list for civilian statutes: one had to write *class*, not *degree*, and *assembly*, not *association*, and instead of writing *citizen* one had to substitute *merchant* or *burgher*.

The latter list, however, was only written, in a minute hand, at the bottom margin of Imperial Directive No. 940, and the clerk had not read this addendum, although the Directive itself was hanging before his very eyes; but as for such terms as *review* and so on, he had learned them on his first day here and had memorized them well. Yet in the paper ready for the regimental commander's signature, which was to be transmitted to none other than Baron Arakecheev, that dread martinet, he had written:

"Having *reviewed*, in accordance with Your Excellency's instructions, the *details* of the *watch*, particularly those picked for service in the suburbs of St. Petersburg and for out-of-town duty, I have the honor to report that all of the said instructions have been *carried out*. . . ."

Nor was this all, by any means.

The first line of the report he himself had transcribed stood forth as: *Your Excellency, Dear Sir!*

Even a little child could not but be aware that a salutation penned in a single line signified a command, whereas in reports submitted by a subordinate, and especially to such a person as Baron Arakcheev, that salutation had to be written not other than in two lines:

Your Excellency,
Dear Sir!
—which signified submission and courtesy.

And even if, when it came to *reviewed* and so forth, it might have been considered that he had not noticed the matter, or that he had not noticed it in good time, in the case of the *Dear Sir!* coming right after and on the same line with *Your Excellency*, it had been none other than himself who had messed things up in transcription.

Thereupon, no longer realizing what he was doing, the clerk sat down to correct the paper with this error. As he was copying it, he quite forgot about the regimental order, although that was far more urgent.

When, however, the adjutant's orderly appeared for the regimental order, the clerk first looked at the clock and then at the orderly—and suddenly thrust out to him the sheet on which Lieutenant Sinukhaev was listed as dead.

Then he sat down and for a long while, still shaking in his boots, kept on writing: *Excellencies, detachments, guards.*

3

At nine, on the dot, a small bell tinkled in the palace, the Emperor having yanked its cord. At nine His Majesty's adjutant entered with the usual report for Paul Petrovich. Paul Petrovich was sitting in the same position as he had yesterday, at a window, with a glass screen around him. For all that, he was neither asleep nor dozing, and his face, too, bore an expression that differed from yesterday's.

The adjutant knew, even as all in the palace did, that the Emperor was irritable. At the same time he knew equally well that the Emperor's wrath was seeking some pretext to vent itself, and the more it failed this, the more inflamed was it becoming. And so the handing-in of the report could not possibly be avoided.

He drew himself up at attention before the screen and the Emperor's back and made his presence known.

Paul Petrovich did not turn around toward the adjutant; Paul Petrovich was breathing hard and at long intervals.

All through yesterday he had been unable to get to the bottom of the mystery of who had shouted "Help! Guards!" under his window, and during the night he had awakened twice, in a dismal mood.

"Help! Guards!" was an absurd thing to shout, and at first Paul Petrovich had merely been slightly annoyed, like anyone who dreams a bad dream and is hindered from dreaming it to the end. For a good ending to a dream does, after all, signify something good. Then, too, his curiosity had been aroused: who had shouted "Help! Guards!" at his very window, and why? But when, after scurrying throughout the palace in great fear, his attendants had been unable to find the fellow, his anger had greatly increased. What it amounted to was this: in the very palace, during the postprandial hour, some fellow or other could create a disturbance and remain undiscovered. To top it off, no one had any idea of the purpose of that shout for "Help! Guards!" It may have been a warning shout from some malefactor, grown repentant. Or it may have been that right there in those bushes, which had been searched three times by now, somebody had had a gag thrust down his throat and then been strangled. It certainly looked as if the earth had yawned and swallowed the fellow. Certain measures ought to be taken. . . . Yes, but what measures could be taken if he went undiscovered?

Measures ought to be taken to increase the guard. And not only here, either.

Paul Petrovich, without turning round, stared at those green, quadrangular bushes, almost like those at the Trianon; they were closely clipped. But that did not help; he still did not know who had been lurking in them.

And he put out his right hand behind him, still without looking at the adjutant. The latter was aware of the significance of this: during his spells of great wrath the Emperor refused to turn round. The adjutant deftly slipped into the extended hand the orders dealing with the guards of the Regiment of the Transfiguration, and Paul Petrovich fell to reading them attentively. Then the hand was again thrust back and the adjutant picked up a quill from a small writing desk, dipped the quill in the inkwell, shook the surplus ink off, and placed the quill lightly in the outstretched hand, managing everything deftly, noiselessly, yet not without soiling himself with the ink. All this had taken him but a moment. Shortly the signed sheets went flying back at the adjutant. He kept submitting sheets and these, signed or merely read through, flew back at him one after the other. By this time he was becoming accustomed to this business and had begun to hope that everything would pass off in this manner, when the Emperor leaped off his elevated chair.

He ran up to the adjutant with mincing steps. His face was red, and his eyes had grown dark. He came right up against the adjutant and sniffed him: something the Emperor used to do whenever he was suspicious. Then he gripped the adjutant's sleeve with two fingers and pinched.

The adjutant stood at attention, one hand holding the sheets.

"You don't know your duty, my dear sir," said Paul hoarsely. "You approach from the back." He gave him one more pinch just for good measure. "I'll knock the Potemkin spirit out of you. Get going!"

And the adjutant, backing out through the door, withdrew.

No sooner had the door closed noiselessly than Paul Petrovich quickly undid his neckerchief and began, ever so slyly, ever so quietly, to rip the bosom of his shirt; his mouth became twisted and his lips began to twitch.

The Great Wrath was beginning.

4

The Emperor had signed the orders of the Regiment of the Transfiguration, but not without making certain wrathful corrections therein. When he had come to "Second Lieutenants Likewise, Steven, Rybid, and Azancheev," he had crossed out all the names save the first, and inserted the hugest of hard-ending marks, thus leaving but one Second Lieutenant, namely Likewise, and then had written above this: "Second Lieutenant Likewise to be put on guard duty." The rest of the order did not meet with any objections.

The order was duly transmitted.

Upon receiving it, the commander for a long while racked his head, trying to recall who this Second Lieutenant with the odd family name of Likewise was. He lost little time in consulting the roll of all the officers in the Regiment of the Transfiguration, but there was no officer with any such name designated therein. Nor was he to be found on the rolls of the rank and file. There was no making head or tail of this thing. There was but one man in all this world who could have understood it rightly—the regimental clerk; but no one had asked him about it, and he had told no one about it. The Emperor's order, however, had to be carried out—or, rather, fulfilled. Yet fulfilled it could not be, inasmuch as in all the regiment there was no Second Lieutenant Likewise.

Therefore, since it was the accepted thing whenever there was any trouble to rush to one's kindred, it was not long before the commander found out that he was of kin to Sablukov, adjutant to His Majesty, and went off at a gallop for Pavlovskoe, the Emperor's country seat.

He found Pavlovskoe in a great state of confusion, and at first the adjutant did not want to receive the commander at all. Then he squeamishly heard him out and was about to send him to the devil (he had enough things to attend to, as it was), when he suddenly knit his brows and gave the commander a lightning glance—and then that glance changed abruptly: it became reckless.

"Don't report anything of this to the Emperor," said the adjutant slowly. "Consider Second Lieutenant Likewise as among the living. Put him on guard duty."

The commander all but collapsed.

Without giving him as much as another look, the adjutant abandoned him to the whim of fate, drew himself up, and strode out.

5

Lieutenant Sinukhaev was but a skin-and-bones lieutenant. His father was physician to Baron Arakcheev, and the baron, in reward for the pills which had restored certain of his powers, had sneaked the physician's son into the regiment. His way of parting his hair was as straight as if with a ruler and his not at all intelligent appearance had proven to the baron's liking. The physician's son was not on an intimate footing with anybody in the regiment, but neither did he shun his messmates. He was not talkative, was fond of tobacco, did not dangle after women, and (which was not at all the thing for a dashing officer) found pleasure in playing the oboe d'amore.

His equipment was always neat and brightly polished.

As the regimental orders were being read out on parade, Sinukhaev, as usual, was standing as stiff as a ramrod and not thinking of anything in particular.

Suddenly he caught his own name and twitched his ears—the way horses do when they are startled out of their meditations by feeling the whip.

"Lieutenant Sinukhaev, having died of a fever, is no longer in the service."

At this point the commander, who was reading out the orders, happened to look involuntarily at the place where Sinukhaev usually stood at parade, and the hand holding the paper dropped.

Sinukhaev was, as always, standing in his place. Nevertheless it was not long before the commander resumed the reading of the orders—true enough, by now not so distinctly; he read aloud the part concerning Steven, Azancheev, Likewise, and so on to the end. The parade began, and Sinukhaev was supposed to go through the drill formations together with all the rest. But instead of doing so he remained rooted to the spot.

He had become used to paying close heed to the words of official orders, as if those words were in a class by themselves, bearing no resemblance to human speech. They had no meaning, no significance, yet they had a life and a power of their own. Their import lay not in whether the order was carried out or was not carried out. The order somehow transmuted regiments, streets, and people, even if it were not carried out —or fulfilled.

When he had caught the words of the order, he had at first remained rooted to the spot, like a man who had not heard clearly. He strained toward those words. Then he had ceased to doubt. The matter the commander had read out concerned him. And, when his column had started off, he began to doubt if he were alive.

Conscious of the hand lying on the hilt of his sword, of a certain discomfort from his tightly drawn sword belt, of the weight of his queue, which he had greased only that morning, he was, so to say, alive; yet at the same time he knew there was something wrong here, something had gone irreparably out of gear. Not once did it occur to him that there might be an error in the order. On the contrary, it appeared to him that it was through some error, some oversight, that he was alive. He had, through negligence, overlooked something and had failed to inform anybody thereof.

At any rate, he was messing up all the drill formations of the parade, standing there on the square like a post. It did not even occur to him to move from the spot.

As soon as the parade was over, the commander swooped on the lieutenant. The commander was as red as a beet. It was sheer luck that, owing to the sultry weather, the Emperor was resting at Pavlovskoe and had not attended the parade. The commander was just about to yap "To the guardhouse!"—but he felt the need of a more reverberating sound to discharge his wrath, and he was just about to start rolling his r's: "You'rre underr arrrrest!" when suddenly his mouth snapped shut, as though the commander had chanced to catch a fly in it. And, for a couple of minutes, he stood thus before Lieutenant Sinukhaev.

Then, staggering back from him as if the lieutenant had been stricken with the plague, the commander went his way.

He recalled that Lieutenant Sinukhaev had been separated

from the service as one deceased and restrained himself, since he did not know how to talk to a man in such a quandary.

6

Paul Petrovich was pacing his room, stopping only at rare intervals.

He was listening closely.

Ever since the Emperor, in dusty boots and traveling cape, had thundered with his spurs through the great chamber where his mother had not yet done with her death rattle and gone out slamming the door, those about him had observed: his Big Wrath would turn into the Great Wrath, while in a couple of days the Great Wrath would end in one of two ways: either in fear or in touched emotion.

The chimeras on the staircases at Pavlovskoe were the work of Brenna, famed for his wild grotesqueness, while the *plafonds* and murals were the work of Cameron, the Jacobin, a lover of delicate pigments that died away under the eyes of all. On the one hand, the gaping maws of lions rampant with anthropomorphous limbs and, on the other, exquisite sensuality.

There were also two lanterns hanging in the grand hall of the palace, the gift of Louis XVI, beheaded just a short time before. These had been presented to Paul Petrovich in France at the time when he had been traveling incognito as Count Severny. They were of fine workmanship, their panels so made that they softened the light. Paul Petrovich, however, avoided lighting them.

Moreover, there was a clock, a gift from Marie Antoinette; it stood on a table of jasper. The hour hand was a golden Saturn holding a long scythe, while the minute hand was a cupid holding an arrow. Whenever the clock struck midday or midnight Saturn would cover with his scythe the arrow of Cupid. Which signified: Time conquers Love. Be that as it may, this clock was never wound.

And so Brenna was out in the garden, Cameron graced the walls, while overhead, in the void under the ceiling, swayed the lanterns of Louis XVI.

During his Great Wrath, Paul Petrovich would actually take on a certain outward resemblance to one of Brenna's chimeric lions. Then, sudden as lightning, rods flailed whole regiments; in the dark of night, by the light of torches, someone's head would be lopped off on the Don; soldiers, scribes, lieutenants, generals, and governors-general would march off on their long trek to exile in Siberia.

His mother, the usurpress of the throne, was dead. Paul had knocked out the Potemkin spirit, just as once upon a time John the Fourth had knocked all the spirit out of the boyars.

Paul had scattered the bones of Potemkin and leveled his grave with the ground. He had annihilated his mother's very taste. The taste of a usurpress! Gold; rooms tiled with china; Dutch ovens everywhere—and a room of blue glass; the vogue of the snuffbox. A show booth at a fair—with Roman and Greek medals of which she had boasted! He had ordered them to be melted down for the gilding of his palace.

But, for all that, the spirit still remained, the flavor remained.

The place reeked of that spirit wherever one turned, and this was perhaps the reason why Paul Petrovich had a habit of sniffing closely those with whom he was conversing.

And, to top it all off, the French hanging lanterns kept swaying overhead.

Fear was closing in on him. The Emperor had not enough air. He feared neither his wife nor his older sons, although any one of these, recalling the example set them by their gay grandmother and mother-in-law, could have stabbed him dead with a fork and taken his seat on the throne.

He feared neither the suspiciously jovial ministers nor the suspiciously glum generals. He feared not one out of all that rabble of fifty million squatting on the tussocks, the swamps, dunes and fields of his Empire, and which he simply could not picture in his mind's eye. He was not afraid of any of them taken individually. But, taken all together, they were a sea, and in that sea he was drowning.

And he ordered moats to be dug, and outposts put up around his castle in St. Petersburg, and the drawbridge to be pulled up on chains. But even these chains could not be relied upon: the sentries on guard over them were men.

And, as the Great Wrath was turning into the Great Fear, the Chancellery of Criminal Offenses would buckle down to its work, and somebody would be hung up on the strappado by his arms, and under another body the floor would yawn, with master executioners awaiting him in the torture chamber below.

Therefore, whenever the sounds of abrupt, stumbling steps, now short, then prolonged, issued from the Imperial Chamber, all would exchange looks of dreary apprehension, and it was rare that anyone smiled.

The Great Fear was in the room.

The Emperor was on the prowl.

7

Lieutenant Sinukhaev still stood on the very same spot where the commander had swooped upon him to haul him over the coals but instead of doing so had stopped, most abruptly.

There was not another soul around.

Usually, after parade, he unlimbered, his hands relaxed and, with a sense of ease, he would head for the barracks. His every limb felt this sense of ease. It became a civilian limb.

At home, in the officers' quarters, the lieutenant would unbutton his coat and play his oboe. Then he would stuff his pipe tight and take to looking out of the window. What he saw was a large wedge of a garden that had been cut down and was now a wasteland, called the Tsaritsa's Meadow. There was no variety whatever about this field, no green life; nothing had been preserved on its sand save the marks of horses' hooves and of soldiers' boots. He found a pleasure in smoking because of all the minutiae connected with it: stuffing the bowl, tamping the tobacco down, lighting the pipe, and drawing the smoke in deep. As long as a man knows how to smoke he will never go to perdition. This pastime sufficed him, since evening would come shortly, and he could go off to visit friends, or simply take a stroll.

He liked the politeness of the common folk. Once, when he had chanced to sneeze, a passing burgher had said to him: "A spoke up your nose: not big—about a finger long!"

Before going to bed he would sit down with his orderly to an amusement that was becoming fashionable: cards. He trained his orderly to play Contra and also Pamphile, and whenever the orderly lost, the lieutenant would slap the fellow's nose with the deck; but when he himself lost he merely refrained from slapping the orderly. Finally he would inspect his equipment, which the orderly had cleaned, would curl, braid, and grease his queue, all by himself, and then lie down to sleep.

But now he did not unlimber; his sinews were cramped, and not a breath was to be heard issuing from his compressed lips. He fell to scrutinizing the parade ground, and it turned out to be unfamiliar to him. At any rate, he had never before noticed the cornices on the windows of the red-brick government building, nor its turbid windowpanes. The round cobbles of the roadways bore no resemblance to one another, like brothers who were unlike in appearance.

In great orderliness, in gray precision, soldierly St. Petersburg was lying before him, with its wastelands, rivers, and the turbid eyes studding the main highway—a town that was altogether unfamiliar to him.

It was then he understood that he had died.

8

Paul Petrovich caught the footfalls of his adjutant, stole like a cat to his armchair standing behind the glass screen, and planted himself in it as firmly as if he had been sitting there all the time.

He could recognize the footfalls of all those about him. Sitting with his back to them, he distinguished the scraping of the self-assured, the hop-skip-and-jump of the flatterers, and the light, ethereal step of those thoroughly terrified. A forthright tread he had never yet heard.

This time the adjutant was walking with assurance; his steps scraped now and then. Paul Petrovich turned around halfway.

The adjutant advanced toward the screen and inclined his head:

"Your Majesty, the man who shouted for the guards was Second Lieutenant Likewise," he said.

"Who may he be?"

The Fear was abating: it was taking on a name.

The adjutant had not expected this question and was taken aback somewhat.

"He is the second lieutenant who was put on guard duty, Your Majesty."

"Why was he shouting?" the Emperor stamped his foot. "I am listening, sir!"

The adjutant kept silent for a space. "Through lack of comprehension," he managed to babble out then.

"Put him through an interrogation and, after a whipping with the cat-o'-nine-tails, to Siberia with him—on foot."

9

Thus did the life of Second Lieutenant Likewise begin.

While the clerk was transcribing the regimental order, Second Lieutenant Likewise had been an error, a slip of the pen, no more. It might have passed unnoticed, it would have sunk into the sea of papers, and, since there was nothing particularly curious about that order, it is hardly likely that historians of a later day would have bothered even to reproduce it.

The carping eye of Paul Petrovich had drawn it forth and with an orthographic sign bestowed a dubious life upon it: the slip of the pen became a second lieutenant, faceless yet bearing a name.

Then, in the sporadic thoughts of the adjutant, he had gained a visage as well—barely glimmering, it is true, as if in a dream. He it was who had called out for the guards under the palace window.

Now this face had taken on firmer lines and had become elongated: Second Lieutenant Likewise turned out to be a malefactor, condemned to the strappado (or, at the best, to the whipping-horse) and Siberia.

This was already actuality.

Up to now he had been a haunting fear of the clerk's, a something that had stumped the commander, and a resourceful stroke of the adjutant's.

Henceforth the whipping-horse, the cat-o'-nine-tails, and the trek to Siberia would be his own, personal affair.

The order would have to be carried out—or fulfilled. Second Lieutenant Likewise would have to pass from stage to stage—from the military to the judicial, and then start over the green road to Siberia.

And that is precisely how things fell out.

The commander of the regiment on whose rolls Likewise was now listed as a second lieutenant called out his name before all the men and officers lined up on parade, in a voice which could belong only to one thoroughly distraught.

Standing off to one side, in full readiness, was the whipping-horse, and two guards deftly buckled its head- and foot-straps into place. Two other guards, one on each side, and each armed with a cat-o'-nine-tails, proceeded to lash the smoothly worn wood; a third was keeping count of the blows, and the regiment was watching.

Since its wood had been well polished long before by thousands of soldierly bellies, the whipping-horse somehow seemed not altogether devoid of an occupant. Even though there was nobody there, it did look, somehow, as if somebody were stretched out thereon. The soldiers, knitting their brows, were watching the whipping-horse from which no human sound came, while the commander, toward the end of this flogging, turned beet-red and his nostrils dilated—as they usually did on such an occasion.

Then the straps were just as deftly unbuckled and, somehow, it seemed as if somebody's shoulders had heaved free of the whipping-horse. Two of the guards stepped close to it and waited for the next command.

When it came they marched off down the street, receding from their regiment at an even stride, shouldering their muskets and, every now and then, eyeing askance, not each other, but the vacancy flanked in between them.

There was a young soldier standing in the ranks, who had had his head shaved for a recruit not so long ago. He had watched the flogging with great interest. To his mind everything that had taken place was quite the usual thing and a frequent occurrence in the military service. But that evening he suddenly took to tossing and turning in his bunk and softly asked an old guard in the bunk next to his:

"Who's our Emperor now, uncle dear?"

"Paul Petrovich, you she-fool," answered the startled old-timer.

"And did you ever happen to lay eyes on him?"

"I did that," growled the ancient, "and so will you."

They were silent. But the old soldier could not fall asleep. He kept tossing and turning. Ten minutes passed thus.

"But how did you come to ask that?" the old man suddenly questioned the young one.

"Why, I can't really say," the young fellow answered. "They're forever saying 'the Emperor, the Emperor,' but just who he is nobody knows. Maybe it's all nothing but talk."

"You she-fool, you," said the old man, and looked uneasily to either side of him. "Keep your trap shut, you hayseed she-fool."

Another ten minutes passed. It was dark and quiet in the barracks.

"He exists, sure enough," the old man said suddenly in the young man's very ear. "Only he's a changeling."

10

Lieutenant Sinukhaev scrutinized the room in which, up to this day, he had been alive and living.

The room was a spacious, low-ceiled one, with a portrait of a middle-aged man in spectacles sporting a clubby queue. It represented the lieutenant's father, Sinukhaev the physician.

Sinukhaev *père* was living at Gatchina, but the lieutenant, as he contemplated the portrait, did not feel any too sure of this. Perhaps he was living there—and perhaps he wasn't. The lieutenant was shying away from a positive answer.

After that he cast a look over the things which had belonged to Lieutenant Sinukhaev: the hautboy d'amour in its wooden case, the curling iron, the small jar of white powder, and the sand shaker—these things in their turn cast a look at him. He averted his gaze.

Thus did he stand in the middle of the room, waiting for something or other. It was hardly likely he was waiting for his orderly. Yet it was none other than the orderly who entered the room cautiously and halted before the lieutenant. He let his jaw drop a little and stood there, gaping at the lieutenant. Probably he had always stood like that when awaiting orders, but the lieutenant, after a look at him as if he were seeing the man for the first time, quickly went out and carefully closed the door after him.

It was necessary for him to conceal his death for the time being, as if it were a crime.

He roamed the streets of St. Petersburg all night long, without even thinking of stepping in anywhere. Toward morning he tired and sat down on the ground near a house. He dozed for several minutes, then suddenly leaped up and started walking again, without looking either to the right or left of him.

Shortly he had left the city limits behind him. The sleepy toll keeper near the barrier wrote down the lieutenant's name in his book absentmindedly.

The lieutenant never came back to the barracks again.

11

His Majesty's adjutant was a crafty fellow and did not confide in any one about Second Lieutenant Likewise and the success of his little dodge. He, even as all of us, had enemies. For that reason he told only a select few that the fellow who had shouted for the guards had been found.

But this had a strange effect upon the feminine half of the court.

To the facade of the palace, which had been built by Cameron, with its columns as slender as fingers stroking a clavichord, two wings had been added, curved like a cat's paws when the cat is playing with a baby mouse. Living in one of these wings was Nelidova, a maid of honor, keeping her virginal state with her retinue.

Many and many a time had Paul Petrovich, shunning the sentries, set out on the sly for this wing, and on one occasion the sentries had seen the Emperor come flying out of there, with his wig all askew and a feminine slipper sailing over his head.

Although Nelidova was only a maid of honor, she had maids of honor all her own. And so, when word reached the women's wing that the man who had called out for the guards had been found, one of the maids of honor of the maid of honor fell into a swoon—not too long a one, however.

Like Nelidova, she was slender and curly, like a Dresden china shepherd boy.

In the days of Elizabeth, the maids of honor had walked about in crackling cloth-of-gold, in susurrating silks, and their paps, seeking freedom, would timidly peep forth. Such had been the mode. As for the amazons of the usurpress's time, with their fondness for dresses of a masculine cut, velvet trains, and star-shaped beauty marks placed in strategic proximity to their paps, they had passed away together with her. And now women had turned into shepherd boys with curly little pates.

And so, one of them had keeled over into not too long a swoon.

Picked up off the floor by her patroness and awakening from

unconsciousness, she told her story: at that fatal hour she had a tryst with a certain officer. She had been unable, however, to absent herself from the room, which was on the second floor, and suddenly, looking out of a window, she had seen that the incandescent officer, having cast all caution to the winds—and perhaps unaware where he was—was standing near the Emperor's own window and signaling up to her.

She had waved her hand, trying to shoo him away, had made her eyes express horror, but her lover had misunderstood her pantomime as a demonstration of his having become detestable to her, and had piteously cried out for help.

That same instant, without losing her presence of mind, she had flattened her nose with her finger into a snub nose and pointed down. After which snub-nosed signal her gallant had become stunned and then disappeared.

She had seen no more of him and, owing to the rapid tempo of their love affair, which had started the evening before, she had not even learned his name.

Now they had brought him out into the open and packed him off to Siberia.

Nelidova became plunged in thought.

Her own affair was on the wane, and—although she did not want to admit this to herself—her slipper had by now had its wings clipped.

She was not on the warmest of terms with the adjutant and did not want to turn to him. The Emperor's mood was dubious. Whenever that was the case, she now turned to a certain person, a civilian, yet one wielding great power, a fellow named Yury Aleksandrovich Nelidinsky-Meletsky. This was precisely what she did, sending him a note by a palace flunkey.

The palace flunkey, to whom transmitting such notes was by no means a novelty, was always struck by the niggardliness of the mighty man. Meletsky was a singer and secretary of state. He used to sing *The Running Rill* and had a passion for little shepherdesses. He looked quite small, had a mawkish mouth, and his eyebrows were shaggy. But, for all that, he was a crafty fellow and, looking up at the broad-shouldered flunkey, he said:

"You may say there is no cause for uneasiness. Let the lady mark time. This whole business is about to be settled."

Yet he himself felt a little uneasy, since he hadn't the least notion how this business would really be settled, and when one of his youthful shepherdesses, who had formerly been a rustic Jennie but was now called Selimena, insinuated herself through his door, he wiggled his eyebrows at her ferociously.

Yury Aleksandrovich's domestic staff consisted for the most part of youthful shepherdesses.

12

The sentries convoying Second Lieutenant Likewise marched on and on.

From toll pike to toll pike, from convict post to fortress, they marched straight ahead, and from time to time looked apprehensively at the impressive void marching along between them.

Convoying some exile to Siberia was no prime novelty to them, but never yet had they had occasion to escort a criminal such as this. When they had left the city limits behind them, they had had a twinge of doubt. They could hear no clanking of chains, and there was no need of urging somebody on with the butts of their guns. But then it occurred to them that this was an official matter and that they had taken a paper along with them. They spoke but little to each other, since conversation was forbidden.

At the first convict post the supervisor had looked at them as if they were mad, and they had been thrown into confusion. But the senior sentry showed a paper which declared that the person under arrest was a secret prisoner and was incorporeal, whereupon the supervisor began to bustle and assigned them a special chamber with three bunks for the night. He avoided all conversation with them and for some reason was so ingratiating that the sentries willy-nilly came to feel their importance.

Their second convict post, an important one, they approached with confidence, their air grave and taciturn, and the senior sentry simply tossed the paper on the commandant's desk. And this fellow as well became ingratiating and began to bustle in the same way as the first.

Little by little they began to grasp that the offender they were convoying was someone of consequence. They became used to the thing and, between themselves, would refer to "Him" or "It."

In this way they had already passed far into the depth of the Russian Empire, along the straight, hard-beaten Vladimir Road.

And the void that was patiently marching between them kept changing: now it would be the wind, now the dust, now the sultriness of summer, a summer so tuckered out by now that it was on its last legs.

13

In the meantime, creeping over the same Vladimir Road, from barrier to barrier, from fortress to fortress, an important order was trying to catch up with them.

"Mark time," Yury Aleksandrovich Nelidinsky-Meletsky had said, and he had not erred in the matter.

For the Great Fear of Paul Petrovich was slowly but surely turning into pity for himself, into a touched mood.

The Emperor was turning his back upon the shrubbery in his topiary garden—shrubbery clipped into the shapes of queer beasts—and, after having wandered in a vacuum, was turning to the exquisite sensuality of Cameron.

He had twisted around his little finger all of his mother's generals and governors-general, he had tucked them out of sight in their country estates, where they were practically doing time. He had had to act thus. Yet what had been the result? A great vacuum had formed all around him.

He had had a box for complaints and letters hung before his castle for, after all, it was he and not some other who was the father of the fatherland. At first this box had remained empty—and this grieved him, inasmuch as a fatherland ought to have speech with its father. Later on, an anonymous letter was found in this box, calling him Daddy Button-Nose and threatening him.

He had thereupon looked into a mirror.

"You are button-nosed, my dear sir; you *are* button-nosed, sure enough," he had wheezed and had ordered the box taken down.

He undertook a journey through this queer fatherland. During it he had sent packing to Siberia a governor who had dared to put up new bridges in his province. His wasn't one of those journeys his dear mother used to take: everything had to be just as it was and not all rigged out. But the fatherland still wouldn't say a word. One one occasion, on the Volga, some muzhiks had gathered around him. He sent a lad out to dip up some water from the middle of the river, so that he might have a drink of pure water. He drank this water and then said to the muzhiks in a husky voice:

"There, I am drinking your water. What are you gaping at?"

And everything again became a vacuum around him.

He did not set out on any other tour and, in lieu of the complaint box, he placed sturdy sentries at each outpost; but he did not know whether they were loyal or not, and he did not know of whom he ought to be wary.

Perfidy and vacuity were all around him.

He discovered a method of getting rid of both—and introduced precision and absolute subordination. The chancelleries buckled down to their work. It was considered that he was taking on only executive powers for himself. But somehow things so fell out that the executive power threw all the chancelleries into confusion, and as a result there was more dubious perfidy, vacuity, and a sly subordination. He pictured himself as a chance-tossed swimmer, raising his empty hands amid the raging waves (he had once seen an engraving like that)—a chance-tossed swimmer that had been but a slip of the tongue uttered by the sea.

Yet at the same time he was, after many long years, the sole lawful autocrat.

And he was oppressed by a yearning to lean upon a father, even if it were but a dead one. He had dug up the grave of the German half-wit who had been considered his father and who had been assassinated with a fork and placed his coffin side by side with the coffin of the usurpress of the throne. But he had done this mostly to avenge himself upon his dead mother, during whose life he had lived the life of one who is, at every moment, condemned to execution.

Yes—and had she been his mother?

He knew some vague things about the scandal of his birth.

He was a man deprived of a lineage, deprived even of a dead father, even a dead mother.

He never let his thoughts dwell on this and would have ordered any man who had the least suspicion of his having such thoughts to be shot out of a cannon barrel.

But at such moments as these he found pleasure even in slight pranks and the diminutive pagodas of his Trianon. He became a forthright friend of nature and longed to have everybody—or at least somebody—love him.

This fit ran its course, and at such times rudeness was considered frankness, stupidity forthrightness, craftiness kindliness, and the Turkish orderly who blacked his boots would be made a count.

Yury Aleksandrovich had a sixth sense when it came to scenting such a change. He marked time for a week, and then scented it.

With soft yet cheerful steps he pattered about the glass screen awhile and suddenly, assuming the protective mask of simplicity, confided to the Emperor everything he knew about Second Lieutenant Likewise—with the exception, naturally, of the detail about the snub-nosed signal of warning.

At this, the Emperor broke into such yapping laughter, laughter so canine, hoarse, and choppy, that it sounded as if he were firing it at somebody.

Yury Aleksandrovich became uneasy. He had wanted to do a favor for Nelidova, whose household friend he was, and, incidentally, to demonstrate his own influence, for, according to the German proverb then current, *umsonst ist der Tod*: all you can get for nothing is death. But laughter such as this could instantly reduce Yury Aleksandrovich to a secondary role or even serve as an engine for his annihilation.

Was it sarcasm, perhaps?

But no; the Emperor had grown weak from laughter. He held out his hand for the quill, and Yury Aleksandrovich, getting up on his tiptoes, read, as he followed the Emperor's quill:

Second Lieutenant Likewise, banished to Siberia, is to be brought back forthwith; promote said Second Lieutenant to Lieutenant and marry him off to the maid of honor involved.

Inspired by having written this, the Emperor took a stroll up and down the room. He clapped his palms and began half-singing, half-whistling his favorite ditty:

Pine grove, my pine grove,
My thick-growing birch grove—

while Yury Aleksandrovich chimed in with:

Lulla, lullaby.

14

A dog that has been bitten likes to go off into a field and treat his wounds with the bitter herbs growing there.

Lieutenant Sinukhaev went afoot from St. Petersburg to Gatchina. He went to his father, not to ask him for help but perhaps just out of a desire to make sure whether he had a father in existence at Gatchina, or whether, perhaps, that father was nonexistent. To the paternal greeting he made no reply, looked about him, and was already set to leave, like a man embarrassed, and even behaving in a namby-pamby sort of way.

But the physician, noting the damage to his clothing, made him sit down and began getting the truth out of him.

"I am not alive," the lieutenant told him suddenly.

The physician felt his pulse, said something about applying leeches, and went on with his interrogation.

When he learned of his son's predicament, he became excited, spent all of an hour in writing and rewriting a petition, compelled his son to sign it, and on the morrow went himself to Baron Arakcheev to submit it with his daily report. He felt embarrassed, however, about keeping his son in his house, and put him to bed in the infirmary, marking on the chart over the bed:
Mors occasionalis
(contingent death)

15

Baron Arakcheev was preoccupied with thoughts about government. For that reason his character lent itself but little to definition; it was elusive. The baron was not vindictive; at times he was even condescending. When some touching story was told in his presence, he would shed tears like a child, and as he walked about his garden he would give a copper to the little wench who swept the paths. Later on, if he noticed that the garden paths were not swept well, he would order the child to be beaten with birchrods. When the chastisement had been administered, however, he would hand over a five-kopek piece to her.

In the presence of the Emperor he experienced a certain weakness akin to love.

He loved cleanliness; it was emblematic of his nature. But he also found real satisfaction when he found shortcomings in cleanliness and orderliness; and, if no such shortcomings materialized, he felt secretly aggrieved. Instead of freshly roasted meat, he always ate salted beef.

He was as absentminded as a philosopher. And, to be sure, German savants found a resemblance between his eyes and the eyes of Kant, a philosopher at that time well-known in Germany: they were of a tenuous, indeterminate hue, those eyes, and streaked over with a transparent pellicle. Yet he took umbrage when someone told him of the resemblance.

He was not merely stingy; he also liked to shine on occasion, as well as to show everything off to the best advantage. For that reason he entered into the smallest details of his household. He pored over the plans and designs of projected chapels, decorations of honor, holy images, or a new dining table. He was greatly taken by circles, ellipses, and straight lines, all of which, intertwining as in the thimble-rigging strap game, resulted in a construction that could deceive the eye. And he loved to take in some visitor, to take in even the Emperor, but would pretend not to see a thing whenever anyone proved cunning enough to take him in. As for taking him in, that, of course, was pretty hard.

He kept a full inventory of the things belonging to each of his people, from his valet down to the least scullion, and he checked all the infirmary inventories himself.

During the organization of the hospital to which the father of Lieutenant Sinukhaev was attached, the baron himself indicated where the beds were to be placed, where the benches were to go, where the house surgeon's small desk was to stand and even what form the clerk's quill was to have: to wit, it had to be plain, without any tuft of feathers, and was to look like the Roman *calamus*, or writing reed. One of the assistant medicos got himself five strokes with birchrods for fancifying his quill with a tuft.

Baron Arakcheev found the idea of the Roman state

absorbing. For that reason he listened to Sinukhaev the physician in abstraction, and only when the latter held out his petition did he read it attentively—concluding by reprimanding the physician because the paper was signed illegibly. The physician offered the excuse that his son's hand had been shaky.

"Ah, my friend, you see that?" the baron responded with relish. "Even his hand is shaky!" And, after a look at the physician, he asked: "And when did the said death befall him?"

"On the fifteenth of June," answered the physician somewhat taken aback.

"On the fifteenth of June," drawled the baron, calculating. "On the fifteenth of June. . . . And now it's already the seventeenth!" he fired point-blank at the physician. "Where, then, has the dead man been for the last two days?"

After smirking at the physician's disconcerted looks, he cast a wry glance over the petition and said:

"There, that's the sort of irregularity one gets. Good-bye for the present, friend; you may go."

16

Meletsky, songster and secretary of state, took chances and often won, inasmuch as he was able to give a soft complexion to everything, in perfect keeping with the delicate pigments of Cameron; however, his winnings alternated with losses, as in the card game of quadrille.

Baron Arakcheev, on the other hand, was of a different bent. He took no risks, he would not guarantee anything. On the contrary, in his reports to the Emperor, whenever he pointed out some abuse, he would right then and there ask for instructions as to what measures were to be taken to do away with it. The belittling which Meletsky risked, the baron in his own case would bring about by himself. But then, the winnings which the baron saw glimmering far ahead of him were great, as in the game of faro.

He informed the Emperor that the deceased Lieutenant Sinukhaev had shown up in Gatchina, where he had been placed in a hospital. In addition to that, he had turned out to be alive and had submitted a petition to be reinstated on the army rolls, which petition, since it called for further disposition, was being duly forwarded. What the Baron was aiming to show through this paper was his submissiveness, that he was the assiduous steward who consults his master on every point.

The reply came shortly—dealing with the petition but, more particularly, with Baron Arakcheev. The decision reached on the petition ran:

"The request for reinstatement of the late Lieutenant

Sinukhaev, struck from the rolls because of death, is to be rejected for the very same reason."

The note sent for Baron Arakcheev's benefit ran:

Baron Arakcheev, Addressed.
Sir:

It surprises me that, although holding the rank of general, you are not yet familiar with the regulations, since you have sent to me, directly, the petition of the deceased Lieutenant Sinukhaev who, besides everything else, is not even of our regiment; the said petition should properly have been sent first to the chancellery of the regiment to which the Lieutenant was attached.

Nevertheless, I remain,
Graciously yours,
Paul

Not "Ever graciously yours," mind you; just "Graciously yours."

And Arakcheev shed a tear, since he hated worse than death to receive reprimands. He went to the hospital himself and ordered the deceased lieutenant to be driven out; he was to be issued some linen, but as for his officer's uniform, which had been entered on the inventory, that was to be kept back.

17

By the time Lieutenant Likewise had come back from Siberia a great number of people knew about him. This was that very same second lieutenant who had called out for the guards under the Emperor's window, had been flogged and sent off to Siberia, and then was pardoned and made a lieutenant. Such were the definitely ascertained details of his life.

The regimental commander no longer felt the least embarrassment about him and simply appointed him now for guard duty, now as officer of the day. When the regiment set out for the summer maneuvers, the lieutenant set out together with the rest. He was a model officer, inasmuch as it was impossible to notice anything wrong about him.

The maid of honor whose not too protracted swoon had saved him had at first been overcome with joy at the idea of being made one with her spontaneous lover. She put a beauty mark on her cheek and drew tighter the reluctant laces of her stays. Later on, in church, when she perceived that she was standing during the wedding rite all by herself, while His Majesty's adjutant was holding the wedding crown over the vacant place next to her, she was on the verge of swooning anew; but since she was keeping her eyes cast down and consequently could see how plump her waistline had become, she thought better of it. A certain mysticism about the rite, during which no bridegroom was apparent, titillated many of those present.

And after a certain time a son was born to Lieutenant Likewise and, according to rumor, the boy favored his father in looks.

The Emperor forgot about him. He had many matters to attend to.

The impulsive Nelidova had taken a back seat and the plump Gagarina had come into her place. Cameron, and the diminutive chalets, and even all of Pavlovskoe, were forgotten. St. Petersburg, squat and soldierly, spread out in its red-brick regularity. Suvorov, that military hysteric whom Paul disliked yet tolerated because he had carried on a feud with the late Potemkin, was disturbed in his rustic solitude. A campaign was in the making, since the Emperor had certain plans. Of these plans there were a great number, and not infrequently one of them would outrace some other. Paul Petrovich's girth increased and his figure sagged. His face turned a brick red. Suvorov again fell into disfavor. The Emperor laughed less and less often.

Once, leafing through certain regimental rosters, he had stumbled upon the name of Lieutenant Likewise and had appointed him to a captaincy; and on another similar occasion, to a colonelcy. Lieutenant-Captain-Colonel Likewise was a model officer. Then the Emperor forgot him anew.

The life of Colonel Likewise flowed on imperceptibly, and all had become reconciled to this state of affairs. At home he had a study all to himself, a room all to himself in the barracks, and from time to time orders and reports were brought in there, without too much wonder being evinced over the nonpresence of the colonel.

By now he was in command of a regiment.

It was the maid of honor who felt best of all, in her enormous double bed. Her husband was getting ahead in the service; she could sleep in comfort; her son was growing up. Now and then the Colonel's connubial couch would be warmed by some lieutenant or captain, or even a civilian. This, however, was the case with many a colonel's bed in St. Petersburg when its lord was away campaigning.

However, once or twice, while the tuckered-out lover was sleeping, she had caught the sound of a board creaking in an adjoining room. The sound came again. Beyond a doubt, it must have been the floor warping, but she had instantly nudged the sleeper awake, thrust him out of the room and thrown his clothes after him. When she had recovered her wits, she could not help laughing at herself.

But this, too, was something that happened in many a colonel's house.

18

The peasants smelled of the wind and the peasant women, of smoke.

Lieutenant Sinukhaev did not look people straight in the eye and distinguished them only by their smell. It was through this sense of smell that he chose each night's lodging, and while doing so he did his best to find a tree under which to sleep, because under a tree one does not get so wet from the rain.

He walked on and on, without tarrying anywhere.

He crossed Finnish village after Finnish village the way a flat pebble, scaled by an urchin, skims across water: without making any contact. On rare occasions a Finnish woman would offer him some milk. He would drink it up standing and then go on. Little brats would become hushed, not daring even to wipe off the whitish snot glistening under their noses. Then the village would close together again in his wake.

His walk had undergone but little change. Because of all his walking it had become sprung, but his sprung walk, quaggy as chaff, even toylike, was still a military walk, an officer's walk.

He did not distinguish directions either. But just the same these directions could be determined. Deviating, making zig-zags that resembled the lightning on pictures depicting the Deluge, he was still going in circles, and these circles were slowly narrowing.

Thus a year passed, until the circle closed on a point and he entered St. Petersburg. Having entered it, he made its circuit, from one end to the other.

Then he began going in circles about the city, and there were times when he kept going in the same circle for weeks on end.

He walked rapidly, still with that sprung, military walk of his, in which the arms and legs seemed to be deliberately dangling.

The shopkeepers detested him. Whenever he chanced to be passing through Merchants' Row, they would call after him:

"Get here yesterday!"

"Try going on backward!"

They said that he brought bad luck, and the country wives who were selling bread and rolls would, by tacit agreement, give him a loaf each, to ward off his evil eye.

Urchins, who in every epoch are superb masters at seizing upon weak points, would run after him and shout:

"Jack-on-a-string!"

19

In St. Petersburg the sentries posted around the castle of Paul Petrovich had called out:

"The Emperor sleeps!"

The halberdiers on the street crossings caught up the cry:

"The Emperor sleeps!"

And because of this cry, as if it were a strong wind blowing, one after the other the shops closed, and the pedestrians hid themselves away in houses.

This meant that night had fallen.

On the Square of St. Isaac the hordes of muzhiks in sacking, driven here from their villages to forced labor, doused their bonfires and bedded themselves down for the night where they were, right on the ground, covering themselves with matting.

The watch, armed with halberds, after calling out "The Emperor sleeps!" had followed his example. A sentry was moving to and fro, like a pendulum, on the walls of the Fortress of SS. Peter and Paul. In a certain pothouse on the outskirts, one of its steady customers, girded with a rope of bast, sat drinking vodka, the Tsar's own wine, with a hack driver.

"It'll soon be all over with Daddy Snub Nose," the hack driver was saying. "I was driving some high and mighty folks. . . ."

The drawbridge of the castle was up, and Paul Petrovich was looking out of a window.

For the time being, on this island of his, he was out of danger.

For the time being. . . . There were whispers and glances in the palace, the meaning of which did not escape him, and when people whom he came upon in the street fell on their knees before his horse they had the oddest look on their faces. This business of kneeling in the street was something he had inaugurated, but now the people plumped into the mire not at all the way they used to do. They did it far too impetuously. His was a high horse, and he swayed in the saddle. He was reining at too fast a pace. The castle was insufficiently protected, too spacious. It was necessary to find a chamber somewhat smaller than this one. That, however, was something Paul Petrovich could not do. There was bound to be some creature who would note the thing at once. "One ought to hide in a snuffbox," mused the Emperor as he took snuff. He did not light the candles. No need of putting people on one's track. He was standing in the dark, in nothing but his linen. He was weighing his men as he stood by the window, crossing the name of Benningsen off his memory, entering that of Olsufiev. The list would not come out right.

"The score isn't coming out right for me. . . ."

Then, aloud, but in a low voice:

"This Arakcheev is stupid. The *vague incertitude* with which the fellow seeks to please!"

By now the sentry on the drawbridge was barely to be seen.

"I ought to . . ." said Paul Petrovich, through habit.

His fingers were drumming on the snuffbox.

"I ought to. . . ." He was trying to recall something, and kept on drumming upon the snuffbox—and suddenly stopped.

Everything that ought to have been done had been done long since, and had turned out to be inadequate.

"I ought to imprison Aleksander Pavlovich—" But he had thought of the wrong thing and made a hopeless gesture.

"I ought to. . . ."

But what was it he ought to do?

He lay down and quickly darted under the blanket—something he always did.

He fell fast asleep.

At seven in the morning—suddenly, with a jolt—he awoke and remembered what it was he ought to do: have some simple, modest person closely attached to him, who would be wholly obligated to him; and, as for all the others, they ought to be supplanted.

And he fell asleep again.

20

That morning Paul Petrovich looked through the orders. Colonel Likewise was suddenly made a general. Here was one colonel who did not importune for estates, did not try to climb up in the world through some uncle's backing, who was no braggart, no whippersnapper. He was doing his duty, without murmuring or raising a fuss.

Paul Petrovich demanded Likewise's service record.

He paused over a paper which stated clearly that at the time when Colonel Likewise had been a Second Lieutenant he had been banished to Siberia for having called out for the guards under the Emperor's window. He recalled a thing or two, as in a haze, and smiled. There had been some sort of frivolous amour involved.

How very handy such a man would be now, who would call out to the guards under his window at a moment of need! He graciously bestowed a country estate and a thousand serfs upon General Likewise.

On the evening of the same day the name of General Likewise bobbed up to the surface. He was being talked about. Someone had heard the Emperor saying to Count Pahlen with a smile—something no one had seen for a long while:

"Wait about encumbering him with a division. He is needed for something which is of the utmost importance."

No one, with the exception of Benningsen, would confess to

knowing nothing about the general. Pahlen kept puckering his eyes. Naryshkin, the High Chamberlain, recalled the general:

"Why, yes, of course . . . Colonel Likewise . . . I remember. He used to run after Sandunova—"

"He was at the maneuvers at Krasnoe—"

"He's related to Olsufiev, Fyodor Yacovlevich, if I remember rightly—"

"He's no relative of Olsufiev's, Count. General Likewise hails from France. His father was beheaded by the rabble at Toulon."

21

Events moved swiftly. General Likewise was summoned to appear before the Emperor. That same day the Emperor was informed that the general had been taken dangerously ill.

He grunted from vexation and twisted a button off the uniform of Pahlen, who had brought the news:

"Put him in a hospital—get him well. And, sir, if they fail to get him well. . . ."

The Emperor's own *valet de chambre* drove to the hospital twice a day to make inquiries about the general's health.

In a great ward, behind closed doors, physicians were bustling about, shivering as if they were the ones who were ill.

Toward the evening of the third day General Likewise passed away.

Paul Petrovich was no longer wrathful. He looked at everybody with misty eyes and withdrew into his own chamber.

22

It was a long while before St. Petersburg could forget the funeral of General Likewise, and certain memoirists have preserved its details.

His regiment marched with its colors furled. Thirty court coaches, empty and occupied, rocked along in the rear. The Emperor had willed it so. The late general's decorations of honor were borne along upon cushions.

Behind the black, ponderous coffin paced his wife, leading her child by the hand. And she was weeping.

When the procession was passing the castle of Paul Petrovich, he himself rode out on the drawbridge to watch it and uttered, as he held aloft his bared sword:

"My best men are dying off."

Then, when all the court coaches had rolled past him, he got off the Latin tag, as he followed them with his eyes:

"Sic transit gloria mundi."

23

Thus was General Likewise interred, having fulfilled in his life all that man may fulfill and with his cup running over: youth and amatory adventures, punishment and banishment, years of service, domesticity, the sudden favor of his Emperor, and the envy of the Emperor's courtiers.

His name appears in the *St. Petersburg Necrologue*, and certain historians mention him *passim*.

One will not, however, come across the name of the deceased Lieutenant Sinukhaev. He vanished without leaving a vestige behind him, disintegrated into the dust, was swept away even as chaff on the wind, just as though he had never existed.

As for Paul Petrovich, he died in March of the same year as General Likewise—from, according to official data, apoplexy.

1927

Rain at Dawn

Konstantin Paustovsky

It was night when the boat arrived at Navoloki. Major Kuzmin came out on deck. A fine rain was falling, the jetty was deserted but for the light of a lantern.

"Which way is the town?" thought Kuzmin. "Dark, raining, the devil knows what not!" He shivered, buttoning his overcoat. A cold wind blew off the river. Kuzmin found the mate and asked him how long the boat would stay at Navoloki.

"Three hours," answered the mate. "Depends on the loading. Why do you want to know? You're going on, aren't you?"

"I have to give a letter to someone. From my neighbor at the hospital—same ward. It's to his wife. She's here, in Navoloki."

"Yes, that's a responsibility," said the mate with a sympathetic sigh. "It's pitch dark, you'll have to listen for the siren, or you'll get left behind."

Kuzmin alighted on the jetty and went up the slippery steps toward the steep embankment. The wind was rustling the bushes. Kuzmin halted to accustom his eyes to the darkness, then made out a depressed-looking horse with a lopsided droshky. The hood of the droshky had been raised, and snores were audible.

"Friend," said Kuzmin loudly, "if the Kingdom of God were at hand, you'd sleep through it."

The driver bestirred himself and got out, blowing his nose on his coattail; this done, he asked: "Are we ready?"

"That we are," assented Kuzmin.

"Where to, then?"

Kuzmin named the street.

"Oh, that's a long way." The driver was anxious. "Up the hill. I couldn't charge you less than the cost of a pint."

He pulled on the reins, clucked to the horses, and the droshky moved off reluctantly.

"Would you be the only driver in Navoloki?" asked Kuzmin.

"There are two of us, both old. The others're away at the war. Whose house you going to?"

"Mrs. Bashilova's."

"I know who she is," exclaimed the driver. "That's Olga Andreevna, Dr. Andrey Petrovich's daughter. Came to her father's house from Moscow last winter and settled there. Must be two years now since Andrey Petrovich died, so the house is hers."

The cab lurched, jingled, and righted itself.

"Keep your eyes on the road," Kuzmin enjoined him. "Don't turn your head."

"And what a road," grumbled the driver. "You'd be afraid

to go down it by day. But night don't matter so much, because you can't see the potholes."

The driver fell silent. Kuzmin lit a cigaret and leaned back in the seat. The rain pattered on the hood. Dogs were barking in the distance. There was a smell of dill, and wet palings, and river damp. "Must be one o'clock, if not later," thought Kuzmin. At that moment a cracked bell did strike one in some bell tower.

"Suppose I spend all my furlough here?" thought Kuzmin. "That air alone's enough to cure all ills, well, that is, any complications to the injury. I could find some little house with a room to rent that looked out on a garden. On fine nights I could open the windows wide and lie in bed listening to the rain falling on the burdocks."

"Not her husband, are you?" asked the driver.

Kuzmin made no reply. The driver thought perhaps the officer had not heard, but decided not to repeat. "Course he's her husband," reasoned the driver, "and people've been gossiping about her leaving her husband long before the war. Must be a lot of tommyrot, that's all."

"Up, you Satan!" he cried, snapping the reins at the bony horse. "You kneading dough with those knees of yours?"

What a nuisance, that boat coming in late at night, thought Kuzmin. Why had Bashilov, his bed neighbor at the hospital, on hearing that Kuzmin would be stopping at Navoloki, asked him to hand the letter to his wife in person? Now he'd have to wake people up, and God only knew what they'd think.

Bashilov was a tall officer with mocking ways, a ready and voluble talker. Before saying anything sharp, he would laugh long and soundlessly. Prior to his joining the army, Bashilov had worked in films as assistant producer. Every evening he would give his ward mates detailed accounts of American films. The wounded men delighted in Bashilov's stories, they looked forward to them, and marveled at his memory. In sizing up men, events, and books, Bashilov was harsh and opinionated, jeering mercilessly at anyone who tried to gainsay him. But he jeered with such cunning, with asides and pleasantries, that only some two hours later did the object of his mockery realize that Bashilov had been insulting him and think of a biting retort. By then, of course, it was too late.

The day before Kuzmin was to leave Bashilov handed him a letter for his wife. Kuzmin for the first time had seen that embarrassed smile on Bashilov's face. And that night Kuzmin had heard Bashilov tossing in his bed and blowing his nose. "Perhaps he's not such a dry stick after all," thought Kuzmin.

"I may be wrong, but I think he's weeping. That means he has it in him to love, and love deeply."

All the next day Bashilov stayed close to Kuzmin. He kept glancing at him, made him a gift of an officer's hip flask, and just before Kuzmin left they drank a bottle of wine between them that Bashilov had smuggled in.

"Why do you keep looking at me like that?" asked Kuzmin.

"You're a good man," answered Bashilov. "You could be an artist, my dear major."

"I'm a topographer," Kuzmin replied, "and topographers are artists by nature."

"How so?"

"They're vagabonds."

"'Outlaw, vagabond, and poet,'" quoted Bashilov, "'who craved to be somebody, but could not.'"

"Who's that by?"

"Voloshin. But never mind that. I've been looking at you because I envy you. That's all."

"Envy me—what for?"

Bashilov twirled his glass, tilted back in his chair, and smiled. They were sitting by a small wicker table at one end of the hospital corridor. Outside, the wind was bending the saplings, rustling the leaves, blowing the dust. From beyond the river a rain cloud was bearing down on the town.

"What for?" echoed Bashilov, laying his red hand on Kuzmin's. "For everything. Even your hand. Not the left, particularly the right one."

"I don't follow you," said Kuzmin and carefully withdrew his hand; the touch of Bashilov's clammy hand was unpleasant; but, so that Bashilov should not notice this, Kuzmin picked up the bottle and poured out some wine.

"Well, so don't follow me!" retorted Bashilov, angered. He was silent a moment, then began to speak, eyes lowered: "If only we could change places! But that's all rubbish, of course. In two days you'll be at Navoloki, you'll see Olga Andreevna. She'll take your hand. That's what I envy you for. Now do you get me?"

"But—what of it?" said Kuzmin, confused. "You'll be seeing her, too: she's your wife."

"For me she's not just a wife," answered Bashilov sharply. "A good thing you didn't say 'spouse'."

"Oh, well, I'm sorry," muttered Kuzmin.

"She's not my wife!" repeated Bashilov in the same curt way. "She's everything to me. My whole life. Well, enough of that."

He got up and held out his hand to Kuzmin. "Good-bye! And don't bear me any grudge. I'm no worse than anyone else."

The droshky was proceeding slowly along the dam. The darkness grew thicker. The rain trickling off the old willow trees had a drowsy sound. The horse's hoofs clattered over a bridge.

"It *is* a long way!" sighed Kuzmin, and said to the driver:

"Wait for me at the house. You'll be taking me back to the landing stage."

"Glad to," agreed the driver promptly, and thought: "No, 'course he's not her husband. A husband would have stayed a couple of days, for sure. He's someone else, a stranger."

Now the road was a cobbled one. The cab began to shake and jingle its iron steps. The driver swerved to the side of the road; the wheels were now churning through damp sand. Kuzmin returned to his thoughts.

So Bashilov envied him, did he? There surely wasn't much to envy. Bashilov hadn't used the proper word, that's all. After his talk with Bashilov by the window in the hospital, it was Kuzmin who began to envy Bashilov. "Again it wasn't the right word," Kuzmin told himself, annoyed. It was not envy he had felt, but only chagrin, chagrin at the fact that he was now, well, forty years old and had never had a love like Bashilov's. He had always been alone.

"The night is dark, the rain sounds in the empty gardens—a strange sort of town that smells of mist from the meadows: that's how life goes by," thought Kuzmin for some reason.

Again he felt a desire to stay on here. He liked these little Russian towns where one could stand in a doorway and see the meadows beyond the river, broad tracks winding uphill, carts piled with hay. This rush of affection took him by surprise. He had been raised in the South and came of a sea-going family. From his father he had inherited a taste for exploring, for maps, and for roaming. This was how he had come to be a topographer. Nonetheless, Kuzmin considered that he had entered the profession quite by chance and that, had he been born in another era, he would have been an explorer, a discoverer of new lands, a seeker after adventure. He liked to think of himself in this way, but in fact he was wrong. There was no trace in him of that kind of man. Kuzmin was shy, retiring, gentle toward others. His graying hair gave his age away, but otherwise, to look at this short, slender officer, one would not have taken him to be more than thirty.

At last the droshky entered the darkened town. In one house alone, perhaps a pharmacy, a blue lamp burned behind a glass door. The road began to slope upward. The driver got down from his seat to ease the ascent for the horse. Kuzmin, too, got out and walked. He was lagging slightly behind the droshky when suddenly he sensed the full strangeness of his life. "Where am I?" he thought, "in a little town called Navoloki, at the back of beyond, with a horse striking sparks with its hoofs. And somewhere near here an unknown woman is to receive— in the middle of the night—a letter, an important and probably a sad one as well. Two months ago I was at the front, in Poland, by the wide, tranquil Vistula. How strange! And not unpleasant!"

They had reached the top of the hill. The driver turned down a side street. Overhead the clouds began to disperse here and there, and in the dark sky a falling star would now and again light up, flash in the puddles, and die out again. The droshky stopped at a house with a top attic.

"Here we are," said the driver, "bell's on the gate, at the right."

Kuzmin groped for the wooden bellpull and tugged at it, but heard nothing except the grinding of the rusty wire. "Pull harder!" advised the driver.

Again, Kuzmin pulled on the handle. Deep inside the house a bell began to ring. But the household remained silent. Apparently no one had wakened.

"Oh-ho-ho," yawned the driver, "a rainy night—that means the deepest sleep."

Kuzmin waited, then rang again and louder. A footstep was heard in the vestibule. Someone came to the door, stopped, listened, then asked with displeasure: "Who's there? What do you want?"

Kuzmin was about to reply, but the driver forestalled him. "Open up, Martha," he said, "Olga Andreevna has a visitor. From the front."

"Who's from the front?" demanded the voice behind the door in the same annoyed tone. "We weren't expecting anyone."

"You weren't, but you've got him all the same!"

The door was half-opened on the chain. Into the darkness Kuzmin gave his name and his reason for coming.

"Gracious me!" said the woman behind the door, fearfully, "you *have* come out of your way. I'll unlock the door at once. Olga Andreevna's asleep. Come in, and I'll go wake her up."

The door opened wide, and Kuzmin entered the dark vestibule.

"Mind the steps here," the woman warned him. Her voice changed, became solicitous. "What a night! Still you got here all the same! Wait a moment, don't hurt yourself there. I'll light a lamp right away—we don't have light at night."

She went off, and Kuzmin waited in the passage. The

fragrance of tea drifted from the rooms and with it some other faint but pleasant odor. A cat came into the vestibule and rubbed up against Kuzmin's legs, purring, then it turned toward the dark rooms as if inviting Kuzmin to follow. Behind the half-open door a feeble light began to flicker. "Come in, and welcome," said the woman.

Kuzmin entered. The woman made a little bow. She was tall and elderly, with a dark face. Trying to make as little noise as possible, Kuzmin took off his overcoat and cap and hung them on a clothes stand by the door.

"Don't trouble yourself, I'll have to wake Olga Andreevna anyhow," said the old woman, smiling.

"Can you hear the siren from the jetty up here?" asked Kuzmin in a low voice.

"You can, my dear man, and very clearly. But you can't come straight off the ship and go straight back on it again! Sit yourself down on the couch."

The old woman went out. Kuzmin sat down on the wooden-backed couch, hesitated a moment, then took out a cigaret and lit it. He was uneasy, and this strange uneasiness annoyed him. He was caught by that feeling which commonly takes over when you find yourself in a strange house amid some one else's life, redolent of secrets and innuendos, like a book on a table left open at page sixty-five. You run your eye over the page and try to guess what the book is about, what it contains. A Turgenev novel with a young girl's fluttering heart and the sun shining through the leafless lime trees? Or maybe Katyusha Maslova's bitter tale?

An open book was actually lying on the table. Kuzmin got up, leaned over it, and, hearing a hurried exchange of whispers and the rustling of a dress beyond the door, he read to himself long forgotten words:

The impossible is possible;
the weary road is light,
when far along the highway,
eyes 'neath the kerchief shine bright.

Kuzmin raised his eyes and looked about him. It was the warm, low-ceilinged room now that roused in him a desire to stay on in this little town.

There is a simple intimacy in rooms like these: the lamp with its matt white shade hanging low over the dining table, the antlers on the wall above the picture of a dog at a sick little girl's bedside. Rooms like these evoke a smile, all so old-fashioned, so long forgotten.

Whatever he saw around him, even the pink shell that was an ashtray, betokened a long and slow-paced life. Perhaps it was an intuition of that easy pace, such as Kuzmin had never known, that brought out the longing in him to stay on and share the life of the dwellers in those old houses, to live serenely through the alternation of labor with rest, of winter with spring, of rainy with sunny days, the longing to steep himself in the life stream, cleansed, free of all spiritual unrest, when even the prospect of old age cannot affright or torment— just as there is no torment in the summer evening sinking gently into the depth of night.

Beside the outdated objects there were other things. On the table was a bouquet of wild flowers, daisies, lungwort, wild ashberries, freshly gathered, it seemed. On the tablecloth lay a pair of scissors and the snipped-off ends of flower stalks. And beside these, the open volume of Blok. "The weary road is light." On the piano a woman's small black hat was lying on a blue plush photograph album. It was not at all an outmoded hat but rather a fashionable one. A wristwatch on a nickel-plated bracelet had been thrown down anyhow on the table. It ticked noiselessly, the hands pointing to half-past one. And again that rather sad—whisper of fragrance.

One section of the window was open. Outside was a lawn set about with begonias, and beyond a wet bush of lilacs glistened in the pale light from the window. A light rain murmured in the darkness, quick drops were drumming on the metal gutter.

Kuzmin listened to the drumming. The irreversibility of each moment has tormented men for centuries, and it was this thought that now came into his head, at night, in an unknown house, which he would be leaving in a few minutes and to which he would never return.

"Is this old age, or what?" Kuzmin asked himself, turning. On the threshold stood a young woman in a black dress. It was clear she had been in some haste to come out to him, for her hair had been sketchily tidied. One braid had fallen over her shoulder, and, without lowering her gaze, with an embarrassed smile, the woman raised the braid and pinned it behind her head. Kuzmin saluted her.

"Do forgive me," said the woman, holding out her hand to Kuzmin. "I've kept you waiting."

"Are you Olga Andreevna Bashilova?"

"Yes."

Kuzmin regarded her. He was taken aback at her youth and the light in her eyes, deep, yet with a certain haze in their depth.

Apologizing for the disturbance, Kuzmin took Bashilov's letter out of a pocket of his single-breasted army jacket and gave it to her. She thanked him and put it down on the piano without attempting to read it.

"Why are we standing?" she said, "please sit down over here by the table, there's more light."

Kuzmin took a seat near the table and asked permission to smoke.

"By all means," said the woman, "I might even have one myself."

Kuzmin offered her a cigaret and struck a match. As she bent toward the light, it shone on her face. Somewhere, Kuzmin thought, he had seen those regular features and clear forehead before.

Olga Andreevna sat down opposite Kuzmin. He waited for her to question him, but she was silent, looking out of the window at the rain still keeping up its monotonous beat.

"Marfa, dear," said Olga Andreevna, "put on the samovar, will you?"

"Oh no, for heaven's sake," said Kuzmin, alarmed. "I'm in a hurry. I've got a cab waiting outside. I've only time to give you this letter and the news of your husband."

"What news?" Olga Andreevna pulled out one daisy and began mercilessly plucking off the petals. "He's alive; I'm glad."

Kuzmin said nothing.

"Just stay," said Olga Andreevna, as if they were old friends, "we'll be able to hear the ship's siren; it certainly won't be leaving before dawn."

"How's that?"

Marfa called from an adjacent room, "We've got a sandbank in the river here, dear man, just below Navoloki. It's dangerous to try to cross it at night. That's why the boat captains always wait till light."

"That's right," affirmed Olga Andreevna. "It doesn't take more than a quarter of an hour to get to the jetty, if you cut across the municipal gardens. I'll go with you. You can pay off your driver. Who brought you, Vasily?"

"I don't know, I'm afraid," Kuzmin smiled.

"Timofey brought him," declared Marfa; she could be heard fitting the tube into the samovar. "Just one cup of tea. Otherwise you're in from the rain and right back out in it again."

Kuzmin consented and went out to pay off the driver. The latter was a long time leaving, stamping about beside the horse, adjusting the belly bands. Returning, Kuzmin found the table already set with old blue china, gold-bordered, a pot of warm cream, honey, and a bottle of wine already broached. Marfa brought in the samovar.

Olga Andreevna apologized for the scanty fare: she was

getting ready soon to return to Moscow, but meanwhile she was working at the Navoloki town library. Kuzmin kept waiting for her to ask after Bashilov, but she did not, and this caused him increasing embarrassment. At the hospital he had already suspected a rift between Bashilov and his wife, and now, seeing her place the letter unread on the piano, he was sure of it; his failure in his duty to Bashilov made him feel very guilty. Obviously she means to read it later on, he told himself. One thing was certain: this letter, to which Bashilov had attached such importance, was of no especial interest here. In short, Kuzmin had not only been of no help to Bashilov but had placed himself in an awkward situation. As if divining his thoughts, Olga Andreevna said: "Don't be upset. There's the mail and the telgraph service—I don't know why he had to put you to all this trouble."

"It's no trouble," Kuzmin assured her hastily, and, hesitating, added, "quite the contrary, it's perfect."

"What's perfect?"

Kuzmin reddened.

"What's perfect?" insisted Olga Andreevna, more loudly, looking severely at Kuzmin as if to penetrate his thoughts, waiting for his reply. But Kuzmin did not reply.

"But what is it that's perfect?" she asked again.

"I don't know how to put it," answered Kuzmin pensively. "This is not an ordinary conversation. We rarely come by all the things we love in life. I don't know about other people, I'm judging by my own lights. The perfect things nearly always pass on the other side. Do you understand?"

"Not very well," replied Olga Andreevna, frowning.

"I can't explain," said Kuzmin, growing angry with himself. "Surely it must have happened to you. From the train window you suddenly see a clearing in a birch grove, you see how the autumn mist will glow in the sun, and you want to jump off the train right there and then and stay in that clearing. But the train goes on. You lean out and look back at the woods and the meadows and the little houses and the country roads speeding away from you, and you hear a distant sound. What that sound is you can't tell. It may be the trees, or the wind, or the humming of telegraph wires. Or the rails singing under the train. It's all gone by in a flash, but you remember it all your life."

Kuzmin fell silent. Olga Andreevna pushed a glass toward him: "Drink your wine. It's Riesling."

"I always expected," said Kuzmin, reddening as he always did when made to talk of himself, "the unexpected, simple things from life. And was happy if I could get them. Not for long, but I was happy."

"And is it like that now?" asked Olga Andreevna.

"Yes!"

Olga Andreevna lowered her eyes. "Why is that?"

"I don't really know, that's how I feel. I was wounded in the fighting on the Vistula and taken to the hospital. Everyone else got letters, but I didn't. There was simply no one to send me any. I used to lie in my bed and imagine—like everyone else, of course—what my life would be like after the war. Naturally, it would be happy and out of the ordinary. When I got all right again, they sent me on furlough. They even told me what town to go to."

"What town?" asked Olga Andreevna.

Kuzmin told her. She did not reply.

"I sat on that boat," he went on, "past villages and landing stages on the river shore. I had a vivid sense of my own loneliness. For God's sake, don't think I'm complaining. There's a lot to be said for loneliness. Then we reached Navoloki. I had been afraid I'd oversleep and miss it. In the night I had gone out on deck, thinking how strange it was that in this enormous darkness covering the whole of Russia there might be thousands of people sleeping under the rain, and that their life stops only while they're asleep, and then only briefly. And the day, when it comes, takes up the threads again—I don't know how to put it—and each thread is someone's destiny, yours and mine. Then I got a droshky and came here, wondering who it was I was going to meet."

"But what is it that makes you happy?" asked Olga Andreevna.

"It's . . ." Kuzmin stopped. "It's everything in general." He was silent.

"Go on, talk, tell me!"

"About what? I've already talked so much. I've said more than need be."

"Tell me about everything," responded Olga Andreevna. She seemed not to have noticed his diffidence. "Anything you like," she added, "though it does all seem a little strange."

She rose and went to the window, pulling the curtain aside. It was still raining.

"What is strange?" asked Kuzmin.

"It's still raining." Olga Andreevna turned back. "A loner, that's what you are. And I am too. And now we've met like this. And all our conversation, hasn't that been strange?"

Kuzmin, perplexed, did not reply. Olga Andreevna went to the calendar and tore off a leaf. "It's the twelfth of June. I'm constantly forgetting how many days there are in a year."

"Three hundred and sixty-five."

"I'm twenty-eight. How many days is that?"

Kuzmin thought. "About ten thousand," he smiled.

"Well, then, setting aside five thousand for childhood, that means five thousand times I've waited, like anyone else, for some miracle to happen, every God-blessed day. But no one, not even a fortune-teller, has ever been able to tell me which one would be the most memorable.

She raised her deep glowing eyes to Kuzmin's. "It's silly, what I'm saying, isn't it?"

Kuzmin wanted to tell her it was not at all silly, but in the rain-sodden darkness beyond the window, somewhere below the hill, the ship's siren sounded a blast.

"Well, now," said Olga Andreevna, as if relieved, "there goes the siren!"

Kuzmin stood up. Olga Andreevna did not move.

"Wait a while," she said calmly. "Let's sit down a bit before the journey, as they did in the old days."

Kuzmin sat down again. Olga Andreevna did too. She became thoughtful, turning away from Kuzmin. Regarding her sloping shoulders, the heavy knot of hair at the nape of her neck, the fine curve of her throat, he reflected that if it were not for Bashilov he would not think of leaving this little town, but would stay on till the end of his furlough, knowing all the while that this woman, so agreeable and yet so sad, was waiting nearby for her most memorable day.

Olga Andreevna rose. In the little vestibule Kuzmin helped her on with her coat. She tied a scarf over her head. They went out together, walking in silence along the dark road. "It's nearly dawn," she said.

On the other side of the river the drenched sky was growing blue. Kuzmin saw her shiver.

"Are you cold?" he said with concern. "It's really pointless for you to come along. I'll find the way myself."

"No, it isn't pointless," she replied briefly. The rain ended, but drops were still falling off the roofs, tapping on the boardwalk. At the end of the street lay the municipal gardens. The wicket gate was open, and beyond it stretched overgrown, neglected walks. The gardens were redolent of the nighttime chill and the wet sand. An old pleasure garden, shaded by tall lime trees, whose leaves were already withering, giving off a light scent. A gust of wind came, and the garden filled with sound for a moment, as if a cloud burst had fallen and ceased on the instant.

At the far end of the garden an abrupt slope overlooked the river, and beyond lay the rainy expanse of early morning, the faint glow of the buoys in the mist, and all the sadness of summertime bad weather.

"How do we get down?" asked Kuzmin.

"This way!"

Taking a path that led straight to the precipice, they came to a flight of wooden stairs that descended into darkness. "Give me your hand," said Olga Andreevna, "quite a number of these steps are rotten."

He gave her his hand, and they began a cautious descent. Between the steps grew grass heavy with rain.

On the last step they halted. The landing stage was now in view and the green and red lights of the ship. A hissing of steam. Kuzmin's heart contracted at the thought that he was leaving this woman, a stranger, yet one so close to him, and that he would say nothing to her, nothing at all. He would not even thank her for letting him find her along the way, for letting him take her small hand in his damp glove, for her carefulness in guiding him down the steps, and for saying, each time a branch threatened to strike him in the face, "Heads down!" Each time Kuzmin had obediently lowered his head.

"Let us say good-bye here," said Olga Andreevna, "I won't come any further."

Kuzmin looked at her. Beneath her head-scarf her eyes were troubled, stern. Was it conceivable that on the instant all this would move into the past and become a heartbreaking memory in her life as much as in his?

She held out her hand to him. He kissed it, scenting that faint fragrance he had first noted on entering the dark room to the sound of rain.

When he had raised his head, Olga Andreevna murmured something, but so low that he did not truly hear. He thought she said the one word, "Pointless." Perhaps she had really said something else; but then the boat called from the river on a high, wild note, complaining of the rain-soaked dawn, of its vagabond way of life in the rain and mist.

Glancing to neither side, Kuzmin ran down to the river bank and along the jetty, pungent with tar and coiled rope, and onto the boat. He went straight up to the deserted deck. The boat was already moving away, its paddle wheels turning slowly. Kuzmin stepped onto the bridge, gazing back at the bluff and the stairs. Olga Andreevna still stood there. Daylight was only just beginning, and it was hard to make her out. Kuzmin raised his hand, but she did not respond.

The boat moved ever farther, sending out long waves toward the sandy shore, rocking the buoys, while from the bank the clumps of willow echoed the beating of the wheels.

1945

Senka

Victor Nekrasov

1

The first half of the day Senka just contrived to keep going, but when, after a short respite, the planes started coming not only out of the sun but from all sides at once, he felt he could go on no longer. His body was shuddering in a repulsive way, and if he so much as let his jaws relax, his teeth started chattering just as they did when he had had malaria. Something seemed to have collapsed in his belly. His mouth was dry and bitter with the taste of tobacco. That morning he had still had a full pouch of tobacco—now there was nothing left of it but dust: he had used up three days' ration before it was even noon.

"There's enough there for two pipefuls," thought Senka, pouring the dust and breadcrumbs onto a piece of paper, "and then. . . ."

But he could not bring himself to think what would happen then. A whole flock ("a hundred" flashed through Senka's brain) of planes with red wedge shapes painted on them now came straight at him. He dropped the pouch and the paper and pressed his head down against his knees, teeth clenched and eyes screwed up tight, and stayed in this position until the explosions stopped. Then he cautiously opened his eyes and poked his head out of the slit trench. Through the smoke billowing off to the left darted the dark wing of a plane marked with a black cross. Senka shut his eyes again. But nothing happened. The aircraft flew off.

"Dear God, what's it all about? Dear God—"

Senka found the scrap of paper and his tobacco pouch, then he tried to roll a cigaret, but his fingers were shaking, the tobacco thinned out, and the resultant cigaret was a poor thin thing.

Titkov—a gunner with Squad No. 2—crept up beside him. His face was dripping with water, and mud plastered his forehead and cheeks. His right arm hung off him like a rag and dragged along the ground. He stopped for a while near Senka in his slit trench and drew a puff or two on the cigaret, then crawled on.

"No more fighting for him," thought Senka, and suddenly began to imagine how Shura, the head nurse, would be bandaging Titkov's arm, he would lie trembling on the cart at the medical aid station, stretched out on a layer of straw.

Aircraft flew over the cluster of trees. A number of men were just passing Senka's trench, and when they saw the plane they spread out in all directions. A warm, heavy body jumped on Senka and flattened him to the ground.

The bombs went on bursting for a long time right beside him; finally, when the explosions ceased, Senka tried to straighten up, but something heavy was lying on him and would not roll off. Senka swore at it, but the heavy thing just went on lying there. He pressed down on the earth with both hands and managed to roll the heavy thing off to one side. A thickset soldier, drenched with sweat, his tunic unbuttoned, was lying beside Senka, staring at him, unmoving.

Senka was terrified.

The day before, when they were going along in trucks to the front, he had seen only horses, swollen, legs spread out, lying here and there on the road. The men had probably been removed somewhere. And now there was this thing, lying right beside him, big, still warm. And the arm thrown back over the head.

Running one behind the other past the shelter trenches went men, weighted down with hand grenades and mess tins, dragging machine guns. A new air attack was in progress.

"Here they come again, the swine."

The din rolled away to one side. Thick clouds of suffocating dust drifted over the ground. Nothing could be seen, neither sky nor trees, nothing but the pale gleam of the gun barrel on the emplacement. Senka looked at it with dislike.

"You rotten stick," he thought, and spread his hand over the gun.

He had not really made up his mind what to do, but simply lifted the gun off the emplacement and, gripping it between his knees, drew back the lock, put his hand over the mouth of the gun, shut his eyes and pressed the trigger.

He did not hear the shot. Something thrust violently against his palm and burnt it. And suddenly his whole body went numb, his fingers dangled nervelessly, streaked all over with thin rivulets of blood that dripped onto his trouser leg. A large red stain spread over the knee.

Someone shouted from just above his ear: "What the devil are you shooting at?"

Senka raised his head. The platoon commander was sitting there, staring at him. Senka blankly stared back at him, then at his hand, then again at the lieutenant, who seemed to be shouting something. Senka did not hear what. He looked at the face, gray with dust, unshaven, he saw the lips moving, the shining eyes sharp with ill-will, but he heard no words. He was conscious only of one thing: in a moment he would be getting out of the slit trench and walking back to the rear, by the river, where there were no aircraft, no soldiers with fixed, glassy eyes, nothing like that. And he sat there, hearing and saying nothing, and then—he did not even remember if it had been the lieutenant who had given him the order or if he had taken it upon himself—he put on his greatcoat, pulled the neck of his bag tight and hoisted it onto his shoulder and, supporting himself on his gun, got out of the trench. He felt no pain in his hand.

From somewhere a lance sergeant appeared. Senka could not remember his name. He had been squatting nearby.

"Take this man to the C.O. and then see he gets to the medics."

The sergeant made some answer or other and prodded Senka in the side with a machine gun.

"Let's get on with it."

And they went on, Senka and a lance sergeant.

They did not find the C. O., but the adjutant ordered him to be taken at once to the medics, who knew how to handle such cases.

"I'd like to shoot him on the spot, but it's not worth the bullet."

Only when they had gone about a hundred yards did the meaning of these words sink into Senka's brain. He turned back, but the adjutant had gone. They went on. A row of telegraph poles lay before them, their wires torn down.

2

The medical corps, set up in a large tent overhung with branches, was filled with soldiers. They lay, sat, or simply strolled about. Nurses in stained and dirty overalls ran in and out of the tent. Large hooded trucks backed and grumbled around the post. Swearing as they went, two soldiers wearing no shirts were bringing out wounded men on stretchers and lifting them onto the trucks. The wounded were silent, looking anxiously up at the sky. Beyond the front line, six or seven kilometers away, planes were launching a fresh attack. The front itself could not be seen, a thicket lay in the way, but the bouquet of smoke from the explosion spreading above it was clearly visible, and Senka felt as if ants were climbing up his back. He turned his head away and watched a truck being loaded.

The lance sergeant sat beside him and smoked in silence. He had not spoken a word on the way. Senka wanted to smoke but could not bring himself to ask.

"He's sure to refuse," he thought, and swallowed his saliva.

A dark-haired little man wearing large round spectacles and a doctor's blouse ran by. He stopped for a second and hastily, not looking at them, threw out, "Self-inflicted, left hand?"

"That's right," answered the sergeant, and got up.

"Bring him in here," said the man with glasses and darted into the tent.

It was stifling in the tent, and there was a strong and disagreeable smell. Wounded soldiers sat along the walls. In the center were two white-painted tables covered with oilcloth. On one of these a soldier was lying with his head thrown back. All you could see was his craggy, unshaven chin. He moaned on a low, monotonous note. He was lacking one leg, in its place was something red, with the skin rolled back and an end of bone sticking out. A tall man, also in overalls, was leaning over him, poking at the red thing with some very shiny object.

"God," thought Senka. "What's that?" and he began to feel sick.

"Take off your shirt—and sit down here."

The little man with spectacles pushed a stool forward with his knee. With difficulty—for his left hand had become heavy and awkward, although it gave him no pain—Senka managed to to roll his greatcoat up over his head and then tried to get his tunic and T-shirt off. The hand would not let itself be pulled out and got caught in the sleeve.

"Why this?" thought Senka. "I'm whole but for the hand. And he wants me to take off my shirt."

"Sit on this stool. How many times do you have to be told?"

Senka sat down and rested his hand, palm upward, on his knee. The blood no longer ran from it, but he could not make out where the wound was: it was all closed up and covered with dirt.

"How old are you?" asked the little man in spectacles, probably a doctor.

Senka did not understand the question.

"Well, what year were you born?"

"Me? in '24," answered Senka hesitantly.

"Born in '24 and healthy as a bull," said the doctor, pinching Senka's taut biceps. "Aren't you ashamed of yourself?"

Senka did not answer.

"You could strangle two Krauts with one hand, instead of which—"the doctor did not finish the sentence but with a quick movement pinched the skin of Senka's belly between his thumb and forefinger and sank a big needle with a glass thing on one end into it. Senka shuddered, not with pain but with surprise.

Then the doctor washed his palm at length with wet cotton wool, and now it began to hurt. Then, without turning, he called to someone: "It's dry now." A nurse brought a bandage in a pair of shining forceps, and the doctor tightly bound the palm.

"That's all. Get dressed."

Senka put on his T-shirt, tunic, and, not knowing whether he was to stay sitting on the stool, shifted a little to one side, watching the legless man's removal from the table.

"Well, what're you waiting for?"

The doctor looked him up and down, and Senka suddenly felt uncomfortable.

"Where's that man, the one who brought you?"

"There, outside."

"Tell him to take you to Tent Four."

Senka went out.

In Tent Four there was one wounded man alone. He was asleep on a layer of straw, his legs spread, his bandaged hand laid on his belly. A sentry stood at the entrance.

Senka shook up the straw, put his rolled-up greatcoat down for a pillow, and stretched out beside the wounded man. Horns were sounding from the trucks outside. Somewhere not too far away the rumbling still went on. Senka lay there and stared at the green canvas ceiling of the tent. Then he shut his eyes and lay for a long time with his eyes closed.

. . . An old mongrel with one eye and a hairless tail ran up. Tail wagging, it licked his hand and ran on. Then a great bowlful of dumplings came up. They were very hot, but his mother kept on ladling out more and more. Outside the window an accordion was playing. He tried to finish the dumplings so as to go and play with the other children by the Enisei River, but remembered that his father had told him to repair the porch. He went to look for the hatchet. . . .

Someone came into the tent and went out again. Senka opened his eyes, but whoever it was had gone. Only the tent flap fluttered slightly, the soldier beside him muttered something in his sleep. Senka closed his eyes again.

The Enisei—what a wide, wide river. And there was a small boat on it. His father was in the boat. There are no rivers like that here. They are always some kind of rusty yellow. And there are no forests here, either. Or do you call those stunted little oaks and ash trees forests?

And in general the devil only knows what it's all about.

They told us we'd come to fight the Germans, but where are they? They brought us here last evening and told us to dig ourselves in. They told us we were right in the front line and that the first echelon was drawn up behind that little hill. But Senka had seen neither echelon nor Germans. He had had his supper off some rusks out of his bag—the field kitchen had got held up somewhere in the rear—and set about digging a small trench. The soil was soft and easy. Senka dug a trench to the depth of his spade, made a parapet on the side where the Germans were said to be, camouflaged it with long grass, scattered some sweet-smelling herb plants on the bottom, and lay down to sleep. The platoon commander left them to sleep till morning. So Senka fell asleep, his rifle gripped between his legs.

And next day . . . when it began . . . when it began. . . .

Their instructor was always telling them that Germans were afraid of the bayonet. So Senka learned to use the bayonet till he could almost lift the dummy target out of the earth it was fixed in. And he could throw a grenade further than anyone in the battalion, even the C. O. And here he'd kept on throwing for two months on end, and what use had it all been? The Germans appeared to be in the air, you couldn't get at them, neither with your gun nor with your grenade.

The soldier beside him stirred, turned toward Senka, made a smacking noice with his lips, and woke up. He lay there awhile looking at Senka, then he sat up, crossed his legs, and asked: "You in the Thirty-Seventh?"

"Thirty-Ninth."

"That's in the second echelon?"

Senka nodded. The soldier smiled. There were large gaps between his blackened teeth, fine wrinkles all over his face, and the short eyelashes over the gleaming little eyes stuck straight out. His left hand was bandaged like Senka's and he had it in a sling.

"You do it yourself?" The soldier gestured with his eyes toward Senka's hand.

Senka felt his ears growing red, but he did not answer.

"Nothing to be scared of. Did you?"

Senka laid his hand—it had suddenly begun to hurt him—on the other knee and fixed his eyes on the toes of his boots.

"What are you, dumb? Got shell shock, have you? What's your name?"

"Senka."

"That's short for Semyon. What's your surname?"

"Korotkov."

"Well, mine's Akhrameyev. Filip Filippovich Akhrameyev. Glad to know you." And he held out his hand.

Senka shook the warm, dry palm.

"You're scared, eh?" The soldier gave a crooked smile and tapped Senka on the knee with his undamaged hand. "No need to be. No need to be scared. You'll get over that. We'll just rest up for a month or so, and then, it'll have healed, little by little, and we'll get away. We won't get a trial till after it's healed, anyway, I'm sure of that." He stretched and yawned. "And maybe we could even lie our way out of it."

Senka remained silent.

The soldier rummaged in the straw and pulled out a flat iron box of the sort Germans use to carry gun parts in and skillfully, using one hand and his lips, he rolled himself a cigaret.

"Course, it's a bit worse in your case. Us fellows were always hanging around the front line, but in the Thirty-Ninth you didn't get nothing of that, bar the bombing. And that's a bullet wound. They're going to start asking questions, finding out things. You shoot through a mess tin?"

"What mess tin?" Senka said, not understanding.

"I'm asking you, did you shoot through your mess tin or a damp rag?"

"No. I just fired, that's all." Again Senka felt his ears glowing.

"Well, I'll be," said the soldier, sighing. "Is that any way to do it? A mess tin or a rag hides the powder burn. And the powder burn—why, that's Exhibit A," and he yawned again. "But never you mind, anyway, we'll get away, don't you fret." He stretched himself out on the straw and smoked in silence, spitting tobacco flakes out to one side.

Senka took out a cigaret butt and smoked it down till it reached his fingertips, then quickly he fell asleep.

3

That evening they were brought millet soup and a piece of bread, then the regimental chemist, a senior lieutenant, came in, took out a sheet of paper and, crouching down on his heels, started to question Senka on where he was born, how old he was, where he went to school, and many other things. Senka replied to all the questions, and the senior lieutenant jotted down his answers. Then the lieutenant read over his notes and ordered Senka to sign each sheet of paper. Senka signed. The lieutenant carefully folded the papers in two, pushed them into a map case, and left without another word.

"He doesn't think of you as a human being," Senka told himself, remembering how he had offered this very lieutenant some homegrown, strong-smelling shag tobacco, so that whenever he ran across Senka after this he would say to him gaily, "So when do we get some more of that strong Siberian tobacco, you old eagle?" But now he had not breathed a word about the tobacco.

"He's just the interrogator," said Akhrameyev from his corner, "that's nothing. It's when the examiner comes, you find out all about it."

"D'you mean there's an examiner as well?" asked Senka.

"I should say there is. He'll be the one to tell you, that's for certain," said Akhrameyev, and got up. "Let's go and see what's happening in the great outdoors."

They went out and sat down at the entrance to the tent. Soldiers were still milling around the dressing station, soldiers covered with dust, their faded field tunics all streaked with black dirt.

A soldier went by, leaning on a stick.

"How's it going out there, brother?" asked Akhrameyev.

"Can't you see for yourself?" the soldier nodded toward the front line then asked where he had to register.

Over the front line German planes were swooping, one after the other. A new kind of plane, not like those they'd sent out that morning—these were small monoplanes that looked like butterflies. They circled for a long time, one after the other, and then fell like stones in an absolute vertical.

"They're the masters, masters of the air, that is. Just look at 'em." Akhrameyev spat angrily. "Do just what they like, they do."

Senka did not answer. He stared at the yellow cloud floating over the front line and again felt something like ants crawling over his back.

"Just try to have it out with 'em, that's all. One of our fighters went up at them this morning. They chased the poor fellow again and . . . And then they shot him down. Went down somewhere behind the woods, he did." Akhrameyev drew a long sigh. "This ain't war, it's wholesale murder."

Senka looked at Akhrameyev out of the corner of his eye. The other was sitting with his knees drawn up under his chin, and he, too, was looking toward the target of the shelling. Then he glanced in Senka's direction.

"Now here's you. A fine, healthy sort of feller. Oughter be getting the best out of life. And what do they do to you? Drive you like a steer right into the bombing. I'm getting on in years myself, but I want my life all the same. Who wants to die—and so stupidly? It's making mincemeat, this is, not war."

"Shouldn't talk like that," said Senka. He did not turn his head.

Akhrameyev laughed, a thin, dry laugh. "Shouldn't, did you say? So what did you push a bullet through your own hand for? To hold back the Germans or what? Don't be a turncoat. You did what you did. And right you were to do it. Means you've got your head screwed on right. But if you'd still been in the front line, you'd have had it blown off by now or be lying on a stretcher, like him." And he jerked his chin in the direction of a wounded man on a stretcher.

It was the same legless man Senka had seen at the dressing station. His face was absolutely white and his beard seemed even thicker than before. His hands were gripping the head of the stretcher and at every step the bearers took, his face twisted with pain.

"What will the poor feller do now?" thought Senka. "He won't be able to do any farm work. Or carpentering. Sitting forevermore and watching others do things. Or, suppose you hadn't any hands." Senka had once seen a man with his arms off right up to the elbows. Couldn't even go to the privy alone, had to ask someone to help him every time.

Senka clenched his fist and stared at it. It was a good hand. Strong. Senka felt a sudden tremendous longing to do some woodwork. His father always said he'd make a good carpenter, with his strength and his accuracy and his keen eyes. It was all in the hands. Can't live without 'em. And again Senka clenched his fist and stared at it.

Akhrameyev was saying something, but Senka caught only the end of it. "What couldn't happen in a month? Have to make the time last, that's what. And, then—"

Senka looked at Akhrameyev. He was sitting as before with his knees drawn up under his chin. Senka suddenly knew that in another minute he would have to punch that yellow, wrinkled face. He didn't even know why or for what purpose. Akhrameyev had done him no harm. He had done the same as he, Senka, had done: shot himself in the palm, so as to—

Senka got up and went to the tent. The sentry by the entrance stared hard at him.

"What's he looking at? Never seen no one before? They should send him over there, to be with the bombs."

When Akhrameyev came into the tent, Senka pretended to be asleep.

4

Senka spent the whole of the next day sitting by the entrance to the tent, looking in the direction of the bomb bursts.

The wounded came in from the front line, and he looked to see if there were any of his friends among them. Some of the men went by from the 5th and 6th Companies; he wanted to stop them, but for some reason did not. They went on into the dressing station, and Senka went on sitting and looking over toward the thicket, where the sky was full of cloud and there was a rumbling sound, where Timoshka was, and Sintsov, and the platoon commander, and some twenty of his other pals, men he had lived with and eaten with, out of the same mess tin, and shared smokes with, one cigaret stub to five men.

It might be they were all gone. And those left alive will see him, Senka, and—

On the third day he saw his company quartermaster at the

dressing station. He had shared the same hut with him at Tatyanovka, in the Kupyansk region. Senka had even made him a present of his belt, a good belt of pale leather and quite new. The quartermaster wasn't a bad sort, the soldiers always had food on the table. And what more can a quartermaster do for the men? Feed them well and give them their change of underclothes regularly. As to the oaths he let out, that was the privilege of quartermasters and top sergeants. And though Pushkov swore prolifically, he took good care of his soldiers.

After his dressing had been changed, Senka went up to Pushkov. He was standing by a desk, waiting for the medical orderly to write him out a requisition.

"How are you, comrade quartermaster?" asked Senka in a low voice and raised his hand to his cap.

The quartermaster eyed him all over and then looked at his hand.

"You didn't stop one, too, did you?" asked Senka, and looked to see where the quartermaster might be wounded.

"No," answered the other shortly and turned his back.

Senka shifted his feet, gazing at the familiar wide back circled with his belt, now grown shabby, and asked again, "Say, what's it like out there? In the front line?"

The quartermaster did not reply, he just stood there and watched the medical orderly rapidly pushing the pen over the paper.

"He didn't hear," thought Senka and prepared to ask again. He wanted badly to know if Timoshka and Sintsov were alive. But just then the quartermaster swung violently round on him.

"Now he's going to let me have it," thought Senka. But no, not a word did he say, he just pushed the piece of paper into his side pocket and went out. Senka stood motionless, then he too ran out.

The quartermaster was standing by the wagons, breathing hard as he shook up the hay.

"Go up and ask him, it may be all right."

The quartermaster was taking the nose bags off the horses and putting the bits back in their mouths.

"I'll go and say it to him right now. They can do what they like about it. I can throw grenades. And carry shells."

He wiped away the sweat starting out on his forehead and went up to the wagon. The quartermaster had already settled himself on the seat. "Comrade quartermaster—"

Pushkov turned. His face looked drawn and old. He had grown much thinner in the past few days. "What is it?"

"Take me with you, comrade—"

He could say nothing more.

"Take you?"

Senka nodded. His mouth was dry and his tongue felt suddenly big and heavy. The quartermaster settled his cape over his shoulders.

"Get up, Sirko," and he jerked the reins.

The wagon shuddered as it ran over the bumpy ground, raising clouds of dust, and then was hidden by the turn of the road. Senka gazed after it, went back into the tent and lay there until dinner time, his face turned into the straw.

After that he went up to no one.

5

Something had changed in the front line. The shooting was coming nearer. Over and around the little clump of trees, first at infrequent intervals, then thicker and faster, shells began to fall. There were so many wounded that they not only filled the tent where he and Akhrameyev were but were laid out on the ground under the bushes. The doctors and nurses staggered around, exhausted. The operating room was in action unceasingly, twenty-four hours out of the twenty-four. Beside it there sprang up great piles of bandages and cotton wool with fat green flies swarming over them, and twice a day these piles were taken away somewhere, only to grow up again a couple of hours later.

"Things ain't so good," said the soldier. "Their planes have it all over us, never give us time to as much as breathe."

The men came from different regiments, different divisions, but they all said the same thing: the Germans are pressing hard, there's no way out of it.

A thin sergeant from reconnaissance, his head shaved to the scalp, was put down beside Senka. His great dark eyes had probably once been full of merriment. He had four pieces of shrapnel in his legs. A fifth piece was lodged somewhere in his collarbone. He lay on his back, but never complained or moaned: he asked constantly for water, being feverish.

"What have they been doing to you?" asked Senka with as much sympathy as he could muster. He was very sorry for the thin sergeant.

"Fell over a mine, during a patrol," said the sergeant, and, breathing jerkily and coughing all the while, he began to tell how he and three other scouts—the platoon commander had been killed and he was replacing him—went out to capture an enemy soldier and, having done this, got lost on the way back, stumbled on a mine field, and he was the only one left alive—the others, including the Kraut, had all been blown to shreds.

Senka listened in silence, watching the sergeant with compassion.

"How thin he is, only a kid," he thought, and mentally compared his own sinewy, muscular arms with the sergeant's thin ones that stuck out of the torn shirt sleeves like a little girl's.

"You were lucky," said Senka.

"I was lucky," said the sergeant, smiling.

"Have you been in it for long?"

"Me? Bless you, since the first day. All the way back from the front line. Third time I've been wounded."

"The third time?"

"That's what I said. At Smolensk, at Rzhev, and now here."

"And you've managed to stay alive?"

"Looks like it," the sergeant said with difficulty, smiling wryly, —smiling was hard for him, it seemed. "Is there a drop of water?"

"I'll get you some right away," said Senka, and ran to the kitchen.

When he came back, the sergeant was lying down and breathing with difficulty. His face had a high flush.

"Must be the fever," said Senka, and put the mug to the sergeant's dry, cracked lips. He managed to swallow a few painful mouthfuls, then threw himself back, swearing feebly.

"Helluva rotten shame," he said. "Shan't be seeing the boys again. All be killed off while I'm getting over this."

"Maybe not all," said Senka.

"Any case, be sent to different regiments. So shan't be seeing them, anyway."

"What happened to you—bones broken?"

"That's right. Both legs."

Senka looked at his legs, so thickly wrapped from thigh to foot as to be almost square; only the tips of his toes showed.

"Seems you'll be on your back a long time."

"That's right" sighed the sergeant, and asked for more water. "Six months lying like a log. And the boys'll be doing the fighting."

He said nothing more but closed his eyes and remained this way on his back for a long time, breathing in short gasps.

"Might die," thought Senka, and felt even greater pity for the thin sergeant. Very carefully he raised the shaven head—it was hot as fire—and put his rolled-up greatcoat beneath it.

During the night the sergeant grew delirious, spoke of Poltava, Klasha, reprimanded a warrant officer, and all night long Senka sat up to change the cold wet rag on his forehead. Toward morning the delirium passed, the fever dropped, and for two hours the sergeant slept peacefully. Senka also had a little nap.

It was only in the morning that Senka noticed the sergeant had the Red Star on his chest. A small chip of enamel had come off one corner. "So young, and he's already got a medal," thought Senka, and ran to get breakfast.

"How did you get the medal?" asked Senka later, feeding the sergeant from a small spoon.

"Got it for whatever they give them for," was Nikolay's evasive answer—his name was Nikolay—as he licked the spoon.

"Had it for long?"

"That's right."

"He's most likely a brave feller," thought Senka. "You can see that from his face. And yet he's so puny and weak-looking."

After breakfast Nikolay needed to relieve himself and Senka ran to get the bedpan (there was only one for the whole medical detachment, so you had to wait in line) and helped Nikolay to use it.

"You're a marvelous nurse," said Nikolay, and these words brought Senka enormous contentment.

When Nikolay was taken away to have his dressings changed, Senka gathered fresh grass and put it under the groundsheet Nikolay was lying on. And at dinner time he begged the cook for an extra helping of meat, but Nikolay had no appetite, and Senka had to eat it himself.

"Nothing wrong with your appetite, thanks be," smiled Nikolay.

Senka was embarrassed and put away his mess tin.

"Can't get anything down, myself. Feel like throwing up all the time."

"It's the fever."

"As for drinking—any time you like I could drink down a bucketful."

"Shall I get you a drink?" asked Senka, reaching for the mug.

"Yes."

Wincing with pain, Nikolay still managed to get down the contents of a half-liter jug, threw himself back on the rolled greatcoat, and lay there gazing at a brilliant patch of blue sky visible through the tent opening.

Around three o'clock, when the sun had grown very hot, Nikolay begged to be carried outside. It was stiflingly hot in the tent, and he had a headache. Senka asked the lieutenant lying in the corner for a groundsheet and spread it out under the bushes so that the sun could not bother Nikolay. He settled himself beside him, driving the flies away from Nikolay with a large burdock leaf, rolling him cigarets—he had already learned how to do this using one hand and his knee—and running to the kitchen to get a light.

Now and then aircraft would fly overhead to bomb the large expanse of dense forest five kilometers away, where the artillery and a cavalry detachment were stationed.

They lay in this fashion, Senka on his stomach with Nikolay beside him on his back, and talked about Junkers and artillery and cavalry, and how the latter was finished as far as this war was concerned. Nikolay knew his aircraft thoroughly, and he taught Senka how to distinguish Junkers from Messerschmitts, and how to shoot at low-flying planes. Then, having had enough talking, they simply lay there, looking at the sky, following the swarms of bombers with their eyes.

Two trucks came up loaded with wounded men. They were quickly unloaded under the trees, and the trucks were driven into the thicket. Solitude once more took over but for the sentry going up and down outside the tent and changing his gun from hand to hand.

"What's he keep going up and down like that for?" Nikolay asked suddenly, looking at the sentry. "There aren't enough men at the front line, but he has to stick around here."

"Regulations, most likely," answered Senka evasively, and busied himself with the groundsheet. "Shall I pull it over somewhere else? Sun's setting."

"Maybe they've got some deserters lying here with us? Eh? What d'you think?"

Senka made no reply. Kneeling, he pulled the groundsheet straight.

"You know," said Nikolay, after a minute's silence, "I get the feeling that the man lying on your other side is one of those 'self-inflicted' cases. He looks like he could be."

"Could be," Senka answered in a vague tone. "Fetch you some water?" He got up. "Think I saw they'd got some fresh in, in the kitchen."

"Never mind, I don't want any. If it was me, I wouldn't be soft on that filthy kind. They give 'em care and attention. Where's the sense of it? Fellers over there," he nodded in the direction from which, day and night, came the grumbling noise, "getting cut to pieces, holding on, while that scum only think of saving their own rotten skins. I'd shoot the whole mess of 'em, the sons of bitches. Gimme one more puff."

Senka handed over the cigaret stub.

"You know," painfully Nikolay turned his head to Senka, "you can pick 'em out right away. Turn their heads away, won't look you in the eye. The rats know they've done wrong." He suddenly broke into laughter. "Look at you, you got it in the left hand, too—just like a 'self-inflicted' bastard. How'd you get it? Bullet or shrapnel?"

"Bullet," answered Senka almost inaudibly, and ran off with the mess tin.

6

That evening the order came for them to move to another place. The whole night was spent in getting ready. Senka himself put Nikolay in the truck and stayed beside him all the time, holding him steady. Nikolay was lying propped up in the cab, where there were fewer shake-ups. As they went over potholes and bumps, he would clutch hard at Senka's hand, but never once did he utter a word of complaint. The road was dreadful.

In the new place Nikolay was all but separate from Senka. For a long time Senka pursued the chief medical officer of the battalion, but he would not listen to him, only turned his back—they were inundated with casualties as it was: the truck carrying the surgical instruments had got bogged down on the way, and fresh batches of wounded were already pouring in. It was only next morning that Senka was able to persuade a medical orderly to get Nikolay placed beside him in a tent where, except for him and Akhrameyev, there were only skull cases.

They slept all the next day.

In the evening the chief medical officer—a corpulent Armenian with sleepy little eyes—came round, looked at Senka's hand, and said he might be discharged in two weeks; Nikolay, however, must be entered on the list for evacuation.

"You'll have to stay on your back for a long time yet, young man. I'm afraid your lung was touched."

Nikolay only sighed.

One day went by, then another, and yet another, but still Nikolay was not evacuated. There were three trucks in all—two one-and-a-half tonners and one three-tonner—and priority was given to the stomach and skull cases. With each day that went by the casualties became heavier. The front slowly but obstinately removed itself to the east. Artillery thundered day and night. Aircraft hung over the front line. The days were hot, the flies overpowering, and in the evening there were mosquitoes. The burning air trembled over the riven earth. Helplessly, the gray leaves of dust drifted about overhead. The lazy July sun slunk reluctantly across a sky pale with heat.

In the tent Senka became known as "Nikolay's Personal Orderly." Scarcely did he leave Nikolay's side, washing him, feeding him, fetching him water, emptying slops. He filched a large brass mug from the kitchen so that Nikolay always had cold water to drink when he wanted it, brought him cherries from somewhere, dosed him conscientiously with a streptocide he had managed to find, gave him his own vodka ration, assuring him he could not drink for the heat, and Nikolay, making a face, not really wanting it, gulped it down with difficulty, so as not to hurt Senka's feelings.

Nikolay grew better. His temperature dropped—never rose now more than a point above normal. At night, when all the tent was asleep and only the seriously wounded stirred and sighed, Senka and Nikolay had long chats together in their corner. Senka loved these evenings. Somewhere over their heads the low-flying aircraft whirred in a manner that was almost reassuring while they lay there, their cigarets winking at each other.

"Ever been fox hunting?" asked Senka.

"No, I never have," answered Nikolay.

"Or hunted bear?"

"Nope."

"So come to my home after the war. I'll teach you to hunt. There's ermine, marten, and gray squirrel where we are."

And Senka gave him detailed accounts of how he and his father would go out hunting in the *taiga* for a whole week, and how the bear had almost torn Tsygan's tail off, and how from that moment on Tsygan's fur had started to fall out, and his tail had become completely hairless.

Nikolay listened, coughing occasionally, and finally asked, "Ever been on a cuckoo hunt?"

"Is there such a thing? What for?" said Senka, laughing.

"Well, *I* have."

"Go on!"

"Honest. They've huge ones over there, great fat things—weigh three-four pounds."

"So where is it they have these four-pound cuckoos?"

"In Finland, that's where."

"Were you in Finland, too?"

"I was. Kiakisalmi—ever hear of it? You haven't? Good for you. I was in the Volunteers then, that's where I got frostbite in these two fingers. And four toes on my left foot."

"And that's where you got your medal?" asked Senka.

"That's right."

Senka waited, thinking Nikolay was about to go on, but he said nothing. So Senka asked: "What did you get if for?"

"You *are* a funny one, Senka. Where's the sense in what for? For war, of course."

"No, I mean—what particular thing?"

"God knows. Went out on a *recce*. Took a prisoner."

"He's hiding the facts," thought Senka. "He's sure to have knocked out a tank. Or captured a general."

For a while they lay there in silence, listening to the crickets. The tent flaps had been tied up, and the stars had come out overhead. Somewhere summer lightning was flashing.

"Oh, Senka, Senka," said Nikolay peacefully. "What a lousy shame we're not in the same unit. I'd have kept you alongside me. Made a great scout of you. You being a hunter means you're a scout. I'd've made you my platoon second."

"I can't read maps," said Senka.

"You'd learn." Nikolay was silent a moment, then sighed. "And tomorrow I'm being evacuated. That's quite certain. Doctor said so. Being taken behind the lines. You'll be fighting, while I'll be lying on my behind at Chelyabinsk somewhere." Again he was silent. "If you knew, Senka, how much it goes against the grain."

Senka made no reply.

More than anything in the world he wanted to be Nikolay's platoon second. How he would have worked for him! And naturally he would have pulled off some very heroic deed or other and got himself talked about. And decorated. What he wanted, of course, was for the heroic deed to be done before Nikolay's very eyes. Or no—better, he would come back to Nikolay, after the heroic deed, wearing the medal on his chest—he didn't mind what medal it was, Red Star or Red Standard—Red Standard was better, of course. And Nikolay would ask: "What were you decorated for, Senka?" and he—casually lighting a cigaret—would answer: "Got it for whatever they give them for." And try as Nikolay might to find out the reason, wild horses wouldn't drag it out of him.

Nikolay was not evacuated next day. A bridge had been blown up, and the trucks had had to take the long way round. Then one of them had broken down, so that only two were now working.

It rained all day. The tent cloth was full of holes, punctured by falling shrapnel, and the rain came in like a shower bath of thin, dribbling streams falling on the soldiers. But no one complained; they had had too much of the grueling heat.

"The boys in the front line'll be having a rest," chuckled the wounded. "Won't have to keep looking up at the sky."

In a neighboring tent Senka had found a dilapidated little book, with the beginning and end missing. It was Gogol's play, "Marriage" and, following the lines with his finger, he read it aloud. And though he read slowly, stumbling over certain words that were unfamiliar to him and awkward, they all liked to listen, and their laughter was ready and wholehearted. Just at the moment Senka reached the place where Podkolyosin jumps out of the window, a soldier in Red Army uniform came into the tent.

"What do you want?" Senka asked him severely, without removing his finger from the book so as not to lose his place. "Can't you see we're busy?"

The Red Army man gave Senka a look of indifference, propped up his gun against the tent pole, and began searching in his pocket.

"How long're you going to be?"

The Red Army man at last drew out the paper he had been looking for and, in a tone as indifferent as his look, he said, "Which are the self-injured cases here? They're to come outside. The examiner's here."

The letters danced before Senka's eyes. He did not even hear his name pronounced. He got up and without a glance at anyone went out.

Then he was standing before a lieutenant with a small moustache. The lieutenant put a question to him. Senka answered. Then the lieutenant told him to sit down. He sat down and began one by one to pull the threads off his bandage. The lieutenant's manner was calm and easy, but he spoke in a very citified manner, and Senka did not grasp everything he said. The lieutenant's words somehow did not take root in his mind but just rolled away. He sat on the ground, his legs crossed tailor fashion, gazing at the lieutenant's round, pink, well-shaven face and thin, threadlike moustache, and waited for permission to go. And when the lieutenant rose and started to fasten his briefcase, Senka realized that the conversation was over and he could go, so he too got up.

He did not go back inside the tent. He lay down on the grass under a battle-riven oak and stayed there till evening. From time to time Akhrameyev would draw close to him. Senka pretended to be asleep. At last Akhrameyev came and sat down beside him. Senka lay there with his eyes shut, listening to Akhrameyev fidgeting and grunting beside him, then he turned and looked him straight in the eye.

"What do you want with me?"

Akhrameyev's lips widened in a crooked smile. "What d'you mean, what do I want? The time's come."

"What time?"

Again Akhrameyev smiled his malicious, strained smile. "What time? Escape time! In two hours it'll be dark. And there's a village near here about three kilometers away. We'll find some stupid village woman who's—"

Senka felt the blood pouring into his face, ears, and neck. "Go to hell." He clenched his fist.

Akhrameyev had been about to say something else but stopped short, looked at Senka out of the corner of his eye, got up, and, brushing the earth off his knees, walked quickly toward the tent. Senka turned over on his stomach and hid his face in his arms.

When it was quite dark Senka went back to the tent. For a long time he stood by the entrance, trying to hear what was going on inside. Then he went in. Nikolay, covered with his cape, was already asleep. Senka brought fresh water from the kitchen, stretched himself out on his layer of straw, and lay all night without closing his eyes. But toward morning he fell asleep.

He awoke late when the others had already had breakfast. There was some buckwheat porridge in a mess tin by his head. Nikolay was lying and staring at something above him. Senka got up. Nikolay did not even move. Senka went out to fetch tea. Then in a low tone he asked Nikolay, "Aren't you going to eat?"

Nikolay did not answer. He went on lying there, looking at whatever it was over his head.

Senka spent the whole day lying under the oak. When he came in again, Nikolay had gone. Another was lying in his place. The mess tin with the buckwheat, now cold, was still in the same place, untouched.

7

Till now no one in the tent had known that Senka's wound was self-inflicted. This may have been because the sentries spoke of it to no one, or because his clear eyes and open face with its light sprinkling of pock marks did not arouse suspicion, or simply because each man was so wrapped up in himself and his own injuries—that tent had mostly the heavy casualties—the fact remained that no one had known about it. And even now that his secret had been disclosed, it could not be said that the occupants of that tent hurled insults at him or behaved in any particular fashion. No, there was none of that. But some indefinable thing, some kind of invisible wall, rose up between Senka and the others. The replies they gave to his questions were reserved and brief. They did not include him in their conversations. Before, in the evenings, the soldiers would ask him to sing to them—his voice was not strong, but it was clear and pleasant—and so he sang to them, not loud, on purpose not to disturb the seriously wounded, old Russian songs his father had taught him. Now they no longer asked him to sing.

And once they spent a long time looking for a knife to cut the bread with, and, though they all knew that Senka had a superb hunting knife of his own with an embossed bone handle, nobody asked him for it and they got the sentry to lend them his.

Senka lay in his corner, watching the flies crawling over the canvas walls of the tent and listening to the artillery fire getting closer and closer. The wounded who had just come in were saying that the Germans had broken through.

That evening a low-flying German aircraft dropped incendiary bombs on the clump of trees. The wounded rushed out of the tent to look. Senka did not stir.

All night long the artillery was moving along the road past the thicket. The heavy equipment went first on tractors, and then the smaller caliber, but this was heavy, too. Senka lay on his stomach, watching, from under the raised sides of the tent, the antiaircraft guns crawling noisily along and the trucks one after the other. There was no infantry. This was the artillery marching. All night it marched.

Toward morning one unit stole in among the trees. The battalion C. O. and the chief medical officer, angry, sweating, dashed to and fro, trying to argue with the gunners. But the gunners paid them no heed and went on placing their guns around the tent, then covering them with branches. The gunners, too, were sweating and angry, their voices rasped.

All day the guns were firing somewhere a long way away. German planes were bombing roads and forests. The wounded came along the road. Not one by one, but in bands of two, three, or five. Some of them walked through the clump of trees—there was a Red Cross sign on the road—others went on farther, dirty, ragged, dragging their guns along the ground.

Some time in the evening the medical corps was given orders to march. The tents were taken down and laid out at the edge of the wood. Heavy trucks came up from somewhere, covered with tarpaulins.

Senka picked up his rolled-up greatcoat and his mess tin and stood by the roadside, watching a truck being loaded with crates. The gunners lined up their guns, one after the other, along the road.

Someone carrying a big bag on his hip—he looked like the medical orderly from Tent Three—ran past Senka.

"What are you standing there for, my boy? Go to the big oak."

"What're we to do there?"

The orderly shouted something incomprehensible and ran on.

Senka went to the big oak. There he found a line of twenty Red Army men and a major, small in stature, wearing a faded forage cap and carrying a great sack stuffed with papers at his side. He was telling them something.

"Left flank . . . left flank," he cried, waving at Senka, who was moving toward him.

Senka took his place on the left flank beside a long-bodied, long-legged man with long whiskers. The soldier's head was bandaged. All the men in the line had suffered some light injury to the hand, or the head, or the neck.

The officer walked down the line and wrote in a small notebook the family name and each man's first name and the unit he belonged to. He wrote down Senka's name last and thrust the list into his pocket.

"Why are they taking our names?" Senka asked the whiskered soldier. The latter looked him up and down. "Don't tell me this is your first day in the Army. Don't you know why?"

"Can they be going to take us out and shoot us—already?" thought Senka, and a lump of sadness rose into his throat. A big truck, splashed with mud, came snorting out of the thicket and pulled up by the oak. Everyone began to get on it. Senka got on with them.

The officer put his head in and asked, "All here?"

"All here," replied several voices from the back of the truck.

"Move it out!" The officer slammed the door. The truck started off.

"Where're they taking us?" Senka asked the man on the bench beside him. It was quite dark now and the men's faces were no more than vague white patches.

"To the front, where else?" a very young voice answered briefly.

"The front?" Senka felt as if everything inside him had come to a stop.

"Didn't you hear that officer? We're going as reinforcements to some regiment or other. All the walking cases."

Senka gripped his neighbor's arm until the joints creaked. "You're lying."

His neighbor swore and pulled away from him. "Are you drunk or what? Laying hands on people!"

Senka did not reply. All of a sudden he saw the sky, immense and high above him, the stars, in all their hundreds and thousands, just like the stars at home on the Enisei, and was seized with a terrible longing to tell someone how good living was at home on the Enisei, much better than here, how you sometimes woke up in the morning and couldn't push open the door to go out, for everything was covered deep with snow. He gave his neighbor a nudge. "Where are you from?"

"What?" The other had not heard.

"I asked you where you're from?"

"Voronezh. What of it?"

"Nothing. Just wanted to know. I'm from Siberia, myself, from the Enisei." He waited for the other to say something, but he was silent, holding on to the bench with both hands. "There's a big river there, the Enisei. Ever hear of it? When she floods in spring, you can't see to the other bank, it's just like the sea. And when the ice breaks free, you've never seen anything prettier. I don't expect the rivers ever freeze over here."

The soldier made no reply. The truck had taken a sharp turn to the right, and they were all pushed to the right side. Senka pulled his cap on tight, so it should not be knocked off and, unbuttoning his fieldshirt, filled his lungs with fresh night air laden with the scent of honey. "It's cooler now, that's good."

"You'll get it warmer in an hour or so," grunted his neighbor sourly and turned his back.

The truck went faster.

They drove on through fields of tall wheat awaiting the sickle, turning now right, now left, through ruined villages, through clumps of trees and small woods. They lowered their heads to keep the branches from their faces. The wind whistled in their ears, and somewhere ahead the red glare of incendiaries flashed like summer lightning, rising slowly and then falling in showers of dazzling sparks.

They sat for a long time beside the wall of a half-demolished barn. From somewhere very near machine guns chattered and mortars exploded. They were given strict orders not to smoke. At last two men came and handed out guns and hand grenades.

Senka did not take a gun, only some grenades—six pineapples and two potato mashers—which he stuffed in his pockets and hung on his belt.

Then they were driven across fields of vegetables to a river and made to sit down in a trench. The trench was deserted. It was one of the old ones that had had time to crumble and acquire a topping of grass.

"The Germans are probably on the other side," thought Senka, and asked the leader, a sergeant, if the Germans were on that side.

"Germans, that's right, Germans, who'd you think? We were there ourselves yesterday, and today it's them. Sit down and don't let them get to this side. Understand?"

Senka sat down as he was bidden, looked over at the other side and fingered the grenades in his pocket, then got them out and placed them in a row before him.

There was a fluttering in his heart, he thought of Nikolay and wanted to hug him hard and tell him that today something was going to happen. What it was he did not himself exactly know as yet, but something very, very important.

8

Toward morning a rumbling noise like tractors rolling began on the other side of the river. But it was still dark and nothing was visible. Then the noise stopped. Frogs croaked. The moon came out. There was talk somewhere in the trenches behind. Two officers came up to Senka, one limping and leaning on a stick. "What company you from, soldier?"

"We don't come from a company, we were sent from medical H.Q." answered Senka, and stood at attention, his arms pressed against the sides of his belt.

"O. .o. .oh," exclaimed the lame officer, vaguely, and after a pause he asked, "Which side did you hear the tanks coming from?"

("So it's tanks, not tractors.") Senka pointed in the direction of the noise.

"The rotten bastards are heading for the bridge," said the lame officer.

The other officer swore. He had the voice of someone with a bad cold. "Where'd you think they'd head for? Of course, they're going for the bridge!"

Again the rumbling noise came across the river, feebly at first, then more boldly. The lame officer leaned over the parapet and put his hand to his ear. "Ten of 'em, couldn't be fewer."

"It'll be light in three hours' time."

"Three hours, or less."

"Oh, hell!"

"What about Sinyavsky? Killed?"

"That's right."

"And Krutikov?"

"Krutikov also. Wish Krutikov were here now. He'd 've jumped right on top of one of those tanks and blown it up on the bridge."

"And not one single pineapple left?"

"You know that yourself."

They were silent.

"Let's go on to the next lot. Ragozin's."

They moved away.

Senka looked after them. For a while their heads could be seen bobbing along over the top of the trench. The moon was already high, and the shapes of cottages could be made out on the other side. They were oddly perched on the slope of the river bank. A church was visible over to the left; only the dome and cross showed through the dense greenery. Upstream, further to the right, something flat and black stretched across the river: this was surely the bridge. Here and there behind the cottages the fine golden rain of incendiary bombs came down from above, revealing little white houses and clumps of trees on the other side in light as clear as day, and, whistling as they came, were snuffed out among the reeds. Red and green dots of light chased and overtook one another, losing themselves somewhere on this side. A mortar would sometimes sound off from the direction of the church, and the shell bursts could be heard somewhere in the rear. There was no response from our side.

At one time, when a rocket went over, Senka saw three men running toward the river and realized that these were Germans. He all but threw a grenade, but just stopped himself in time—the river was wide, at least eighty meters.

Again footsteps came along the trench. Senka turned. It was the same couple who had gone by a while before.

"So what's the picture?" one of them asked, stopping beside Senka.

"Not too bad. They only fire a few rounds at a time, comrade— Senka halted, not knowing how to address him,

"Lieutenant," the officer finished for him and asked if he had a match.

"Only a flint and steel," answered Senka.

"Hand it over here."

Senka felt in his pocket and took out a fuse about half a meter long, a flint, and a steel ignition pan—all carefully wrapped in a cloth—and handed it to the lieutenant.

"We'll be just here," said the lieutenant, and went a short way on along the trench.

Senka again leaned his elbows on the parapet and gazed at the opposite bank. He could hear the officers' repeated attempts to strike a light from the flint and steel—the fuse would not ignite, it seemed—then one asked the other the time.

"Twenty-five minutes of two."

There was a silence.

"Better make up our minds, Lyonka. Be too late an hour from now."

"You're right."

"Who can we send? I've only got three men, and Stepanov says two of those are wounded. What's the use?"

"How many grenades?"

"Oh, enough and to spare, as they say. Five crates full. Got to be careful how we throw them, though. Krutikov's gone. And Stepanov's only good for pissing in his pants."

"Well, what about the lot the medics sent?"

"Oh, look at them, what are they? A bag of invalids. Can't ask them to do anything—only let you down, that's all they're good for."

There was a long silence. Their presence could be guessed only by their glowing cigarets. Then the officer called Lyonka said: "That means . . . one of us two. You or me."

"How you? With your leg?"

"Well, you don't throw grenades with your legs. My arms are perfectly sound."

"And you with your left hand couldn't even throw within ten meters."

"What I could or couldn't do is beside the point—those tanks'll be across in an hour."

And as though to confirm his words, the same rumbling sound as before came from the other bank.

Senka strained his eyes at the place where the noise came from, but could see nothing; he took the grenades off the parapet, tightened his belt, pulled his tunic straight in front, and put his rolled greatcoat over one shoulder. Thrusting the grenades into his pocket, he went up to the officers.

Somewhere at a distance a rooster crowed.

Somewhat hesitantly the first tank came out of a half-demolished hut and, as if uncertain whether or not to go forward, waddled slowly toward the bridge. No one fired at it. The regiment had no artillery.

The tank climbed slowly toward the bridge. Stopped. It fired three times, the shells bursting a long way behind Senka. It climbed onto the actual floor of the bridge. Another tank came from behind the hut.

Senka picked up a bunch of grenades and pulled out the middle one. Three other bunches lay on the grass beside him.

Caterpillars churning, the tank went slowly on. It was gray; on its side was a black cross outlined with white. Beside the cross, a patch of bright red, was a painted image of a wild beast rampant.

"Like in the picture." Senka recalled the pictures of tanks he had been shown in the dugout. "There's the fuel tank, that's the engine. So that means the first goes under the tracks, and the second in the fuel tank, and then—"

Senka raised himself on one knee. He steadied the other foot against a root. Some briars were in his way. Senka carefully broke them off, then he took up the bunch of grenades and examined the safety catch.

The tank was crawling on the bridge. The bridge floor curved under its weight and, had there not been the noise of the caterpillars, a crack would probably have been heard.

The tank passed over three of the arches of the bridge. There were still two left. Behind, another tank had already climbed up to the bridge floor. A third was crawling along the bank.

Senka looked at the sky—it was clear, there was no trace of cloud—at the bushes, the sand (a dazzling yellow in water); he gritted his teeth, flung up his arm with all the strength he could muster, and hurled the bunch of grenades right under the caterpillars. Then another. Then, rising to his full height, he threw the third.

A great globe of flame sprang up to the sky. On the other bank a machine gun opened fire. Senka dropped to the ground, his hand on another set of grenades; he picked it up and threw it after the others. It didn't get as far as the bridge, but fell into the river. An enormous spout of water rose into the air, and the ground beneath Senka trembled.

The tank was on fire, sending out puffs of thick, sooty smoke. Men ran over the bridge to the other side. The second tank began to pull back.

Senka pulled his cap down over his eyebrows and, bending, ran toward the white cottage he could see between the pines.

He was already near the cottage when behind him something fell with a stupefying crash. Senka turned in his tracks. Two arches of the bridge were on fire.

There were no longer any tanks to be seen.

A twisting black column of smoke rose slowly up to the sky, and the sky was a brilliant blue.

1950

Biographical Notes

Babel, Isaac E. (1894–1941).

Born in Odessa, the son of a Jewish merchant. Studied in the Odessa School of Commerce. Resided in Kiev, Petersburg, and Moscow. Served in various professions (as clerk in the Commissariat of Education, as a printer, and as a soldier in Budyonny's cavalry). Began writing in 1915. His first stories printed in 1916 in Gorky's almanac, *Letopis* (Chronicle). Arrested in 1939. Died in a concentration camp, probably in 1941.

His main books: *Red Cavalry* (Konarmiya, 1925); *Short Stories* (Rasskazy, 1925), *Odessa Stories* (Odesskie rasskazy, 1926).

His plays: *The Sunset* (Zakat, 1928), *Maria* (Mariya, 1935).

Grin, Alexander S. [Grinevsky] (1880–1932).

Born in Vyatka, the son of a Pole, who was exiled for the 1863 uprising and settled in Vyatka as a subordinate clerk in the provincial hospital. Like Maxim Gorky, Grin had no formal education. He lived in poverty, tried many professions, wandered through Russia, often on foot. He spent short periods in Odessa, Baku, the Urals, trying to earn a living. He was a volunteer soldier, and for a short period was involved in revolutionary work (through the Social Revolutionary party), was arrested, and imprisoned in Sevastopol (1903–1905), where he began writing. During the Civil War he served in the Red Army. After 1920 Gorky arranged better living and writing conditions for him in Petrograd. He died in Stary Krym, in loneliness and poverty.

His main books: *Island Reno* (Ostrov Reno); *The Day of Vengeance* (Den vozmezdiya, 1913); *The Famous Book* (Znamenitaya kniga, 1915); *The Adventure Seeker* (Iskatel priklyucheny, 1916); *Heart of the Desert* (Serdtse pustyni, 1924); *Red Sails* (Alye parusa, 1924).

Ivanov, Vsevolod V. (1895–1963).

Born in the Semipalatinsk district, near the Kirghiz steppe (today Kazakhstan), he was the son of a village teacher. He attended a village elementary school and later the school of agriculture, but did not finish his studies. Worked in varied professions, in the circus, as a salesman, and as a typesetter. He took an active part in the revolution; according to his memoirs, he belonged simultaneously to two parties, the Social Revolutionaries and the Social Democrats. His first published story came out in 1916 and was praised by Gorky. In the late 1920s he moved to Leningrad. Later he resided in Moscow, where he died.

His main books: *Partisans* (Partizany, 1921); *Colored Winds* (Tsvestnye vetra, 1922); *Blue Sands* (Golubye peski, 1923); *The Return of Buddha* (Vozvrashcheniye Buddy, 1924); *Armored Train No. 14.69* (Bronepoezd 14.69, 1925); *Mystery of Mysteries* (Taynoe taynykh, 1927); *The Adventures of a Fakir* (Pokhozhdeniya fakira, 1934); *Parkhomenko* (1938).

Nekrasov, Victor P. (1911–).

Born in Kiev, he studied architecture and drama and for several years worked in the theater. During World War II he fought with the combat engineers and participated in the battle of Stalingrad. In 1957 he traveled in France and Italy. In 1962 visited the United States and Western Europe, which he described in a series of reports published in *Novy Mir.*

His main books: *In the Trenches of Stalingrad* (V okopakh Stalingrada, 1946); *In My Native Town* (V rodnom gorode, 1954); *Kira Georgievna* (1961).

Pasternak, Boris L. (1890–1960).

Born in Moscow, the son of Leonid Pasternak, a painter. His mother was a pianist. Studied law at Moscow University and philosophy at the University of Marburg. Seriously interested in music, under the patronage of Scriabin, he thought of becoming a composer and pianist, then gave it up. Began writing poetry *c.* 1914. He became not only one of the greatest of Russian poets but also an important innovator in Russian prose. For a brief time he belonged to the moderate group, called "Centrifuga," of the Moscow Futurists during World War I. In the early 1920s he was associated with the Futurist journal *Lef*, whose chief editor was Mayakovsky. Between 1937 and 1944 his publications were mainly translations from Shakespeare (the dramas) and Goethe (*Faust*). Resided in Moscow and its suburb, Peredelkino. His principal writings are:

Poetry: *A Twin in the Clouds* (Bliznets v tuchakh, 1914); *Above the Barriers* (Poverkh baryerov, 1917); *My Sister Life* (Sestra moya-zhizn, 1922); *Themes and Variations* (Temy i variatsii, 1923); *The Second Birth* (Vtoroe rozhdenie, 1931); *On Early Trains* (Na rannikh poezdakh, 1944); *When It Clears Up* (Kogda razgulyaetsya, 1959).

Prose: "The Childhood of Luvers" (Detstvo Luvers) and "Aerial Tracks" (Vozdushnye puti), in *Short Stories* (Rasskazy, 1925); *Doctor Zhivago* (*Il Dottor Živago*: Feltrinelli, Milano, 1957).

Nobel Laureate, 1958.

Paustovsky, Konstantin G. (1892–1958).

Born in Moscow, the son of a railroad clerk, a descendant of the Cossacks of Zoporozhe. His childhood was spent in the Ukraine. He finished the classical gymnasium in Kiev. Studied first at the University of Kiev, then at Moscow University. World War I interrupted his studies. He published his first story in 1911, but later ceased writing to wander through the country, trying various professions, such as streetcar conductor, hospital attendant, factory worker, sailor, teacher, and journalist. He took part in World War I as a hospital attendant at the front. During the Civil War he fought in the Red Army. Began writing again in 1924 and published his first book in 1926. Thereafter he devoted himself completely to literature. He traveled constantly throughout the country. During World War II he worked as a war correspondent on the southern front. Died in Moscow.

His main books: *Coming Boats* (Vstrechnye korabli, 1928); *Kara-Bugaz* (1932); *The Lake Front* (Ozerny front, 1933); *Colchis* (Kolkhida, 1934); *The Romantics* (Romantiki, 1935); *Summer Days* (Letnie dni, 1937); *The Northern Tale* (Severnaya povest, 1939); *Storm on the Steppes* (Stepnaya groza, 1945); *New Stories* (Novye rasskazy, 1946).

Pilnyak, Boris A. [Vogau] (1894–1937?). Born in Mozhaisk (Moscow district), the son of a surgeon who came from the German settlements on the Volga. Studied at the Moscow Institute of Commerce. Began writing at fourteen. His first famous book was *The Naked Year* (1922). During the Revolution he lived in the provincial town of Kolomna. Later he traveled in Germany, England, Japan, and America. In 1929 he became head of the Moscow section of the Soviet Writers Union. In 1937 he was arrested and disappeared.

His main books: *The Legend* (Bylyo, 1919); *The Naked Year* (Goly god, 1922); *Heartsease* (Ivan-da-Marya, 1923); *Machines and Wolves* (Mashiny i volki, 1925); *Ivan Moscow* (Ivan Moskva, 1927); *Mahogany* (Krasnoe derevo, 1929); *The Volga Flows into the Caspian Sea* (Volga vpadaet v Kaspiyskoe more, 1930); *O'Key, American Novel* (O'Key, Amerikansky roman, 1932).

Platonov, Andrey P. (1899–1951). Born near Voronezh, the son of railroad worker. After finishing parochial school, he began working on the railroad (1913); later he tried various professions, as locksmith and electrician. From 1918 to 1924 he studied at the Polytechnic Institute and became an engineer. Began publishing in 1918, first poetry, then prose. In the late twenties he moved to Moscow and became a professional writer. He was sharply criticized for his story, "Vprok" (In Store, 1934), and was not published again until World War II. In 1946, after the criticism of his story, "The Return" (Vozvrashchenie), his works did not appear again until the XXth Congress.

His main books: *Epifansk Flood Gates* (Epifanskie shluzy, 1927); *Inspired Man* (Sokrovenny chelovek, 1928); *The Origin of a Master* (Proiskhozhdenie mastera, 1929); *Under the Sky of My Country* (Pod nebesami rodiny, 1942); *Toward the Sunset* (V storonu zakata solntsa, 1945).

Tarasov-Rodyonov, Alexander (1885–1937?). Born in Kazan, the son of a surveyor. He studied at Kazan University in the law faculty. Became a member of VKPb (the Bolshevik party) in 1905. In 1914 he was drafted and became an officer. He participated in the 1917 Revolution as a Bolshevik.

Began writing after the Civil War. A proletarian writer, he was printed in journals such as *On Guard* (Na postu), *Young Guard* (Molodaya Gvardiya), *October* (Oktyabr). *Chocolate* (1922), the most important of his writings, was used against him after his arrest in 1937.

Tsvetaeva, Marina I. (1892–1941).

Born in Moscow, she was the daughter of Ivan Tsvetaev, an eminent scholar and professor of fine arts in the Moscow University. She studied unsystematically at various schools in Moscow, Lausanne, Freiburg, and at the Sorbonne. She began writing poetry at the age of six, in Russian, French, and German. Her first volume of verse was published when she was sixteen. She married Sergey Efron, who joined the White Army during the Civil War. This and other circumstances caused Tsvetaeva to emigrate (1922), first to Germany, then to Czechoslovakia and France. Her life as an émigrée was hard, and soon she found herself in conflict with other émigrés. Shortly before World War II she returned to Russia. Evacuated from Moscow, she committed suicide in the provincial town of Elabuga.

Her main books of poetry: *Evening Album* (Vecherny albom, 1910); *The Magic Lantern* (Volshebny fonar, 1912); *From Two Books* (Iz dvukh knig, 1913); *Parting* (Razluka, 1922); *Craft* (Remeslo, 1923); *After Russia* (Posle Rossii, 1928); *Poem of the End* (Poema kontsa, n.d.); *Rat Hunter* (Krysolov, n.d.).

Prose: *Prose*: (Proza, Chekhov Publishing House, New York, 1953); *My Pushkin* (Moy Pushkin, Moscow, 1967).

Tynyanov, Yury N. (1894–1943).

Born in the Vitebsk region, the son of a physician. He finished the gymnasium in Pskov and then completed his studies in Petersburg University in the faculty of philology (1918). Tynyanov was an eminent philologist and literary theoretician. One of the founders of the Russian Formalist school, he was also a talented prose writer, a theoretician of film, and the author of several scenarios. One of the latter was modeled on his story, "Second Lieutenant Likewise," first published in 1934. He traveled in France, Germany, and Czechoslovakia. Resided in Leningrad, where he died.

His main books: (1) literary theory: *Dostoevsky and Gogol. On the Theory of Parody* (Dostoevsky i Gogol. K teorii parodii, 1921); *The Problem of Verse Language* (Problema stikhotvornogo yazyka, 1924); *Archaists and Innovators* (Arkhaisty i novatory, 1929). (2) Novels: *Kyukhlya* (1925); *The Death of Vazir Mukhtar* (Smert Vazir Mukhtara, 1927, known in English translation as *Death and Diplomacy in Persia*); *Pushkin* (1936). (3) Short stories: "Second Lieutenant Likewise" (Podporuchik Kizhe, 1927); "The Adolescent Vitushishnikov"

(Maloletny Vitushishnikov, 1933).

Zamyatin, Evgeny I. (1884–1937). Born in the Kharkov region, into the intelligentsia. He studied at the Polytechnic Institute in Petersburg in the faculty of naval engineering. He began writing in 1908, the year in which he completed his studies. His book, *Things Provincial* (first published in a journal in 1911), brought him renown. He traveled in Turkey, Greece, Palestine, and England. In 1917 he returned to Russia. There he became a leader of young writers, especially the group known as the Serapion Brothers. In 1929 he was head of the Leningrad section of the Soviet Writers Union. In the early twenties he taught literature at the Polytechnic Institute in Leningrad. In 1931 emigrated to Paris, where he died.

His main books: *Things Provincial* (Uezdnoe, 1916); *The Islanders* (Ostrovityane, 1922); *On the Outskirts* (Na kulichkakh, 1922); *Three Days* (Tri dnya, 1922); *We* (My; first published in New York in English translation in 1924); *Scourge* (Bich bozhy, 1938).

Plays: *The Lights of St. Dominique* (Ogni Svyatogo Dominika, 1922); *The Flea* (Blokha, 1926).